WALKING SHADOW

GREG DORAN

WALKING SHADOW

Love, Loss and Shakespeare

Incorporating The Dying Diaries *by Antony Sher*

BLOOMSBURY PUBLISHING
LONDON · OXFORD · NEW YORK · NEW DELHI · SYDNEY

BLOOMSBURY PUBLISHING
Bloomsbury Publishing Plc
50 Bedford Square, London, WC1B 3DP, UK
Bloomsbury Publishing Ireland Limited,
29 Earlsfort Terrace, Dublin 2, D02 AY28, Ireland

BLOOMSBURY, BLOOMSBURY PUBLISHING and the Diana logo
are trademarks of Bloomsbury Publishing Plc

First published in Great Britain 2026

Copyright © Gregory Doran, 2026

Gregory Doran is identified as the author of this work in accordance with the Copyright, Designs and Patents Act 1988

All rights reserved. No part of this publication may be: i) reproduced or transmitted in any form, electronic or mechanical, including photocopying, recording or by means of any information storage or retrieval system without prior permission in writing from the publishers; or ii) used or reproduced in any way for the training, development or operation of artificial intelligence (AI) technologies, including generative AI technologies. The rights holders expressly reserve this publication from the text and data mining exception as per Article 4(3) of the Digital Single Market Directive (EU) 2019/790

Bloomsbury Publishing Plc does not have any control over, or responsibility for, any third-party websites referred to in this book. All internet addresses given in this book were correct at the time of going to press. The author and publisher regret any inconvenience caused if addresses have changed or sites have ceased to exist, but can accept no responsibility for any such changes

A catalogue record for this book is available from the British Library

ISBN: HB: 978-1-5266-9437-9; EBOOK: 978-1-5266-9661-8

2 4 6 8 10 9 7 5 3 1

Typeset by Six Red Marbles India
Printed and bound in Great Britain by Clays Ltd, Elcograf S.p.A

To find out more about our authors and books visit www.bloomsbury.com
and sign up for our newsletters
For product-safety-related questions contact productsafety@bloomsbury.com

To Richard, the best of best friends,
with thanks and love

Life's but a walking shadow, a poor player
That struts and frets his hour upon the stage
And then is heard no more.
Macbeth (Act 5 scene 5)

Contents

Introduction ... 1

THE DYING DIARIES ... 11

THE FOLIO ROADSHOW ... 101

Part One

Chapter One: Stratford-upon-Avon ... 105
Chapter Two: The UK Folios ... 112

Part Two

Chapter Three: Westward Ho! ... 145
Chapter Four: North of the Border ... 159

Part Three

Chapter Five: Germany ... 173
Chapter Six: The Great Libraries of Dublin, Cambridge and Oxford ... 185

Part Four

Chapter Seven: California ... 207
Chapter Eight: 'The Great Literary Slug' ... 221
Chapter Nine: January 2023 ... 227

Chapter Ten: Stratford, Westminster Abbey, Windsor Castle 234
Chapter Eleven: 'Slippery Times' 243

Part Five

Chapter Twelve: Japan and 'The Unknown World' 255
Chapter Thirteen: Australia 270
Chapter Fourteen: New Zealand and a Māori Love Story 277
Chapter Fifteen: Cape Town 286

Part Six

Chapter Sixteen: North American Folio Roadshow I:
    Chicago to Boston 295
Chapter Seventeen: The Book World's Jekyll and Hyde 321
Chapter Eighteen: North American Folio
    Roadshow II: Connecticut to Texas 330

Part Seven

Chapter Nineteen: Vancouver 357
Chapter Twenty: Foliomania 361

Epilogue 370
Acknowledgements 374
Image Credits 378
Index 382

Introduction

On a December night in 2021, I lost half my life: Antony Sher, actor, writer, artist, husband and my life partner of thirty-five years.

He was diagnosed with cancer that June. The original prognosis was five years. That soon whittled down to just six shocking months, and on 2 December 2021 I lost him. 2.12.21 – the date engraved forever on my heart.

Tony started to write a journal about what was happening to him. He called it *The Dying Diaries*. As with all the books Tony wrote, *The Dying Diaries* are brutally honest and raw. I wrote a diary too in those last months, rather more mechanically, in order to keep on top of everything, trying to comprehend the incomprehensible, to control the uncontrollable.

I took compassionate leave from my role as Artistic Director of the Royal Shakespeare Company to care for him. After he died I stepped back from the job. Losing Tony, leaving the RSC and moving from Stratford, and the house we had made our home for so long, was challenging. Shakespeare helped.

I set out on a quest. 2023 was the quatercentenary of the publication of the First Folio, the first collected edition of Shakespeare's plays. If his friends John Hemmings and Henry Condell had not pulled that miraculous volume together we would have lost half of those astonishing works. No *Macbeth*, or *The Tempest*, no *Julius Caesar*, or *Twelfth Night*, or *The Winter's Tale*.

We have our own First Folio at the RSC in Stratford. I would show it to the acting companies each time I did one of the plays within it. I decided to celebrate the 400th anniversary by trying to see as many of the other copies in Britain as I could. Then it snowballed. The second part of this book recounts that journey.

When I got back home I finally felt able to read Tony's *Dying Diaries*. That allowed me to begin properly to face what I had been running away from. I decided to edit our two diaries together, to trace our shared experience of an event which we all encounter: our shared experience of dying — not of death — which I discovered, however much we are loved, we ultimately and inevitably face alone.

Greg Doran

John Kani and Antony Sher in *Kunene and the King*

A month after Tony's funeral, Lilah discovered a set of five light-blue, half-bound exercise books. Inside the first one, in Tony's tight, neat writing, was the short title: *we have no shadows in Camden*. The Sea Point, Esher, Lot's Wife, Camden Sequence in all. I opened the first exercise book at random. The first page bore the following:

YEAR I

[...]

It names the afternoon session, and prays to the gods that I might now fall in the schoolyard. Strikes, and subsequently that I be dead.

The Runner with a prologue (seated).

PROLOGUE

A year ago, in the theatre, I was playing the role of South African Theatre's great actor dying of lung cancer.

A month after Tony's funeral, I began sorting his desk and found one of the A4 spiral-bound exercise books he always used to write in. On its cover was a yellow Post-it listing the short stories he had written during lockdown: The Wonder, The Sea Point House, The Man Who Woke Up Happy. *Six of them in all. I opened the cover expecting to see one of his early drafts. Instead I found the following:*

YEAR OF THE SATSUMA

The dying diaries

A diary of dying
by
Antony Sher
(24.8.21—)

It wasn't the alternative subtitles that got me, it was the date, and the fact that I could now fill in the missing part, 2.12.21. The day, fourteen weeks later, that he died.

He began with a prologue. Here it is:

PROLOGUE

A year ago, in the theatre, I was playing an old South African Shakespearean actor dying of liver cancer.

Now, in real life, I am an old South African Shakespearean actor dying of liver cancer.

Who says that actors don't take their roles home with them?

The play was *Kunene and the King* by John Kani.

When John and I were together in *The Tempest* in 2009 – him playing Caliban, me Prospero in an RSC/Baxter Theatre co-production – he asked me to have coffee with him one morning and told me that he was thinking of writing a play for the two of us. His plans for it were still very unformed at that point, but he thought it might be about a white actor and his black dresser. This sounded a bit like a South African version of my cousin Ronald Harwood's famous play *The Dresser*, but I encouraged John to proceed. I was just immensely flattered by the idea of being in a two-hander with John, like those great pieces he performed with Winston Ntshona in the 1970s – *Sizwe Banzi Is Dead* and *The Island*, which they conceived and created along with Athol Fugard.

I heard nothing more about the project for the next decade.

Then in 2018 I suddenly received an email from John, saying, 'Remember that play I wanted to write for us? Well, I've done it and here it is, and please let me know what you think. Give my regards to Greg.'

I read the play immediately. My role was still that of an actor, a Shakespearean actor, but his role was now of a professional medical carer, who is assigned to the actor because he has terminal liver cancer. I emailed back: 'I think it's basically terrific – so I've given Greg more than your regards, I've given him your play to read. This could be one for the RSC.'

Greg agreed with me. The play was basically terrific – funny, moving, full of raw living politics, and, perhaps best of all, offering an extraordinary picture of how Shakespeare is viewed by different cultures (in the play, the actor is an expert practitioner of the Bard and the carer is a devoted fan). Greg felt it needed some work. But the RSC might fund workshops and then produce it in collaboration with a South African partner, which turned out to be Cape Town's Fugard Theatre.

John couldn't believe his good fortune. I believe he has my first email – saying I was showing the play to Greg – framed on his wall.

With Janice Honeyman as our director – she'd worked with both of us many times, including *The Tempest* and this would be her fifth

RSC production — we held two invigorating workshops, the first where John and Janice joined me in Stratford, the second when I joined them in Johannesburg. Both with RSC assistant director, Nel Crouch, serving as an invaluable script editor and researcher.

As we worked through the text testing the scenes by reading them aloud, then doing alterations or sometimes even re-ordering certain sequences, I was deeply impressed by John's openness in allowing his script to be changed. Research-wise we could supply some of it ourselves. The play is set in 2019, twenty-five years after the first democratic elections in South Africa, and John knew all about the history of his country during and after apartheid. And the Shakespeare play which my character was hoping to do before he dies is *King Lear*, which I had just played in Stratford, London and New York, so I had a good knowledge of which quotes to choose and why.

But our main topic of research was cancer. I remember us saying to one another that there wouldn't be a single person in our audiences who didn't have some personal experience of the disease, either directly or second-hand, and that we had a duty to honour them and to get our facts right.

Together we interviewed medical experts, visited hospices, watched documentaries, read articles, then struck gold when we made contact with Kathryn Mannix, the author of *With the End in Mind*, a remarkable book about dying which relates her encounters with various patients when she was an oncologist. One of her chapters called 'Little Dancer' led to a complete rethink of our third and final act. In the chapter Kathryn Mannix describes the effects of a particular drug on a dying patient who is suffering extreme nausea: it causes her to be very hyper, mentally and physically, 'dancing' through her last hours of life. What a brilliant solution for us — to create a strange upbeat tone for the concluding phase of a story, which otherwise would inevitably have a gloomy, dying fall.

Kathryn Mannix agreed to come on board as the production's technical adviser.

We rehearsed at the Fugard, then opened in Stratford — to tremendous reviews, including a five-star rating from Billington in the *Guardian*, then played the Fugard, and then finally reassembled for a West End run at the Ambassadors, starting in January 2020. And that's where my story really begins.

I turned the page to the first chapter.

Saturday 14 March 2020

A matinee day. Throughout my fifty-odd years as an actor, I've never got used to doing a show twice a day and frankly never ceased to hate it. You feel like videotape, which someone runs through, then rewinds, then runs again. But my matinee-day blues are tempered on this occasion because we have only two weeks left to run.

It's crazy, I know. I'm tremendously proud of being in this show and of its success, yet I can't wait for it to be over – as with any show I've ever done. When it comes to creativity, I'm impatient and easily bored, so I'm not really a theatre actor by nature. The endless repetition defeats me.

Finally, the long day comes to an end. I find Tim West and Pru Scales at the stage door. They've waited to say hello and well done. Tim played the Fugard a couple of years ago, with his son, Sam, in Caryl Churchill's *A Number* and had a good time there. I chat with them, then climb into the pre-ordered taxi which is waiting for me next to the stage door and head for home, relishing the thought of a peaceful Sunday ahead.

Little do I know that I will never return to the stage door, or this theatre, or any theatre, and I will never work as an actor again.

Tony had written one more entry describing the erratic way in which lockdown had finally been imposed and how we promptly made our way home to Stratford-upon-Avon, to the house we rented from the RSC on the edge of the Welcombe Hills. The rest of the pages were blank. Lying beneath it were two of the black sketchbooks in which he used to write his diaries, assiduously labelled in the top right corner with the dates. The first diary began in April of that year and ended in the week he began drafting 'Year of the Satsuma'. The second diary took him until five days before his death.

Tony had always written a diary. In the last few weeks of his life we had gathered them all together, hundreds of them going back to his teenage years. He would read them through in a rather listless way. At one point when he seemed very far away, I asked him if he was all right. 'I'm reading my life,' he explained. 'It's not an easy read.' Occasionally he would choose an extract to read to me. There was a wonderful description of his beloved Table Mountain, and another recalling how we had once watched from the cliff top as a group of seals chased a shoal of sardines into Bantry Bay, while noisy gulls and mute cormorants took advantage of the feast, diving into the kelp-filled ocean. Layer upon layer of life.

He told me to do what I liked with his diaries, probably burn them, but that I should at least read these last two. I couldn't. And didn't. For over two years. But then I did. So what follows is an account of dying, from the person facing death and the one left behind.

THE DYING DIARIES

Year of the Satsuma: A Fable of Living and Dying

Tony Sher and Greg Doran's parallel diaries
from June–December 2021
subsequently woven together by Greg

(Tony's entries are in roman; *Greg's entries are in italics*)

JUNE

'Life's but a walking shadow'

Wednesday 9 June 2021: Diagnosis

4.15 God. Just received a phone call from Dr Shearman. He'd seen my ultrasound scan from this morning. Reports that there are two dark patches on my liver. Will have to do more scans.

I asked, 'How sinister can this be?'

He said, 'I can't say. Not till we've done the further scans.'

It must be cancer.

He said they could be birthmarks.

Then why haven't they shown up before?

No – it's cancer.

Probably explains why recently I have felt iller than before.

Cancer.

Don't know what to think.

Other than I'm not 'getting away with it' any more.

Sat in shock outside, waiting for G to come home.

I went through every detail: having to tell family and friends, having to choose chemo or not, the final few days, etc.

And will it be one of those slow, lingering cancers, or one of the fast ones?

Looked around the garden – particularly beautiful, everything blooming – and wondered whether I'd see it next year. Poured a glass of champagne. Amazing how fast the anaesthetic of alcohol works. The word 'cancer' was still stuck in my head but there was now a nice numbing distance between it and me.

G took the news with a kind of blank shock. Said 'whatever happens, we'll go through it together'.

Tony is waiting for me at the front door. His gastroenterologist, Dr Shearman, has rung to say two 'patches' have appeared on his liver. We go into the garden to discuss.

Later that evening, I have an hour-long international call with our RSC America Board, about possible future plans. Hard to concentrate.

Saturday 12 June
After siesta, went for a pee. Felt a bit faint halfway through, finished peeing (thank God) but then a dizziness overwhelmed me and I fell backwards, between toilet and bath, hitting both and all stuff in between: toilet roll holder, toilet brush holder, etc. G dashed to my help. He couldn't get me up at first. Then did, and onto bed. Bad bruising and scratches on right arm, but it could've been worse. Very, very shaken though.

A little later, lying back on the bed, he shudders with the weird sensation of falling backwards through the mattress. I know this is hypertension, but don't know what to do about it.

Sunday 13 June
Have to use stick indoors now, but determined to have the pre-birthday treats we've lined up for today. Breakfast and lunch on our splendid new patio at the fence in the garden. Best restaurant view in Stratford.

Monday 14 June: Tony's seventy-second birthday
I refuse to write up my birthday in black,* but it was a very strange and quite worrying day.

On waking, dizziness very bad. G went off for an early walk on the Welcombe Hills with Catherine Mallyon,† a two-and-a-half-hour catch-up. He was just popping home afterwards to collect his stuff and go to work, but found me on the bed, looking very white. He cancelled going to work today.

---

* Tony would write his diaries in blue Pentel pens, or black, depending on his mood.
† RSC Executive Director.

We rang Dr Alia, and (bless this new Medical Concierge service) she came round an hour later. Checked blood pressure, pulse and urine (all normal). She confirmed that the 'falling through the bed' feel is hypertension. That the dizziness could be from anxiety (which is immense) about next week's CT scan. Anyway, it was a godsend having G home for the day. And we did manage to create the semblance of a happy birthday.

Message on my phone tells me that I have tested positive for the coronavirus and must immediately self-isolate for ten days. In my hurry to complete my lateral flow test (which the whole company working in the building have to do every seventy-two hours) and, in my resolute determination to keep optimistic, I have ticked positive instead of negative.

Wednesday 16 June

11.40 a.m. Appointment with Dr Shearman, Stratford Hospital.

As always with doctors these days, I went in having rehearsed a fight. Thought he'd say he couldn't comment on results of the ultrasound scan till after the CT scan next Tuesday.

I was wrong. He was fully willing – and had indeed pre-decided – to talk about the results.

The fact is they seem very conclusive.

I have primary liver cell cancer.

Two spots, one quite big, 65 mm (size of a satsuma, he said) and one smaller, 25 mm (size of a walnut).

A liver transplant is out.

The first treatment they'll try is zapping the two spots with chemo. If this fails, they'll open me up and burn off the spots physically.

Wouldn't give any prognosis at this stage.

He asked if, in the light of this news, I'd still be staying up here or returning to London for treatment. I replied: 'Greg is my strength, and he's here, so I'll be here.'

So treatment will be in Coventry.

Generally I felt relief more than anything.

So it is cancer. Good to have the word said out loud and calmly by a medical person (rather than my uninformed nightmare images of it).

It doesn't sound ultra urgent, or ultra critical yet.

Came home in a strange mood, oddly lighthearted.

Tony opens the front door. 'Bad news, I'm afraid,' he says. Dr Shearman has confirmed that the dark patches are indeed cancer. I find myself reeling. I had not expected any diagnosis until the CT scan next week. I am not ready to hear this.

We sit on the bench in the garden, watching the field. The sheep have gone now. I suppose they have been taken away to be shorn, so the grass is tall and the clover and the buttercups have grown in dense swathes.

I think that until now G still imagined it could be something other than cancer.

But the thing we've always dreaded – one of us going before the other – it's happening now.

Not sure when – a couple of years? Five? But it's happening.

I said I wanted to go to bed early, curl up and have Mommie come and tell me it'll be all right.

I fetch bowls of strawberries perhaps to signify that our approach will be defiant, optimistic and cheerful. As the light fails, the sycamore is suddenly illuminated in a brilliant blade of saffron-coloured light.

I told G he should phone Ruth.*

They spoke for a long time.

He said he wanted her strength, but instead just felt like howling. Ruth said she'd tell Mark and Jo.

Finally in bed.

G was getting into his side. I cried (at last), saying: 'You've forgotten that Mommie's got to come and say it'll be all right.'

He came over and kissed me. Said, 'It will be all right. Together we'll make it all right.'

Thursday 17 June

During the day, a different thing took over. Aftershock. It always amazes me how powerful aftershock is. The first time you hear or experience something bad, an in-built resilience protects you from

---

* Greg's twin sister. His two older siblings are sister Jo and brother Mark, who is a doctor.

the worst of it. But the day after it hits you like a club – again and again.

Phoned Randall and Joel* to tell them. Both shocked. I make the calls short.

Friday 18 June
Funny day to end a funny week: you could say I had my birthday and my deathday in the same week. Idea occurred to write a book about this experience, from diagnosis to death. Asked G, 'What shall I call it? Year of the …' He said insistently, 'Well, it'll be more than a year for a start!'

Strange thing. G and I ran out of things to say to one another today – which <u>never</u> happens. Everything normal but with a strange silence to it. Emotion comes at unexpected moments: him snuggling his head onto my shoulder for a snooze in front of the telly, him bringing me a little treat, a made-up dessert of double cream and raspberry jam.

Cold, grey, pouring with rain. Impossible to believe this is close to midsummer.

Saturday 20 June
Final run-through of the Henry VI Part One *Open Rehearsal project in the Ashcroft Rehearsal Room. No cameras.*
Peonies in abundance in the garden.

Monday 21 June
Thought for the day:
I'm not scared of death itself. To an old man, it has its appeal: a good deep sleep where you don't have to keep getting up for a pee.
But I am scared of the effect of my death on Greg.

The structure of the new Garden Theatre going up in the gardens behind the Swan. Arrival of the crew to film Henry VI Part One. *They watch a run-through. This evening we work through the scene between Suffolk (Ollie Johnstone) and Margaret (Minnie Gale) for cameras, to catch Shakespeare's*

---

* Tony's brothers in Cape Town.

multiple and innovative use of asides. Minnie's bump is showing. She is due in November with her second child.

Tuesday 22 June
Company have morning free, which allows me to accompany Tony to Stratford Hospital for an ultrasound scan.

A boring hour beforehand, when you have to slowly drink a mixture which will help them see your insides. Then the scan itself was remarkably quick, just the tube passing over and round you twice while you hold your breath each time.
Now the wait for the results.
All my life I've waited for results:
Exams
Getting into drama school
Auditions
Reviews
When will I stop waiting, when will I <u>be</u> the result?

Wednesday 23 June
Well, here we are. The day.
At least the weather is glorious. 'Got a nice day for it then?'
1–4 p.m. The strangest few hours I've ever known.
What other situation in life puts you in a position of waiting to hear about your death? (Murderers on trial, I suppose, in places where there is capital punishment.) After lunch, tried snoozing on our new garden chair on the patio, but it was impossible. Just keep going through different scenarios of what might happen at the meeting with Dr Shearman at 4.40 p.m.
G was at the theatre, doing a run of the show, which is live-streamed tonight. He's told a couple of his colleagues he might not be present for the recording. He got home at 4.15. I was waiting at the open door, fully ready, cap, bag, stick – feeling stranger by the moment.

At the Grafton Suite, in Stratford Hospital, Dr Shearman gently takes us through the detail of the CT scan. Tony has hepatocellular liver cancer. It's primary and there is no evidence of metastatic spread; it hasn't infected his surrounding organs.

Shearman is recommending sending Tony to the consultant gastro-enterologist at University Hospitals Coventry, so he can be assessed by a multidisciplinary team. The first step will be an MRI scan. It is probable that they will take a targeted chemo approach to 'zap' the two patches and seal them up to prevent spread. He described this as TACE (transarterial chemoembolisation).

Tony felt reassured that, although he has liver cancer, he is living with it, not dying from it.

Dr Shearman was running late, and didn't see us until 5.00.

It struck me that I'd never seen his face – because of the Covid mask – and wouldn't recognise him in the street.

A masked messenger with life-or-death news.

He didn't start off with any of the lines I had scripted for him – people never do – but instead took G through the story so far. Then showed us the CT scan (no surprise ... well, it did prove there is no cancer anywhere else in my body) just the two lesions, the satsuma and the walnut.

I said, 'But something the size of a satsuma in my liver is quite seriously big, isn't it?'

He said not. The liver is the biggest organ in the body, and the satsuma was only about 10% of it.

Still sounds a lot to me.

But his manner was determinedly low key throughout, non-dramatic, calming.

He wouldn't be specific. Wouldn't say what stage the cancer was at, or whether we'd caught it early or late. On the other hand he communicated no sense of special urgency.

And he certainly wouldn't give a prognosis: time left to live. 'I've learned over the years,' he said. 'I can't change the past and I can't predict the future.'

Instead, he explained he'd be handing me over to the oncology unit at Coventry Hospital. They'd discuss my case next week, and then they'd probably want a first consultation with me the week after. (No urgency again.)

And that was basically it.

When G and I got home, we both said we felt calmer than we had since first hearing that devastating word, cancer. Shearman hadn't given us good news, but he'd given us clarity, and a plan. That was good.

I urged G to go to the theatre tonight and be present for the live stream. It'd be good for everyone. He agreed. But first we sat in the garden and had a G&T.

We looked across the field to the walnut tree, currently in magnificent bloom. 'And to think I've got this walnut-sized thing inside me.'

'And a satsuma thing.'

'That's it,' I said. 'The title of my book: The Satsuma and the Walnut.'

'Sounds like an Aesop's fable,' he said.

'And that's even better,' I said. 'The Satsuma and the Walnut: A fable of living and dying.'

G went to the theatre.

I had supper and sat outside again. For hours. Relishing the birdsong, the late sunlight on the field, relishing life.

Next thing, G was home, glowing. The live stream had gone magnificently.

We sat there a bit longer, very contentedly, then went to bed saying, 'What a day!'

Thursday 24 June

During phone call with Randall, he asked, rather touchingly, 'Any chance of you guys coming out here at Christmas time?' ... I told him we'd think about it (though the idea of travelling does not sound very feasible).

Friday 25 June

There are times when the cancer thing feels like it never happened, just a bad dream, and I got away with it again!

Then something happens.

This afternoon it was a letter from Dr Shearman summarising our last meeting. In it, he refers to two or three lesions. Where did the third suddenly come from?

Saturday 26 June

Sorrento's lunch where T persuades G he has a lot to live for. I ended up making quite an inspiring little speech.

Sunday 27 June

Today at lunch (delicious slow-roast lamb shoulder) we discussed South Africa at Christmas, and thought maybe we should pursue the idea …?

Told Randall on the phone – to cheer him up – only for him to tell me that Covid has got so bad in SA now, Ramaphosa is addressing the nation on TV tonight to announce a new strict lockdown.

Monday 28 June

This cancer thing is like a bomb in our household. For most of the time it sits there unobtrusively and we just move around it, getting on with our lives. But then it goes off.

Today it went off twice.

G suddenly broke down. Told Catherine the news about me. Catherine, who is marvellously compassionate and sensible, sent him home. He arrived in tears. An email came from Catherine saying he should take a few weeks off work. It's the best thing, time to readjust to living with the bomb, before continuing to do his job to the best of his ability.

Then in the late afternoon I started to have to dump, not diarrhoea exactly, but urgently having to go. Got worse in the evening. We found we had only three Imodium tablets from long ago (expired). I took them, but it kept happening, now bleeding and hurting. G discovered there was a pharmacy still open near the hospital and went and bought a pack of Imodium. Do I take another? Trying to decide I gradually became hysterical, crying and shaking all over, saying, 'This is it. This isn't ordinary diarrhoea – this is the other thing happening!' G calmed me, said I was just remembering Verne's terrible bouts. [*Verne, Tony's sister, died of cancer aged seventy-one.*] I felt traumatised all the same. Eventually took another tablet, plus a sleeping pill and got to sleep.

Tuesday 29 June

My big fear – of the attacks going on through the night – didn't happen. I slept quite well.

Jesus, what happened?

The bomb – that's what happened.

Odd thing. We were watching the 6.30 ITV news and realised there was an important match in the Euro 2021 tournament – England versus Germany fighting to be in the quarter-finals – and that there was just fifteen minutes to go. G suddenly said, 'Let's watch to the end'. So, as we very occasionally do (like the '95 Rugby World Cup final in South Africa) we found ourselves watching <u>sport</u>. Very exciting. And then England won – which was, apparently, remarkable. Strange and rather wonderful to be part of a moment of joyful national hysteria.

The second night running had multiple dumping. Got very upset again. G tried to help but I snapped at him, and drove him away. <u>Must be careful of this</u>. It's what happened between Verne and Joan. As Verne's fear grew, she took it out on Joan. <u>Must not let this happen with me and G</u>. I'm feeling more repulsive than ever at the moment. But I must stop making myself repulsive to G. (Even though it would help him when it gets to grieving time.)

Wednesday 30 June

Joan rang from South Africa. She mentioned that, as part of Pride Month, there was a showing of the documentary made about their wedding – Joan and Verne's. I'd forgotten that, because their wedding was the first same-sex wedding to have a proper Jewish ceremony, it became the focus of a film about the whole struggle to change the law.

Tammi, Joan's daughter, emailed us the link and we watched after supper. We both began crying during the intro, and never stopped. Tears of joy, pride, grief. There's Verne looking absolutely <u>radiant</u>, someone who hated the limelight, yet is glowing with happiness at the centre of this public event – and this is long before her diagnosis. And there's G, and Randall, and us all – all looking so <u>young</u>, and so full of pure delight.

JULY

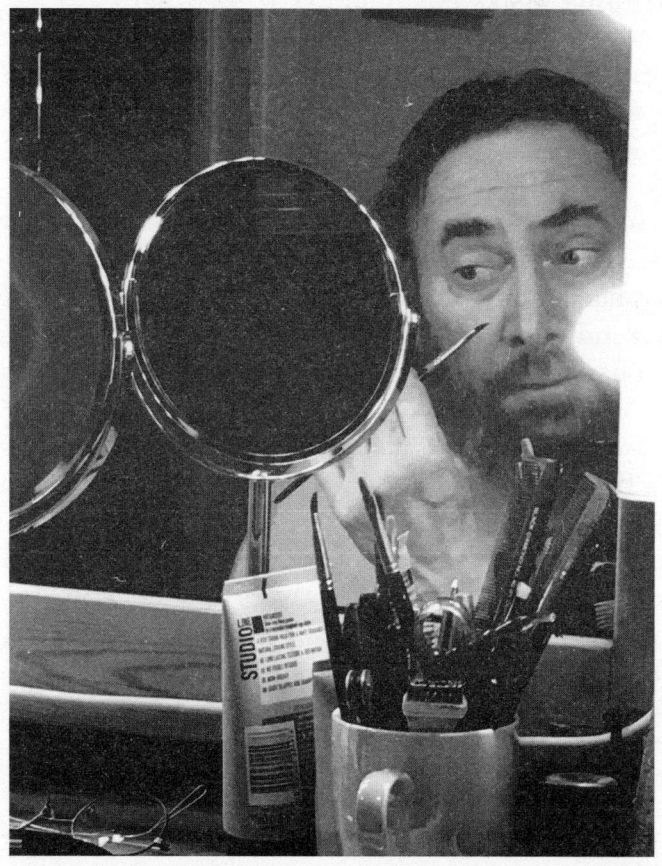

'If it were now to die'

Thursday 1 July 2021: MRI scan

Fairly unpleasant business. Stuck in a narrow tube for about twenty-five minutes. Not for the claustrophobic. They give you instructions through headphones but the radiographer had a thick accent, and I couldn't understand what he was saying. And holding your breath for long stretches, while wearing a fucking Covid mask! The whole thing took some panic management.

Got home just in time to see new animals being released into the big field (it's been empty for weeks since the sheep went): five cows, three brown and white Herefords, and two glossy black Gloucesters. Thrilling to have such big beasts living next to us.

In the evening, having a bit of unusual warmth and light, we stayed outside and had one of our 'good talks' about the situation. I confessed that for years I had been thinking about suicide in the event of G going first.

> G: And how were you going to do it?
> Me: Going to Dover, and jumping off the White Cliffs.
> G: Dying by falling? Oh no, I'd hate that.
> Me: Be exhilarating for a second or two. The rush of white. The sense of stepping off England. But then I realised that I couldn't do it anyway, because in order to get down to Dover and find the right bit of cliff, I'd need <u>you</u> to organise it.

We laughed.

Friday 2 July

Meeting with the doctor at Coventry Hospital. G with me.

The news was bad.

My liver, with its longstanding disease and scarred by cirrhosis, isn't strong enough to withstand any invasive treatment, whether the zaps or chemo or the burning out of the two lesions.

I said, 'Dr Shearman was unable to give a prognosis, and I'm finding that's making me very anxious. Can you give one?'

She said, 'It's very difficult. I've had to do this so often, and it's so difficult ...'

(I wasn't quite sure if she meant difficult for her, personally, or difficult because it's hard to pin a time on these things. Maybe both.)

'... But if we can strengthen the liver and give treatment, about two years.'

'And if you can't?' asked G.

'Then ... less.'

We didn't press her on what that meant.

I was still reeling from the two years.

Wasn't expecting the figure to be so low. And it could be much lower.

I had two instant physical reactions:

I felt slightly faint.

I started coughing – a small cough, but with the kind of tickle that stops you from talking. I thought: but I must talk more; there's more to ask.

Both the cough and the faintness passed.

So we did talk a bit more, like whether we could do any of the procedures closer to Stratford, and a chat about diet.

She said that obviously alcohol should be cut out completely, but this was my choice.

I said I would think about it, but I knew there was nothing to think about. Of course I'd carry on. It still gives pleasure, it still worked as an anaesthetic to what was happening.

We were silent on the way home: we couldn't talk in front of the taxi driver.

The weather was fairly bright at least, so we sat in the garden and shared our shock.

'Was it the moment she said two years?' I asked.

'Yeah,' he said.

'And actually it could be less.'

'Yes.'

We'd gone full circle. When Dr Shearman first phoned with news of the two 'shadows' on my liver, and before the word 'cancer' had been spoken, we'd fantasised the worst. One of those 'just a few months between diagnosis and death' cases. And now, after different pieces of information and different assumptions (during which we grew more hopeful) we've come back to this very grim possibility.

We began to talk in a less frightened way, about practical things, like the ways that I could die at home, by creating a downstairs bedroom (maybe convert my studio) and maybe getting a carer, maybe even a full-time one (who could live in the granny flat).

We noticed that the buzzard was in the field. It's always exciting to see it. But then, as it flew away, G exclaimed: 'It's carrying something. We've never seen that before? What is it?'

'My liver?' I suggested.

We went to make crucial calls, people who needed to know immediately. Ruth said, 'It's not the years in your life, it's the life in your years.' We ordered fish and chips. Before going to fetch them G suddenly said calmly: 'I didn't know you were going to leave me like this.'

I took a while before answering, 'I didn't mean to.'

He nodded, then said, 'Shall we go to Table Mountain and jump off together, holding hands?'

'Except we'd probably choose the wrong spot, and just end up hurting ourselves badly. The sides aren't steep, they're very slopey.'

As we got into bed I said, 'I have officially rewritten the greatest poem about death. It now goes:

"Do not go solemn into that good night,
Laugh, laugh against the dying of the light".'

Saturday 3 July

G's aftershock very extreme today. Began weeping at lunch, said: 'I haven't had a chance to howl', and then did precisely that: deep sobs, those high-pitched cries which break my heart.

This thing is going to be much tougher for him than me. All I have to do is die. He's got to carry on living without half of himself. That's how we've always been for one another.

Sunday 4 July
We're still very emotional. Music tends to set me off, even if it isn't sad.

At odd times I watch G just doing everyday things, and I cannot bear, <u>I cannot bear</u>, the thought of him doing these things, alone and lonely, when I am gone.

We wondered if this state – living with the knowledge of the cancer – will become normal, the new normal, and we'll get used to it.

G and I had a strange discussion this evening about what to do with all my stuff. My paintings, for example. G shocked and sad to hear I don't care what happens to them.

A strange moment, yes, when you look at what you've collected preciously through your life, and now think about throwing it all away.

Tuesday 6 July
Jan rang from South Africa. Full of love. [Janice Honeyman, who directed Tony in *Kunene and the King*]. She said, 'I can't believe it – you rehearsed for this!'

Wednesday 7 July
Early evening. G stepped out onto the loggia to look at the garden. I watched him. Evening light, the sound of birdsong, and a picture of him strolling this way and that, thinking about what needs planting or dead-heading, etc. The frame of the doorway made him look further away than he was, and there was a separation between us that I found poignant. There he is alone, like he will be, seeking comfort from his garden, and here I am, my dead spirit, observing him, unable to make contact. I became very upset, but wiped it away before he came back inside.

Thursday 8 July
Good news. The doctor at Coventry has arranged for me to have a fluid drain of my stomach on Monday. At last something is happening.

Friday 9 July
G had an astonishing dream during the night ... (G rarely remembers his dreams, or tells them to me). Us in the car, me driving, trying

to get into a parking place, overshoot it, continue reversing, picking up speed, rain, night-time, going faster and faster, completely reckless. G jumps out of the car, but his foot catches in the seatbelt …

It's astonishing because, unlike most dreams, it's so easy to interpret:

G, who likes to be in control, isn't in control (I'm in control or my cancer is) and my behaviour (i.e. my cancer again) is lethally dangerous and will kill.

G went to do our weekly big shop at Waitrose. Couldn't find a can of consommé (in case I have to have light meals) and broke down. There, in the middle of the condiments aisle.

When he told me about it he broke down again: 'I can't bear the thought of living without you, there'll be no point!' He tried to work out his immediate future – should he resign, take a sabbatical or what? I urged him not to make any big decisions – not until things are clearer about my prognosis. Maybe after Monday's draining procedure.

Saturday 10 July
It continues: grey day after grey day. It's impossible, incredible, intolerable.

The buzzard is visiting the big field all the time these days. Whenever he comes the crows make a fuss and drive him away, mobbing him. He normally submits, though in a lazy almost mocking way – he could have 'em all for breakfast – but today he kept coming back and at one point in the afternoon, hung in the air right above us on the patio, closer than he's ever been. A magnificent sight: the rich brown topside of his torso and wings, the light creamy feathers of his underside, and this against a rare bit of blue in the sky. Our blue-sky buzzard.

'It's a blessing!' G said.

Sunday 11 July
I'm going to die, I am actually going to die.

This keeps hitting me in a stark, jolting way. Yet I am still not sure I _actually_ comprehend it.

It's causing depression and strange drowsiness. I can't stop falling asleep. A rehearsal for the Big Sleep?

A day for sports fans.

At Wimbledon, the men's final this afternoon.
At Wembley, the finals of Euro 2021 this evening.
Incredibly, we watch both.

As the Wimbledon match finished – Djokovic winning – I became very emotional. That could be the last Wimbledon I see.

'What is it?' G asked.

'Oh, just Djokovic's interview – when he said that as a kid in Serbia he'd fantasised about Wimbledon, and even built a version of the trophy from scraps of things he could find, and now here he was holding the real thing. It just hit me. Childhood dreams and adult achievements. I dreamed big too, but I never achieved major success like this.'

'Nonsense!' said G.

A little later, we were sitting in the window, and the grey day began to rain again. How was this possible – for summer weather never to come?

'You bastard!' I shouted at God. 'And for my last summer!'

G waited a bit, then said, 'You're not allowed to say that. And I know that's what you were thinking at the end of Wimbledon too. You're not allowed. Otherwise we'll just be counting every minute.'

Incredible build-up to tonight's Wembley match. There's talk of making history – England haven't won a major tournament in fifty-five years – dangerous talk, the kind of talk the Devil hears and likes.

And, sure enough – England lost.

Monday 12 July

A grim day ahead. Draining the excess fluid from my stomach – takes six hours apparently.

Coventry Hospital for 9 a.m. Here things got grimmer.

Despite having arranged it all, the hospital was suddenly short of beds and there wasn't one for me.

We'd have to do it on Wednesday.

Came back to Stratford with a new kind of low.

My prognosis is that I might only have a limited time to live. But no one is in any rush to help.

The draining procedure could result in the liver becoming a bit stronger – able to withstand some cancer treatment – but whey-hey, what does a day or two matter?

Wednesday 14 July
Hard to believe but today's visit was worse than Monday.

Great difficulty getting the drain into the right spot on my abdomen (there's the danger that it could puncture an organ). They decided they would have to do an ultrasound-guided insertion of the drain needle. But they'd have to find out when a radiologist was available. Did I want to wait?

T decides that the NHS are too busy, and that he needs private attention.
  'Why not go back to London?' I ask.
  'Because our surroundings, the big field, the cattle, the buzzard – give me a peace of mind which London could never do.'

Thursday 15 July
Had one of my lowest days, probably because of yesterday's fiasco at the hospital. Feeling of hopelessness, which manifested itself, oddly, as extreme drowsiness. Kept dropping off <u>all</u> day.

At one point the cows came to graze by the fence. G went over, and struck up a friendship, scratching their muzzles and even blowing in their nostrils.

I watched, amused and touched. There he was again, my Greg, looking further away than he actually was, entertaining the cattle.

Friday 16 July
The weather suddenly glorious: hot, bright, the full summer treatment. My spirits soar. It's incredible – how the presence of light affects me.

Tony is a creature of his homeland. He loves the heat. He would be happy with constant sunshine, and occasional turbulent storms, like the ones they get in Jo'burg, with earth-shaking thunder and lightning. Distinct polarities. My quiet brand of Englishness delights in 'weather', in its infinite congruities of grey, with the surprise of sunshine.

Napped on the patio bench, this evening while G watered the garden. Felt such peace and safety. Me lying here, him pottering around nearby.

Decide <u>this</u> is how I'd like to die.

'If it were now to die, 'Twere now to be most happy' (Othello)

Saturday 17 July
Summer in full glory.
    Meanwhile the world is going mad. Covid is raging out of control again, but the government decided months ago that this coming Monday was Freedom Day – the lifting of <u>all</u> restrictions – and are going ahead with it.
    In South Africa, there are riots in the streets – to protest about former President Zuma going to jail, because he's refused to stand trial for fraud, and explain the billions of rand that went missing under his regime. Their supporters don't protest with ordinary marches, and articulate speeches; they protest with looting and stealing, Zuma-style.

Tuesday 20 July
They decide no point in the drain. Tony relieved. But sinister sense this meant less than two years.

Saturday 24 July
Heatwave over. That low, soiled-white sky is down over us again, robbing everything of shape or shadow. My own light seemed to be turned off with the sun. Had one of my worst days of fatigue … sleep-walking through life. Or is it … the Walking Dead?

Friday 30 July
Not very inspiring visit to the hospital. Only treatment sorafenib. But side effects, and could make my liver <u>worse</u>. Doctor said that if I wanted to proceed I could see the oncologist who'd want to do a liver biopsy, before putting me on the drug. Or I could do nothing … prognosis … a year. We drove back in heavy rain. If this was a movie … the world just looked utterly bleak.

Saturday 31 July
Lunch at Sorrento's. Ordered two favourites: G had Dover sole. I had *Fegato alla veneziana* (tender strips of liver with onion).
    Halfway through meal, I asked, 'How's your sole?'
    He answered, 'Hurting.'

I looked up in surprise, then caught on.
He asked, 'And how's your liver?'
'Yes, hurting too.'
You couldn't have made it up: soul and liver.
Late afternoon, suddenly G rushed out of his study and stood in front of me, eyes wide and frightened, saying nothing. I didn't know what on earth was going on. G's silence went on and on.

I said: 'This is frightening me. Worse than anything you have to tell me.'

He tried writing on my notepad, gave up, and went into the front room. I followed. He managed to say, 'Can't speak … maybe … stroke?'

I rang Mark. He said, 'Get an ambulance immediately. Tell them he can't put thoughts into words. There's a danger of clotting.'

I rang 999.

They said they were on their way.

I got ready to go with him. They arrived ten minutes later.

Said they'd do an assessment on the spot.

G was asked if he was under any special stress. I volunteered the info about my cancer.

I phone Mark and hand phone to ambulance man.

Shock not stroke, hospital not required.

Huge relief.

They went (they'd been v. nice and helpful).

G and I stared at one another in amazement.

The stress we're under is incredible.

AUGUST

'O, that this too, too solid flesh would melt…'

Sunday 1 August
With no treatment in over two months, T has had enough, and concludes that the NHS is too slow.

The doctor said possibly just a year left. That's this time next year.
 Me gone. G alone.
 Impossible to conceive.
 When will the pain of cancer arrive to help convince me?
 Meanwhile this too, too solid flesh still seems so solid, that you can't imagine it melting, thawing, and resolving itself into a dew.
 I can honestly declare that the strangest thing that's ever happened to me in my life is dying.
 So ... just party? The latter half of my final year (as per the prognosis) is going to see me tired, sick, in hospital, or having care, all sorts of indignities, so for now ... just party.
 Of course, there is another option to when things get bad – Dignitas. Must discuss with Greg.

Thursday 5 August
To Chipping Camden and Broadway. Thumping rain. Both shows cancelled in open-air theatre.

Friday 6 August
Hospital. Long-awaited meeting with oncologist. Kept waiting an hour, then seen by the trainee who says T could have three to six months left. Came home again in shock. We need a second opinion.

We watch Jackie Mason DVD. Lovely to cry with laughter tonight rather than the other kind.

Saturday 7 August
Zoom call with the specialist.

Sure enough he swept away all the stuff we'd been told by Shearman, the Coventry oncologist and the trainee, and said we needn't bother with sorafenib (we could do better than that). He assured me I would not be dying of cancer, but living with it for some time.

After the call we were in shock again but nicely so. This was the first potentially good news we'd had. But then we Googled him only to find he is being investigated by British Medical Council 'for promising patients more than they could deliver'.

'Oy,' I said. 'We've got enough problems already without now having hired Dr Crippen to help us!'

Maybe because of this unease, we ended up having a terrible row. The trigger was trivial (me not being able to get comfortable with the sofa cushions) but of course it was really about the anger, shock and terror we've both been experiencing over the last two months.

Sunday 8 August
Woke sad. Had a long talk in bed. We resolved to be more careful with one another. And to have a good day.

Monday 9 August
Extreme anxiety all day. NHS won't show my ultrasound, CT, or MRI scans to the Harley Street doctor (that the specialist has arranged for us to see while he is away). About to cancel the doctor, who then says it would be sufficient to see the radiologist's report. Dr Shearman brings them round personally this afternoon. He's a good man.

Tuesday 10 August
To London to see the doctor in Harley Street.

In a moment of unexpected indiscretion he mentioned the 'trouble' that the specialist is in, so 'he won't be taking charge of my case any time soon'.

Sent us to have blood test a few blocks away. It was shocking how difficult I found the walk, one hand on a stick, the other linked through G's arm. Just another old man hobbling around the Harley Street area.

Monday 16 August

It's extraordinary how stress registers in G's face. Not when he's directing (you never see him stressed then) but in personal matters, like our current situation. He looks pale and tired, very tired – the lines round his eyes are deep, the bags under his eyes are heavy. The flesh of his whole face is heavy. And he looks ten years older. It distresses me to see him like this.

Good news from Warwick Hospital. Liver biopsy on Friday. But then an email saying can't guarantee a bed. Kafka couldn't make it up.

Evening news. Shocking images from the fall of Kabul. A huge US troop carrier (filled with American citizens, embassy staff, etc.) heading down the runway before takeoff, but surrounded by Afghan people charging alongside, desperate to leave as well. Two of them actually clambered onto the outside of the plane, and then fell to their deaths as it rose into the air.

Tuesday 17 August

Message from Harley Street doctor. It wouldn't be safe to try any treatment other than sorafenib. So despite their initial boasts … the Harley Street big shots have not bested the country doctors. It was like getting the shock of the initial diagnosis all over again.

I'm dying. Probably soon.

The recommended specialist turned out to be facing charges for misconduct. In late November, it was announced that a medical tribunal had found him guilty on several counts and he was suspended from practice and narrowly avoided being struck off for misconduct.

Wednesday 18 August

Official letter from trainee oncologist. Prognosis: three months. But from when? Probably two and a half by now. Have lovely lunch with lots of wine.

Discuss changes to the house. Converting studio into our bedroom – we went in there and I said, 'Yes, this would be a good room to die in.'

I email Catherine Mallyon to ask if we can do alterations, assuring her we'll pay. Later she replies having spoken to both chairs, yes to the alterations, no to us paying for them – very heart-warming.

Thursday 19 August

Harley Street doctor rings. Said he didn't need to wait for the results of biopsy. I said I wasn't sure I wanted to take sorafenib, might prefer to just let this thing take its course. With me continuing to enjoy the good things of life (good food, incl. salt! And good wine) while I feel like I do presently, which is kind of fine.

He said that of course I was free to choose this alternative course and if I did he estimated that I had three to four months. I said I'd talk it over with G.

We do.

So I don't need to do the biopsy tomorrow, which I had been dreading. Making the decision gave me my first feeling of power and freedom since the whole fucking thing started. <u>I'm</u> taking control. And I'm not going to do anything I don't want to.

But I also felt a new kind of fear. A truly deadly fear (in every sense). Three to four months.

Friday 20 August

G taking compassionate leave, with immediate effect.

'Till when?' I ask. 'End of the year?' he replies. I'm sure I won't reach Christmas, but I hope I reach his birthday on 24 November. He says his compassionate leave will have to be explained to the company, the Board, and the Arts Council, some kind of story is bound to get out. The RSC press office will make a statement.

He reads me Sonnet 66: 'Tired with all these for restful death I cry.'

Particularly striking is the last couplet. Having listed all the things he hates about life he concludes:

> Tired with all these, from these would I be gone,
> Save that, to die, I leave my love alone.

As so often with Shakespeare lines which had simply seemed like poetry, suddenly speak to you directly. It's startling.

Monday 23 August

Woke to the greyest of grey Monday mornings. Felt more depressed than I have so far. This situation is hopeless. Life without being able to think about the future is hopeless.

G came back early. It was sunny, so we sat in the garden. How I rejoice in his love for and knowledge about nature.

We listened to a woodpecker doing its odd Morse code routine on a nearby tree, and he explained that woodpeckers don't eat the wood they peck away but it's simply a way of getting to the bugs under the bark. Then he communes with the cows again ... now we watched a neighbour's cat hunting a vole in the grass just behind our fence ... We said it was almost as exciting as watching the lion kill just below our verandah the last time we were in Mala Mala.

Laughter returned to our day.

T in a fury over cling film. He has managed to get it all tangled up and impossible to unwind.

I was about to throw it away, but he made me keep it, so when I found it I would remember him kvetching, 'and you'll laugh'. And we did now, in one another's arms.

Another Jackie Mason tape. What a joy, what indescribable joy. At one point G thought I was having one of my weeping breakdowns. Extreme laughter producing the same kind of uncontrollable hysteria. My fave line was when he was talking about Moshe Dayan, and how he never knew what was going on in the Six-Day War because of his eye patch: 'It's a good thing the Arabs came from the right side!'

Later, when we were preparing for bed, G recalled a trip to Brazil which he had made for a project for the Worldwide Fund for Nature. One of the indigenous people there, the Kayapo, have no word for tomorrow.

That must be useful for when they are dying.

Tuesday 24 August
This morning I woke with a little start. I had felt a little touch on my shoulder and heard a voice say gently 'withdraw'. I was in a kind of cage, it had been protecting me. Now it was removed. Withdrawn.

Don't know why, but suddenly started writing the book about this – Year of the Satsuma: the dying diaries.

Later, when I mentioned it to G, I said, 'obviously, you'll have to write the last few entries'.

'Oh no,' he said. 'You can ghost-write them yourself.'

Wednesday 25 August
A call with Marietta [Young, Tony's art therapist].

When I mentioned that I was having new strange feelings – we have no experience of dying – she used a wonderful phrase: 'The unthought known', meaning thoughts that we didn't even know we had are surfacing, and becoming known.

She talked of celebrating my good fortune in having found great love with G, and accepting that the parting which will now happen through death is the price one pays.

Also of celebrating my creativity: 'What a rich thing it is,' she said; 'people who live without it don't know what they are missing.'

When I told her that, despite G's constant care and love, I still have alarming amounts of feeling completely alone dying – she said that a human being's most intense experiences can only be alone.

I feel much better for this!

Stratford Hospital

An odd situation.

Four people in a room – Dr Shearman, his specialist nurse Laura, Greg and me – talking calmly about one of the people dying, and that one person being me.

If this was a scene in a film, the director would be saying, 'I think the patient should be a bit more upset. Or at least the partner should be.' But no we were just v. polite and attentive as Dr Shearman and Laura talked through the various at-home nursing systems available, and different sorts of pain management. Though it came as a (nice) surprise to hear that there may not be any real pain. On the other hand, there might be some episodes of encephalopathy – confusion and not knowing how to do the simplest things like putting on a jacket. (Jesus Christ, sounds like dementia. I thought I'd escaped that by dying early, but now it seems like that is thrown in into the bargain too.)

Dr Shearman said that it shouldn't be stressful to me as I wouldn't know about it – but could be stressful to G. I saw him flinch.

The whole session had a dual feeling – of it being totally unreal, and of it being reality kicking in.

Came home, shocked all over again. G said, 'Maybe we're still in denial.' Could be. Ninety-five per cent of life is still completely familiar and ordinary.

Thursday 26 August

District nurse came round. Discussed things like wheelchairs, hospital beds, special cushions and mattresses (to prevent bed sores). After she'd gone G & I said to one another, 'Who are all these people who keep coming round to discuss these very serious things? What's it got to do with us?'

G shared a sweet thing with the nurse: 'We're making sure we laugh as much as we cry.'

Friday 27 August

As arranged, HRH phones: about 7 p.m.*

When it came to it he was comforting, full of praise – said that Falstaff was his favourite of my performances: 'I'll never forget it' – and gratitude for the work I had done.

When we finished – 'Bye bye, Tony' sounded almost emotional. I was very touched.

But I said to G: 'Mind you, when Robert Stephens was dying, Charles personally went to his bedside in the hospital. Not just a phone call.'

G said: 'Have you got deathbed envy?'

Not going to live to see Charles's Coronation. Was looking forward to saying we knew a king personally. (Agh, c'mon, don't mock me – I'm a little Jewish boy from Sea Point. I wasn't expecting to know a king.)

---

* Prince Charles had once described Tony as his favourite actor. As President of the RSC he had seen most of Tony's work there.

Tuesday 31 August
Over the last two days G has been cataloguing all my paintings and drawings. At first I found the process depressing … going through them was a chore … but then I began to be surprised and delighted by some, particularly ones in folders, which hadn't been framed and which I hadn't seen for a while.

SEPTEMBER

'Every third thought shall be my grave'

Wednesday 1 September
Something sinister about the turn of the month. I was told I had three to four months to live. I think I must start saying three.
 Another Marietta session:
 Dying is living. Being. Breathing.
 Letting go of the sadness that I won't see Cape Town again. She stresses the phrase 'letting go'. Not fighting it.
 Told her that I was still drinking but there was a power in that (to counter the astonishing, utter powerlessness of dying): doing something I shouldn't. And confessed that the whole of my drinking was a kind of slow sweet suicide, in response to my disappearance in my career. We described it as 'grabbing a drink angrily'.
 Told her about my surprise and delight as G & I go through our photo albums – how handsome we are. Both of us. Not only him (who has always been) but ugly little me too.
 She reminded me of how my stage fright was cured by doing *Primo** with love. (In the letters I wrote to him.) Could I deal with my death-fright with something similar? Love.
 I asked about the portfolio of my drawings done in our early sessions and of the possibility of her coming to Stratford.
 11.30. Nurses from Shakespeare Hospice come round. I told them the story of us visiting the hospice as research for *Kunene and the*

---

* Tony's one-man play about the Holocaust survivor Primo Levi.

King. One of them asked what it feels like: having acted the part, and now living it? I replied, 'I preferred acting it.'

Said to G that if I could choose the perfect way to die it would be like this – in this house with him constantly here at my side.

Sitting here at my desk this afternoon at the dreaded empty hour of 3 p.m. staring out at another dreaded grey day in the field, I realised that I was stuck in one of those dreaded times. With absolutely NOTHING to do.

So why not die?

Thursday 2 September

Woke to another grey day of nothingness, but decided to cherish it more. Things may be physically difficult for me currently (unpacking the shopping, getting up and down the stairs), but it's nothing to what's coming, when I'll be so feeble I'll just lie in bed all day, dozing and fading.

Several nurses have suggested getting in a hospital bed, which would make things easier for me: being able presumably to control lying down or sitting up. But that'll mean no longer sleeping next to G. Can't bear the thought of it. I can't live without sleeping next to G. How can I die without it?

And what about peeing and dumping? Does that mean that hateful thing, a catheter, and an adult nappy? Such quiet horrors in store.

Friday 3 September

So here I am again...paralysed by inactivity.

There are things I could be doing:

1) Working on *Prospero and the Spirits*. A couple of years ago, I started a big oil of this, after I realised the coloured pencil original was fading fast, but never had the appetite and abandoned it. Only the head and top half of Prospero is painted but I want to cut it out and give it to Janice as a (death) gift. Just needs a bit of scrubbing around it with white spirit to soften some crude lines and shapes.

2) Writing the *Dying Diaries* book.

But I don't have the energy for either at the moment.

Dying creates such an overwhelming feeling of pointlessness.

On the other hand, there's Marietta's phrase 'with love'. Find motivation to work through doing it with love. But for who? Maybe me.

Sun came out and we lunched on the patio. It was like being on holiday.

Evening. Mike Theodorakis died yesterday, so we watched *Zorba* again tonight. God, it's a fine film. Felt very proud of my 15-year-old self for recognising why it was different from Hollywood films, and so much better. That European filmmaking, so much more beautiful, brutal and honest. And what a delight to realise that Zorba is Falstaff: a loser who is also a life force, and can endlessly bullshit his way into work and fortune.

Saturday 4 September

Dream. G & I are listening to the radio. We hear: 'The death has been announced of the actor Sir Antony Sher. Tributes have come in from …'

We look at one another in shock. Then I stumble towards the radio, wondering if the report is true.

Don't know if it's because of the dream, but felt distinctly weaker today. Has the dreaded new phase started? We were told three to four months but we were never told from when. Maybe I've just weeks left …?

Evening, watched *Gloria* with Julianne Moore, such a tremendous actress. What is it? Something like M. Streep has, a combination of vulnerability and humour which can break your heart.

It did break G's heart tonight: her portrayal of loneliness. At bedtime he spoke about his fear of being alone, and we both began weeping uncontrollably. Then he yawned. And then we laughed uncontrollably.

He yawns a lot these days. It's not tiredness, it's one of the most surprising signs of anxiety.

Sunday 5 September

We've been praying for just one more completely sunny day, and today we got it.

Breakfasted outside, lunched outside, had supper outside, and spent all the time in between outside.

It was exquisite.

My siesta was truly special. Dozing in the lounger, under the 'dangling apricock'* tree, feeling it brush my arm from time to time, gazing at its leaves above me, layers of light and shade, and then the clear blue sky beyond, and all around birdsong from the big field and its trees. I slept deeply, beautifully, and when I woke the geraniums around the sundial seemed to spring across the lawn at me like someone giving a nice surprise. The colour! That velvety orange-red colour. I saw it as only a very sick person can, as if for the first time.

But, despite these pleasures, the strange new fatigue was there again. It's cured (temporarily) by alcohol, when I am suddenly infused with energy again, so is it the sickness getting worse or the drinking getting more demanding?

This evening, after yet another bout of drowsiness, I said to G: 'I've got to stop doing dying acting.'

He said: 'Yes. Act Five acting.'

We roared with laughter. In the big tragedies, Act Five is often a slow, doom-laden fall, and one of G's most frequent notes is 'Stop showing me you are in Act Five. Your characters don't know what's going to happen in the next half hour, so how do you?'

Tuesday 7 September

Sudden crack in the big sycamore tree. And a shower of leaves. Had a branch broken? No, it was just a shift in the atmosphere, autumn coming. Never noticed that before – autumn coming with a crack.

Wednesday 8 September

A new season normally comes with a wind. The arrival of spring is a beautiful warm breeze; today's version was less attractive, with a slight chill on its edge. Unmissable.

Friday 10 September

The RSC press announcement of Greg's compassionate leave.

Marietta session. She pointed out that this situation (i.e. dying) was so utterly new as an experience that I needed to invent new thoughts,

---

* The Gardener in *Richard II* refers to the 'dangling apricocks' in his garden. Ours never produced any fruit.

new feelings to deal with it. I told her about something that had been disturbing me: the few times I've seen a dead person close to & how each had shocked me. Nothing peaceful about any of them. What will I look like? She suggested I use the image of myself having those exquisite siestas on the sunny days, earlier this week. I liked that.

We talked about continuity, things which will go on after my death. Like the garden. And Greg's love for me. I mentioned that I'd already told G that he mustn't close himself off to a new relationship, a new partnership.

'Oh, bullshit!' she exclaimed, laughing but serious, too. 'You can't go there at the moment. What nonsense. Where did you get such nonsense from, such bullshit.'

I roared with laughter: I'm going to write in my diary that in twenty-five years of therapy with Marietta this is the first time she has ever told me I am talking bullshit.

By now, (noon) messages were pouring in from people who had heard the news. Judi Dench saying she was holding us tightly in her arms. Rufus Norris (NT) describing me as a cultural icon.

Saturday 11 September: Compassionate Leave

A single bright yellow lime leaf spinning and dancing outside the kitchen window this morning, a tiny miracle. It is tugging on an invisible thread of spider web, but as other leaves tumble around it in an early gust of autumn, this luminous little spirit refuses to fall, and pirouettes to its own silent orchestra. Tiny things seem precious now.

Yesterday the RSC announced that I would be taking a period of compassionate leave to look after Tony. Tsunami of emails. I rang Thelma Holt just before the company meeting. In the swirl of reactions which follow she gets the prize, emailing to say a case of champagne is on its way.

And Dominic Cavendish in the Telegraph, *mourning the end of our working relationship*, which I read to Tony at the breakfast table over our Saturday morning boiled eggs.

'Odd to read my obituary,' says T. 'It's a rave!' I say, 'a five-star obituary from the Telegraph!' And I read it to him:

> 'The RSC's power couple, now forced to retreat from the spotlight, were responsible for a Golden Age of Shakespearean

production' ... 'That partnership has served as a guarantor of quality for the past decade, upholding the RSC's sense of mission in its mixture of long-honed expertise, star quality and interrogative curiosity. For commentators like myself and I suspect many audience members the Doran/Sher 'project' represents a gilded era of Shakespearean production, when a deep-rooted understanding of the text, immaculate handling of the language and an aversion to facile modishness held sway. It wasn't avant-garde but nor was it fusty – very often it dazzled. In the security of his relationship with Doran, Sher has brought a slew of towering performances to the stage. Theirs has been one of the great partnerships of British theatre. Its abrupt end has shocked the industry.'

Dark humour sustains us both in this dark time. And we laugh at silly things. We started watching Once Upon a Time in America, *the Sergio Leone epic mobster movie set in Jewish Brooklyn. It has a great score by Ennio Morricone. Which prompts Tony to remember a little song we made up: 'Any old iron, any old iron, any Ennio Morricone', except we can't quite remember how we made all the syllables fit, which keeps us chuckling in bed for ages before we settled to sleep.*

We have progressively been clearing things. We had already brought up all his old diaries, and stored them all in a large plastic trunk. We have worked methodically through all his drawings, and sketch books and artwork. There is a personal folio with intimate drawings, and raw psychological portraits; a general folio of his drawings; with an A4 folio of smaller drawings which he did in the seventies.

On Saturday morning I took a snapshot of Tony's studio, as ordered and tidy as it has ever looked with vase of sunflowers dazzling the room. In the afternoon Tony's niece Heidi and her husband Ed arrive with a vanload of stuff from the eaves of the house in Islington. By the time the unloading had finished the tables were completely stacked both above and below.

The amount of stuff is overwhelming.
My beautiful studio turns into a junk yard.
But it'll be good for me to share the sorting of all this, rather than have Greg have responsibility alone when I am gone.

I try to identify what's in the boxes. Some are filled with old videos. Some with old cassettes. Some with old computer discs we can't play any more. The cassettes are mostly accents people have recorded for Tony to study: a Cookham accent for Stanley Spencer, a Turkish accent for Shylock from Joan Washington.

'Krapp's spool of life is almost wound, and the silent tape is both the time it has left to run and the silence into which he must pass.'

The first big item is a dusty cabin trunk. Tony's been dying to look at this. It's the trunk he brought over from Cape Town when he first arrived in the UK in 1969, and took with him after drama school to the Liverpool Everyman. There is a paper sticker on the corner with the address: Liverpool Everyman, Hope St, Liverpool, from a time before postcodes.

There is a thin paper poster on top. It's for The Bespoke Overcoat *with an unmistakable Sher cartoon. It's at the Weismann theatre in Cape Town, 'an Esther Caplan production'.* There is pencil drawing of his art master McCabe, who nurtured the young prodigy's talent, and was then hurt when little Ant decided he was going to try for a career in acting not art. There is a magazine cutting with colour photographs of* Richard II *at Maynardville, the Shakespeare theatre in Cape Town. It could easily be an English production from the early sixties. But there at the back standing in attendance upon the king is a rather short herald with the unmistakable profile of a young Antony Sher.*

There are old exercise books filled with drafts of plays. 'Not plays,' Tony says. 'They are film-scripts.' He and his tight little group of school friends used to make cine-films, and here I suspect they are, all jumbled up in a little square leather 'Dunlop' box. 'Don't you want to see them?' I ask. 'We couldn't possibly, it would be far too much trouble,' he sighs. 'Not enough time left. Just throw them away.' I put them all to one side.

We start on the manuscripts of his books, beginning with Year of the King. *We have already found some sketches which had never made their way into the book, and which had nearly been lost in a flood at home in Islington back in January. Amazing drawings of Tony trying out different animal looks, the wild boar, a bull, a sort of bison.*

---

* Auntie Esther was Tony's 'elocution' teacher, and eventually his brother Randall's mother-in-law.

Then we try and file Middlepost. *Here is a letter from Carmen Callil* [the founder of Virago Press, then managing director of Chatto & Windus] *in which she calls Tony's first novel the best novel that could ever be written about South Africa, about immigration and the Jews … Pretty hyperbolical praise. I read it out to Tony who bats it back with 'and she said of my next novel "I hate it".*

The drafts of the other three published novels, Indoor Boy, Cheap Lives, *&* The Feast *make their way to satisfyingly neat piles, and we ditch the trim little desk-box full of computer disks.*

In the middle of the morning, a van draws up on the street. It's a blow-up mattress and cushion for Tony, with a pump for each. The mattress and cushion are to prevent bedsores for when Tony is confined to bed, as apparently we have to expect. Not yet, I want to shout at the nice delivery man as he demonstrates the pump action.

There is a little leather suitcase, which Sandra Smith and the Wig girls gave Tony at the end of a long Stratford season before he went on tour to Newcastle and elsewhere. It stayed with him for years, until the handle fell off and had to be replaced with string. But it still has the brushes with which he applied his make-up like painting a portrait in the long half-hour before any show.

There are plastic bags retrieved from his dressing room at the Ambassadors after Kunene and the King *closed with the rest of the West End, in March 2020. There are twenty different-sized paint brushes, and the pot he keeps them in. There are paint sticks in ivory and white and crimson lake, little circular and triangular wedges of sponge, Kryolan Professional Powder, with a Woods & Windsor powder puff to dust off the excess. There's a big red tub of Leichner removing cream, and Nivea facial cleansing wipes to wipe it all after with a nice cold glass of Chablis at the end of the show.*

Monday 13 September

They talk of your life flashing before your eyes before death. Happened to me literally today as we began the gargantuan task of sorting the mounds. What to keep, what to chuck? Things from way-back-when cropping up. My first self-portrait aged about sixteen, with toothpick and smoking jacket. Pompous little boy. I suppose he's sad too, but I just want to give him a slap.

Surprised to find my acceptance letter from Webber Douglas.

Surprised to find my acceptance letter from Liverpool Everyman.

Delighted to find Andrew Motion's letter about the manuscript of *Middlepost*. He gave me an object lesson in creative writing.

Going through some lever arch files of special letters in the garden this afternoon. Robert Stephens asking Tony if he would play Iago to Robert's Othello. Nigel Hawthorne on his disappointment at the critical response to his King Lear with Ninagawa. Alan Dossor lamenting the closure of the Liverpool Everyman. McKellen, Stoppard, Berkoff, the Kinnocks, Archbishop Trevor Huddleston, and Helen Suzman. And very funny ones from Terry Hands.

Email from my new literary agent having read *The Sea Point House*.* All I could've hoped for. So it might get published after all. I won't be around to see it but nice to leave behind.

Tuesday 14 September

We've had a flood of emails, texts, letters. Among all the famous names, the most touching was from Rosinda, who used to clean for us. And an equally touching phone call from Ralph Sher, my favourite cousin, trying to be cheerful, refusing to believe it's final.

Several people have suggested that G and I try and find some beauty in this strange time. It's not a word I'd ever thought of, but they're right, and it's happening. We are having some beautiful times, mostly laughing together, crying together too. We've never been so close.

Tuesday's job is to sort the scripts. One box delivers some surprises from the very start of his career. Scripts from the Everyman: Tarzan's Last Stand *in which he played Enoch Powell;* John, Paul, George, Ringo and Bert, *the Beatles show which took him to the West End;* The Government Inspector *from the Lyceum in Edinburgh;* Teeth and Smiles *from the Royal Court, though we can't find his script for* Cloud Nine. *His research material for Mike Leigh for* Goose-Pimples; White Man Blues *by Adrian Mitchell; and Carl Sternheim's* Knickers *from his time at Nottingham Playhouse under Richard Eyre. A play he did at the Bush, one for the King's Head, another by Edward Bond for Gaysweatshop, with a rather accurate cartoon of Bond himself on the front cover.*

---

* The unpublished novel Tony wrote during lockdown.

So far only one page has emerged for Singer, *with a jovial sketch of Peter Flannery, but the other RSC plays are here.* Molière, *and* Tartuffe; *Peter Barnes's* Red Noses *and David Edgar's* Maydays; *and TV scripts for* Collision Course, *and for* The History Man. *And the film script of* Shadey.

And, of course, the Shakespeares.

Wednesday 15 September

Jim comes up for the day. [Jim Hooper, Tony's previous partner.] It was lovely, chatting, looking at photos and drawings. Nevertheless I was aware of a veil of self-control, thin as tissue paper, keeping my feelings in. It almost tore open as we hugged goodbye. (Beforehand G had said, 'Don't think of it as the last time you are seeing one another.' But of course it was.) But I held it in. Afterwards thought to myself how stupid, how English. I should've just wailed.

Anyway, as he stepped out of the front door, there was a movement on the ground below us and we all looked down to see a snake uncurl and slither itself across to the herb box, disappearing behind it. It was enormous. About five feet. G said it was a grass snake, but do they really grow to that size? Very thrilling.

Reminded me of one of my favourite D. H. Lawrence poems, 'Snake':

> A snake came to my water-trough
> On a hot, hot day, and I in my pyjamas for the heat
> To drink there.

When Jim had gone, G remarked that snakes are supposed to be a symbol of immortality.

'Boy, did it get the wrong address!' I said.

We had one of our really good laughs.

Call from the new literary agent. He had given me some notes in his Monday email, but said I didn't have to implement them. The book was ready to be sent out now – to find a publisher. But I love notes so I said I'd do them and get revised draft to him soon.

Friday 17 September

Ruth arrives, G's twin sister. A true gift for Greg, and a blessing – how they will talk over the next few days.

Beth and David [daughter of Tony's brother Joel and her husband] drive up from London for visit. She's seven months pregnant and radiant with it. (Oh dear, will a birth and a death happen at the same time?)

Also Ruth's eldest, Evan, arrived (he's doing a course in London), a handsome charming bright twenty-eight-year-old.

Also Mark and Jo.

Everyone here to say hello to Ruth. It's good for me to be distracted from my thoughts, enjoyable too.

Monday 20 September
Weather so splendid we decide on a braai, and everyone comes along again.

When I first got my diagnosis I said I was going to party towards death, and then let painkillers take over. Pleasure and painkillers – that's the way to go. So far lots of pleasure …

But a sad/beautiful moment when the Doran siblings took a selfie of themselves. They were there without me.

Later had a secret cry in Greg's arms. Emotion still very close to the surface.

Tuesday 21 September
While G and Ruth go off on long walks and talks I work on the book. That joy again.

At night, a full moon. Will this be my second last?

Wednesday 22 September
Time for Ruth to leave. I've been dreading this moment. My tissue-thin layer of control is no match for the moment when it comes. Can't stop hugging her. I whisper: 'Take care of him.' We all get very upset. And then G drove her to the station.

Thursday 23 September
A beautiful day. Spend most of it in a writing ecstasy (G working next door), breaking off to lunch outside together, and me to siesta in the garden – one of those glorious fresh air siestas. At drinks in the evening, the sky is a clear vista of foreverness. A perfect day.

Saturday 25 September

G has resolved to cook all my favourite foods during this strange limbo time we're in. Today he tackled the Big One. Bagels.

Not those soft rolls with a hole in the middle which you get in shops but genuine, homemade, shtetl-style bagels. Grannie Annie taught Katie [the Sher family 'maid' in Sea Point] the Plungyan recipe and no one in the family has been able to make them since.

Today I try making proper shtetl bagels, as Tony calls them, while he prints out the draft of The Sea Point House *which he has been working on all week. He's nervous because he fears the printer will conk out before he's done. He calls me through. Somehow the skin on his left forearm has torn over a purple bruise. I get some TCP and cotton wool and the plasters, and tidy him up. This keeps happening now. His shirt sleeve has a patch of dried blood at the elbow, but he doesn't want to change his shirt. He's too busy. 'Life is too short,' he smiles, 'literally.'*

At bedtime, said to G, 'I'm not scared of death, but am very scared of the next phase arriving. No more up and down stairs, more and more confined to bed.'

We cheered ourselves up by developing our new chant further, realising the rhyming potential of the Yiddish word faygeleh (gay) which G had first heard on the Jackie Mason DVD.

> I'm not a faygeleh bageler
> I'm a faygeleh bageler's chum ...

Getting sillier and sillier, we laugh ourselves to sleep.

Sunday 26 September

Oich. Overnight, the bagels, doing their eighteen hours wait in the fridge, have swollen, lost their holes, and look like what G calls 'floury cowpats'.

Still – we've yet to taste them.

G starts the last part of the process, triple boiling them and baking them.

Well, the bagels are a triumph. Lacking in holes maybe, but otherwise the real thing to a tee: crisp golden brown on the outside, soft and chewy within. I had mine with egg mayo and cheddar cheese. G had lox and cream cheese. Katie's bagels are back!

Monday 27 September

Rain is back, greyness and depression. Apart from everything else, I've finished the book, and sent off the revisions and have <u>nothing</u> to do.

Also, as we creep towards October, and my death date (which we don't strictly know, and certainly don't try to name), I'm feeling a strange new sensation. I want to change my mind.

I want to stop dying.

Maybe I could still take sorafenib, and gain a few more months? No – remember that instead of my present lifestyle, which is still quite normal, I'd be constantly going to clinics, I'd be feeling sick from the side effects. I'd be alive longer, yes, but wretched.

This is the correct way but it's becoming alarming.

Agent loves the rewrites. Wants to start approaching publishers by the end of the week.

Wednesday 29 September

Marietta. Told her how, over the last few days we've been sorting the studio again, archiving some things and dumping others. I've been shaken by the process, and less curious than I would have been in different circumstances. Marietta said here was another example of the cancer forcing me to <u>invent</u> new ways of thinking and feeling. Being shaken and curious at the same time: opposites, pulling in different directions, yet having to function together.

We talked about perfection. A lot of my artwork disappoints me. Only a very few are seriously any good.

Talked about 'paying the price' for happiness. I said I only felt that in terms of booze. I knew I was drinking too much and I'm paying the price. But I wouldn't change it if I had to do it again – I enjoyed it too much.

Evening. Watched the film *Supernova*. God, talk about too close for comfort. The story of a middle-aged gay couple, one of whom is very ill – with growing dementia – the other is acting as his carer. We wept and wept. Colin Firth and Stanley Tucci are superb, completely convincing – touching and kissing one another with the true tenderness of long-standing partners. What idiot said straight actors can't play gay?

Greg continues to make special dishes for me, dishes from my youth. For supper, green bean bredie. With beans instead of tomatoes. Delicious. So familiar from so long ago. Jesus, I'm lucky to have G.

I dread the arrival of October. During the pandemic we used to say 'It's Thursday ... Again!' The weeks seemed to turn round so quickly, and Thursday meant putting the order out to Paddock Farm for meat for the weekend and finding out which dustbins this week. Now, the days are shortening. Like our days together.

Yesterday we had another blitz on Tony's room. By five we had sorted all the programmes, first night cards etc., joined them to the scripts and put them all into the cabin trunk. They fitted perfectly. What a treasure trove. As the last one went in, and the groaning tables had finally been cleared of dusty cardboard boxes, I felt a quiet sense of triumph and of a job efficiently and imaginatively done. But Tony had removed his glasses and was wiping away tears.

How insensitive I had been. We were packing away a career of fifty years. As I locked up the trunk, he felt the snap of finality.

Thursday 30 September: the last day of September

Eve. A minor disagreement about our cleaner Nadia coming tomorrow, exploded into a terrible incident. To win a cheap point I said, 'Well, I'll just die, and get out of your way.' I knew this was wrong, taboo, off-limits completely. G responded by sweeping everything off the table, walking out, slamming the door and going to bed.

Thank God Tony came up and apologised. Eventually went back downstairs. And in silence watched The Repair Shop. *But I became overwhelmed. Tony said I mustn't hold it in. I said if I started to cry I was afraid I wouldn't be able to stop. All I can feel is an abysm of emptiness I am being dragged inexorably towards. I could hear myself making these horrible noises.*

Some sort of battle royal going on in the back field. Gatling-gun cries of the magpies, attracting a squadron of jackdaws who come swooping in from over the ridge. I can hear a crow squawking behind the fence which is where the action is centred, but I can't see. The jackdaws dive about, the magpies following. There is even a hobby hovering on a higher plane but following the action. The blustery day echoes the turmoil of the event. And now it's all over.

OCTOBER

'I didn't realise that dying meant actual dying'

Saturday 2 October
G has got the RSC to send over a newly mastered copy of the archive 'film' of *Richard III*. In fact, it's just one motionless long shot from the back of the auditorium, done on all shows as a record. G wants to watch it with me. Anyway, we only watch the first few minutes: 'Now is the winter ...' my voice is surprisingly light and inexpressive (when Roger Allam comes on as Clarence, you hear a <u>real</u> theatre voice). But my body compensates and the crutches are impressive.

Then, with me still feeling today's odd new fatigue and depression, G proposed the latest Jackie Mason DVD we've got. *The World According to Me*. For the next one and a half hours laughter went through me like a gust of fresh air. Then we saved the second half for later. Said to G, 'If only there was an endless supply of Jackie Mason shows I'd get through whatever this cancer can throw at me.'

By bedtime feeling very frightened. Who knows, this process might not be long and drawn out but quick and unexpected (like in the middle of tonight).

Monday 4 October
A new plan this morning. Instead of him getting up, coming downstairs for breakfast and then going back up to wash and dress, he would wash and dress before coming down, meaning one less trip to and fro, which exhausts him by the time he gets back down and robs him of energy at the start of the day.

Over lunch he asked me (eventually when he could get it out), 'When I die ...' he hasn't ever said that so openly, or without any prelude, 'When I die, will you ring Randall first, and then Joel, and then Jim. It's been preying on my mind.'

'*We must talk about the funeral too,*' he said. Oh dear.

Sandra Smith came round on Saturday, to cut my (very long) hair and for her and Matt to witness us sign our wills, which I posted this morning.

Tuesday 5 October

Tony wobbles getting up from his armchair this morning. He's panting more, and thinks perhaps he needs to keep his stick with him now. He leans against the door frame, with his head in his hand.

We attended to the paint cupboard in his study to prepare for some work today on Prospero, the cut-down portrait in oils that Tony wants to work up for Janice. He'll complete it in acrylics.

Tuesday 5 October

Encouraged and bullied by G, I finally did the bit of work on the Prospero picture. With G acting as my assistant, I sat in front of the picture – stuck to my drawing table angled up. Odd feeling – to be doing artwork again. Quickly realised why I had been avoiding it. My hands shake badly, and G had to keep moving my chair back, then forward again, for me to gain perspective on it.

Struggled. Thought I'd achieved it, then decided no. Usual thing with me and artwork.

Wednesday 6 October

Marietta call. I'd emailed her the Prospero portrait and we discussed it. I said it was a double portrait: a) the character of Prospero, frowning with concentration as he works out his revenge strategy; b) the actor, me, sitting backstage between scenes bored, pissed off – doing the show again – and wondering how long before the first drink.

We discussed why I became an actor. 'You didn't have to,' she said. 'We don't have to do anything we don't want to.'

'The irony is,' I replied, 'these days I can hardly do anything whether I want to or not.' For the record, I told her I loved acting – in rehearsal, in that delicious, bubbling stew of creativity. It was only the endless repetition of performance that I hated.

The district nurse rang – their weekly check-up. I told her about the new disintegration this week. Was that normal? She replied, 'I'm afraid it is – at this stage.' What stage, I wondered – did she have an

EDD on her file. Estimated Death Date? After the call I said to G: 'I keep getting frights from this. It's like I didn't realise that dying meant actual dying.'

After watching a wildlife doc, *Serengeti*, G and I rejoiced that we share a love of wildlife. All those safaris, and trips, my God, the things we have seen together. What a privilege. What a beautiful part of our love.

Thursday 7 October
[Written in black pen.]
> Writing this diary is becoming harder and harder. My shaking hand, my weak eyesight. Might have to stop.

[Then in blue pen.]
> ... That said, must record watching a home movie this evening, on the trip to Middlepost* which G and I took in 1993, with Ralph, Myra and Dad. Very moving. Especially Dad. (He would die later that year.) All through my youth I was irritated by how muddled his communication was. He'd tell stories and forget what point he was making. Here he is in this film still doing it. But it's poignant now. And he communicates much better with the Cape Coloured people,† who come up to pay their respects – in Afrikaans of course. Maybe that's it. He spent his life having to speak his second language, English.

How strong and handsome G and I look, what a great couple. But I am still speaking in that strange false posh accent, in which I played Richard III. Wonder when I finally got rid of it?

Friday 8 October
Dr Alia visit. She reassured me about 'the change' that's happened to me over the last week. Said it might continue like this for a while and then dip again, or not. No two people go on this journey in the same way.

---

*Subject of T's first novel: a small 'dorp' or village in the Karoo where the Shers would go on family holidays.
† 'Cape Coloured' is a term used in South Africa for a specific racial classification referring to people of mixed European, African and/or Asian heritage.

Another episode of *Serengeti*. We couldn't stop laughing when they showed a pride of lions stalking gnu and remembered Billy Connolly's sketch (possibly his best sketch ever) on selfsame situation with head lioness whispering to her sisters on either side 'Eh, Agnes … 'Ere Betty …' gesturing the best manoeuvre for attack. We became completely hysterical.

Saturday 9 October
Despite a good nine hours sleep, I had severe fatigue all day. It's a horrible feeling. That irresistible downward pull.

Discussed the funeral. The favourite choice is Holy Trinity. But would they let a faygeleh Jewish alte kaker have a service in there? I suppose the Actors' Church in London is a working Church too, and they allow it. G says he will talk to the vicar.

Saturday 9 October
Four months today since we heard about The Satsuma and the Walnut. Made bouillabaisse last night as a special treat, the Julia Child recipe, with halibut, hake and cod loin.

Tried a stool in the shower. Sitting to wash. Then putting the stool on carpet to dry (G helping). Felt easier, but vaguely humiliating. This is also part of the next stage.

This week's deterioration in his energy levels depresses him. The doctor said that this was a step, but not an indicator of the speed of the progress of the disease. He could remain at this stage for some time. T very anxious for her not to estimate an ETA. In fact got me to waylay her en route to see him to ask her specifically to avoid doing so.

Monday 11 October
G emailed the vicar and he replied in a flash, saying yes of course, they'd be honoured.

But I feel honoured, too, more so than if it was Westminster Abbey. Shakespeare's church!

Watched home movies, which G has had transferred to DVDs. Very strange to see. From when Joel was a small baby to Randall's wedding.

Tuesday 12 October

Mustered the energy and courage and <u>finally</u> did one of the drawings I had been planning: 'Done from Death'.

Worked on my drawing fast – about one and a half hours – moving between a chair at the upright drawing board and one on my desk.

Fairly pleased with the outcome, though it was more active, more ferocious than I had planned. More like someone howling, raging (against the dying of the light) than dead. When G saw it, he said it represented dying not death. Realised why. The features are too animated. For example, the brow is twisted and agonised, but death would unclench muscles. They'd be smooth. Everything would be blank, except for the fallen mouth.

This was the perfect example of what art therapy seeks to reveal. The brain sets out to do one thing, the hands and the heart do another. My hands and my heart know I'm not dead yet, and don't want to show it. So I'll have to master them and do it again.

Bright morning, Tony sat in his studio and drew. A Lear-like sketch on the drawing board. Him, but in a sort of harrowing wind tunnel of grief, gaping mouth but too tired to scream, and eyes closed but not in death, perhaps to prevent seeing what approaches. He's sketching the next part he has to play.

Wednesday 13 October

G helping me to wash, dry and dress in the morning is a great help – yet sad too: step by step I am becoming an invalid.

Last night in bed, Tony frightened. 'It's happening so fast,' he said. 'We don't have much time left.'

'We've got to enjoy the "now, now, very nowness" of things,' I said. 'Look what happened today, when we looked through the portfolio of art therapy pieces that Marietta had sent up, I saw work that you have done over twenty-five years that I have never seen before, and they were wonderful.'

And they are: haunting, disturbing, angry, but all done with astonishing imagination. There are recurrent issues: cocaine addiction, alcohol, the intruder dream. Of the monster waiting outside a locked door. Fear, a slouching black hyena, the fear of being on stage and losing your lines. The fear of stage fright.

> *There is one of his mum's huge claw-like hand, her wrist bangled in gold, her fingers jewelled, her nails plated in scarlet varnish, holding out a peppermint cream to a tiny child – Tony.*
>
> *He's settled down to his weekly chat with Marietta now. I've dressed him, made him a fried egg and carried through his coffee. A quiet hour.*
>
> *The bed arrived just after lunch. I resented it as soon as it appeared, pushed it against the wall and quickly covered it with travel rugs to disguise it. It's as if he's brought the coffin in.*

The hospital bed arrives (supplied by the NHS). It's brutally shocking. Both G and I feel this. An image of disease, dying, death here in my beautiful studio, my beautiful room. It upset us in a weird way. We became strangely angry with one another, and oppressed by our constant proximity. How bizarrely fear affects one. I left him alone and went to watch a DVD on my computer.

The DVD was *Primo*.

Much more than my performance and adaptation or Richard's direction [Richard Wilson] or Hildegard Bechtler's design, I was struck by Primo Levi's achievement. His creation of this journey through hell. His setting is one of the most epic and evil atrocities which mankind has ever known – its scale is apocalyptic, and he's just one little man, yet by giving evidence as an ordinary individual he somehow manages to show the whole giant picture. This description of his book has been given 1,000 times before, but it struck me anew today. Felt very proud of having represented it with the simple power of our show, but in terms of my performance, I tend to go a bit too fast, not allowing things to land or linger, and so end up displaying one of my faults as an actor: being too efficient and in control, not spontaneous enough, not human enough.

Thursday 14 October

My fatigue today is incredible, unrelenting, depressing. I can <u>feel</u> myself dying. It's shocking. My instincts sense it could be very soon.

People who write to us (letters, emails, gifts, love, keep pouring in) say they can't imagine what we're going through.

No, well, I can't either.

Yet we are going through it, and it's surreal, because some of the time things are rather ordinary and nice.

After my siesta this afternoon (on the new bed, a bit uneasy) and when drowsiness returned, instantly, G suggested we watch the rest of the Jackie Mason DVD. Within seconds I am wide awake, and crying with laughter. It's like you are being carried through the air.

Friday 15 October
Busy morning. Have just got Tony settled for a doze on the horrible new hospital bed. Before he closed his eyes he got frightened. He said the doctor had told him to reconcile himself to a time when he won't be able to get out of bed by himself. And that a team of carers will have to come and care for him, bath him etc. Tears sprang to his eyes. 'But what about peeing and dumping?' he cried. 'Don't worry about that yet,' I said, 'don't let that trouble the now.'

'I can feel myself slipping away,' he said. 'It might happen sooner than we think.'

I watch him snore gently. Taverner's 'Song for Athene' in the other room.

Sunday 17 October
Keep resisting visitors, but always enjoy it when they come. Lovely lunch today with Mark and Angie, and Ben Tyreman. Together we filled out power of attorney forms.

Monday 18 October
Watched two films: *Sunday Bloody Sunday* – such tenderness – and *Mrs Brown* – part of its excellence stems from the fine, fine script. An excellent actor in it playing Disraeli, but nothing came of him.

Doctor reports that blood test results are OK. Thank God, no transfusion.

Our comedy fix tonight was *An Audience with Kenneth Williams* … bliss, bliss, bliss.

Tuesday 19 October
One of those days – woke up feeling noticeably worse than yesterday. Scared the shit out of me.

In the morning, with nothing to do, and unable to stay awake, began watching *Sophie's Choice*. If Brando's *Godfather* is the best male performance I've ever seen, Streep's Sophie is the best female performance. Got halfway through before lunch.

Afterwards siesta. As G helped settle me onto the hospital bed, he leaned over and kissed me. It affects me strangely. I saw the same thing happening, with us in the same position, but me dead, him saying goodbye. I became very upset.

Tony restless today. He is reluctant for me to set the bed up with all the new sheets, not even the pillowcases. But he settles back, and I take off his socks, pull the 'best friend' green waffle blanket around him and lean over to kiss him. He suddenly gasps, 'I get a terrible image each time you lean over to kiss me on this bed,' he says. I know what he is thinking and cannot bear it.

Over G&Ts in the big window, said to G, 'Remind me again, why you were against the Dignitas idea.'

My concerns were not about Dignitas as such, but about the legal and moral issues of assisted dying being adopted in this country. I worry about the mental strain it would put on the sick and the elderly, thinking they were a burden on their relatives. I worry about the terrible extra pressure on the disabled community. I worry about the slippery slope. But I told Tony that if that is what he wanted of course I would be right there, and would book our tickets to Zurich.

As we talked it through, I realised that, apart from the incredible strain of organising it all, once it was over G would have to return home alone. I couldn't bear that thought.

I said, 'OK then, not Dignitas. What about a glass of champagne?'

Wednesday 20 October
Best Jewish joke I ever heard:
  Solly finally decides to tell his 90-year-old mother he's gay.
  She responds by asking, 'Does that mean you put your mouth on other men's private parts?'
  'Yes, Mother, I do.'
  'Oh, Solly,' she says, 'and you wouldn't even try my kishka.'
  Marietta. Done as a three-way call, with G. Having finally admitted he needs help, he asked me to organise it. But now on the call, he's totally calm, charming, articulate and unstressed.

Throughout these sessions on dying, M has used the word 'continuity': how, when I am gone, the world will continue in all its magnificence, and that I should take comfort from that. Today, she used the word in a new context: 'The continuity of Greg.' How I should take comfort in the amount that G could still achieve, and maybe he and I should talk about that, and I could help, with his decision-making? He wasn't comfortable with it, wasn't able to look at his life beyond me. When in quick succession he will lose his husband, his job and his home. He's also scared of bursting the bubble: the aura of normality which still exists in this house.

After the call he said he was not sure whether he wanted to continue three-ways, or switch to one-to-ones, or not do them at all.

Getting up from my siesta, saw the sky was clear blue. Wondering if it was mild enough to sit out, opened the front door to test the air. A blast of cold freshness, sunlight, wind, golden leaves all rustling.

Beautiful. Moments of life you only see clearly when you are dying.

Wrapped up warmly, we had tea in the garden. Then it clouded over quickly and we never got to see tonight's full moon (so is this my last?).

Thursday 21 October

Waking the usual sensation. Abandoning the joy of bed, where I feel totally well, to sitting up and feeling everything drain from me: energy, wakefulness. Now I feel totally unwell.

I think either:

Maybe today's the day

Or:

Maybe I'd like to die now.

Friday 22 October

This email from Jo Jelly* broke my heart:

Dearest Tony. You changed my life. You broadened my understanding of acting and Life. Marrying you was one of the best and most productive actions of my life and I thank you with all my heart, where you'll always have a place. With lots of love, Jo.

---

* Jo and Tony married in 1979.

By coincidence, I recently found, while sorting my papers, the Certificate of Naturalisation for my grandfather Joel (Dad's dad), it's dated 11 April 1903. It states that he's from Plungyan (so they use the Yiddish name) in Russia, that he's been in the Cape Colony for seven years (having arrived in 1896), that his occupation is a shopkeeper, and that he lives in Middlepost, Calvinia. I'd always assumed that he exchanged his Lithuanian (Russian) citizenship for South African citizenship, but of course SA was a British colony then, so instead he became British.

If I had known that, and produced this document in 1968 when I arrived here, would I have automatically inherited his British citizenship? Would my whole frightening struggle to find a way of staying and working in the UK have been unnecessary? That's an amazing thought.

Very bad drowsy day.

Because I'm taking no cancer medication, there are no side effects to distract me. My experience of dying is clean, clear, terrible.

Maybe similar to what infants experience but in reverse. They are slowly waking into life, I'm slowly fading from it. But both of us have this half-conscious view of the world. Now there's sunlight on the window, now there's rain, now someone walks past me, now the sound of cutlery going in and out of a drawer, now the fridge door opens.

I sit nodding off, feebly fighting it.

I hobble around, wearing a constant tired scowl.

As I fall asleep, comforted myself with images of different people hearing the news.

Saturday 23 October

Went in to dinner – to find G crying quietly in the pantry.

'What's brought this on?' I asked.

'Just catches me unawares,' he said.

We hugged, crying together.

This situation is mad.

It's like some kind of parable.

Eve. Watched episode one of *Succession*. Brilliant. Brian Cox magnificent. B is my generation (one year older) at the height of his career, power, earning capacity. Jealous, *moi*?

The feeling of unwellness is subtle yet overwhelming. There is a low sound of laboured breathing at my neck like it's someone else, someone who embarrasses me — following me everywhere. And my eyes are half-lidded, as though sedated or drunk. My view of life is of half the world, the lower half.

Gris round yesterday afternoon as T snoozed, which was of course a tonic. Loo sent a box of almond macaroons, delicious.

King Lear *running through my head last night. As we went to bed I had to trot back downstairs in my birthday suit to check a line:*

> Men must endure
> Their going hence, even as their coming hither.
> Ripeness is all.*

Why ripeness? Couldn't remember. But it's because Gloucester has just said he doesn't want to go any further, but just sit and rot where he is. Rot/Ripe.

He listens to Edgar's words and then adds, 'And that's true too'. John Barton's favourite line.

Montaigne argued that learning to die is essential for learning to live. Perhaps in philosophy for once in my life, I will find consolation or a way of helping Tony prepare. God knows. Anything.

Sunday 24 October

Had a tirade this afternoon about how this current feeling of fear and dread — something awful about to happen — has been with me all my life.

> Fear of school (especially PT)
> Fear of exams
> Fear of the army
> Fear of going overseas
> Fear of getting into drama school
> Fear of drama school
> Fear of how to stay and work in this country
> Fear of my gayness

* King Lear (Act 5 scene 2)

Fear of (as an actor) being known to be Jewish
Fear of (as a civilised human) being known to be a white South African.
Fear of every role I have played
Fear of every medical test I have had (prophetic)
Fear of shoulder replacement
Fear of open-heart surgery
Fear of knee surgery
Fear of the new person I've become: obese, unbalanced, limping
Fear of the day G and I went to Dr Shearman for the actual diagnosis
Fear ever since.

Sunday 24 October
King Lear begins to preach to the blinded Gloucester on the heath. I can hear Tony's delivery of those lines now:

When we are born we cry that we are come
To this great stage of fools.*

You might expect him to continue with this philosophical enquiry into the nature of life with an account of what death means ... but he gets distracted instead with a new military stratagem, and ends the speech running off shouting 'kill, kill, kill'.

The culinary experiment of the week: one of Tony's favourites: Tongue. Paddock Farm had agreed to source one and get it peeled and cured for a week in brine, and cooked. Don't know what I was expecting but this rigid vacu-packed joint arrived on Friday, looking exactly as if it had been made by the RSC prop department.

Monday 25 October
Odd sense of the beginning of another week, and a determination to make each day happy in some way. But anxious, it's the last week of the month. The fact that British Summer Time ends soon and the days are getting darker won't help Tony's mood. He was crying in his sleep early this morning. I wanted to wrap my arms around him, but didn't want to wake him.

---

* *King Lear* (Act 4 scene 6)

We've had lunch now, a favourite, Caesar salad, but for the first time he couldn't finish it. He's dozing here with me in the front room on his chair, while the beautiful andante from Mozart's Piano Concerto No. 12, played by Alfred Brendel, lulls him on the CD player. There is an exquisite theme in the centre of the piece which I find so beautiful. It may be a tribute by Mozart on hearing of the death of Johann Christian Bach, who was Mozart's mentor while in London. Before he settled Tony said: 'You know that expression people use "half dead", well, I'm experiencing that for real.'

Tuesday 26 October

Appalling night of no sleep, then a day of the worst drowsiness yet. Tried watching *Room With a View*. What on earth is this story about? A piece of fluff passing itself off as great literature.

Wednesday 27 October

Marietta. Used my drawing 'Seventy' for discussion today. The self-portrait I did after my seventieth and the heart operation. Expresses the same thing I am experiencing now: total shock at what's become of me. This isn't my body. This isn't me.

G is endlessly patient and attentive, but I remain unresponsive, scowling, withdrawn. We eat meals in silence. I think I'm subconsciously punishing him for being well. It's ridiculous.

Made a resolution at bedtime to make more effort tomorrow, to cover up my feebleness more, to engage more.

Tony had another restless night. Yesterday the occupational therapist, Heidi, came round with her trainee nurse, Eko. She advised on everything from the height of Tony's chair and the sofa, to getting a 'glide-about' commode, and shower chair. Side protectors for the hospital bed, and the dangers of crocs. A possible banister instalment and newel post addition, and a lip for the studio to allow the wheelchair access. A bit exhausting all in all, though very well meaning.

Tony had a good conversation with Randall on the phone this evening. With his new hearing aid, (which Tony bought for him) he can now hear his brother, which will ensure they can talk from now on without the frustration of Randall not really catching what is said.

Thursday 28 October

Thursday again. Terrible night. I must finally have dropped off because I had a dream and think I must have cried out. I heard Tony say, 'It's all right, it's all right!' I thought I saw him, standing on his side of the bed, with his light on and leaning towards me. I heard myself ask, 'What's happening?', but now it was dark again. The nightmare developed into being alone in a smashed-up room in a dingy flat and trying to protect myself from something outside. Pretty clear that anxieties about what happens afterwards are beginning to surface in my subconscious.

Odd light outside. Slanting under rain clouds. It lit the field, making it bright green an hour or so ago, but now it feels, with the river-flow of bright clouds in the distance, as if it predicates a day of angry weather. The light outside has shifted again. To flat gloom. I think I preferred the dramatic lighting. It feels weirdly as if something is going to happen today. I wonder how close we are.

I fear that lack of sleep will make me tetchy. Knowing that he is likely to go in his sleep makes me feel as if I am about to be robbed, and what is most precious to me stolen behind my back. As I write I am listening intently to any creaks from the bedroom above.

There is tension in the field. The crows have just fled the sycamore flying stage left, and all the pigeons took off, fleeing stage right, suddenly the wind has dropped completely and the squirrel on the fence post has frozen, listening. Footsteps upstairs.

So today I cut Tony's hair. A fairly nerve-wracking experience, having never cut anyone's hair before. There was a stage when I thought he looked like Sarah Miles, tarred and feathered in Ryan's Daughter. *We have taken it right down so he can wash and care for it easily. But his scalp is quite scruffy where the skin flakes in patches. But it is not obvious to him, so that is good.*

We did a big haircut this morning: hair to a No. 3, beard only a bit longer. Will make hair washing in the period ahead easier. It was fun, like doing a new look for my next part – Dying Man – and I felt no drowsiness. And G and I were really <u>engaging</u>.

I was so nervous that when the phone suddenly rang on the desk in the bedroom, I bit my tongue. It's quite a deep bite, and right in the middle. But the tongue seems to be a rather resilient organ, and after mouth-washing it a few times, it already feels on the mend.

The phone went several times. The district nurse; the delivery company about to deliver a whole load of stuff: bedside supports, inflatable cushion, an extra pee bottle etc.; and the surgery trying to arrange a Covid booster for Tony.

And the front doorbell went. That turned out to be a real delight. A package of two delicious Kobe steaks from Thelma, all packaged and wrapped in freezer bags. There are also instructions about how best to serve.

Eve: watched *An Evening with Peter Ustinov*. The man was a genius. Such subtlety and grace to his work, but hilarious, too.

Friday 29 October
I mentioned to the substitute doctor (Dr Sam) that the district nurse had suggested I talk to her about liquid morphine as a help with my breathlessness. I thought morphine was for the very last stage, but to my surprise Dr Sam recommended it and by noon I had some.

Dr Sam said that on the plus side it would help my breathing and bring a sense of wellbeing. The negative side – it would cause drowsiness. More? I couldn't do more. Anyway, took 2.5 ml and almost instantly fell into a deep sleep for an hour. Then went into the kitchen for lunch, and again it lived up to its reputation. I was less breathless and felt very chirpy. At 2 p.m., and overcome by another deep, hour-long sleep. Decided not to take more until bedtime. Dr S was very relaxed about freedom of usage.

So I'm a morphine man now. Like the sound of it.

After lunch he settled for another doze while I got the yeast ready for our second batch of bagels. Then I slipped back to sit opposite him in the window. I am writing a chapter in the book on Venus and Adonis, *and the workshop where the puppeteers created the figure of Death for the first time, lots of cardboard and gaffer tape, sash cord and toilet rolls. I tried to describe the moment when they made Venus swing happily from Death's little pinkie, and how it captivated me, a highly original version of the danse macabre.*

Suddenly, Tony shuddered. He sat bolt upright, his eyes flickering in a shock reaction, and then he went still. For a second I thought this is it – here is the moment. Breath held. Then he came to.

He said he had felt as if someone had grabbed him in his sleep, and their face, close to his, was whispering in his ear, and yet he could still see me sitting there. I worry that this may be some hallucinogenic effect of the morphine. But it scared me stiff, and I think it did him, too. And what I couldn't stop thinking was that, like Holbein's famous woodcuts of the Dance of Death, the grim-grinning ghost had come for Tony.

We feel as though we have heard from pretty much everyone we know … with the odd exception of Simon Callow.

Saturday 30 October
Thelma Holt had herself driven up from London. As gifts, she had already arranged for genuine Kobe beef to be sent to us and today she arrived with another case of champagne. It was a joy to see her. Thought how blessed we were to have had such an extraordinary woman in our lives: one who had the power to make impossible projects happen.

NOVEMBER

'Thou met'st with things dying, I with things new born'

Monday 1 November
Secret Fear.
    Today becomes November.
    I think my death will be in November.

Email from Simon Callow. We expected him to make contact among the very first. Now he explains, saying that knowing that Tony was terminally ill had paralysed him.

> I could scarcely engage with the information – it simply seemed impossible. Tony and I have travelled through life with such strange synchronisation, often separated by oceans and continents, too often not seeing each other or even communicating, but never, in my case, certainly, unaware of each other, as if we were brothers, or each other's shadow, partly defining each other – sometimes by the parallels and sometimes by the divergences – partly echoing each other in hauntingly different ways.

Tony delighted to receive it. He wrote back immediately wishing he could reply in detail:

> Wish I could write a book about this whole journey. Dying is the strangest thing people will ever experience. But its most overwhelming feature (if you don't have pain, which, luckily, I've been spared so far) is the intense, non-stop drowsiness. I'm writing this now with my lids half closed, and my fingers fumbling on the keys.

Simon wrote back saying how haunting he found Tony's letter: 'I wept when I read it, but not for pity, or even for sadness. It was for the simple beauty and profundity of it. You really are facing the Mysteries, now. How deeply I wish you could write a book about the journey you're on.'

These two men, both Geminian, almost twins, born a day apart, finally became friends two decades ago when Tony admitted in an article he wrote about playing Leontes in The Winter's Tale *that, though he never suffered from sexual jealousy, he had from the professional kind, and that from a very early point in his career he thought Simon was having his career. They met for lunch and Simon admitted that he thought exactly the same thing, and they became friends.* 'What an extraordinary story we've lived through,' *Tony wrote,* 'sometimes intertwining, sometimes not.'

Simon writes how lucky both men have been in the 'steadfastness' of their partners. Simon married his partner Sebastian Fox in 2016. 'For flighty, divided creatures such as you and me, that rock solidity is a gift beyond purchase.'

Then Simon adds his own gift: 'What you wrote made me think of the four extraordinary songs by Richard Strauss, the last music he ever wrote.' *He continues:* 'Strauss, like Stravinsky, was a Gemini, sometimes too clever for his own good, but always with a thread of redeeming wit running through everything.' *And sweetly he sent Tony the translation of the text of Eichendorff's poem, the final part of the* 'Four Last Songs'.

We listened to Schwarzkopf singing 'Im Abendrot' – At Sunset – suffused with a sense of calm, of acceptance.

'Wir sind durch Not und Freude Gegangen Hand in Hand;
vom Wandern ruhen wir beide nun überm stillen Land.'

'Through sorrow and joy, we have gone hand-in-hand;
we are both at rest from our wanderings now above the quiet land.'

Tuesday 2 November
7 a.m. Very grateful for the extra hour of light this morning. Having turned the clocks back, on Saturday night, though it is now dark by 5 p.m. it's light by 6.30 a.m. again, which feels like a reprieve, for the hours in the day, which I get to myself to write before Tony emerges. I have bathed, and dressed because we are expecting a delivery today ... of more 'stuff': some armrests for the bed; a shower chair with arms; and some chair-raisers.

The syrup-coloured sun just cresting the horizon flushes the horse chestnut in golden light.

This week, quietly, I need to find out about funeral directors, and confirm how the process of having a service at Holy Trinity and getting a cremation done is all interwoven.

Tony says he likes the idea of some of his ashes being portioned out: save some, so our ashes can be buried together under a tree in the Theatre Gardens with a little sign; have some scattered from Big Rock. I like the idea of being scattered from Clopton Bridge so they float past the theatre and the church over the weir and are gone.

Depressed. The morphine hasn't really helped. Like every other cancer idiot in the world I fell into the trap of saying I can beat this.

Wednesday 3 November

I've got terminal liver cancer. I'm going to die.

The completeness, the finality of the fact which I am facing up to as I lie in bed, this is overwhelming, there is nothing to be done. I have no options.

Marietta proposed an idea: that I say to myself: 'I choose Death.'

This sticks with me during the day. There's something too crude about it – a line from an action movie – but if I made it 'I choose to die …'

That's better.

Can't work it out yet.

It mustn't just be pretence.

Taking control when there's none to be had.

On the other hand there is something very powerful.

The swans on the Avon are dying. An outbreak of avian bird flu has hit the population of eighty birds, and literally decimated them. Twelve have died already. Fifteen per cent. Inordinately sad.

G back from the vicar. The challenge is how to have a church service without there being too much 'church' in it. I don't want hymns, I definitely don't want an organ playing. G thinks they can work round these things.

A rather fun session discussing invites and songs/speeches.

Noticing that in talking or emailing others, I say 'we'. As though G & I are both dying. He isn't, but he's holding my hand every step of the way. It's enormously comforting to say 'we'.

I barely have any energy/interest for emails. Favourite thing is sitting in my chair in the big window, opposite Greg, as he works. But means I spend all day there, often dozing.

Watching Tony sleep I remember a line that Michel de Montaigne wrote about his beloved Etienne de La Boétie. 'If pressed to say why I loved him, I could only reply "Because I was I; because he was he".'

Eve: another of G's astonishing meal treats. A fresh grilled Dover sole from Rick Stein's famous restaurant in Padstow, which we always meant to visit but never did. Delicious beyond belief.

After an episode of Succession, *he said he wanted to go to bed, but for once I just wanted to stay and watch some crap TV. And for a second I made him feel, albeit fleetingly, that he was a burden. 'Don't you usually help me up?' was all he had to say for me to feel wretched, and selfish, and lonely.*

Saturday 6 November
This afternoon I suggested we sat outside and got some fresh air. Not a particularly nice afternoon, but we put on his coat and scarf and he sat in one of the new deck chairs. I decided to sweep the loggia of leaves, and then, as he seemed fine just watching me potter, I cleared away the steamer deck chairs, and the parasol, and the new furniture from the patio (encrusted with fallen yew berries) and put the braai into the loggia too.

And of course all I could think was 'This is the last time ... if this comes out ever again, he won't be here'. I know he's thinking the same thing.

It's 4.15 and getting dark already.

The day was grey, but not too cold. Sat outside, wrapped in jersey, jacket and scarf – oh the fresh air! – while G packed away the garden chairs and furniture for the winter.

When we moved back inside, he said, 'It's not fair. Where's it all gone? Where's the light?'

Monday 8 November
Watching a rather beautiful documentary on Truman Capote and Tennessee Williams on BBC4. We are approaching ten to nine. And Tony suddenly flags.

'Would you mind ...' he said.

'Of course,' I said, '... if we go to bed?'

'Yes, please.'

'Of course.'

But as I help him up off the couch he seems exhausted, thin, had enough.

I follow him up, holding his hips from behind and lifting him as he chooses to climb the next step. I don't know if I am helping. I hope so. He doesn't say. He's too tired.

Tuesday 9 November
Delicious task this morning. The destruction of those paintings of mine that I hate. I've left it a bit late, don't have the strength for stabbing and slashing attacks I'd planned, but compromise by doing the first cut on each one myself, then let Greg finish them off.

    Latest thought about my dying motto:
        Dying is part of me.
        It has not come from Mars.
        My height is part of me.
        Gayness is part of me.
        Acting is part of me.
        A certain talent is part of me.
        A leaking heart valve, and autoimmune hepatitis is part of me.
        (And so on ...)
        Dying is part of me.

Didn't fully sustain me through the morning though. At about noon started to feel a kind of panic attack. The drowsiness was overpowering me again (despite another twelve-hour sleep) and, in trying to resist it, felt I was writhing around within myself. I <u>wasn't</u> myself. Was this death close to?

    G suggested a nap. I did for an hour. Felt better. Had a G&T. Felt almost normal.

Once I had got him to bed last night I could see Tony was troubled. He struggled to say, 'I think ... We may have reached the time when I stay in bed ...' Today it is exactly five months since the diagnosis. So we have defied the three to four months. If the prognosis is right at three to six months then we have another four weeks. Impossible. He talks about making sure things are all clear and ready, 'if I die suddenly ...'. Oh please don't let that happen, not after so long at each other's sides.

I check a website for what needs to be done.

The press is full of 'necrophilia outrage', a man raping the cadavers of over 100 women in hospital mortuaries in Tunbridge Wells. How would you deal with that if it was your daughter, your sister, your mother, your gran? Would you want to know?

And there is one grim laugh as I tell him that the funeral director has suggested that we could separate the funeral in Holy Trinity and the cremation at Oakley Wood, which could happen the following morning.

'But that keeps you hanging about.'

'Yeah, in a mortuary,' he laughs, 'who knows what could happen!'

Wednesday 10 November

Slept a glorious thirteen and a half hours.

But once ensconced in my big window chair, the drowsiness overcame me – a panickiness.

Afternoon, G went for his Covid jab.

What if he has a car accident? What if it were serious or worse?

Devastating in these circumstances.

But a great short story plot. The wrong one goes first.

Thursday 11 November

Thursday ... again!

Just given Tony 1.5 ml of morphine and put him down on his bed in the studio. Taken his socks off, given him his 'best friend' blanket, and left the little Shakespeare brass bell on his bedside table. Come back to my chair to cry. He is slipping away.

When I got up this morning, I was so worried about going out to do the morning shop that I had to check he was still breathing before I left. We had to get him up early (i.e. 9.30) now, because the doctor was visiting.

Gift from Ian McKellen. He had asked if we wanted anything, 'Anything ... Caviar? Or Eccles cakes?' I plumped for the caviar. But this is Beluga Caviar, amazingly generous of him. We had some on little horn spoons with vodka. Perfect. And Thelma sent a couple of Japanese scarves.

Saturday 13 November
Schloffed on our bed upstairs. Coming down afterwards, Cuban music was playing on the radio. G led me into a salsa, or rhumba of whatever it's called. For a few beautiful minutes we danced.

But then we sat down for a routine task and we're suddenly struck dumb. It was ordering a new wine supply as the last one gets depleted. How long do we order for? We were both stumped for a reply, but tried to talk normally while avoiding one another's eyes. It felt like one of the most uncomfortable shocks we've had in this situation, perhaps because it was over such an ordinary thing. It came from nowhere.

I am letting him sleep in this morning for as long as he wants. I won't disturb him, and will take up a glass of juice when I hear him stir. His appetite has dwindled rapidly. He ate half an Eccles cake in the afternoon (yes, a dozen Eccles cakes arrived from Sir Ian this morning), and had half a bowl of chicken consommé for lunch.

Today I am making a requested meal: Oxtail stew, slow-cooked for six hours, in Jamie Oliver's 'insanely delicious' recipe. I'll make it today so it can be warmed up for Sunday lunch, and then he can have as much or as little as he wants.

Climbing the stairs to bed every night is getting harder and harder for Tony. So I remind him of a story, part of our own mythology.

We spent our honeymoon in Uganda in the Bwindi Impenetrable Forest searching for mountain gorillas. We immediately learned two things: 1) why they are called <u>mountain</u> gorillas, and 2) why Bwindi is called the <u>Impenetrable</u> Forest. We were advised to hire a couple of porters at base camp 'to carry our water bottles', which we did – and hired two very strong-looking young women. Tony found the climb really tough. And even though we were told that a troop of gorillas was just over the next rise, a few hundred metres further up the slope, Tony said he didn't think he could make it, and to leave him there and go on ahead alone without him. I wouldn't have it, and we hauled him up the remaining mountainside, with the porters taking a buttock each. And we had one of the best experiences of our lives, watching these gentle giants.

So I stand behind him at the bottom of the steps, grab his hips in both my hands, and support his weight. It's much easier for him to heave himself up now, and we climb the wooden hills to Bedfordshire together.

Sunday 14 November
Got Tony down to sleep, with his 1.5 ml of oramorph. He's not quite rested yet. I am sitting here watching and typing. Rachmaninoff's Vocalise on CD. It premiered in 1916 in Moscow. There is a dies irae disguised in the opening melody, and an underlying melancholy, which must reflect the composer's mood as Russia endured the First World War. Rachmaninoff once wrote: 'Music comes straight from the heart and talks only to the heart: it is Love! Music is the Sister of Poetry and her Mother is Sorrow.'

Oxtail for lunch today. He ate a tiny bit really, but I am delighted to watch him sucking the bones.

Monday 15 November
G had fruitful hour-long conversation with Bloomsbury about his book.* They'll decide at their next board meeting, about 18 Dec.

A small sharp blade went through me.

So I'll never know.

Tuesday 16 November
By chance my new literary agent got in touch today. To update me but there's no news, good or bad.

Day of worsening symptoms.

Loss of memory. Can't think of certain names or words. Drives me mad. The other night at bedtime, couldn't think of the word for the stewed fruit we have in the morning. Only came up with compost. G told me it was compote. Didn't matter but I need to unload my niggling worry onto my bedtime pad.

I've simultaneously lost my voice and my hearing. When I speak it sounds like a blurred echo. At times, so bad I can't carry on.

For the first time in a while I took a nasty trip on my way to the loo, and almost fell. Then a calamity waiting to happen. My penis has shrunk, and is difficult to find among the surrounding skin and scrotum when I need to pee in an emergency, like now. Ended up

---

* *My Shakespeare*, finally published in April 2023.

wetting pants and knickers. Much snarling anger. G, very calming, fetched dry clothes and washed the wet ones.

Wednesday 17 November
Marietta. Used sketch of Cecil Bloch* about to be hit by the train in his suicide, death just a fraction away. Which is how it feels to me too. It's such an alarming situation that I have to show this crude raw drawing of it.

Could only last half the call. Partly because of weak voice. Partly because I have little left to say. After call, G observes that my next Marietta session, next Wednesday, will be his birthday. I've been wondering if I'll make it. Still not sure.

Eve: another of our big Shakespeare discussions: him reading the latest chapter of his book, me offering editing advice. These have been a wonderful conclusion to the Shakespeare part of our life.

Thursday 18 November
Watch the tavern scene from *Henry IV Part One*. We laughed and wept our way through it and he ended by saying, 'I am so proud of that'. The scene itself is one of Shakespeare's masterpieces, so alive, spontaneous and rich. And I think G really did come up to the mark. We all did – to be fair. There's not a fraction of A. Sher visible in this J. Falstaff.

Thursday (again). His voice is getting very dry and hoarse, sometimes a sort of squeak at the end of the day. But we still sit for our long afternoon chat. Yesterday I had drafted a chapter on Lear, and he gave brilliant editing notes, no, more than just editing notes, structural shifts and emphases which really bring out what I actually want to say, and have the emotional content which I keep shying away from.

Then he talked about how much these chats about so many different Shakespeare plays meant to him, how he looked forward to them.

Oh, and I cast Richard III yesterday. Arthur Hughes has radial dysplasia, his 'little arm' as he calls it. He is twenty-nine years old. It might be a leap of faith, but I think it's a positive step into a bleak future. I haven't told Tony.

---

* an old school friend of Tony's.

Not quite sure why. It's the first work Zoom call I have made in ages. It seems like an attempt to move towards the closed door.

Friday 19 November
Beth gave birth last night. A week over, but in good health, a little girl. No name yet. Much happiness and relief. Special relief for me personally. This was another milestone, which I wondered if I'd make. Thank God I did. Wouldn't've wanted to win this particular race.

Message from Beth's mum, Eileen, with photos. Mother and baby look well.
  'Thou met'st with things dying I with things new born'.
  I hear Tony suddenly crying in the kitchen and go to hug him.
  To cheer him up I put on Miriam Makeba and we danced (sort of). He sat, lifted his arms, and rocked from side to side, grinning from ear to ear. Dancing has always embarrassed him, but he loves it when I dance about the kitchen for him.

Told Dr Alia I'd been experiencing a fast heartbeat and tight chest. Asked if my kind of condition could lead to death by heart attack? She was a bit shocked by the frankness of the discussion (and, God, could I ever have imagined having it?) but said yes it could. And if it did G was to call the ambulance, and have my respect form standing by for them. No hospital. No bringing back to life. Just making patient peaceful.
  I tell G my hope to make it to his birthday.
  He's shocked. So soon?
  We've each got a (secret) prognosis.
  For the first time I've admitted part of mine.
  We cry together.

Friday 19 November
Get up at six to answer RSC's appeal for help on the messaging. I have had to cross Tony's name off the statement, as I could not bear to see it in print next to the words 'we are sad to announce ...'.

Sunday 21 November
Beautifully sunny morning, we sit in the window. The beech tree on the drive of The Hill is aflame in copper and gold behind the walnut tree.

Tuesday 23 November

Tony having enormous trouble dumping. Dr Sam proposes that Tony is severely constipated and she needs to examine him. And then prescribe an enema and a course of laxatives. Tony endures the humiliation of a finger up the bum, but it proves she's right. There is a hard blockage which Tony won't be able to shift on his own. T seems relieved when she has gone that he knows the problem.

There is a flurry of activity as the prescription lands at the Stratford Pharmacy, and when I check I can pick it up they say they don't have it in stock. Won't be until tomorrow. This doesn't seem good enough to me, and while T is taking his afternoon schloff, I ring back the nurses, and they sort it so I can collect it at the Rosebird Centre pharmacy next to Waitrose. Which I do, and am back in time for the next district nurse, Jade, to administer the enema, which doesn't seem half as bad as anticipated. It works fast and in minutes we have Tony on the commode, and hear a blast. Great relief.

This morning I bring up his juice as normal, and also a coffee to make sure things move. But I can see how tired he is. After the shower as I lead him back into the bedroom his wrists seemed crankier than usual, cracking as he grips me tight. Now, he is sleeping soundly in the window. I have washed his daytime jumper, overnight, as it was getting a bit grubby down the front, and have ironed two of his favourite shirts, with the vital breast pockets he likes.

Wednesday 24 November

When I went up to wake T this morning at about ten thirty, he whispered hoarsely 'I have something to tell you', as I leaned closer he said, 'I made it to your birthday'!

He told me later that he had tried writing the card to go with the flowers last night, and decided to write two different versions, one if he survived the night and the other if he didn't.

Oh Lord, to be able to pray.

Richard Sharples arrived with Tony's bust. He took the original reference photos in 2016 when Tony was playing King Lear. It's a powerful object made by his own brilliant process of 'growing' copper. In Richard's own words 'it produces these exquisite organic forms which for me embody the relationship between growth and decay which is so central to us as human beings'.

Richard wrote later: 'I can honestly say it's been one of the most challenging, strangest and above all saddest and upsetting projects I've ever done and yet weirdly I think it might turn out to be one of the best pieces I've ever made.' And he went on: 'The reason for doing this particular sculpture was because it felt important to me to do it ... seeing two people I dearly love going through something so shockingly painful and not being able to help them or change the situation. The sculpture felt like a way of channeling that frustration into something creative ... I'm sure you're aware it comes from a place of love.'

Tony dictated a note to Richard: 'What a magnificent achievement. I can't tell you how touched I am by it. Greg told you I'd used the word "noble". Can I please retract it? "Noble" is too precious; this bust is rough, raw, tender, alive, full of humanity, vulnerability, anger. Can't find the words.'

And then unexpectedly my sister Jo appeared. She's come all the way down from North Wales just to say 'Happy Birthday'. We took some photos of the bust with Tony and with Richard and Jo, and a birthday photo together.

Thursday 25 November

It's no good, everything is decaying very fast. I list it for G:

At the time of the diagnosis (June) only needed a stick outside.

Then needed one inside. But still very mobile.

Then needed G on other arm.

This is now a real struggle.

When, this evening, G suggested some new improvements, I snapped, 'Stop having so many good ideas.'

After a moment's pause, we both burst out laughing – one of our first good laughs for several days.

Meanwhile, Janice is proving a gigantic friend. From the start she's been ringing constantly, emailing, sending nostalgic photos of our times together, etc. Now after big fights with the visa office, she's finally got one and is coming over in a couple of weeks.

Friday 26 November

G had a seriously good new idea. Use the wheelchair/commode just as a wheelchair. All journeys easier for me, though backbreaking for him. But it's like everything else he's done during this: make it more comfortable for me.

But he was exhausted by bedtime and low-spirited. I must remember to say thanks to him all the time.

A step change.

Just before 10.30 Tony called from upstairs. He had got himself into the bathroom OK but was really struggling to walk. I thought he was going to collapse. I helped him back into the bedroom, got him dressed eventually, and down the Everest of the stairs. He had no appetite at all at breakfast, and didn't even consume the tiny helping of compote he had served himself.

I cancelled my appointment with the osteopath. I suggested that we use the wheelchair downstairs from now on. We tried it and it does work.

He is sleeping now and I am feeling shaken, and inadequate, and exhausted.

Saturday 27 November

Slept and dozed for fifteen and a half hours.

G had a new brainwave for morning, washing and dressing. All done on a high stool at bathroom sink. This process linked to the wheelchair downstairs made life 100 per cent easier.

Bad news from Janice. New Covid virus in SA. Very bad. All travel banned for months.

This was Tony's last entry.

THE LAST FIVE DAYS

'Break heart, I prithee break'

Sunday 28 November

It started to snow first thing yesterday morning. The tail of Storm Arwen, which has been battering the north-east coast. The snow melted but the low temperature stayed.

Since Friday the situation has deteriorated in terms of Tony's mobility. The move to the wheelchair downstairs has vastly improved his mood, and relieved him in terms of struggle. I am coping OK with the chair. It's tougher over carpet and there is a bump in the tiles in the bathroom. I tell him he has to look out for his extremities, elbows, knees. And then I manage to trap his foot in a door. Estates are coming on Monday to put a lip in on the studio doorway.

Yesterday he didn't get up until noon. We decided still to have our boiled egg, Saturday morning routine, but it threw the day out from our schedule of new constipation medicines. So I made proper chicken soup ('Jewish penicillin') and built the first fire of the season.

The district nurse phoned to say they have a Zimmer frame she could bring round. And might be able to get another wheelchair for upstairs. Tony would be so happy about that. The effort to get him up and down stairs is still worth it so he can sleep in his own bed, but who knows how much longer.

I am committing the last things we say to each other at night to memory, just in case. Last night after the usual 'I love you', 'I love you too', 'sleep well', 'and you …'. I could see his mouth was dry and he kept trying to moisten his lips. He didn't want to get up again. Getting in had been such an effort. So I suggested I could syringe some water into his mouth. It worked very well. 'Another good idea,' he smiled.

As he finally turned out the lights and could stretch in his own bed, he sighed, 'Ahhhh, glorious.'

Monday 29 November

9 a.m. Not sure why I am writing all this down. To remember, I suppose, in case I forget details, or timings that the nurses need to know. Perhaps it just helps me cope.

Last night, I heard Tony stir about 4.45, getting himself ready to get up and use the pee bottle. Then I heard a cry. He had slipped off the bed and onto the floor. I switched on my bedside light and stumbled round the bed. He was very awkwardly placed, and though I tried to get his legs straight, there was simply no way of getting him up. I also realised that if I did try and manhandle his 14-stone weight, that I was likely to injure my back, and then I would be of no help to him at all.

I phoned the night-time assist number, but they told me they couldn't help and I needed an ambulance, so I phoned 999 at 5.10. They said they would send an ambulance but it might be a while. I got Tony into a T-shirt and pants, put the phone within reach and lay with him on the floor wrapped in my arms. Another operator rang an hour later, and asked the same questions. Clearly they were determining a priority list. Two hours later, one did turn up. The attendant told me that if I had said that Tony was having trouble with his breathing (which is true in fact as he has a problem with breathlessness now) then I would have got a faster response, but she said she hadn't said that!

They brought in a sort of lilo cushion which they slipped under his bum, and then pumped up. Amazingly it raised him to a sitting position in moments. They got him onto his feet and onto the bed, and both left the room discreetly as I helped him to the pee bottle. They then did some observations, blood pressure, heart rate, etc.

The healthcare professional, Janine, was very helpful, and I asked her about how I could get Tony further on the bed, and she showed me how to use the sliding sheet, which Moira, the original district nurse, had brought. It's another very clever piece of kit. It's a folded loop of very slippy material. You lay it on the bed, get the patient to lie on it and then slide them further on. Asher, the male nurse, suggested that if you move the legs then the patient can often move their bums over themselves.

So we are having a time of it. Yesterday, Heidi, the occupational health nurse, arrived with two Zimmer frames for Tony. And suggested she would bring another commode, too. She has suggested a seat elevator, for the chair in the front room cos she does not like how low it is. But we were not so sure about that.

Dr Alia arrives later and the district nurse, Heather, has just rung to check in and will be over at two-ish. So we will no doubt need a conversation about whether we can still manage the stairs after the events of last night.

Another snowfall overnight, and an orange sun slanting over the field earlier, very beautiful. Last night, a cup of chicken soup in front of the fire, and watch some of Tick, Tick Boom! *The show features an actor playing Stephen Sondheim, who died two days ago, aged ninety-one.*

Sam from Concierge Medical arrived as Steve from RSC Estates appeared to put in the lip for the studio. She came up to see T in bed, and is clearly concerned at the rate of deterioration in a week. He is still sleeping now (3.30). We had some of the special milkshake before he went off. He is determined not to miss going downstairs, but I suspect he's here for the evening.

Tuesday 30 November

Wrong! And a big mistake. We should have taken the slip from the bed as a warning to act fast and not delay. The district nurse said yesterday not to leave it too long. So Tony did get up yesterday afternoon. We dressed and came downstairs, with me having to guide his foot at each step. He had another cup of chicken soup. We finished Tick, Tick Boom! *and by eight he wanted to head upstairs again.*

As normal, I slowly pushed from behind, but he just didn't have the strength to make each step, and suddenly he started falling backwards. On to me. Don't know how we made to the top, but by the time we did he was wobbly and frightened. So was I. I propped him against the bathroom door post and flew downstairs and back up with the wheelchair, and gently lowered him into it. We somehow managed to get him into bed.

We determined that this was the last time we could do this and in the morning would have to get professional help to get him back downstairs.

But in the meantime we still had the night, with its inevitable bladder requirements to get through. I said he had to call me – that was what I was there for. He called first at 11.15. I couldn't believe it was only 11.15.

At 12.15 there was another call. He was very thirsty and wanted me to keep giving him syringes of water, which although I was happy to do I realised would just create more urine to pass during the night. He complained of very dry lips and I hit on the idea of cutting up an orange from the fridge which worked wonderfully. At 2.20 he called again.

He didn't stir again until 7.30 when I got up to go to the loo. My relief that the night was at last over was overwhelming. Even though I hadn't got a wink of sleep, listening to his breathing and anxious that he would need another pee.

I got up and, after getting him to the loo, he went back to sleep. Estates came with a mattress at 9.30, and they went off to get a divan to go with it. So I now have a bed for the studio. We are waiting for an ambulance to come now.

Dr Sam from Concierge phoned around ten and I said I needed her to help co-ordinate the help we need, whether it was Shakespeare Hospice, or the district nurses or the instant responders, or just the ambulance. So at 12.00 Dr Alia arrived, and shortly after Ellie from the instant responder team, who eventually rang again for the ambulance. They may be here in the next five hours, but probably not before. In fact, mercifully, the ambulance crew, beefy Ama and strapping Brenda, arrived by 2.30. They were very bright and jolly, and managed the job of getting Tony downstairs very quickly and efficiently.

Then we had the Shakespeare Hospice arrive: Alison and trainee Alice. Explaining what help might be available. Morning and night two assistants to help get him up, washed, dressed, etc.

I think we watched Succession *before bed this evening. Relieved not to have to climb back upstairs to get him to bed.*

Wednesday 1 December

God, things are moving horribly fast.

Tony is very resistant to the idea of a catheter, but after Monday night he agreed he needed to have one fitted, and the district nurse arranged to bring them this morning.

But last night, our first in the studio, with me next to him in the bed the Estates team had delivered, we had a continuing nightmare of needing to pee. Once we tried getting him to stand so he could reach the pee bottle but he couldn't stand. Once we tried me hunkering in front of him so he could keep himself sitting on the side of the bed, and me trying to hold the pee bottle, but that didn't work either. Getting him back onto the bed at one point, he couldn't get far enough up the bed, and when we did manage to move him to his satisfaction, he felt strangled by his T-shirt, so I found a pair of scissors and cut it up the front.

After a restless night he woke at 6.45, probably because of the light in the room, and wanted to get up. I said I thought we should sleep in a bit more. But he said he wanted to try going to the downstairs loo. I wheeled him there, and he tried standing to pee into the bottle again, but couldn't. The cushion was not on the wheelchair at this point so I suggested that I put some newspaper on the floor under the commode, and that he just pee on that. Which worked a bit. I had put a shirt on him backwards to keep him warm, and aware that as the newspaper hadn't come, and was due then, that I didn't want to find us crossing the hall as the outside light came on and the newspaper man got a shock!

Dying is all about pissing, shitting and trying to sleep.

Yesterday, when he came round, he said he felt there was someone at his side, and he was waiting to see what they would do. Any conversation at all is now nearly impossible, as he can't find the words, and can't speak as his voice seems dry.

I remembered that he had a Marietta session at noon, and said I would ring her to let her know that he couldn't make it. Of course this led to her asking me how I was coping, and me trying not to open the floodgates, but realising yet again that I was not coping and blaming myself, for being inadequate and not up to the job. The 24/7 nature of the job is tough.

2 p.m.

District nurse came this morning, as I was trying to count out Tony's pills for the week. I had tried to delay her, as Tony and I needed further conversation about the catheter and the bed. I had already got tetchy, because getting him up so early had meant I couldn't bath, even have a coffee, and he was demanding (in his now squeaky abbreviated way) to know about the catheter.

The nurse said we had to get him onto the bed. I tried getting him up from his chair twice, but his legs couldn't support him, so the nurse said we would have to get the ambulance to move him, and then, when he was on the bed, someone would return to apply it. She then left.

In the meantime, Tony wanted to pee. I suddenly realised I had no idea how we were going to manage that. I phoned the nurse back, as she had used my mobile to call me earlier. 'I'm afraid you'll just have to manage,' she said. She had left pads. The hospice lady yesterday had left pads.
But what do you do with pads?

Ambulance arrived half an hour ago. I immediately phone the district nurse to say come with catheter now! But they decided they didn't have the right equipment to move him ...

5 p.m.

Ambulance get support from Warwick to bring a hoist, to get Tony out of the chair in the lounge and onto the bed in the studio. Big Viking 'Matt' leads the charge. As soon as he is there I ring the 'icebar' number to say he is ready. They tell me it might not be today. I plead. The woman on the phone says that the delay has been because of confusion over Concierge Medical. Apparently any catheter has to be authorised by his NHS doctor and though they have now got that permission from Dr Hall it is too late to get it done today. Though I could get Dr Alia to do it. She would be authorised to do so. I ring her. Good news. <u>You</u> can do it. But she can't, or it's too long since she did one so understandably she is declining.

Then Tony says he needs to get up and pee. I try to explain that we might have to use the pads, cos it had just taken three paramedics and me to get him into bed. I can't manage or risk getting him out of bed now. I ring the hospice and they say they'll try and send someone round right away.

7.10 p.m.

Helen (in lilac) and Alice (in blue), from the Shakespeare Hospice turned up. I took them through to the lounge to tell them where we were and how, frankly, I needed help. When they came through they explained how to use the pads. They helped him pee into the bottle and then used the sliding sheet to get Tony comfortably up the bed. They left promising to have someone come in later to check all well.

Calm.

Then, Tony says he wants to go through and watch telly. I say he can't, that he will now have to stay in bed. After a while he says I have to help him onto the commode because he needs a dump. I remind him of the events of the last two days, and say I can't do it by myself. He keeps trying to put his legs over ready to get up, and I keep insisting that he stay there.

Then he says I am torturing him.

That stings.

I take the armrest off the wheelchair commode, and wheel it round to the left side of the bed. I lower the bed to the height of the commode wheelchair. I say I am doing this against my will, and am very scared about how to get him back on once I have got him there. He insists, albeit through drooping eyelids that he has to do this, he can't crap his own bed. I protest, and get tetchy and irritable, but help him to slide onto the commode. He can't get far *enough back. And his penis can't get into the hole. He says he can't go. And he wants to get back on the bed now. I ask him what I do in an hour's time when he wants to do the same thing? I suggest he take some docusate and we wait a few minutes for it to work. In the meantime he has peed on the floor a bit, which I wipe up.*

He then says he has to get back on the bed. I say we should give the docusate chance to work. Maybe wait until six. It's quarter to. I feel like Nurse Ratched except she never lost her cool. She never implored a patient to apologise or take back an accusation of torture. I counter, saying I feel bullied. This is really terrible. At that point Jenny the nurse arrives.

I am terrified that because Tony's still on the commode, like the nurse this morning she will say that she can't apply the catheter, and go. Luckily Jenny is not only a 'Catheter Queen' but a queen of curds and whey, and helps me get Tony onto the bed. Wipes his bum, helps use the sliding sheet to get him up the bed, and applies the catheter with really minimum discomfort. Tony lying quietly now. Coughing a bit occasionally. I am at his desk, with no light other than the iPad. Perhaps we'll have a quiet night at last.

Calm.

Then Tony wants to get up to dump. Is certain I have misunderstood instructions. I turn into Nurse Ratched again. Not that she ever raised her voice or had to push the patient's legs back onto the bed, when they kept trying to get out. Can't believe I have reverted back to square one quite so soon. I tell him if he doesn't listen to me, if we can't co-operate in this, then I will have to admit defeat and take him to hospital, despite the respect report. This is what needing a crap can do. Eventually he listens. I think he listens. I ring Shakespeare Hospice who are meant to be checking in. 'Have you got a bedpan, Greg?'

Of course I haven't got a fucking bedpan.

'Roll him onto his side and make sure the pads are beneath him.'

So I do. And he gives in. And it all works. And he calms down. We are calm together. He asks if I am coming to bed soon. I say yes.

But the Shakespeare Hospice workers are now on their way. I will waylay them, and thank them, but he has now accepted some morphine and might, please God, might sleep through. The hospicers have just arrived. They will order a bedpan in the morning. And perhaps Tony needs those adult nappies to be comfortable. But he is right. This is torture.

At 9 p.m. I email my siblings in distress:

I know this is the sickness in his liver now affecting his brain. This is the encephalopathy Dr Shearman warned us about. He is frightened and his closest love is forcing him to crap himself.

I wish you guys lived closer. Everyone is offering help, wonderfully, but most would require more effort from me. And I just don't have that reserve of energy.

I am going to creep into the bed we have had put in next to Tony's and just hope he sleeps through.

Your brother with so much love

G

Thursday 2 December
T sleeps through until about 4.30 a.m.

Then he kept saying 'OK' and reaching his hands out. I gave him some water, and tried to explain that he couldn't get up yet. That I needed help. I gave him 3 ml of morphine to help him rest, for a few more hours, and then at 5.15 a zopiclone, but he dropped it in the bed.

Now it's 10.30 and he is saying 'OK' again. It's the mantra.

The nurses arrive. The freshening up they do is a GREAT thing. Bedbath, change pad, cream elbows, and heels, check catheter (tooth-brushing needs more co-operation from patient), pull him up bed and make him feel calmer. Give him a dose of oramorph before they leave. The nurse suggests perhaps putting that on a drip, so he doesn't get too agitated.

11.20. Tony very distressed. Begging me to help him get out of bed, and trying to do so on his own. He knows this is his deathbed, and he must, MUST, get out of it. Raging against the dying of the light. Tried to give him some grapes. And then he started getting angry, then helpless, then frightened. But no conversation just the same refrain. 'OK, help me, help me.'

2.45. The refrain has continued throughout the afternoon. I rang the district nurse, but she said wait an hour until the midazolam kicked in. I am sitting on the staircase outside his room, just out of his line of vision, weeping. 'Greg, Greg, help me, help me.' I feel like a first-time parent outside their new baby's bedroom hearing them cry, but trying to resist rushing in to comfort them.

Just as I think I can't bear any more, I hear a car in the drive. It's Mark.

Later, after Tony has fallen asleep, and as I continue to sit by the bedside holding his hand, Mark makes me some food. Proper food.

Friday 3 December
Tony died a few minutes before midnight, last night.

I was lying next to him, and heard his last breath. It was 11.53.

I had been dozing, and woke to hear the rhythm of his breathing change.

Then the gap between in-breath and out-breath became a long pause. And then it stopped.

I turned on the bedside light. Felt his forehead, and knew.

I reached over and kissed his brow, the image he had dreaded seeing. I told him I loved him, kissed his lips, and whispered for his soul to go.

Then I called Mark.

He came downstairs, felt Tony's pulse, put his hand under Tony's nose to feel if there was any breath, and confirmed it.

In the living room the clock on the mantelpiece struck midnight. 'We have heard the chimes at Midnight, Master Shallow.'

Before covering his face with the sheet, I kissed Tony's hand, and said to my brother, 'I am going to take his ring off.' It slipped so easily from his delicate thin finger. I put it on my left pinkie. Where it will now stay.

I switched out the light. As I left the room I turned to the man I have loved with all my being for thirty-five years, and said, 'Thank you.'

He was 'my all the world'.

Break heart, I prithee break.

THE FOLIO ROADSHOW

PART ONE

From Stratford-upon-Avon to Skipton

Chapter One
Stratford-upon-Avon

Our Theatre Copy of the First Folio (and how we nearly gave it away to the Pope)

We are in the Palazzo Pio in Rome, a stone's throw from St Peter's Basilica. It's November 1964. The Sala Grande is packed with two thousand dignitaries of the Catholic Church. In the central aisle His Holiness Pope Paul VI sits enthroned. On stage, performing a forty-five-minute recital of extracts from Shakespeare, are three leading actors from the Royal Shakespeare Company: Dorothy Tutin, Tony Church and Derek Godfrey. The occasion marks the Vatican's unprecedented decision to participate in the global celebrations for the quatercentenary of Shakespeare's birth. It is the first theatrical performance before the pontiff in centuries.

The RSC have decided that it would be appropriate to bring along our First Folio, and the insurance company has agreed, setting the rate at £25,000 with the stipulation that, though the actors may fly to Rome, the folio must not. The production manager has duly boarded a train to the Holy City with his precious cargo, wrapped in brown paper, tied with string and placed in a locked briefcase chained to his wrist. If the plane crashed the folio would have been lost for ever, but if the train crashes the chances are that the folio would survive, even if the person attached to it did not.

I am not sure who thought it was a good idea to bring the folio to Rome, as the papacy generally does not get a good press in its pages. Had nobody read *King John*? However, it was placed on a lectern, and some passages would be read directly from its pages during the recital, and that seemed fitting.

Pope Paul VI watching the performance in the Palazzo Pio

According to Tony Church,* who had put the event together, several Roman Catholic members of the company had given the actors 'little crucifixes and rosaries for the pope to bless, a customary procedure when you have an audience with the pope'. So on being congratulated by His Holiness, both Tony Church and Derek Godfrey held up their hands, containing these holy objects, over which the pontiff made the sign of the cross. On impulse, Dorothy Tutin seized the folio from the lectern and held it up for his blessing, too.

Unfortunately, Pope Paul misunderstood the gesture and muttering what a beautiful memento of the occasion it would be, he took the folio and handed it to a waiting cardinal who promptly marched off down the corridor with our First Folio under his arm. Tony Church described the incident as 'an episode of unscheduled but sublime farce'.

But as he contemplated the prospect of finding himself liable for the £25,000 insurance (and was no doubt wondering if it could be deemed an Act of God), Dr Heenan, who as Archbishop of Westminster was the spiritual head of the Catholic Church in

---

* In his autobiography *A Stage for a Kingdom*.

England and Wales, stepped in to save the day. A swift piece of episcopal diplomacy prevented an international incident, and the folio was retrieved from the Vatican vaults.

The Library at the Shakespeare Birthplace Trust (SBT) in Stratford-upon-Avon, which looks after our First Folio, has a file of photographs and newspaper articles from the time, which documents the incident. Here is a clip from the *Coventry Telegraph*, showing Dorothy Tutin snapped by paparazzi in her snowball hat as she arrives at London Airport. She tells the story of the near papal purloining to a reporter, and another clip prints a subsequent denial by the Vatican.

The SBT also have a copy of the recital performed that afternoon. It includes some surprising choices. Dorothy Tutin had famously played Viola at Stratford, which might account for the two scenes from *Twelfth Night* in the programme, but she had also played Portia in *The Merchant of Venice*. To include a scene before His Holiness in which a Jewish merchant is condemned for his lack of mercy and lectured about the value of Christian justice might seem provocative, but I believe it was deliberate.

The trial of the Nazi Adolf Eichmann in Jerusalem in 1961, just three years before, had brought the Holocaust back to the forefront of public consciousness. The RSC's own production of Rolf Hochhuth's controversial play *The Representative* about alleged papal complicity in that persecution opened at the Aldwych in London the previous September and had roused tensions about the Catholic Church's involvement.

The recital took place at the height of the Second Vatican Council, intended to modernise the Catholic Church. Pope John XXIII's initiative to open a window to the modern world had been taken over on his death by Paul VI. The impact of the decisions made by Vatican II were far-reaching, and included authorisation for the mass to be spoken in the vernacular, and to be addressed facing the congregation.

Among the sixteen official declarations made by the Council, one of the most significant was 'Nostra aetate'.* It discussed the Church's relationship with other faiths and in particular its anti-Semitism.

---

* Its name comes from the first words of its opening sentence. 'Nostra aetate' means 'in our time' in Latin.

Before his death, John XXIII had drafted a statement which he had wanted to be read out in churches across the world. It said: 'Forgive us for the curse we falsely attached to their name as Jews. Forgive us for crucifying Thee a second time in their flesh. For we knew not what we did.' The authenticity of this prayer was later disputed, but its spirit was embodied in the declaration.

At dinner after the recital, Archbishop Heenan told Tony Church that he had been pleased at the inclusion of the trial scene, because he had been especially keen to urge his fellow Council members to amend that ancient edict which condemned all Jews perpetually for the crucifixion of Christ. The declaration had been passed by a large majority, but it is nevertheless still shocking to learn that out of nearly 2,300 of the assembled clergy eighty-eight voted against it.

★ ★ ★

2023 was the quatercentenary of the First Folio. At Stratford-upon-Avon we had been planning our response for a while.

The year 2016 (which marked four centuries since Shakespeare's death) had been a big one for the RSC. We had mounted a season which demonstrated some of our top priorities. We created a national tour of *A Midsummer Night's Dream* with Bottom and the Rude Mechanicals played by fourteen local amateur groups with 580 school children across the nation performing as Titania's fairies, while on our main stage we hosted the biggest celebration of Shakespeare across the art forms, from ballet and opera to musical theatre, jazz and rap in a live concert broadcast worldwide by the BBC. In that busy season, Paapa Essiedu became the first black actor to play Hamlet for the company. I directed Tony as King Lear, and Simon Russell Beale as Prospero. *The Tempest* was created in collaboration with Intel (and in association with Andy Serkis's The Imaginarium Studio), and used bleeding-edge performance-capture technology to make Ariel flame amazement as a digital avatar on stage in real time.

2023 would be tougher to market. Celebrating a book published seven years after the author died would definitely be a harder sell. Nevertheless I felt it was an important anniversary to mark. Perhaps the best way of celebrating the achievement of the 1623 Folio in 2023 would be to mount a season of some of the plays we would have lost without it: *Macbeth*, *As You Like It*, *Julius Caesar* and the very first play in the 1623 Folio, *The Tempest*. I would do the very last play in the folio, *Cymbeline*. And then it would be time to step down as Artistic Director after a decade at the helm, and spend whatever time Tony and I had left, together. Our best-laid plans were foiled by a global pandemic, and my own life was about to change for ever.

The idea of a folio quest emerged gradually. I knew there were about fifty copies of the First Folio all around the United Kingdom. I got a laminated map from Stanfords in Covent Garden, pinned it to the back of my study door, and with a packet of coloured dots tracked where they all were. They were widely spread from Leeds to Longleat, from Skipton to the Isle of Bute. I wondered how many I could visit in its quatercentenary year. My sister Jo had a question. Jo has a knack of getting straight to the point. She looked me in the eye and said, 'So let me get this right, Greg. You are going to try and see fifty copies of the same book? Why?'

I explained that, inspired by our own Theatre Copy and its intriguing story, I realised that every copy of the 1623 Folio is different. I wanted to track that miraculous book's progress around the country and understand a little more of Shakespeare's complex legacy. Nevertheless, my canny sister had at once acknowledged the essential absurdity of my zealous pilgrimage, and exposed its probable true purpose as a massive piece of displacement activity.

★ ★ ★

The RSC's collection facility in Stratford-upon-Avon contains thousands of items: costumes, props, prompt books, designs, as well as a large collection of paintings. The one I have come to see is a portrait. Robyn Greenwood, the Collection Manager, takes me to the stacks to find it. She pulls out one of the racks and there is an Edwardian gentleman in a high collar and ample moustache. It is Sir Sidney Lee by Alfred Wolmark. But who is he?

Sidney Lee was born Solomon Lazarus Lee (the family had changed the name from Levy sometime before). Apart from his work as editor of the *Dictionary of National Biography*, and writing a book on Stratford-upon-Avon, he was a distinguished Shakespeare scholar. He set out to establish how many copies of the First Folio there were in the world and published his findings in a census in 1902. The census lists 160 folios, which he classifies into a sort of hierarchy of excellence: perfect, imperfect and defective copies.

Robyn is anxious to know where our folio appears in the list, and I have brought along my own crinkly copy of the original census. *Class 1 Division A (in good, unrestored condition)* starts with ten copies in the United Kingdom, first in public institutions and then in private hands, and then the same for the United States, of which there are only four. Next is: *Class I Division B (in good condition, but with occasional leaves either supplied from another copy of the First Folio, or repaired, i.e. mended, mounted, or inlaid)*.

There was a huge trade in perfecting First Folios by plundering other folios.* Sometimes the owners wanted the pages remounted, sometimes into larger sheets, or inlaid onto new paper if the page was damaged. Then there is a third division, C, which are those *in good condition, but with leaves supplied from later folios*.

'So is our copy in that division?' pleads Robyn, sounding discouraged. Scanning the list, we are now up to forty-three. Next we get: *Class II (Imperfect) Division A (in good condition, but with a few pages missing, and occasionally other slight defects)* and *Division B (in fair condition)*. Now we are up to 105 copies. 'Don't tell me the Theatre Copy isn't in the top 100.'

According to Lee, our copy is in *Class II Division C (in moderate condition, with most of preliminary and other missing leaves in Facsimile or from later Folios)*. Our entry is number 107.

CVII   STRATFORD-ON-AVON   —   SHAKESPEARE MEMORIAL LIBRARY. History: *acquired by James Orchard Halliwell-Phillipps c 1865; sold with other books from Halliwell-Phillipps's library in July 1889 for £95 when it was acquired by Charles Edward Flower, of Stratford-on-Avon for presentation to the Memorial Library there.*

Charles Edward Flower was a member of the local brewing family, and he raised so much money for the building of the original

---

* Eighteenth-century Shakespeare editor George Steevens called this process of revamping First Folios 'Vampment'.

Shakespeare Memorial Theatre that he was known locally as 'Self-raising Flower'.

Lee continues: *To this copy originally belonged the early proof impression of the portrait, which was detached by Halliwell-Phillipps, and was sold ... in 1897 to Marsden J. Perry Esq., Providence, Rhode Island USA.*

'What?' cries Robyn, outraged. 'So our copy originally had the famous Droeshout engraving, but this Halliwell-Phillipps cut it out and sold it to a man in the States. We need to get out to Providence, Rhode Island, track down our Droeshout engraving and bring it back.'

The Sidney Lee Census isn't the only census of First Folios ever done. Veteran folio hunter Antony James West conducted one which he published in 2003, and Eric Rasmussen incorporated that work into a census published in 2012. The Rasmussen/West catalogue lists 232 copies. Since it was published, three more First Folios have emerged: one on the Isle of Bute, one in Saint-Omer and one in Warwickshire, at Shuckburgh Hall, which was sold at auction at Christie's (with a Second, Third and Fourth Folio) for £2.48 million in 2016.* A more recent online survey, The Shakespeare Census, presents only extant copies, and precludes folios which are missing, having been lost or stolen. Their total is 228. We think that there were originally 750 printed,† so about a third remain.

So I am setting out on a sort of Folio Roadshow, to see as many of the fifty First Folios in the UK as I can, though some of those are in private hands.

---

* It was sold again privately at Sotheby's in 2025.
†Though a recent study of watermarks suggests the print run could have been as high as 1,200.

Chapter Two

The UK Folios

Birmingham

I opened *Richard III* at the Royal Shakespeare Theatre in June 2022. I had officially stepped down as Artistic Director in April, and the search was now on for my replacement. I would enjoy the title of Artistic Director Emeritus until the end of 2023. In July, I travelled up the road to Birmingham to visit the very first folio on my Roadshow.

Centenary Square was named in 1989 to mark 100 years since Birmingham received city status. In the centre is a ten-metre-high mechanical raging bull. It represents the industry of Birmingham and was the highlight of the opening of the Commonwealth Games in the city a few weeks earlier. It roared into the Alexander Stadium, snorting smoke from its nostrils, and won the heart of the crowd. That day Birmingham felt like a very proud city.

The animatronic bull stands in front of the library, a people's pleasure palace which opened in 2013. It's an arresting piece of architecture, the Hanging Gardens of Birmingham, a ziggurat of gold and silver filigree tiers, constructed of interlocking rings. They are intended to remind us of the city's jewellery quarter nearby, though Brummie wits have described them as bedsprings under a mattress. The whole edifice is topped off with a gilded rotunda which houses a Victorian treasure, the Shakespeare Memorial Room; and that's where I am headed.

The world's first great Shakespeare Library was built here in Britain's second city and yet until recently it had fallen into obscurity. Ewan Fernie is a professor at the Shakespeare Institute in Stratford and it is his mission to reintroduce the city and the world to one of its greatest assets.

Ewan is the director of the 'Everything to Everybody' Project. The name is inspired by the library's visionary founder, a radical young thinker called George Dawson, who sought to establish a 'cultural commonwealth' in his adopted town. He was a passionate advocate of working-class education and self-improvement, and campaigned for a free library for all of Birmingham's citizens. 'The time has come,' said Dawson, 'to give everything to everybody.'

On the tercentenary of Shakespeare's birth in 1864, Dawson and his friends decided that Birmingham should be the home of the greatest collection of Shakespeare books in the world, and insisted that it should be housed in the most beautiful room in the town and should be freely available to everyone. The first Shakespeare library opened in 1868. Dawson believed that beauty and art should not be the private right of the rich, but should be common to all.

I meet Ewan in the Shakespeare Memorial Room. This beautiful oak chamber was built as a place of study and contemplation, like the *studiolo* of an Italian Renaissance palazzo. The marquetry and metalwork bursts with exquisite foliage and flowers. But when the city's third library was constructed in 1974, in a brutalist concrete design, there was no place for this Victorian jewel box, and it was dismantled, stored – and ignored. Now miraculously reinstalled at the apex of the new library, it looks splendid. Even the scrolling painted plasterwork ceiling has been reinstated, though the glass-fronted bookcases no longer actually house the collection.

In comparison to the room, the First Folio Ewan shows me is not very grand. The edges and corners are worn and scuffed, and several pages have been stamped 'BIRMINGHAM FREE LIBRARY REFERENCE DEPARTMENT' in purple ink (a practice frowned upon today). What makes this folio special is the pioneering spirit which brought it to Birmingham in the first place.

There had been a proposal to acquire a copy of the First Folio for Birmingham as early as March 1870, when the famous London book dealer Bernard Quaritch wrote tantalisingly of a copy that had come into his possession. 'The volume is in my private room, locked up, and the key is in my pocket ... a volume like that cannot be shown to everybody.'

At £520, however, the asking price was too high,* and the purchase was declined. Quaritch then marketed it as 'the finest and tallest copy ever offered for sale' … 'in the most desirable condition' and added 'as the opportunity may not occur for many years, a spirited collector should take advantage of it'. The advert adds condescendingly, 'There is a further folio offered to the less wealthy'.

It was fortuitous that Dawson and his colleagues turned down Quaritch's 'absolutely perfect' copy, as the library then burned down in 1879, destroying all but 500 of the 7,000 volumes it contained. By the time the new library opened in 1882, Dawson and his committee had found another, humbler copy, again from Quaritch, at the more affordable price of £240.

However, I wondered where the marvellous original folio that Quaritch offered had ended up, having made such a narrow escape. Which august institution or lucky private buyer was now the proud owner? Quaritch may have purchased it at the sale of the library of Clement Tudway Swanston (1783–1863), a barrister and QC who also owned slaves, having inherited a plantation in Antigua. But, intriguingly, nobody seems to know where that volume went. No folio census currently mentions it.

However, the copy that Dawson and his committee eventually secured is the only copy of the First Folio in public ownership. Birmingham can be very proud of that.

Like Dawson, Fernie is passionately committed to a truly democratic culture. He and his team have not only created an exhibition displaying some of the Shakespeare Library's collection of books and prints and playbills and translations of the plays in many different languages; they also aim to reconnect all of Birmingham's communities with the city's Shakespearean heritage, reaching out to schools and families, finding ways to elicit a response to this hitherto neglected treasure.

In fact the city hosts a second 1623 Folio. A privately owned copy held by Birmingham University has a claim to be one of the earliest copies to be printed. A scrap written in a seventeenth-century hand and pasted into the first binder's leaf reads *February 24 Tuesday*. That date fell on a Tuesday in 1624, perhaps suggesting the volume was purchased within three months of publication.

---

* The equivalent in purchasing power of around £80,000 today.

The British Library

On a warm July afternoon in the British Library on Euston Road I got myself a crash course on how the First Folio works as a book, with the Head of Printed Collections, Adrian Edwards, and his colleague Christian Algar. They make a great double act: Adrian a light tenor, very precise and neat, and Christian the bass, larger and bearded.

The British Library have five copies of the First Folio. We look at one in the public display front of house. It's a copy that was owned by three eighteenth-century editors – Lewis Theobald, Dr Johnson and George Steevens – and the man who effectively owned the copyright on Shakespeare for most of the eighteenth century, the bookseller Jacob Tonson. Then I am taken 'backstage' to see their four other folios, all spread out on grey Styrofoam blocks before me. They are all very different, whether in terms of provenance, or bindings, or annotations within them. The first volume we look at is the Phelps copy, the last one purchased by the British Museum, back in 1922.

'Why did they need another First Folio when they already had four?' I ask. But what makes the Phelps copy so special is immediately apparent on the first page. The Droeshout engraving, that most famous of celebrity mugshots, looks odd. Something is wrong. Shakespeare's head seems to be floating on his standing collar, like John the Baptist's head on a plate. 'We call this early proof impression of the portrait the first state.'

'The early proof impression?' So this is just like the one James Orchard Halliwell-Phillipps cut out of our Theatre Copy.

'This is how the engraving first gets printed,' Adrian continues. 'It is clearly an early copy, and Droeshout looked at it and decided to make some changes. On the copies you see elsewhere, he has added shading between the hair and the collar. This is one of only four known to exist.'*

Had Mr Halliwell-Phillipps kept his scissors to himself, our copy would be one of only four in the world.

---

* I later see the other copies in the Bodleian Library, Oxford, and the Folger Shakespeare Library in Washington, DC.

'Are you still in the market for more First Folios?' I ask. 'Did you have agents at the Sotheby's auction in New York last week?' The latest folio to emerge (the William Stuart Stirling Crawford copy) went up for sale the week before, alongside a previously unrecorded copy of the Declaration of Independence, and a collection of Sex Pistols material (including a press release by Malcolm McLaren, autographed lyrics by Johnny Rotten and a promotional poster for 'God Save the Queen' owned by Sid Vicious). The folio went under the hammer for $2.47 million. The British Library were not bidding. They have enough folios.

Next, we look at a copy owned by Thomas Grenville, a politician who had been Lord of the Admiralty for a short period (1806–7). He bequeathed his large collection of books to the British Museum, including not only this First Folio, but copies of both the first and the second major books ever printed by movable type in the West: a Gutenberg Bible (1453) and a Mainz Psalter (1457).

Grenville, like many wealthy book collectors of his time, had had the folio rebound in sumptuous full goatskin, known as red morocco, and gold-stamped with his elaborate crest. It's a very handsome copy indeed with gilded edges. The pages have had to be trimmed in order to apply the gilding. Untrimmed pages, I learn, have rough-cut, or 'deckled', edges. Deckle-edged books were the original standard in publishing. Until the nineteenth century all books were printed this way on handmade paper. I notice the edges are not only gilded but embossed.

'It's called goffering,' says Christian, 'after *gaufre* – the French for waffle. The ornamentation is created by heated finishing tools.' 'Goffering' – another great word.

There are single words on the bottom far right of every page. These anticipate the first word on the following page, and are called 'catchwords'. They are there so that the printer can quickly check they have the pages in the right order. But there are also odd single letters and numbers at the foot of the page, which don't appear on every one. 'What should that alphabetical position portend?' I ask my captive expert librarians. It turns out these hieroglyphics are there to assist in the binding process. The readers may make use of the page numbers, but the printers and binders putting the printed sheets together need help.

'Ah, that's the gatherings,' says Adrian, and he dashes off to find three sheets of paper to explain. While he is gone, I ask Christian to explain the blotchy printing.

'The men who applied the ink to the type had these big leather inking balls, sometimes known as "dog's bollocks".' Apparently, they had to be soaked in urine to keep the leather pliable, and were also called 'dabs'. You needed to be a 'dab hand' to apply the same amount of ink with the same amount of pressure, or the print would be patchy. 'That's what's happened here,' says Christian. 'I suspect they were much better at it at the start of the day, and by the end of the week it got worse and worse.'

Adrian is back with his three sheets of paper.

'So folio just means leaf in Latin. The First Folio is made up of these large sheets of French rag paper. They are roughly twelve inches high and about nineteen inches wide. Each of these sheets when folded in half makes a folio.'

'Like foolscap?' I ask.

'Yes. It's just slightly taller than A4,' he replies.

'The name foolscap actually comes from the watermark of a jester's cap and bells, dating back to the fifteenth century,' Christian adds helpfully.

'And if you count each side of the folded sheet that gives you four pages. Fold it twice and you get sixteen pages, and you have the size of a quarto, like the small single paperback editions of the plays.'

Adrian then puts his three sheets of paper together, folds them in half, then places the little six-page booklet in front of me. 'These individual folded quires are sometimes called "sixes", for obvious reasons, or "gatherings". So the first page is given a signature code, say A1, on the "recto" side, the side facing you. And the other side of that page – the reverse, or "verso" side – doesn't need signifying. The recto side of the second sheet is then called A2, and similarly the third sheet is given the signature A3. Then you turn the page to the centrefold of that gathering (or quire), and you don't need to put in any more letters or numbers because the remaining pages of the gathering are attached.'*

---

* The second Birmingham copy demonstrates the importance of those signature letters. A leaf of the text of *As You Like It* was originally incorrectly printed R2 instead of R. When they came to put the play

'So the next gathering starts with B, the next C, right through the twenty-three letters of the alphabet,' says Adrian.

'Twenty-three?' I say. 'Aren't there twenty-six letters in the alphabet?'

'Not in the Jacobean period.' And Adrian and Christian start recalling which letters were not used: 'j and u and w'.

'But here's an anomaly,' says Christian. He turns to *Troilus and Cressida*. 'This play got left out and had to be inserted later. They didn't want to confuse the binders by using an alphabetical signature. So what do you get? This little character ...' and he points to what looks like a reverse P, or a paragraph mark.

'It's a pilcrow,' says Christian. What a fabulous name. And I listen as the two book-loving librarians go into a riff about the pilcrow: 'Born in Ancient Rome, refined in mediaeval scriptoria, and finally rehabilitated by the personal computer.'* In the days before printing, the pilcrow would be elaborately decorated by the specialised scribes, or rubricators, but as printing advanced spaces would be left at the start of each paragraph for the rubricators to perform their artistry. But the spaces were far too many for the rubricators to keep up with, and eventually were left as blank spaces, hence the introduction of the indented paragraph. All hail the pilcrow.

'Goffering', 'deckle' and 'pilcrow', I think to myself, like Andrew Aguecheek, 'I'll get 'em all three already'.

But I am still intrigued that *Troilus and Cressida* was left out of the folio. We turn to the contents page, which lists all the plays. I count them. There are meant to be thirty-six: there are fourteen Comedies (starting with *The Tempest* and ending with *The Winter's Tale*, in no discernible thematic order as far as I can see); ten Histories (bookended by *King John* and *Henry VIII* with the two tetralogies in between in chronological order of reign not of writing); and then eleven Tragedies (starting with *Coriolanus* and ending up with *Cymbeline*). So only thirty-five plays listed. And no *Troilus*

---

together the compiler picked up a corrected version of the page, but then, instead of adding the next leaf, picked up the same page but with the uncorrected R2 signature. It makes a confusing read with Jaques repeating 'All the world's a stage'.

* They rave about a recent book on typography by Keith Houston called, wittily, *Shady Characters*.

and Cressida. Whatever the controversy surrounding its inclusion it meant it was too late to insert on this contents page.*

The last folio we look at was once owned by George III, and bequeathed to the British Museum by his son George IV, in 1823.

'It's in pretty poor condition,' says Adrian. 'It's got foxing and black spot all over it. It's riddled with holes and tears, resulting in the loss of text on almost every page. There is another folio originally owned by George III at Windsor Castle which is in much better condition than this one, so obviously George IV decided to keep the better copy for himself.'

But the most fun feature of this folio comes at the end of *Henry IV Part Two*. Next to the final word, *FINIS*, there are pencil sketches.† On one side, the face of a young man in a Caroline collar, with long hair and heavy eyebrows. It might be a self-portrait, and copies the pose of the Droeshout engraving, staring directly at the viewer and showing the left side of the face. On the other side is a drawing of a cannon. We ponder if it's a reference to Falstaff's line about the ragged recruits being cannon fodder – 'food for powder, food for powder' as Sir John sneers. But then just behind the cannon I notice the unmistakable phallic doodle of a cock and balls.

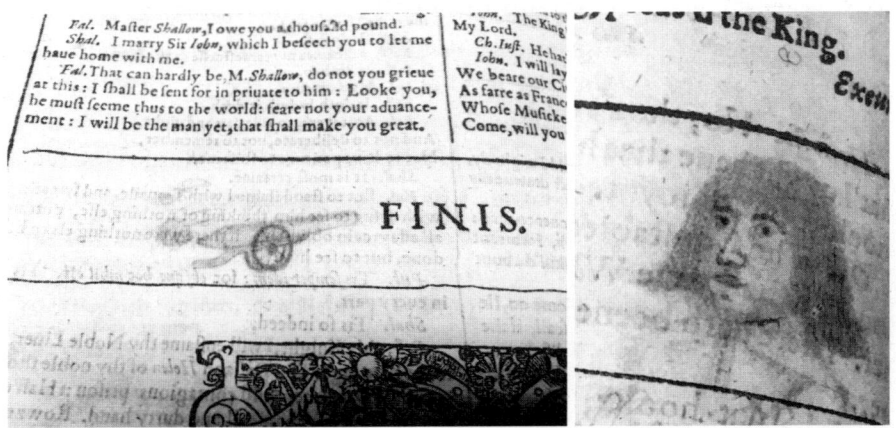

Pencil sketches in the BL Folio

* On many copies I will later see the title has been inked in between the Histories and the Tragedies.
† In the Folger Library there is a folio containing a child's drawing of a house.

'And do we think that has some reference to the cannon?' I ponder out loud. 'Well,' offers Christian, 'the cannon is aimed at the word "FINIS".'

Guildhall Library, City of London

'Of all the extant First Folios, our copy is the closest to its place of origin,' boasts Dr Peter Ross, the Principal Librarian at the Guildhall Library. And he is right. The print shop of William Jaggard and his son Isaac at the sign of the Half Eagle and Key stood on Aldersgate Street across from where the Barbican tube station stands today. It's roughly a ten-minute walk north-west. I have just done it to get here this morning. But there is an even closer connection, for the men responsible for publishing the First Folio lived just yards away. Dr Ross points out of the window of the John Stow Room where we are standing.

'See that little park just across Love Lane?' he asks. 'Well, that is built on the site of St Mary Aldermanbury. Both Hemmings[*] and Condell worshipped in that parish, and as all the city parishes were so tiny they must have lived quite close to where we are now standing,' he says proudly. John Hemmings and Henry Condell were Shakespeare's colleagues, running a company of actors, assembled in 1594 under the patronage of the Lord Chamberlain, the man in charge of entertainment at court. They eventually established themselves at the Globe Theatre on the South Bank, with Richard Burbage as their leading actor. The Lord Chamberlain's Men, with Shakespeare as their principal dramatist, then became the King's Men on the accession of King James I in 1603. Shakespeare wrote exclusively for this small group of actors for nearly two decades. Perhaps not surprising then that Hemmings and Condell should make such great efforts to preserve his legacy.

We turn to the front of the folio. On the pages following the Droeshout engraving Hemmings and Condell published two letters. The first is addressed 'to the most noble and incomparable

---

[*] John's name is printed twice as 'Heminge' and once as 'Hemmings' in the folio. I have chosen to adopt 'Hemmings' throughout the book, as it makes the double act of Hemmings and Condell easier to say. Condell's name is printed both as Henry and Henrie on pages facing each other in the folio.

pair of brethren William Earl of Pembroke etc. Lord Chamberlain to the Kings most excellent majesty, and Philip Earl of Montgomery etc.' and the second letter is addressed 'To the great variety of readers'.

I read out some of the elaborate prose of the first letter. 'There is a great difference, whether any book choose his patrons, or find them: This hath done both,' and then a masterly piece of flattery: 'The volume ask'd to be yours.'

But there is a semi-religious fervour in the language Shakespeare's friends employ: 'The most, though meanest of things are made more precious, when they are dedicated to Temples. In that name therefore we most humbly consecrate to your highnesses these remains of your servant Shakespeare.' This is surely the trigger of what George Bernard Shaw two and a half centuries later would define as 'bardolatry'.

The second letter is more jaunty, addressing all readers: 'from the most able to him that can but spell.' And they are quite direct in their sales pitch: 'Well! It is now public and you will stand for your privileges, we know to read and censure. Do so, but buy it first.'

They then point out why the potential buyer should consider this purchase: 'Where before you were abus'd with diverse stolen and surreptitious copies, maimed and deformed by the frauds and stealths of injurious imposters, that expos'd them: even those are now offered to your view cur'd, and perfect of their limbs; and all the rest, absolute in their numbers, as he conceived them.'

Then comes my favourite line: '… who as he was a happy imitator of nature was the most gentle expresser of it. His mind and hand went together and what he thought he uttered with that easiness, that we have scarce received from him a blot in his papers.' They finish with a flourish which will echo down the ages: 'Read him therefore, and again and again.'

I decide to pay my respects to Messrs Hemmings and Condell, and after my chat with Dr Ross I walk over to the little garden across Love Lane from the Guildhall Library. Various office workers are perched on benches in the shade. A team of City gardeners are sweeping and raking the little park. This 'green' open space where St Mary's Aldermanbury once stood, where John Hemmings and Henry Condell worshipped with their families, is now a memorial to them. We owe these two men a huge debt. Had they not pulled together all Shakespeare's plays in a folio edition, only the plays already published in the single smaller quarto editions would have survived.

The plinth of polished pink granite bears a Victorian bust of Shakespeare modelled on the funerary demi-figure in Holy Trinity Church. Unkindly, Pevsner's guide calls it 'stodgy'. Further plates on its flanks give more detail about Shakespeare's colleagues. Henry Condell lived in the parish 'upwards of thirty years'. He had nine children, eight of whom were baptised in the church, and six buried there. Condell was buried here on 29 December 1627, just four years after the First Folio was published.

John Hemmings was, it seems, similarly 'philoprogenitive'. The bronze plaque reads that he and his wife had fourteen children, 'thirteen of whom were baptised, four buried and one married here'. Hemmings was also married at St Mary's, and indeed he was buried in the churchyard, too, in October 1630, just three years after his fellow parishioner. So these two members of the King's Men had twenty-three children between them. Neither of their wives' names appear on the monument, but let's mention them here. John was married to Rebecca, and Henry to Elizabeth.

Rebecca was the widow of William Knell, an actor with the Queen's Men, who had been killed in a duel with another actor, on tour in Thame in Oxfordshire in 1587. I think John must have loved Rebecca, as in his will he asks to be buried as close to her as possible.

Hemmings was originally a Worcestershire man, from Droitwich (twenty-odd miles north-west of Stratford-upon-Avon), and was just a couple of years younger than Shakespeare. He was a grocer by trade, and became the business manager of the Globe. We think he built and operated the tap house next door. We hear of him in a poem written about the burning down of the Globe in 1613, where he is described weeping at the playhouse's destruction:

Then with swoll'n eyes, like drunken Flemings,
Distressed stood old stuttering Hemmings ...
    'A Sonnet Upon the Pitiful Burning of the Globe Playhouse'

Henry Condell (or 'Harry Condye', as he is named in the poem*) hailed it seems from East Anglia, and may have been the son of a fishmonger in Norwich. He and Elizabeth Smart married in the church of St Laurence Pountney.

The friends' parish church where they both served as churchwardens was destroyed by the Great Fire of London in 1666. It was rebuilt by Christopher Wren, only to be bombed in the blitz in 1940. The marble inscription reveals that the fabric of the church was removed to Fulton, Missouri, in 1966, and restored as a memorial not to Hemmings and Condell but to Sir Winston Churchill, in recognition of his famous 'Iron Curtain' speech delivered at Westminster College in Fulton immediately after the war in 1946.

The bust is swagged with droopy cobwebs, which seem dustier in the hot sunlight. The gardeners have left their rakes and tools around the monument and are bagging up the weeds. One of them has stopped to open the pack of bottled water sitting on the bench. I ask him if I could use his long-handled brush to sweep the cobwebs off the bust. 'Knock yourself out,' he says, a little bemused by the request. So I give the statue a sweep, like a barber giving his client a little brush-down at the end of the job.

★ ★ ★

In his will, Shakespeare left twenty-six shillings and eight pence each to Hemmings and Condell, and to the great Richard Burbage, to buy mourning rings. Stanley Wells suggests that this might have been to secure a pact to memorialise him after his death by publishing his plays. Perhaps this was the trigger for Hemmings and Condell to collect together and publish all Shakespeare's plays. After all, if his rival playwright Ben Jonson could do it (he published his collected works in 1616) then surely a folio edition of Shakespeare's plays would be a great commercial proposition.

The King's Men paid playwrights for their plays (£6–£8), which they then owned. After the play had been performed they might sell

---

* Shortening his name to Condye would suggest the stress should fall on the first syllable, 'Cóndell', as opposed to 'Condéll'.

them to different booksellers who then owned the exclusive rights to print and publish the plays. An avid theatregoer who wanted to buy a copy of a play by Shakespeare might therefore have to do some walking. They could buy *Othello* at the Eagle and Child, in Britain's Bourse, the new shopping arcade recently opened in the Strand. They could walk up Fleet Street and buy *Romeo and Juliet* under the dial of St Dunstan's, or *A Midsummer Night's Dream* at the sign of the White Hart, a little further along. Or they could walk up to the north-east corner of St Paul's Churchyard, where a whole menagerie of booksellers had their stalls or stations: Matthew Law, at the sign of the Fox, sold history plays from *Richard II* to *Henry VI*; you could buy a quarto of *King Lear* at the Pied Bull, or *The Merchant of Venice* over at the Green Dragon. *Titus Andronicus* was available at the Gun.

Hemmings and Condell needed help to pull off such an ambitious undertaking as this folio edition. They were theatre men, they knew little about publishing. They would need a syndicate both to finance and to organise the printing. On the morning of Wednesday 8 November 1623, two key members of that syndicate met up. William Jaggard's 28-year-old son Isaac walked over from their printing house in Aldersgate to St Paul's Churchyard, to the Black Bear, the shop owned by the veteran publisher Edward Blount, a man by now in his early sixties. Together they headed the short distance to Ave Maria Lane at the top of Ludgate Hill to the Stationers' Hall. There they were met by the Master Dr Worrall and the Under Warden Mr Cole, and entered 'Master William Shakspeers Comedyes Histories, and Tragedyes' in Liber D, the fourth volume of the Company Register. Or at least they registered their rights in the unpublished plays the King's Men owned. They paid seven shillings for the privilege. They would have to negotiate separately with all those different booksellers to lease them the rights to reprint the plays they owned. Only then could their scheme succeed. And soon customers would be able to buy all Shakespeare's plays in one volume.

★ ★ ★

If there was a pact to publish the plays, Burbage could not be part of it as he died four years before the folio was published, though it is possible that his death was another prompt. The public outpouring of grief over Burbage's death threatened to eclipse the mourning for King James I's wife, Queen Anne, who had died ten days before. He was buried in St Leonard's, Shoreditch, with the best epitaph any actor ever had: Exit Burbage.

Dulwich College

Richard Burbage's great rival was Edward Alleyn. Just four months older than Burbage, Alleyn was the star of the Lord Admiral's Men, the rival company run by his father-in-law Philip Henslowe at the Rose Theatre, just yards from the Globe on Bankside. Alleyn originated three of Christopher Marlowe's overreaching heroes: Dr Faustus, Barabas in *The Jew of Malta* and Tamburlaine the Great.

I have come to Dulwich to see a folio at the 'College of God's Gift', founded by Alleyn in 1619. The notion that the folio in the library here might once have been owned by Alleyn is attractive.

Dulwich College holds many great treasures of Elizabethan theatre, like Edward Alleyn's Diary; one of only six surviving 'platts' (or plots) of a play which were hung up backstage to keep the actors on track during the performance; and Philip Henslowe's Diary, his account book of the daily takings at the Rose, undoubtedly the single most important document of early modern English theatre history. Besides these wonders their First Folio is a little disappointing. It is very fragmented. There are two bound volumes: Comedies and Histories, and six pages of *Romeo and Juliet*. Nevertheless, there can be few folios outside the famous Folger Shakespeare Library in Washington, DC which can be seen in such a special context of surrounding material.

In fact, it seems likely that the Dulwich Folio was the gift of an actor called William Cartwright. Cartwright, whose father knew Alleyn, had been a player in the reign of Charles I, and after trading as a bookseller during the Commonwealth became a founder member of the newly re-formed King's Men at the Restoration, under Thomas Killigrew.

On my way back I stop in at the Dulwich Picture Gallery to see the portrait of Richard Burbage. The painting is oddly small. It is dwarfed by its gold frame. The accompanying label suggests the portrait 'was likely intended to be sewn into a larger canvas. A common practice that explains its odd shape.'

'I always had you in mind when I was writing this' – that's a line any actor loves to hear a writer say. But imagine if those parts included Romeo, Richard III, Henry V, Brutus, Hamlet, Shylock, Macbeth, Coriolanus, Othello and King Lear – a lifetime's career of great roles. Over two spectacular decades, Shakespeare wrote that very line of parts for this particular actor.

And they were not the only roles Burbage originated. Ben Jonson wrote the virtuoso comedic role of Volpone for this great actor; as well as Subtle, one of the duo of conmen in *The Alchemist*. Thomas Heywood wrote the severe husband Frankford in his devastating play *A Woman Killed with Kindness* for Burbage, while he also triumphed as the murderous Duke Bracciano in *The White Devil* by John Webster.

Burbage did a good line in grief. 'My grief no heart, my thoughts no tongue can tell,' laments Old Hieronimo, the grieving father in Thomas Kyd's *The Spanish Tragedy*, one of the roles he is credited with playing. But his forte seems to have been parts which could express furious jealousy or characters hell-bent on revenge. Thomas Middleton wrote the vengeful Vindice in *The Revenger's Tragedy* for him and John Marston created the mercurial Malevole for Burbage, in *The Malcontent*. Indeed, it's possible that the popularity of the whole genre of Revenge Tragedy could be ascribed as readily to Burbage as to any writer of the day.

The Dulwich picture might be a self-portrait, though the only extant documents mentioning actual painting by Burbage refer to payments for decorative heraldic work. However, the character sketch by Thomas Overbury of *An Excellent Actor* is thought to be of Burbage and it notes: 'He is much affected to painting, and tis a question whether that make him an excellent Player, or his playing an exquisite painter.'

As I stare at this actor with his strong nose and kind hazel eyes, he reminds me of Tony, and I think of all the many portraits Tony did of himself in many of Burbage's roles: Richard III, Shylock, Macbeth and Lear, as well as Vindice and Malevole. Surely Burbage, like Tony, played Leontes and Prospero, too. How striking that both actors were artists.

It is not surprising that the stable of Elizabethan and Jacobean playwrights liked writing for Burbage. One of the many elegies and poems published at his death says he added 'grace to the Poets' labours' and suggests that he was responsible for turning many a playwright's words into something special:

... He *made* a Poet,
And those who yet remain full surely know it,
For, having Burbage to give forth each line,
It fill'd their brain with fury more divine.

And perhaps it was the same with his relationship with Shakespeare. Perhaps without the talent of an actor like Burbage, Shakespeare would not have been able to write his plays in the way he did; perhaps they inspired each other, and Burbage filled his brain with divine fury.

When we were rehearsing *Richard III* a few months ago in Stratford, we did a first run of the play. After the first four acts, Arthur Hughes (playing Richard) admitted that he was knackered, and he still had the fight in Act 5 to go. I think that is exactly what Burbage must have said to Shakespeare: *Will, don't get me wrong, it's a great part, fantastic, but never do that to me again!* And after that Shakespeare never does. The leading character always gets a rest in Act 4: Macbeth during the England scene; Hamlet while Ophelia goes mad and dies; Lear through the blinding of Gloucester to Dover; and Leontes has the sheep-shearing scenes in Bohemia to put his feet up. Tony always said that a crucial part of the rehearsal process is building up the stamina to play these great roles and learning how to pace yourself.

As I leave Dulwich I am suddenly hit by a black wave. What am I going to do with all Tony's paintings? Once the new Artistic Director is announced, I know I will have to move out of our house in Welcombe Road in Stratford. Where will I put everything?

My grief no heart, my thoughts no tongue can tell.

Northward Ho! Manchester

Radio 4's *Front Row* has invited me onto the programme to reflect on my decade as Artistic Director. Nick Ahad is an expert at putting his guests at ease and I soon feel we are just old mates chatting on the sofa. He asks me about the issues we faced and the challenges we met, about the diversity on our stages which I championed, and the criticism we received for doing it. He also asks what I think about what the next incumbent will need. 'Resilience,' I say, without thinking too much.

Before the interview I have arranged to visit the splendidly neo-Gothic Rylands Library, in Deansgate in the heart of Manchester. It has been affiliated with the city's great university since 1972. My guide is the Rare Books Librarian, Jane Gallagher. John Rylands was Manchester's first multimillionaire. His fortune was founded on cotton. When he died in 1888 his wife Enriquetta intended to build the library in his name. Instead, she built him a cathedral, in dark red Barbary stone from Penrith.

At one end of the reading room nave stands a marble statue of Rylands himself, and at the other end under a stained-glass window stands the formidable Enriquetta. She was born in Cuba, and had been the companion to Rylands's first wife, Martha. She married John eight months after Martha's death. He was seventy-four. She was thirty-two. Enriquetta decided to spend half of her husband's fortune on building the library itself and half on the collection. In 1892 her first significant purchase was the Spencer library at Althorp. The 5th Earl Spencer had become strapped for cash. In the late summer of that year, 600 cases of books were packed and dispatched to Manchester. The 5th Earl was said to be uneasy that his precious collection should be destined for smoggy Manchester. Enriquetta persisted. But she faced further opposition in the press. This article, with its racist overtones, appeared in a weekly gossip newspaper called *Modern Society*:

> We see the purchase of the Althorp library by Mrs. Rylands is confirmed, but not the gift of it to Manchester. We trust this magnificent collection will not go to that dirty, uncomfortable city. What do unsavoury Greek shent-per-shenters and uncultivated boors want with a library, and such a one? Besides, they have not enough light to read by, and the books they already have are wretchedly kept.

Enriquetta's stated wish was 'that this library shall be of use in the widest sense of the word: for young students as well as for advanced scholars. It is not to be a mere centre for antiquaries and bibliographers.' If Enriquetta's ambitions for the library were not quite as fully democratic as George Dawson's in Birmingham, nevertheless she was a remarkable philanthropist.

Jane shows me into the Bible Room, a study originally intended (as the name suggests) for theological contemplation. The Bible Collection at the John Rylands Library is one of the finest in the world, spanning six centuries and more than 400 different languages and dialects. Today, a different sort of worship is on offer. Among Lord Spencer's books was not only a First Folio, but also a copy of the first edition of the sonnets (1609). I am excited to see it before me now. There are only twelve other extant copies of this book in the world.

The title page includes a note recording a purchase price of 5d. Edward Alleyn recorded his acquisition of 'a book Shaksper sonets' among 'Howshowld stuff' (household stuff) at a cost of five pence, too. Could this be his copy? But then Jane points out an inscription. It's quite hard to read but has generally been translated as: 'Commendations to my very kind and approved friend.'

'To my very kind and approved friend' ... hmm ... that pentameter sounds familiar. What does Petruchio call his friend Hortensio in *Shrew* – 'My best beloved and approved friend'; and how does Othello address the Venetian senate – 'My very noble and approved good masters'; and in *Henry IV Part One*, Archibald is described as 'That ever-valiant and approved Scot'. The dedication is followed by an enigmatic sequence which some have read as the initials B. M. with a flourish at the end. But it immediately strikes me differently.

'Could that not be the date?' I ask Jane, '23 : M :) – 23 May – and might the dash not be a figure 9 suggesting May 1609?' If that's the case then it would relate to the date that the publisher Thomas Thorpe entered the sonnets in the Stationers' Register: 20 May 1609.

A decade before, in 1598, Francis Meres in his treasury of wit, *Palladis Tamia*, had written that 'the sweet witty soul of Ovid lives in mellifluous and honey-tongued Shakespeare, witness ... his sugared sonnets among his private friends'. This looks like the sort of inscription Tony would scribble to me in the first copies of one of his books after publication. So could this be the publisher's handwriting ... or could it even be ... the author's?

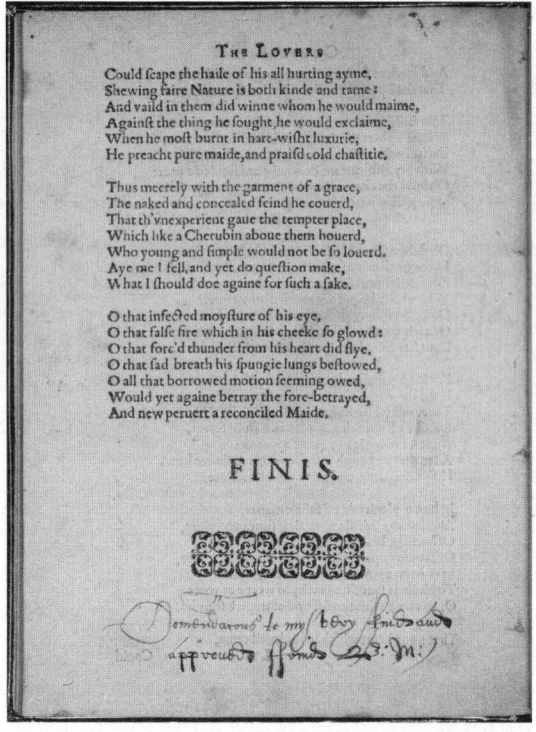

The dedication note on the 1609 Sonnets *in the Rylands Library*

★ ★ ★

With train strikes disrupting the rail network, I have enlisted the help of a very dear old school friend, James Robertson, to drive me around to the next two folios on my Roadshow. We head north, skirting the Trough of Bowland to Stonyhurst College.

Stonyhurst

It's 1605. On the night of Tuesday 5 November, five-year-old Helen Wintour saw a group of men arrive at Huddington Court, six miles east of Worcester. They had ridden hard and looked wild and frightened. Helen's father Robert was there, and her uncle Thomas and several others. Her mother Gertrude hurried her to bed with her sisters. Early in the morning, having heard mass in the secret chapel, the men galloped away. It was the last time Helen would see her father or uncle.

They were all part of a failed conspiracy to blow up the Houses of Parliament, in a desperate attempt to restore England to the Catholic faith. Had they succeeded, the king, the royal family and all the lords temporal and ecclesiastical attending the state opening of Parliament would have perished.

The man occupying the cell next to Robert Wintour in the Tower of London was Guy Fawkes. Their whispered conversation was recorded and read out at their trial. On 30 January, Wintour was dragged on a hurdle to St Paul's Cathedral, hanged by the neck from a scaffold, and before he expired was cut down and eviscerated, his heart pulled out still beating, and presented to a roaring crowd. His body was then hacked roughly into quarters and parboiled. Three other of his co-conspirators were executed with him. The following morning the rest, including Helen's uncle Thomas, were hauled to Old Palace Yard in Westminster, and, opposite the building they had tried to destroy, were executed, too.

Robert's wife, Gertrude, never recovered from the shock. Within two years, poleaxed by grief, she was dead. Her ghost is said to walk Huddington Court on the anniversary of her husband's execution to this day. Little Helen would grow up to look after her family and run the household of Huddington Court. And, like the two priest holes hidden in her home, she learned to conceal her Catholic faith, which was only strengthened by the trials she endured.

★ ★ ★

In the Shakespeare First Folio preserved at Stonyhurst College in rural Lancashire, I find the Porter scene in *Macbeth*. The Hell Porter welcomes an equivocator on the primrose path to the everlasting bonfire: 'Here's an equivocator that could swear in both the scales against either scale, who committed treason enough for God's sake yet could not equivocate to heaven.' It's a reference to the trial of one of Robert Wintour's acquaintances, the Jesuit Father Henry Garnet.

Garnet had written a pamphlet, *A Treatise on Equivocation*, in 1598. It was a justification for (and instruction in) the use of carefully worded language to avoid self-incrimination and prosecution, a legitimate strategy he argued to save the lives, for example, of those Catholics who illegally housed and supported Jesuit priests. To the Protestants this defence was lying by another name. Garnet had learned about the gunpowder plot through the confessional, but refused to break his sacred oath to reveal that information. He equivocated about precisely what he knew when he was captured and interrogated by the Privy Council. Sir Edward Coke described his equivocation as 'open and broad lying and forswearing'.

Garnet was sentenced solely for having advance knowledge of the plot and was executed in May 1606, the year *Macbeth* was first performed at the Globe. A devout Catholic witnessing that execution collected some of the straw from underneath the scaffold on which Father Garnet's blood had fallen. On one husk they saw the face of the martyred priest in the splashed blood. The relic was smuggled out of the country and remained in the possession of the Society of Jesus, before being lost during the French Revolution.

Another Jesuit priest who, like Garnet, was caught up in the furore around the gunpowder plot, and was also tortured and executed, was Father Edward Oldcorne. When in the sequence of hanging, drawing and quartering the executioner decapitated him, the force of the blow expelled one of his eyes. *Out vile jelly*. It was scooped up as a relic. As I read the Porter scene in the Stonyhurst Folio, I am shown that very eye, preserved in a small circular silver reliquary. One side is engraved with the words '*OCULUS DEXTER P ED OLCORNI SOC IESU*' (the right eye of Fr Edward Oldcorne Society of Jesus). The other side has an eye-shaped aperture, filled with glass and fringed with lashes.

As I hold it in the palm of my hand all I can see is a brown, shrivelled circle of gruesome gristle, but what that eye must have seen. It is a potent reminder of the febrile, fractured post-Reformation political world which Shakespeare had to navigate.

★ ★ ★

Stonyhurst College is the oldest surviving Jesuit college in the world, tracing its existence back to 1593, when it was founded in Saint-Omer, near Calais, then part of the Spanish Netherlands. It counts among its alumni Sir Arthur Conan Doyle, creator of Sherlock Holmes. The Jesuit poet Gerard Manley Hopkins taught there.

The college stands in acres of land, about fifteen miles from Preston, where I went to school. We used to play Stonyhurst at rugby and hockey. Well, I didn't, I was sports-averse, but James Robertson ('Jimmy' to us then) certainly did, and my old school friend accompanies me here today. James remained in the area, became a doctor, and brought up his family here in the picturesque Ribble Valley. Though we have always stayed in touch, it's been pretty much on a Christmas card basis, but since I lost Tony, reconnecting with friends has become really important.

James introduces me to Dr Jan Graffius, Curator of the Archive for Stonyhurst. We are in the Arundell library. Seeing a First Folio here reinforces my understanding of the context in which Shakespeare was writing his plays. Apart from Oldcorne's eye, there are other remarkable artefacts of Catholic history. Here is a human skull, not another contender for Yorick, but the rescued cranium of John Morton, councillor to three kings during the Wars of the Roses: Henry VI, Edward IV and Henry VII. Morton supported Richmond in his claim to be king against Richard III.

He appears as the Bishop of Ely in *Richard III*, whom Gloucester humiliates by getting him to run for strawberries from his garden in Holborn. Morton was a patron of Thomas More and funded his studies at Oxford. More recorded Morton's memories of the tyrant king, whom he believed was responsible for the murder of the Princes in the Tower. Astonishingly here, too, in the Arundell library is Thomas More's brown beaver hat. It brings the past vividly close.

Jan asks if we have time to see an exhibition which she has curated, called provocatively 'Hot Holy Ladies'. The phrase is a sarcastic insult which dates back to 1602, aimed at some of the strong-minded Catholic women who supported the Jesuit mission. They achieved extraordinary acts of religious defiance and cultural creativity in the shadow of state-imposed religious intolerance and persecution. Most striking is the work of Helen Wintour, who as a little girl saw her father ride off to his death in the aftermath of the gunpowder plot. As an adult she became the centre of a network of erudite, charitable, recusant women.

Several dazzling seventeenth-century chasubles hang before us, illegal vestments for a proscribed religion. They are embroidered in gold thread incorporating pearls, rubies and opals. Secret codes are embedded in the needlework, and symbols such as dewdrops, roses and flames of fire, encoded acts of devotion and of defiance. On the white Alleluia chasuble used at Easter, Helen has dared to stitch her own name, countering state oppression with her exquisite artistry.

Jan shows us a pedlar's chest which was discovered walled up in nearby Salmesbury Hall. This wooden cylindrical trunk, covered in pony hide, had been used by the itinerant Jesuit priests, moving between households in Catholic Lancashire, to carry the chalice, pyx and other implements necessary to celebrate mass. They made use of the packhorse routes which threaded over the fells to avoid being arrested by the state watchers.

When they arrived, the holy fathers would unpack the tools of their devotional trade and don the vestments kept for them in hiding. 'You can imagine how they must have sparkled in the candlelight,' says Jan. 'Living in such isolation, amid such state hostility, the beauty of the needlework they accomplished must have allowed these recusant women and their families to feel some element of control over the chaos and fear of their existence.'

How these astonishing works have survived at all is miraculous. Some were discovered in what was thought to be a trunk of rags in the attic, when the kitchen cat had her kittens. It makes me wonder how any of the folios survived the turbulence of that riven century.

★ ★ ★

Back in the Arundell library, Jan has a series of other books, which she thinks might interest me. School plays are a strong Jesuit tradition, and here are copies of some early stage adaptations. The first school Shakespeare play might have happened at Saint-Omer, where it is known that from 1623 they had a First Folio (only recently rediscovered). But unlike the experience James and I had at the all-male Preston Catholic College, where I got to play Lady Macbeth, the boys were not originally allowed to play women, and so all the female parts were re-gendered. In *The Tempest*, Prospero has a son called 'Mirando', though I did not get to find out what his relationship with Ferdinand was; presumably just good mates. In *Hamlet*, the Prince's mother becomes Uncle Donald and even more intriguingly Ophelia is renamed Eric.

Skipton

James and I drive forty minutes or so up the Ribble Valley to our next folio. We skirt Pendle Hill, home to the poor women tried, condemned and executed for witchcraft in 1612; and arrive in Skipton, 'the Gateway to the Dales', just across the Yorkshire border. Here I find one of the most intriguing folios I have so far encountered on my Folio Roadshow. At the Craven Museum, in the heart of this little market town, we are met by Lead Curator Jenny Hill and her assistant Charlotte Craig. I ask Jenny how Skipton came to own a 1623 Folio in the first place.

'A wealthy local businessman called John Wilkinson purchased the book in the early 1900s,' Jenny tells me. The Wilkinsons were mill owners and John's father spun cotton at Primrose Mill in nearby Embsay from 1854. Over the years, with the advent of the Lancashire cotton famine, brought about by the American Civil War, he began to manufacture tobacco as well and in 1890 this took over the whole mill. John Wilkinson died in 1919 and left all his possessions to his sister Ann. Included in these was his Shakespeare First Folio.

'Then when Ann died in 1936,' Jenny concludes, 'she chose to leave it to the town, which is how it arrived here at the museum. But for some unknown reason the librarian at the time decided that it wasn't a First Folio after all, it was a Second Folio and it was downgraded. And from then on that classification was always assumed to be correct.'

'So, this isn't a First Folio?' I bumble, confused. Jenny continues: 'It wasn't until 2003, when a new census of Folios was being drawn up by Anthony James West, that he came up here to the museum, took one look at our folio and said it was a First Folio after all. Well, you can imagine the excitement!' It was a big moment for Skipton. A local campaign managed to raise the money to build a secure room and a theft-proof display case, and they even got Patrick Stewart, a great Yorkshireman, to record the voice-over describing the treasure.

I ask Jenny to tell me how the cotton mill owner got hold of a folio in the first place. Jenny grins at her colleague Charlotte. One theory is that it came from nearby Ponden Hall. Ponden had one of the largest private libraries not just in the West Riding, but in the whole of Europe. Charlotte has a theory about some of Ponden Hall's close neighbours who might have used their library.

'Well, Ponden Hall is just two or three miles across the moors from Haworth.'

'Oh, no!' I gasp 'From Haworth Parsonage, where the Brontë sisters lived?'

'That's right,' says Charlotte. 'I used to work there.'

'Are you saying that the Brontë sisters might have read this copy of the First Folio?'

'We know they used to borrow books from Ponden Hall. But I can't prove they read this folio.'

'Just say it!' I explode. 'Let somebody else disprove it. Oh, that is fantastic. What about that!'

James smiles wryly. He thinks I'm mad. Jenny and Charlotte very kindly took the folio out of its case and carried it upstairs for me to examine more closely. While they were doing so, I did a bit of research. I remembered a reference to a letter Charlotte Brontë had written to a school friend about Shakespeare. By the time Jenny and Charlotte had laid out the folio upstairs, I had found the letter online.

Jenny points out that the folio is missing quite a few pages, and doesn't have any of the Comedies. So I tell them about Charlotte's letter dated 4 July 1834, to Ellen Nussey. 'Ellen was her best friend at school,' Charlotte interjects.

'If you like poetry let it be first rate, Milton, Shakespeare, Thomson, Goldsmith, Pope (if you will though I don't admire him), Scott, Byron, Campbell, Wordsworth and Southey. Now Ellen don't be startled at the names of Shakespeare, and Byron. Both these were great men and their works are like themselves. You will know how to choose the good and avoid the evil, the finest passages are always the purest, the bad are invariably revolting you will never wish to read them over twice. Omit the comedies of Shakespeare.'

Omit the comedies of Shakespeare. And the Skipton copy has no comedies.

'Perhaps Charlotte ripped them out,' Jenny laughs.

'This just gets better and better,' I say. 'Charlotte, you've got to get this story out there.'

Once we have all calmed down a little, I tell Jenny that despite its now even more fascinating history, I think it might be the grubbiest copy of the First Folio I have ever seen. 'Could you not say "grubbiest",' Jenny grins. 'Could you perhaps say "well-loved"?'

The well-thumbed Skipton copy has become one of my very favourite copies of the First Folio, whether or not anyone can prove that the Brontë sisters ever read it.

A Wild Goose Chase

I had been invited to speak at a conference organised by the British Shakespeare Association, of which I had just been made an honorary member. It was held at the University of Liverpool, right next to Paddy's Wigwam, as the scousers called the Metropolitan Cathedral of Christ the King, the mother church of the diocese of Liverpool in which I grew up. We made a family pilgrimage from our home just outside Preston to see this marvellous concrete shuttlecock when it was consecrated in 1967.

I climbed the great white staircase stretching up from Hope Street to visit the cathedral again, and gazed at its circular interior illuminated by stained glass in a trinity of colours which lend the church a special grace. I sat in one of the pews which circle the high altar, and quietly yearned for the certainties of the faith I held as a child, and how it might have sustained me during Tony's final days. I felt the same at his funeral in Holy Trinity Church in Stratford. Would my eroded faith have provided consolation in my grief? Certainly my parents had derived great strength from their Catholic faith. Or, like C. S. Lewis, would I have been angry with God for taking my beloved away from me? Would it have been easier with someone to blame?

In *A Grief Observed*, Lewis details the bewilderment that he felt after his wife Joy Davidman's death, as well as his painful impressions of life without her. He questions the nature of grief and whether or not returning to normality afterwards is even possible. The period of his bereavement was marked by a process of moving in and out of various stages of grief and remembrance. Lewis ultimately redefines his own characterisation of God: experiencing gratitude for having received and experienced the gift of a true love. Perhaps that transition will come, as grief transmutes into happy remembrance.

★ ★ ★

At the Liverpool conference I was introduced to one of the other speakers, Richard Dutton, a retired English professor from Ohio State University, who was born locally in Cheshire. He was interested to hear about my Folio Roadshow and confided that he knew of an undiscovered copy.

From 1999 to 2000, he had been awarded study leave from Ohio State to prepare a Revels Plays edition of Ben Jonson's *Epicoene, or The Silent Woman*. He knew that Warrington Library had a copy of Ben Jonson's 1616 Folio of his works, and applied to see it. The librarian brought him into the director's office and opened a large safe. But as they extracted the Jonson, Professor Dutton noticed another old volume beneath it and asked what it was. Apparently the librarian admitted that it was in fact a Shakespeare First Folio (it had come to the library from the clearance of a farmhouse in the 1920s), but that they didn't like to advertise the fact.

I decided to investigate. I emailed Warrington Public Library. The following day the Strategic Library Manager got in touch saying it had been passed to her, and how could she help? I asked if the director's office still had a safe in it, if the 1623 Folio was still there, and, if so, whether they would be prepared to acknowledge it, or could tell me where it had gone.

The librarian responded swiftly saying how fascinating this all was. There was indeed still a safe in the office but it had no books in it. She had worked at the library for over twenty years, and did recall that some valuable items had been auctioned off about fifteen years before. But she would do some investigating, ask some retired colleagues and get back to me.

How thrilling. If I can actually manage to help uncover a lost First Folio, that would be a fantastic result for the Folio Roadshow.

In 2002, around about the same time as Professor Dutton was shown the copy in the Warrington safe, there was another folio story which hit the press not twenty-five miles away in Stockport. A 'humble housewife' discovered she had been left a First Folio by a second cousin twice removed whom she had never met. She even appeared on the *Richard & Judy* show on TV. There was considerable controversy surrounding the bequest, which was disputed. The 'housewife', Anne Humphries, realising what a fuss had been stirred up, and what the costs of keeping a First Folio in her house in South Bramhall might entail, had the folio auctioned in October 2004. It went to a private owner 'in the Far East' for £160,000. Whether or not this story had a bearing on the lost Warrington Folio I didn't know. But it struck me that the two things might be related.

Had all the frenzy surrounding the Stockport Folio made the Warrington team reluctant to engage in another potential media circus? Might this explain why whatever happened to the Warrington Folio had been kept under wraps? But four days later the librarian sent me an email from her retired colleague, saying that the volume in question was not a First Folio – despite that being the legend – but a Second Folio, and that as far as she could remember it was sold at auction at Christie's in London for about £8,000.

I asked a contact at Christie's to check their records. They came back to say they thought the confusion might arise from a copy of the Poems Christie's sold in 2006 for £7,000 which was consigned from Warrington. So it appeared that Warrington never had a First Folio. My correspondent said she was sorry to disappoint, admitting, 'I was quite excited for a minute there!'

I was still left with questions that troubled me. Would a distinguished scholar of early modern drama have mistaken a First Folio for a small book of poems? Would the archives at Warrington not have yielded a more definitive record? Ah well, I thought (in a phrase Shakespeare invented) perhaps it was just 'a wild goose chase' after all.

★ ★ ★

'A pattern to all princes living'

When I chose to complete our RSC journey through the entire canon with *All's Well that Ends Well* it sounded like a neat idea, a tidy way of wrapping up the work of nearly a decade. Life and a global pandemic messed that up. And we never got to do the production of *Henry VIII* we had planned. Now it's August 2022 and Blanche McIntyre's production of *All's Well* has opened in Stratford, and *Richard III* returns to the rep for another month or so. As a little press boost, the Comms team have arranged for Arthur Hughes and me to visit the Leicester car park where the real King Richard's body was uncovered a decade ago, back in 2012.

There is now an impressive £4 million visitor centre which tells the whole story of Richard from Bosworth to burial. We peer at a remarkable 3D printed reconstruction of the king's skeleton. It reveals his adolescent early-onset scoliosis in a painfully corkscrew twisted spine with pronounced curvature. He must have been in considerable pain and yet proved himself a substantial warrior in battle. Our admiration for the man rises higher. We also look down into the actual archaeological trench in which Richard's remains were found, having been buried over 500 years ago. Remarkably, they were discovered in the first trench dug, just six hours into the two-week planned excavation. It is covered in a glass floor and, as you stand above the grave, it provokes thoughts both contemplative and troubling.

'As a disabled actor,' Arthur says, 'I've spent a lot of time understanding the psychological shape of Richard III. To finally understand the physical shape of him and to know that he was a disabled man is very important, as it is to be playing this very famous disabled part, which historically has – not enough – been played by a disabled actor.'

As we leave, Arthur and I take a look at the statue of Richard that the Richard III Society commissioned in 1980, and which was moved to this site behind the cathedral, where Richard was reinterred in 2015. Heroically holding his crown, and raising his sword in righteous battle, he looks like a romantic Henry V, but with long, flowing hair. But surely if the venerable society genuinely want to rehabilitate Richard's reputation, now that they know he was indeed a disabled man, and the discovery of his severely twisted spine is irrefutable proof that his disability was not just the product of the Tudor propaganda machine, then they should take down this statue and replace it with an image which honestly represents his disability.

Shakespeare may have invented Richard's implication in the murder of his brother Clarence, and historians continue to debate precisely what crimes he may or may not have committed. But he probably did have Hastings executed, and wiped out Elizabeth Neville's family, her brother Rivers and son Grey, and it now seems more and more likely that he was indeed responsible for the murder of the Princes in the Tower. But even if all these accusations could be definitively disproved, and he is considered a man 'more sinned against than sinning', then all the more reason to celebrate his achievements as perhaps the most famous differently abled man in history.

Back home from Leicester that evening, RSC chair Baroness Shriti Vadera phones to tell me the Board have finally chosen my replacement. The joint application by Daniel Evans and Tamara Harvey has won them the job. Excellent choice. They would not be programming until 2024. Tamara, who has a young family, would be moving into the house in Welcombe Road.

A week later, I am giving a few notes during the warm-up and fight call of *Richard III* when news comes through from Buckingham Palace that the Queen has passed away at Balmoral, at the age of ninety-six. We have already been alerted that all events should go ahead; nevertheless it seems appropriate to say a few words before the production. RSC Executive Director Catherine Mallyon joins me on stage just before the show. As Catherine makes the announcement, there is a groan from the house. Some but not all had heard. I then offered some thoughts. It seemed to me that the Queen had always displayed those 'king-becoming graces' that Shakespeare enumerates:

> As justice, verity, temperance, stableness,
> Bounty, perseverance, mercy, lowliness,
> Devotion, patience, courage, fortitude …

And that, as Shakespeare at the end of *Henry VIII* has Cranmer prophesy of the baby who will become Queen Elizabeth I, she had proved:

> A pattern to all princes living with her,
> And all that shall succeed.

Then I said: 'Long Live the King.'

★ ★ ★

Before I can move all the stuff from Stratford I need to get our house in Islington in order. I have just discovered it needs a new roof. I need to squeeze two households into one, before I start rehearsals for my last RSC show, *Cymbeline*, next March.

Moving out of the Welcombe Road house is going to be tough. I walk into Tony's studio, the room in which he died. It is full of light. His beautiful studio with its teak floor made up of planks from the old RST stage, salvaged after the redevelopment, the very boards trodden once by legends: Olivier, Gielgud and Ashcroft, and later by Tony himself.

Oddly enough, a pair of the crutches he used as Richard III are propped by the table. In the corner is a large black plastic storage trunk in which we packed all his diaries. His latest ones, those he had written after his diagnosis, lie stacked on his desk. He told me I should at some point read these. I pick one of them up, but can't open it. I just can't find the courage to face this. Not yet.

PART TWO

The Folio Roadshow Continues: 'Westward Ho!' and North of the Border

Reading a First Folio

Chapter Three
Westward Ho!

I am heading to the West Country. I will drive down to Bristol and Bath and then back to London, stopping off in Longleat, Wilton, Winchester, Arundel and Eton. This will take my folio tally to twenty-five.

Longleat

Longleat House in Wiltshire may be famous for the lions in the safari park in its grounds, but it is one of the finest Elizabethan houses in England. Along with Burghley, Hatfield and Hardwick, Longleat is one of the great 'prodigy' houses built by wealthy courtiers to accommodate Queen Elizabeth I and her court on her summer progresses around her kingdom. It is beautifully situated with the Wiltshire Downs to its south, Salisbury Plain to the east and the Mendip Hills in the distance. I am in the old library on the top storey of the house. The mullioned bay windows in front of me look out onto the rolling lawns dotted with trees and lakes designed by Capability Brown. Curator Dr James Ford is telling me the intriguing story of Longleat's possible connection to Shakespeare.

In Whitsun week in 1594, the sixteen-year-old heir to the Longleat estate, Thomas Thynne, a student at Oxford, went with some friends to the Bell Inn in Beaconsfield on the London Road. There he met a girl called Mall. She was the same age as Thomas, dark-haired and vivacious. They fell for each other immediately and later that night in an upper chamber of the inn they were married by candlelight.

Mall's real name was Maria Touchet. The Touchets and the Thynnes were deadly enemies. Since the days of their grandfathers Thomas and Mall's families had been in bitter dispute. They decided to keep their marriage secret, and did so for over a year. But by the time it came out, the feud had deepened, and the two households 'From ancient grudge break to new mutiny'. Fighting between the factions resulted in a fatal stabbing. The story spread like wildfire through the court. Did Shakespeare hear of it, and capitalise on the scandal? Did he incorporate the Thynne family saga into *Romeo and Juliet*?

When Thomas's mother, Joan, found out she was furious and tried to have the marriage annulled. However, when her husband, Sir John Thynne, died in 1603, she could do nothing but watch as her son and the daughter of her inveterate enemy inherited the Longleat estate. The story of these lovers might not have ended in their suicide, but it was still star-crossed. Maria bore her husband two sons, but having had a premonition that she would die in childbirth she had her portrait painted in the hopeful flush of her third pregnancy. Her sad foreboding came true when she passed away giving birth to that child. Her portrait still hangs at Longleat.

The Longleat Folio has been in the possession of the Marquess of Bath for generations and is beautifully bound by the great eighteenth-century bookbinder Roger Payne. But sitting next to these splendid folios, Dr Ford has put out something even more tantalising for me to see.

The Peacham drawing is described as the only contemporary illustration of a Shakespeare play (*Titus Andronicus*) in performance. Henry Peacham's name appears above the sketch. Though I have seen it reproduced many times, now I have the privilege of examining it close up. Titus's eyes are beautifully drawn, and I can see his individual toes, in his sandals.

Titus is a play I know well, as it was the first time that Tony and I worked together as director and leading actor, in a production at the Market Theatre in Johannesburg in 1995. The drawing seems to show the opening scene of the play. Here on the left is Titus, 'bound with laurel boughs', having returned to Rome after a ten-year war with the Goths. Behind him in sixteenth-century armour bearing pikes are two of his sons. At his feet kneeling in supplication is Tamora, Queen of the Goths and his prisoner. Behind her

The Peacham drawing

are two of her sons, with their hands tied. Next to them is Aaron the Moor.

The drawing often comes up in discussions about costume in Shakespeare's day. Is Aaron wearing black face paint, perhaps of soot and oil? Is that a black curly wig on his head; black gloves on his hands; black stockings on his legs? Titus seems to be draped in a toga which has led scholars to insist that the Lord Chamberlain's Men adopted Roman dress for those plays set in Ancient Rome. I would suggest that is not a toga, but the 'palliament of white and spotless hue' offered to Titus by his brother Marcus in the same scene, signifying he is a candidate for emperor of Rome.

> Be candidatus then, and put it on,
> And help to set a head on headless Rome.
> *Titus Andronicus* (Act 1 scene 1)

Aaron is holding a drawn sword and may be indicating the beardless Alarbus, Tamora's youngest son, who has been picked out to be sacrificed. Or is he just pointing to the tip of his sword, suggesting the weapon is intended for Titus? Either way this action doesn't occur in the scene. Aaron remains silent throughout it. Nor does he have a sword, as he, too, is a Roman prisoner. But he will be the agent of the violent destruction that ensues. So, rather than depict a specific scene, I think the Peacham drawing is a bit like a modern film poster, where the leading characters are all assembled as dramatically as possible in the same shot.

After Longleat, I drive south-east to Wilton, just outside Salisbury. The library at Wilton House does possess a First Folio, but it's the Ben Jonson Folio. I ask the librarian if there is no record of the Shakespeare Folio. There must have been a copy here at some point, surely? Wilton was the home of that 'incomparable pair of brethren' William Pembroke and his brother Philip, to whom John Hemmings and Henry Condell dedicated their folio. In the Double Cube Room, Van Dyck's colossal painting of Philip and his family dominates the far wall, while the portrait of William, pictured holding his white staff of office as Lord Chamberlain, stands to the left of the fireplace. Perhaps in my travels I will discover the copy that must once have been here.

Next I am heading across the chalk downlands of Hampshire to the primal heart of England, the royal seat of the kingdom of Wessex, Winchester.

Winchester

The cross of St George hoisted above the Norman tower of Winchester Cathedral is flying at half-mast to mark the close of the second Elizabethan era. The doors are thrown open wide and entrance charges suspended to receive the hundreds of people who have come to pay their respects to Queen Elizabeth II and sign the Books of Condolence laid out on candlelit tables in the long nave. Before the high altar, the Queen's photograph is placed on a Union Jack with a spray of lilies and behind it the rood screen is uplit in a soft magenta.

I am on my way across the Cathedral close, past the Pilgrims' School, and through the King's Gate to find the Warden's Lodge of Winchester College. The outgoing headmaster Tim Hands invites me into his study for coffee, to tell me a little about the history of this distinguished school (founded by William of Wykeham in 1382) and to find out about my quest.

The 1623 Folio at Winchester College was donated by one of the housemasters whom the boys called Chawkers. The Rev. C. H. Hawkins set up a Shakespeare Reading and Performing Society in 1869 and enjoyed playing the leading parts himself. There is a scrapbook in the library with hand-tinted photographs of Chawkers playing a rather hammy Shylock, a doleful Hamlet wringing his hands and being stared at by one of the boys, dressed as his mother, Queen Gertrude. There is alas no photograph of Chawkers in his final appearance as King Lear.

But he is responsible for a tradition of performance at the college which goes on to this day, and in one particular way directly connects to Shakespeare performance at Stratford. For one of the Rev. Hawkins's pupils was a young Frank Benson, the man who would go on to run the Shakespeare Memorial Theatre until the Great War.

I have a soft spot for Frank Benson. He was a quixotic actor-manager, had a profile to grace a Roman coin and was a keen sportsman. He was famed for choosing his Stratford companies more on the basis of their cricketing skills than their acting talents. Donald Sinden used to tell the story of the season in which Frank was appearing as both Shylock and Henry V. The plays in the repertoire shared a number of scenic elements including a wall, which Frank as the young warrior king would pole-vault over with great dramatic flair at Harfleur, with the cry, 'Once more unto the breach, dear friends, once more, / Or close the wall up with our English dead'.

One matinee Frank was pacing around backstage waiting for his first entrance. The cue came, he grabbed the pole, vaulted over the wall, and suddenly realised he was dressed as Shylock, and the matinee was *The Merchant of Venice*. Without a pause he shrugged and began, 'Three thousand ducats, well'.

Benson recalls his days at Winchester ('where the boys are all men') and writes how he was recruited as a member of Chawkers' Shakespeare Society, where he was cast in such roles as Rosalind, Constance and Cleopatra. 'At first I distinguished myself; then I degenerated into an exaggerated melodramatic rendition of the parts entrusted to me. The school paper referred to me as a burlesque of a third-rate actress.' How is it that a bad review can stay with you for a lifetime? Chawkers took Benson aside and told him he had told the school paper to say that: 'You needed it. Come to me for the next reading and we will remedy the defects.' Benson remained profoundly grateful to Chawkers for the grounding in Shakespearian analysis he gave him.

★ ★ ★

The Eccles Room of the Fellows Library at Winchester is housed in a building that was once the brewery until the college stopped making its own beer in the early twentieth century. Here, amid thick walls of knapped flint and limestone, with early autumn light streaming through the leaded windows, Richard Foster, one of the college dons, shows me Chawkers' Folio. Its binding in mottled calf is one of the shiniest I have seen.

'It's a rather "unspecial" copy,' Richard admits. 'In fact about one-sixth of the text is missing, so you don't have to be too careful with it. There are one or two interesting annotations though,' and he points me to *Henry VI Part One*. An unknown hand has written: '10,000 beauties she can spare and yet outshine the fairest face.' And then the name Molly Fawley. 'Is this a schoolboy crush?' I ask Richard. He tells me my guess is as good as his.

There are several rather waxy, oily, blotchy stains in this copy. 'Never try and identify stains,' he says. 'It leads to horrible speculation. It might be chewing gum.' Richard then places in my hands a scruffy eighteenth-century quarto volume stuffed with notes. It is Lewis Theobald's own copy of Alexander Pope's 1725 edition of Shakespeare. This is the very copy Theobald used when searching for evidence of his fellow editor's incompetence so that he could expose him in print. It was one of the great editorial spats of the century.

When Theobald published his findings in *Shakespeare Restored*, two years later, Pope was furious. Pope's edition might have been sloppy, but Theobald was relentlessly pedantic, and Pope was spiteful and vindictive in return. In revenge, he would effectively destroy Theobald's reputation by making him the chief dunce in his satirical epic poem, *The Dunciad*, forever branding poor Lewis as 'Piddling Tibbald'.

Richard has more of Winchester's treasures to share with me. Here is a copy of Lucian not only owned by Ben Jonson but signed by him, too. It also bears his own motto. It reads *Tamquam explorator sum*

Ben. Jonson (Just like an explorer: Ben Jonson). We know of nearly 200 books that Jonson possessed. I presume that Jonson also had a First Folio. But if so, where is it?* Jonson lost part of his library in a fire at his home, in the very same year the folio was published. He wrote a poem about it: *An Execration upon Vulcan*.

> And why to me this, thou lame lord of fire,
> Thou might have made me perish, piece by piece,
> To light tobacco, or save roasted geese,
> Singe capons, or poor pigs, drooping their eyes:
> Condemned me to the ovens with the pies;
> And so have kept me dying a whole age,
> Not ravished all hence in a minute's rage.

Susan Hill, in a chilly ghost story called *The Small Hand*, imagines her protagonist, a book dealer, coming across a copy of a First Folio with Jonson's signature, in a monastic library high in the mountains of the Vercors in south-east France. 'The place smelled as all such places do, of paper and leather, polish and age and wisdom – a powerful intoxicant to anyone whose life has been bound up, as mine has long been, with books.'

Eton

The Eton First Folio was bequeathed to the college library by an old boy. It is certainly the largest copy I have seen. It has 100 extra pages bound into it. They are filled with engravings of figures from the plays, not characters and scenes, but of the real people depicted, the kings and queens, dukes and lords, and some of the famous locations where the plays are set.

But I am completely captivated by one image. It looks like someone has attempted to incise a new copy of the Droeshout engraving. The doublet is almost finished, the shape of the standing collar has been outlined, the cross-hatching behind the demi-figure is complete. But the face is missing. There are ghostly outlines on the head and hair, the beard and moustache. If you look closely the left

---

* William-Henry Ireland apparently tried to mock up a folio owned by Ben Jonson.

The faceless Shakespeare

eye emerges faintly, and then a shadow of the right eye. What has happened? Has the engraver made a mistake and had to abandon the plate? If so, why does this print of it exist at all, and why has the compiler of the enlarged edition included it in this folio? When you stop puzzling how the image ever came about, you see it afresh for what it is: an image of a faceless Shakespeare.

When he turned sixty, Tony embarked on a huge painting of his life. *The Audience* depicts a dilapidated auditorium populated by people who had an impact upon him: his heroes and villains, portraits of his family, actors he admired and the great roles he played. He called it 'a dream-like map of my life'. There are threads linking characters across and between the rows. One such thread follows a floppy Salvador Dalí supported by crutches, watching a dysmorphic Francis Bacon hand Michelangelo's self-portrait as a flayed skin (from *The Last Judgement*) to Shakespeare. 'Michelangelo died the year that Shakespeare was born,' Tony wrote, 'and there is no better example of genius being handed on.' But Shakespeare is blank-faced 'since I have no idea what he was actually like as a man'.

Why do I respond to the depiction of a faceless Shakespeare? I think because we all tend to cast Shakespeare in our own image, alert to those places where he catches and articulates our own perspective on the world, conveniently skipping over those passages where he does not.

Two days after my visit to Eton, on Monday 19 September, a large screen was erected on the stage of the RST so we could broadcast live the Queen's state funeral for anyone from the town who wanted to come and pay their respects. I would be there to greet them with Catherine Mallyon and other members of the team. I put on my black suit. I hadn't worn it since Tony's funeral ten months before. I found the typed eulogy in the inside pocket. Tony had insisted that I spoke. 'Start with a joke,' he had said, 'to warm them up.'

'How are you doing?' colleagues ask. 'Fine,' I lie. In *Richard II*, the Duchess of Gloucester (Jane Lapotaire in my production), mourning her murdered husband, catches the long process of grief exactly when she says, 'For sorrow ends not when it seemeth done'.

Arundel

The ancient turrets of Arundel Castle rise grandly on the edge of the South Downs, looking out across green water meadows to the English Channel. It is the seat of the Dukes of Norfolk and has been there since the Norman Conquest. In one of these turrets I meet John Robinson, the castle's archivist. 'Ah,' he says, removing his glasses and rising from his desk, 'you're the Shakespearian, yes, you look Shakespearian.' His full-length portrait in his regalia as the Maltravers Herald Extraordinary rather dominates the cramped stock room. 'That's my dog, Galba,' he says pointing at the painting to a little terrier at his feet. But he doesn't explain why he named his pet after the sickly Roman emperor who succeeded Nero.

'I am one of those human playing cards who lend a splash of colour to state occasions.' He was part of the procession that carried Her late Majesty to her final resting place, the previous week. John is in his mid-seventies and speaks with the choice relish of the well-bred English aesthete he is. 'It was a marathon, I must say,' John adds. 'The dress rehearsals took place in the small hours, which ended with us marching for nearly four miles, through London and Windsor Great

Park, in full ceremonial dress. Fine for the younger members, but gruelling for those of us of riper years.'

John's employer, the 18th Duke of Norfolk, in his role as Earl Marshal, was responsible for all the ceremonial arrangements for the Queen's funeral. His ancestor, Thomas Howard, the 3rd Duke, appears as a character in Shakespeare and Fletcher's *Henry VIII*, where he leads the conspiracy to pull down Cardinal Wolsey. Thomas Howard was the uncle to two of Henry's wives, Anne Boleyn and Catherine Howard, both of whom lost their heads. The Howard family persisted in their Catholic faith, and, not surprisingly, Thomas eventually fell foul of the king, and only narrowly avoided execution when Henry died. He found favour again under Henry's daughter 'Bloody' Mary as she reasserted Catholicism.

John leaves the archivist Roz to show me Arundel's copy of the First Folio, chuckling at the calculation we have spotted in the margins of *Richard II*: $17 \times 7 = 119$ and there is a scribbled sum on a page of *A Midsummer Night's Dream*: £11.2s.0d + £9.11s.7d = £20.13s.7d. Later John takes me on a tour of the castle. We come across one of those paintings that you know so well, and are thrilled to find in reality before you. Here is Thomas Howard's son, the poet Henry Howard, Earl of Surrey, the first writer to introduce the iambic pentameter into English verse in his translations of Virgil's *Aeneid*.

It's a ravishingly Italianate painting. The red-bearded Earl leans insouciantly on a broken pillar, kid gloves in hand, dressed in a chocolate and cream embroidered doublet, a fur demi-cape draped nonchalantly over his shoulders, and very short trunk hose, showing off his long legs in white stocking-tights. His stare is confident, reckless maybe, even a tad disdainful. He knows he is superb. Within a year of this portrait, he will be arrested, charged with treason and beheaded on Tower Hill, the last person to be executed by Henry VIII.

'And here is the 11th Duke. The one who we think purchased our First Folio,' John says.

'Ah,' I say, 'the famous "Drunken Duke".'

Charles, the 11th Duke, was an extrovert, who despite the steadfast example of his predecessors, renounced his Catholic faith for reasons of political expediency. He was so large, he was thought incapable of passing through a doorway of ordinary proportions, and was noted for his aversion to washing. A friend of 'Prinny', the Prince Regent (the dissolute son of George III), Charles was frequently caricatured in satirical cartoons by Gillray, in his slovenly attire.

As John Robinson waves me off, and I am driven away in one of the tourist buggies down the long drive of Arundel Castle, I feel delighted to have met the Maltravers Herald Extraordinary, who heads back to his turret to continue his work.

★ ★ ★

The College of Heralds plays a significant role in the history of the First Folio. A close friend of the printer William Jaggard was the Rouge Croix Herald, Augustine Vincent. The College of Arms was a stone's throw from the North Churchyard of St Paul's, the centre of the London book trade. Jaggard had crossed swords with the York Herald, the notoriously dyspeptic Ralph Brooke. Brooke was (as Pisanio says in *Cymbeline*) 'as quarrelous as a weasel'. In 1602, he challenged the heraldry that the Garter King of Arms had granted to John Shakespeare, the father of William Shakespeare, on the basis of low social rank, but was defeated. He then deceived a fellow herald, whose work he regarded as slovenly, into granting arms to a local hangman. The king threw both heralds into the notorious Marshalsea prison to teach them a lesson.

In 1619, Brooke produced a book of genealogy, but when a number of serious errors were revealed in it, he blamed his printer. William Jaggard was nearly blind by this stage in his life. His friend in the fractious College of Arms came to his aid. Augustine Vincent wrote a book exposing the genealogical mistakes Brooke had made and invited Jaggard to include a frontispiece defending himself against weaselly Brooke's accusations. It is a scathing riposte. He marshals his arguments with great rhetorical eloquence and concludes with a flourish: 'howsoever it hath pleased God to make me, and him to style me a Blind-printer ... it is no right conclusion in schools, that because Homer was Blind and a Poet, therefore he was a Blind-Poet. Farewell.'

The matter took up much of Jaggard's time and energy, and was in all likelihood a greater focus for him than the printing of the Shakespeare First Folio. In thanks for his help, Jaggard presented a copy of the finished folio to the Rouge Croix Herald, Augustine Vincent, writing on the front, *Ex Dono Willi Jaggard Typographi. ao. 1623*, the gift of William Jaggard Printer, anno domini 1623. In fact William Jaggard died before the printing of the First Folio was complete, which somehow makes the existence of this early copy with its note from him even more poignant. When this volume turned up in Lincolnshire in the late nineteenth century it became one of the most sought-after copies in the world, and caused a most unseemly battle.

★ ★ ★

In April 1891, a book dealer from Southeran & Co. was invited to view the library of a stately eighteenth-century pile near Lincoln called Canwick Hall. The dealer found the library being used as a billiard room, and when he explored the coach house there were piles of old books gathering dust on a high shelf. He asked a young man who worked on the estate for help. As his assistant threw down the books, there was one tattered unbound volume tightly wrapped with rough twine. As the agent from Southeran's began to examine it his helper called down 'That's no good, Sir, it's only old poetry'. It turned out to be the very copy that William Jaggard had presented to Augustine Vincent.

The owner of Canwick Hall was a gentleman by the name of Coningsby Sibthorp, whose family were mentioned in the Domesday Book. Southeran's gained his permission to tidy up the folio, replacing a couple of missing pages and giving it a splendid new binding complete with Mr Sibthorp's coat of arms. When Sibthorp comes up to London with his wife to reclaim his property, the book dealer offers the couple the book, or a cheque for £3,000. He has already alerted that most voracious of folio buyers, the American collector Henry Clay Folger, to the discovery of the book, and Folger is desperate to get his hands on it. Sibthorp, however, declines the cheque and Mrs Sibthorp explains that they will only spend the money, but they will keep the book. Folger is disappointed but, as the presence of the book is still little known about, decides to bide his time.

Unfortunately for him, Sidney Lee (the man who assembled the First Folio census a few years later) gets wind of this important copy and writes an article about it in the *Cornhill Magazine*. The cat is now out of the bag, and Folger decides to act quickly via the book dealer. However, Sibthorp, now aware that his property is in fact a national treasure, has no plans to sell it, declaring he would not part with it for £5,000, an impossible amount to countenance for the sale of any book.

Rashly, Folger calls Sibthorp's bluff and offers him £4,500 and is roundly and flatly refused. Eventually after some quiet negotiation on the book dealer's part, and agreeing to throw in a beautiful case for the book, a deal is struck, and Lloyd's of London confirms it will insure the volume for its passage across the Atlantic. However, Folger then learns that the book is not in fact complete (facsimile pages have been inserted), and suggests a discount, stating that he requires the right to examine the book before the sale is confirmed. At which point Sibthorp withdraws the sale altogether.

When Folger tries again, without haggling this time, Sibthorp raises the sum to £6,000. Folger, who has remained anonymous up to this point, now breaks cover, and, despite his book dealer's advice, writes direct to Sibthorp with an offer of £8,000, at that time the largest sum ever paid for a single book. He makes the mistake, however, of referring to the folio as 'Our Shakespeare', and the offended Sibthorp retorts that it is most certainly 'not our Shakespeare, but My Shakespeare', and insists that the dealer refunds Folger's money.

This ferocious book battle is recounted in edifying detail by Andrea Mays in her book on the Folgers, *The Millionaire and the Bard*. She describes it as re-enacting in miniature 'the larger cultural conflict between the two worlds, revealing a more elemental struggle between American triumphalism and British decline'. Eventually, Sibthorp accepted an offer from Folger. Mays writes that the episode proved to Folger that, despite Sibthorp's 'feigned indifference to wealth, and pose of cultural superiority, an Englishman could, in the end, once tempted with enough money, usually be induced to part with treasures'.

But unbeknown to Folger, Sibthorp's wife had died in the interim, and perhaps he no longer cared about the book or the pestering it had entailed. Perhaps, rather than exposing a truth that everyone has a price, the story reveals the absurd rapacity of the rich

American who believes his wealth entitles him to anything. Perhaps Mr Sibthorp had the last laugh. Folger made sure that his prize possession's connection to Coningsby Sibthorp and the trouble he had caused him was eradicated by nominating his new volume as Folger 1,* and referring to it as 'the Vincent copy', after the Rouge Croix Herald, Augustine Vincent, friend of William Jaggard.

---

* Of the seventy-nine he purchased before his death.

Chapter Four
North of the Border

Edinburgh

'I'm sorry it's a bit dreich today,' says my host, apologising for the soggy weather. I am sitting in a sort of glass promontory. To my left is the mediaeval crown steeple of St Giles, the High Kirk of Edinburgh. Arthur's Seat is away off to my right. I am in a reading room attached to the top floor of the National Library of Scotland. The library's Curator, Graham Hogg, is drawing back the blinds to give me the maximum effect of the panoramic view.

He's brought in the two copies of the 1623 Folio that the National Library look after. One is on deposit from a private collection, which I have been given special dispensation to see, and the other is the library's own copy, and we begin with that. Graham opens it to the Droeshout engraving.

'Good Lord!' I cry. 'He looks like Quasimodo! What has happened?' It's true, Shakespeare looks like Charles Laughton in *The Hunchback of Notre Dame*. His left eye seems to have slipped down his face. On closer inspection I realise that someone has pasted a paper patch over the original engraving and then tried to draw an eye on it, in sepia ink. How did the damage occur? Did someone deliberately target the eye? And how did they ever conclude that the ugly patch was an acceptable solution?

The Quasimodo Shakespeare is intriguing and upstages pretty much anything else of note in the National Library's copy. But if that folio was slightly damaged, the copy from the private collection, a very fine copy, was nearly totally destroyed. It had a narrow escape when fire engulfed Sotheby's warehouse in Covent Garden in 1865.

Quasimodo Droeshout engraving

There is a newspaper clipping from *The Times* between the binder's leaves which details what was lost in the fire. The folio had been in the library of the Earl of Charlemont, a passionate advocate for Irish independence and a Knight of the Order of St Patrick. The article reads: 'Lord Charlemont's fine library was in large part destroyed in the fire; it just happened that at that moment Halliwell-Phillipps had some of the rarest of the Charlemont Shakespeare and other books on loan at his house in Old Brompton, and these escaped the fate of the others.'

And so James Orchard Halliwell-Phillipps re-enters our story, as gallant saviour of the folio. In truth, this eminent Shakespeare scholar was an undoubted protecter of Elizabethan Stratford-upon-Avon, an unashamed Shakespeare fanatic but also without doubt an unscrupulous opportunist. He is going to play quite a large part in our tale.*

★ ★ ★

---

* See Chapter Eighteen.

The oddity of the first state of the engraving in the British Library copy with Shakespeare's head on a platter, or the Quasimodo version in the Edinburgh Folio, or the faceless rendition in the Eton Folio, all contribute to the fascination this image holds. But a visit to the folios held at the Senate House Library of the University of London made me look at the engraving in a different light.

One of their copies belonged to the Edwardian lawyer Sir Edwin Durning-Lawrence, prominent Unitarian, member of the Liberal Unionist Party and Bacon-backer-in-chief. I was shown his copy in the library which bears his name, a reconstruction of his study from his grand residence in Carlton House Terrace, complete with original bookcases and furnishings. There is a photograph of the honourable member for Truro outside the Commons in one of the expensive silk top hats for which he was famous.

We have a look at the Droeshout engraving. In his book, with its 'does-exactly-what-it-says-on-the-tin' title: BACON IS SHAKESPEARE, Durning-Lawrence states definitively and irrefutably: 'There is no question, there can be no possible question that, in fact, it is a cunningly drawn cryptographic picture.'

His argument focuses on the back of the left arm which, he insists, 'does duty for the right arm'. 'Every tailor will admit that this is not and cannot be the front of the right arm, but is, without possibility of doubt, the back of the left arm.' In fact Sir Edwin got the head of the Tailors and Cutters Guild to corroborate his revelations. He suggests that if you look at the front of the left arm 'you at once perceive that you are no longer looking at the back of the coat, but at the front of the coat'.

He then turns his attention to the face: 'Now ... you see the mask, especially note that the ear is a mask ear and stands out curiously; note also how distinct the lines showing the edge of the mask appear.' He then adds helpfully: 'Perhaps the reader will perceive this more clearly if he turns the page upside down.' And he triumphantly concludes: 'The reader will I trust now be able to perceive that this portrait is correctly characterised as cunningly composed of two left arms and a mask ... in order to reveal the true facts of the authorship of the works to those who are capable of grasping the hidden meaning of his engraving.'

I can hear disdain here for us poor ignorant mortals from the Baronet. I can hear him employing the rhetorical skills he must have used in Parliament: 'England is now declining any longer to *dishonour* and *defame* the greatest Genius of all time by continuing to identify him with the mean, drunken, ignorant, and absolutely unlettered, rustic of Stratford who never in his life wrote so much as his own name and in all probability was totally unable to read one single line of print.' As he builds climactically to his big Churchillian reveal, I can almost see Sir Edwin remove his shiny top hat and wave it in the air:

> The hour has come for revealing the truth. The hour has come when it is no longer necessary or desirable that the world should remain in ignorance that the Great Author of Shakespeare's Plays was himself alive when the folio was published in 1623. The hour has come when it is desirable and necessary to state with the utmost distinctiveness that BACON IS SHAKESPEARE.

Glasgow

My favourite page in the First Folio is headlined *The Workes of William Shakespeare, containing all his Comedies, Histories, and Tragedies: Truly set forth, according to their first ORGINALL.* Then follows: *The names of the Principall Actors in all these Playes*, twenty-six names in two columns, beginning with William Shakespeare, Richard Burbage and John Hemmings: a roll call of the actors who made Shakespeare.

I'm looking at this very page in the conservation lab of Glasgow University. The Book Conservator, Keira McKee, is preparing the book for its 400th birthday outing next year. She has been doing a 'risk-reduction' exercise on the folio as she describes it, not restoration but preservation, not trying to take it back to what it was, but supporting it so it can still be used, read and enjoyed. Her colleague Julie Gardham, Senior Librarian and a proud Liverpudlian, points out the outstanding feature of their copy. 'Now this is the page which you would like, Greg,' she says. 'The one which acknowledges the actors. But look at this ...'

Someone has annotated the list, highlighting eleven of the names. The writing is scratchy and untidy and a little hard to read.

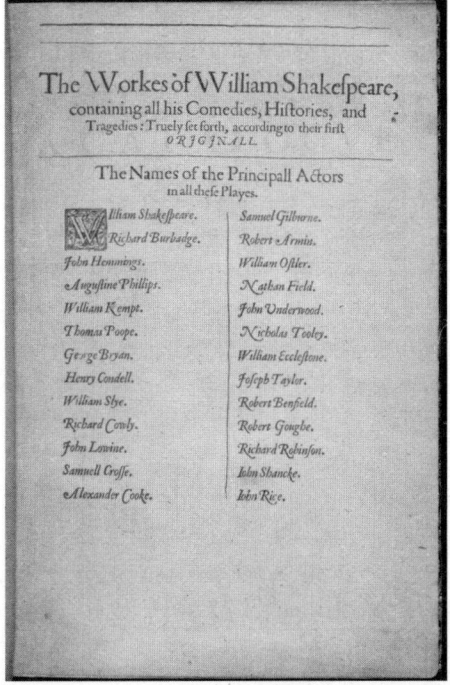

Page of actors' names

Shakespeare and Burbage have been double underlined in heavy black ink. Under Shakespeare it seems to say *least for making*. Does that mean he was least well-known for acting and most for playwriting? Julie suggests 'It could be *ceast for making* meaning that he gave up acting to concentrate on writing.'

Under Burbage it reads *by report*, which suggests that the writer, though they might never have seen the great actor on stage, knew those who had. No notation against the name of the famous clown William Kemp, who created Dogberry (and probably Bottom and Falstaff), but that is not surprising as he fell out with the company and left before the Globe opened in 1599, twenty-four years before this book was published.

But my heart skips a beat when I read under John Lowin, *by eye-witnesse*. Whoever scribbled these notes had actually seen John Lowin perform. Lowin was a big man, he took over the role of Falstaff 'with mighty applause'. Of the thirteen names in the second column, seven consecutive names have been underlined. Beside

William Ostler it says *hearsay*, and the next four names, Nathan Field, John Underwood, Nicholas Tooley and William Ecclestone, have variations of that note: *so too, so to chief, so too a little*. But then under Joseph Taylor it says *know*. And the same under the next name Robert Benfield – *know*.

I feel as if I am back in the tiring house of the Globe Theatre spotting the actors as they come off stage, or hanging around John Hemmings's tap house next door after the show, hoping to have a few words, like the fans in Stratford who crowd the stage door with their programmes ready to be autographed, or who make their way to the Dirty Duck on the off chance of bumping into their favourites.

'Do we know who wrote these notes?' I ask Julie.

'It may be Lorenzo Cary, he left his name on a page of *The Two Gentlemen of Verona*, a little further on.' Lorenzo was the son of Elizabeth Cary, the first woman to write a play in English. *Mariam, The Fair Queen of Jewry* was published in 1613, the year Lorenzo was born.

And what of those other names?

Nathan Field (or 'Nid' as Ben Jonson called him) was the son of a Puritan preacher, who had inveighed against the theatre. His father died when he was a baby, and would not have approved when thirteen-year-old Nid was impressed into the Children of the Chapel Royal at Blackfriars. He would become one their brightest stars. In his enigmatic portrait (which I saw in Dulwich Picture Gallery) he wears a white silk shirt with black embroidery work, and holds his hand over his heart.

William Ostler was married to Thomasine, the daughter of John Hemmings. Nicholas Tooley was apprenticed to Richard Burbage, and lived with the family in the parish of St Giles Cripplegate. John Underwood, who was a mainstay of the company for many years, even named one of his children Burbage, after the great actor. Tooley died just six months before the folio was published and Underwood the following year. William Ecclestone, who became a sharer in the King's Men sometime between 1614 and 1619, disappears from the record in 1623. So, of all the actors whose names are underlined in the Glasgow First Folio, only John Lowin, Joseph Taylor and Robert Benfield are still alive within a year of the publication of the folio.

Why is this page here? There is very little reference in the Folio to the life of these plays on the stage, and no reference to their company title, the King's Men. Why insert a list of actors, 70 per cent of whom have already died? It is surely a tribute to their part in the creation of these plays.

The King's Men that form the acquaintance of our excited annotator is a very different troupe from the men who entertained Queen Elizabeth and King James at their respective courts. John Lowin was among their number, but he is the only one of the old guard left. Joseph Taylor joined the company when Richard Burbage died, and took over his roles, making him the second actor ever to have played Hamlet.

I feel exhilarated by this folio, and thank Julie and Keira for sharing it with me. Now I am meeting up with my sister Jo, and heading to see Scotland's fourth 1623 Folio, whose existence was only revealed to the world in 2016.

Bute

On the train from Glasgow Central Station we watched a whole weather front barge down the Firth of Clyde. Gales were due to blow in from the west, and we worried that the ferry might be cancelled.

At Wemyss Bay, an Edwardian covered ramp sweeps in a great arc down to the dock, ensuring that transferring from train to ferry is as convenient and dry as possible. Luckily there were no cancellations, and we made our way on board. Around the clock tower, grey seagulls seemed to hang suspended facing into the wind, watching men in high-vis jackets packing the ferry with its cargo of drive-on cars. The passengers all looked as if they made this trip every day, and few paid any attention to the scenery. We settled in seats up front and watched the rain dash against the windows as the ferry set out across the gunmetal water.

A young woman with a beaming smile greeted us as we arrived at the ancestral home of the Marquesses of Bute. Elizabeth Ingham is the librarian at Mount Stuart and had agreed to show us around. The family no longer live here and it is now owned and run by a trust.

The fortune that the 3rd Marquess (1847–1900) inherited with the title at the age of six months would make him the richest man in the world. In 1870 he rebuilt the house as a Gothic Revival palace and spent a fortune shipping in tons of Carrara marble to build the chapel, like an extravagant wedding cake with an elaborate spired tower; and a flamboyant colonnaded marble hall with specially woven tapestries; and a lantern tower boasting large stained-glass windows depicting the signs of the zodiac. It all feels over the top.

One of the biblical friezes on the staircase shows Adam naming the animals, and unlike any mediaeval depiction of the scene, there is a wallaby among the beasts. The 3rd Marquess, as well as being an art collector, introduced exotic wildlife to the island, including beavers, porcupines and wallabies. The last of these exiled marsupials died when it was hit by the island's first car.

Eventually we arrive at the library. Scotland's fourth 1623 Folio was not, strictly speaking, unknown. It had been listed in the typed catalogue of the Bute family library as early as 1896, but its existence seems never to have been made public. The most obvious difference with this folio is that it is divided into three separately bound volumes. The 4th Marquess commissioned a fresh Arts and Crafts-style binding for the three volumes for his library in Belgrave Square. On the outbreak of the Second World War, the books were moved to Scotland for their care and safety, and the folio volumes were relocated to the Blue Library here at Mount Stuart.

Elizabeth tells me that this copy once belonged to the eighteenth-century editor Isaac Reed, who produced the first 'variorum edition' of Shakespeare, the first to acknowledge and compare the editorial choices of previous editors. But then Elizabeth revealed a feature which suddenly made my hair stand on end. We scanned the final page of the folio to see how it had been made up. Next to the watermark there is a long streak down the page. Elizabeth produced a small torch. 'Can you guess what it is?' Jo and I shook our heads. Elizabeth explained.

Imagine we are in a paper mill in Normandy – England had no substantial paper industry in the seventeenth century so all the paper for the folio was imported from France. Piles of linen rags have been

Woodcut of 'The Papermaker' from *The Book of Trades*

collected, sorted and shredded, and then ground between enormous granite millstones, rotated by the flow of river water cascading over the mill wheel outside. The rags are then boiled for hours, until they break down into a pulp, a slurry of cellulose fibres, which is then strained and drained into a vat. The 'vatman' takes a rectangular wooden frame called a mold. It has a series of wooden ribs placed vertically across it. Each rib is laced with a 'chain' wire. Attached to the chain wire is a lattice of closely spaced horizontal 'laid' wires.

He fits the sieve-mold with a deckle* (a narrow rim or fence, which will keep the newly formed paper in bounds) and dips the mold into the warm, steamy water, scooping the pulp into the frame. At this point the pulp, called 'stuff', looks thin and milky. The water runs through the mesh leaving a thin layer pressed against the screen. The vatman then shakes the mold from side to side to form an even sheet. Within seconds the stuff binds and knits together into a mat, coalescing into a large folio sheet of paper. It is then flipped out of the frame by the 'coucher', and placed between layers of felt, stacked

---

* Hence the term 'deckled' edge, which I encountered at the British Library (see Chapter Two).

in a 'post' of perhaps 250 sheets by the 'layer' then pressed to squeeze out the excess water. After pressing, each sheet is then hung up to dry in the drying loft.

It is at the moment in the process when the sheet is lifted off the mold in the clammy heat that a bead of sweat rolls down the vatman's arm and across the paper, leaving the mark we can see to this day across the chain lines of the Bute Folio.

'These marks are sometimes called "Vatman's Tears",' says Elizabeth.

This visible dribble is actual seventeenth-century DNA from the Normandy paper mill: a vivid insight bringing you closer to the process of the production of this mighty book, and the effort it took to make it.

★ ★ ★

As I prepare for my first folio foray abroad, I wonder when the 1623 Folio left Britain for the first time. As far as we know it was purchased in The Hague by a Dutch diplomat called Constantijn Huygens. He signed his name ('Constanter') in the copy now in the Folger Library. The date – 1647 (now only detectable under UV light) – suggests that Huygens probably bought the volume from a bookseller fleeing the English Civil War.

Huygens was a talented poet of the Dutch Golden Age. He learned English while in the employ of the English ambassador at The Hague, worked as a diplomat in London for over a year in 1622, and became friendly with John Donne. He translated his poem 'The Triple Fool' into Dutch.

As I researched his life I discovered that, after a long courtship, he had married a woman called Suzanna van Baerle, in 1627. He called her 'Sterre', his star, and referred to their marriage as 'two minds joined in a single mind'. I recognise that. Shortly after the birth of their fifth child, Suzanna died. Constanter was in his early forties, and though he lived another fifty years, he never remarried.

Reading of the Huygens' life together, their devotion to each other and the stimulation they derived from each other's company, I came across this: 'On the death of Sterre'.* This beautiful poem

---

* Literal translation by Bart van Es (April 2024).

begins with a feeling of panic that I find familiar as the widower-poet wakes in confusion and cannot find his beloved:

> Do I dream, and is it night, or has my Star vanished?
> I wake, it is the height of day, and I do not see my Star.
> Oh heavens, which forbid her sight to me,
> Speak in human language and tell me where it is that my Star has vanished!
>
> Heaven thunders, I feel it in my stones,
> And tells me that my Star is there in heaven
> Where she sees God and where God sees her
> And – for there is laughter there – they are laughing at my idle tears …
>
> Come, death, free me swiftly from these fevers.
> I long, in the eternal light, to see there, floating freely
> My heaven, my body, my God, my Star, and me.

Though I can find no such consolation in the hope of reunion after death, I am moved by the poet's elation, how he is uplifted by the memory of his dead wife, and can transform his grief into joy. Tony was my 'Sterre' – just to hear his laughter again would be consolation enough.

PART THREE

Curing the Soul:

Germany and the Great Libraries of Dublin, Cambridge and Oxford

Old Library, Trinity College, Dublin

Chapter Five
Germany

One dark early morning in October I was sitting on a German railway station platform waiting to board a train to Cologne, when a pigeon on one of the girders above my head crapped all over my sleeve. I couldn't help wondering if this was a scatological critique on the futile notion of my whole journey.

I am venturing farther afield on my Folio Roadshow. We first hear of Edward Blount's syndicate project to produce a folio edition of thirty-six Shakespeare plays in an announcement of the books to be sold at the Frankfurt Book Fair in October 1622. So, 400 years later, I want to be there and find out a bit about Germany's famous love for *Unser Shakespeare* ('Our Shakespeare'). I am starting in the ancient city of Köln.

Cologne

Sidney Lee described the Cologne copy I am about to see as *Class I Division A*, one of fourteen perfect copies in the world and therefore one of the most valuable. I had been met at the Bahnhof by the Vice President of the German Shakespeare Association, Dr Roland Weidle, who took me to the Universitäts-und-Stadtbibliothek in Universitätstrasse, and introduced me to Dr Christiane Hoffrath, Head of the Archive.

We went up to one of the reading rooms where the precious volume was brought in to me. I hadn't been allowed to see where it was stored as this is a very treasured possession of the university and its security is taken very strictly and seriously indeed. In fact, the assistant who brought in the book kept her face to the wall, and didn't turn round until Dr Hoffrath returned, when it was ceremoniously revealed and set out on the desk.

'So this is the Carysfort-Proby-Newton Copy,' says Dr Hoffrath. A series of bookplates back up her claim. And there is a pasted-in newspaper clipping which discusses the value of early perfect editions quoting the editor George Steevens writing in 1785: 'The First Folio usually valued at seven or eight guineas ... now realises £400–£500, if in a perfect state. There is however "much virtue in if". Imperfect copies are nearly as plentiful as blackberries, but we do not believe that there are above a dozen absolutely perfect ones known to exist.'

We can accurately trace the value placed on this copy through its detailed provenance from the £410 which James Orchard Halliwell-Phillipps paid for it in 1867 to the £880 the 5th Earl of Carysfort spent in 1888 to bring it into his library at Elton Hall, near Peterborough. Quaritch's bought the folio for £6,100 in 1923 and sold it for £10,000 to a New York dealer, who sold it on four years later to Edward Newton of Philadelphia for £12,000. That collection then sold in 1941 with the folio selling as a separate lot for $22,000. Then the University of Cologne bought all four folios for DM425,000 in 1960. Dr Weidle points out that, though that sum would then have converted to about £36,000, today the amount paid would be more like £300,000–£350,000.

But as I was carefully working my way through this extremely valuable, perfect copy, with its pages as pristine as if they had just been printed, watched by Dr Hoffrath, the Head Archivist, and her colleagues, and by the Vice President of the German Shakespeare Association, I turned to *Henry VI Part Three*. There was a sharp intake of breath. A torn page corner lay tucked in the gutter in the centre of the book. Whoever was responsible for this outrageous act of vandalism had clearly decided that if they needed the perfect place to hide this poor torn-off page corner it would be in *Henry VI Part Three*. As we all contemplate the solitary fragment, I say: 'Please could everyone here witness that I am not responsible for this.'

The laugh breaks the ice and someone says, 'Perhaps we can sell it. It would fetch thousands', and then we conclude that this, too, is part of its story, just as we are now part of its story.

Berlin

The Berlin Folio has one of the grandest of homes. It is kept in the Staatsbibliothek zu Berlin-Preussischer Kulturbesitz on Unter den Linden, the central boulevard which leads to the Brandenburg Gate. The grand library courtyard has a splashing fountain and red Virginia creeper climbing the classical pillars. The Berlin copy was donated to the Staatsbibliothek in 1859 by William I, King of Prussia, and may have been a gift from Queen Victoria.

We are in the office of Dr Andreas Wittenberg, a grey-haired academic with kind eyes. His colleague Dr Silke Trojahn has joined us and Professor Anne Enderwitz, who has been contacted by the German Shakespeare Association to assist my visit. Anne is a lovely bright spirit, who, despite teaching in the English Department at the neighbouring Humboldt University here in Berlin, has never seen this First Folio either. As with so many of my visits, it is affording an opportunity for the people who work in proximity to these treasures to take a close look at them.

Dr Wittenberg's English isn't as fluent as Anne and Silke's but he becomes especially animated as we discuss the fine tooling on this nineteenth-century brown leather cover by the renowned binder Francis Bedford. I don't think I have ever particularly noticed the tooling before, but he gets very excited about the work along the edges of the inside cover. He suddenly darts to a drawer at the back of his office and returns with what looks like a very old pizza cutter. The cutting disc (which is removable) has the pattern along the edge. You can attach different bronze wheels with varying designs to the shank, and once you have brushed the surface with a little glaire[*] and have applied gold leaf to the wheel, having warmed it up on a little stove, you can roll out the continuous pattern onto the leather.

As Dr Wittenberg demonstrates, he no longer needs help translating. 'But you must notice,' he says, 'how the tooling extends out from each corner.' All turn-ins are filled with a gold-tooled design of flowers and leaves at the outer edge with a double gold fillet near the inner edge. 'But again,' says Wittenberg, 'see how the pattern meets perfectly at the corners. There is the craftwork.' Delicious.

---

[*] Another great word I have learned on my Roadshow: it's an adhesive made from egg whites.

Frankfurt

Frankfurt is the book centre of Europe, and for the next five days it hosts the Buchmesse. That's why I am here. While most books originally offered at the fair were in Latin, by 1618–19 booksellers advertised books in English in printed catalogues. The Londoners' catalogue for the Spring 1622 Frankfurt Fair announced that English supplements would be included thereafter. Among the English titles listed in the very next catalogue, for autumn 1622, was *The Comedies, Histories and Tragedies of Mr William Shakespeare*. Exactly 400 years ago this month. But they jumped the gun by one year. It didn't come out until the autumn of 1623.

The Fair's origins are said to go back to the twelfth century, and it is still going strong more than 800 years later. But it is not Frankfurt's only claim to fame in the world of books, as Johannes Gutenberg, the inventor of printing, lived and worked here from 1454 for three years. A statue on the Roßmarkt celebrates the fact. Here is Gutenberg flanked by his patron Johannes Fust and his printer Peter Schöffer.

Before heading to the site of the Fair itself to meet up with some of the Bloomsbury team, I head to the Goethe Haus, the birthplace and childhood home of the great writer. Goethe wrote of Shakespeare, in his essay *Literary Criticism* (1771): 'The first page I read made me a slave to Shakespeare for life. And when I finished reading the first drama, I stood there like a man blind from birth ... I realised and felt intensely that my life was infinitely expanded.' He wrote his most Shakespearian play, *Goetz von Berlichingen*,* here at the Goethe Haus.

Dr Joachim Seng gives me a detailed tour of the house, from its elegant parlour with a large stove in the corner to the kitchen with its brass moulds and woven baskets hanging in racks along walls hand-painted with flowers. The actual house was destroyed in the bombing of the Second World War, so I am surprised to see how entire the reconstruction is. It was all designed to be ready for the Goethe bicentenary of 1949, part of the effort to re-establish a new German identity after the war.

---

* The RSC produced *Ironhand* adapted by John Arden from Goethe's *Goetz von Berlichingen* in 1965.

Eventually, Joachim and I retired to a bar next door and had (of course) a frankfurter and a beer. As we ate, we discussed the German love of Shakespeare. I wondered why there were in fact only three First Folios in Germany. If it had been sold at the Frankfurt Book Fair in 1623, why were there not more copies here?

It's because Shakespeare really only becomes *Unser Shakespeare* when he is translated and retranslated, by Schlegel and Tiecke, and then by Hans Rothe, or Frank Günther. There is no real interest in the original, as expressed in the First Folio. Germans, he said, are used to watching Shakespeare in translation, in contemporary idioms, so they are not interested in 'authenticity' or in versions that sound archaic, or self-consciously poetical. So their engagement with Shakespeare's language is kinetic, constantly shifting and embracing new ideas. It is always contemporary. Dr Seng's view made a lot of sense to me.

★ ★ ★

Here in Frankfurt in 1568 a Book of Trades was published which provides an insight into the book-making industry back then. The *Ständebuch* illustrates 114 different professions including the crafts of the papermaker, the book printer and the bookbinder. The woodcuts were created by Jost Amman (1539–91). Each is accompanied by an eight-line verse describing the trade. These are notable because they were written by Hans Sachs, the cobbler-poet, whom Wagner celebrated as the hero of his opera *Die Meistersinger von Nürnberg*. Here is a translation of Sachs's verse accompanying the bookbinder:

> Binding books of all sorts 'tis my call,
> Religious and secular, large and small,
> In parchment or in boards of wood
> My studs are strong, my closures good
> I add nice clasps and stamps to embellish
> Then I press the books with relish
> And gild the spines of some I do
> I earn good money at it, too.

Woodcut of 'The Bookbinder' from *The Book of Trades*

By a window of blown-glass panes a man sews a book together at a sewing frame. Hemp cords hang from hooks on the frame. Having built up each quire, one on top of the other, he sews the gatherings together.

In the foreground the bookbinder with corky forearms sits on a log stump with a laying press on his lap. He is 'ploughing' the book, trimming the edges, by running the bladed plough over the book block firmly held in the press, in preparation perhaps for gilding. In a finishing press, leaning against the stump, is a volume with its spine and raised bands already covered in leather.

Around the bookbinder lie further tools of his trade: a bow saw and a draw knife, a block plane and a paper-beating hammer on the floor, and, hanging neatly on the walls behind him, an orderly array of long-handled tools: a polishing iron, a roller and burnisher. There are balls of linen thread, and hemp cord, a gimlet, rasps and files and an axe. Many of these tools are woodworking tools. Some say that *beech*, the wood in which many mediaeval books were bound, and *book* come from the same Germanic root – *Bōk*.

The woodcuts in the Frankfurt *Ständebuch* give me an insight into how the First Folio was created. I can imagine the paper mills, the print shops and the binderies which produced the books I have been visiting. I get a clearer picture of the book trade in Shakespeare's day.

In London it revolved around the churchyard of St Paul's Cathedral. I have often tried to picture the place. The old cathedral had stood for half a millennium, and once boasted the longest nave and the tallest spire in the kingdom. That spire had collapsed in the reign of Elizabeth, struck by lightning in a thunderstorm in the summer of 1561 during which the roof caught fire and 'the very bells melted'. Sixty years later the ancient cathedral is in a calamitous state of disrepair.

The walls of the cathedral itself were pestered by 'wall creepers', a sort of shanty town of illegal dwellings. According to the Elizabethan antiquarian John Stow, some began, as 'low sheds but [are] now high houses'. Sea-coal smoke rising from their chimneys has corroded the cathedral's mediaeval walls. Tourists have carved their names into the leads on the roof and raucous jackdaws and crows nest in every crevice of the crumbling walls.

The churchyard is centred around an open-air pulpit, an octagonal construction of stout oak with a leaded roof, called St Paul's Cross. When King James came to the cathedral in 1620 he heard a sermon here. For over two hours, the Bishop of London delivered 'a pathetical speech' on the perilous state of the building. After which the king ordered that all the houses that had been built in the vicinity of the cathedral 'to the annoyance and blemishing of it and the churchyard' should be pulled down by the following Whitsuntide. 'Somewhat a hard case,' wrote John Chamberlain to a friend, 'for more than 2,000 souls are to be turned out of house and home.' Very little was done.

In his witty *Microcosmographie* (1628), John Earle gives us an aural portrait of the cathedral and its precincts. 'It is the ear's brothel,' he writes, 'and satisfies their lust and itch.' 'It is a heap of stones and men, with a vast confusion of languages ... nothing liker Babel.'

> The noise in it is like that of bees, a strange humming or buzz mixed of walking tongues and feet: it is a kind of still roar or loud whisper. It is the great exchange of all discourse, and no business whatsoever but is here stirring and a-foot.

Playwright and pamphleteer Thomas Dekker notes in *The Gull's Hornbook* how the cathedral has been turned into a public parade, known as Paul's Walk, where gallants strut up and down, showing off their fashionable clothes, before making their way to 'the new tobacco office, or amongst the booksellers, where if you cannot read, exercise your smoke, and enquire who has writ against this divine weed'.

People advertise their wares in one corner and even barter for hire in another. Falstaff in *Henry IV Part Two* describes how he hired Bardolph, with his carbuncle-covered nose, for a servant in the nave of St Paul's. Porters use the church as a shortcut to lead their loaded mules down to the dock on the river. It is a 'thieves' sanctuary'; 'idlers and masterless men' sleep rough on the pews.

The place stinks.

> No easement, but against the temple walls
> No other place to piss or make laystals.*
> From 'The Complaint of Paules' by Henry Farley

Outside the north door of the cathedral the Swiss traveller Thomas Platter notes 'a vessel … for passing urine, giving a pleasant odour to the passers-by!'. No wonder St Paul's Walk was known as Pissing Alley.

It is within this foul-smelling, overcrowded, noisy precinct, in the north-east corner of the churchyard, that the book trade has flourished, a chaotic assembly of variously constructed shopfronts or stations, their painted signs prominently on display, some more familiar to us as pub signs like the King's Head or the Golden Lion, alongside the Angel, the Parrot or, more exotically, the Brazen Serpent and the Tiger's Head.

It is here in early November 1623 that Shakespeare's First Folio is set out for sale for the first time, in unbound sheaves on the wooden stall which projects from Edward Blount's shop, the Black Bear. On the posts which hold up the awning, copies of Martin Droeshout's engraving of the playwright are pinned up as advertising, bearing witness to his celebrity, albeit seven years after this death.

---

* Laystalls were places for holding cattle going to market, and by association where dung accumulated.

Having purchased your copy for fifteen shillings, you could take it away and have it bound to your own specifications, or, for another five shillings, you could choose to have it bound in plain calf, and the loose quires would be taken to the binderies a short walk across the yard from Blount's shop, nestled between the great smoke-blackened buttresses which support the cathedral chancel.

★ ★ ★

Today's Frankfurt Book Fair is huge, a thousand times the size of St Paul's Churchyard. It occupies over four million square feet, and is the world's leading venue for printed and digital content. Over several acres, in many interconnected pavilions, the world's publishers host stands displaying their latest and their future titles. Publishing experts meet up to exchange ideas, be inspired and do deals in a jumble of foyers and open stages, workstands and catering stalls with ramps and escalators and signs.

I meet my contact at Bloomsbury, who wants to know how my journey down from Berlin went, whether I have dinner plans and if I found a reasonable hotel. He tells me that, like the hotels, the Frankfurt sex workers double their prices during big trade fairs. The auto show is boom time; the butchers' convention is famously busy, but when the Buchmesse is on, they complain they are virtually redundant as the book dealers are all sleeping with each other. He is intrigued that Shakespeare has a connection to Frankfurt. But I am still baffled by it. Why did the syndicate of London booksellers who produced this sales catalogue for Frankfurt assume that these books would sell? A book of plays ... in English! Isn't the notion of selling Shakespeare's First Folio in Frankfurt a very risky adventure?

And who went out there that Michaelmas? Isaac Jaggard? No, too busy printing books at the Barbican. Edward Blount perhaps? And did he take stock with him, or just hope to drum up deals? Did he fill a waggon-load with these large, heavy books with over 900 pages each? How many did he think would be worth taking? Did he drive them down to Dover, board a ship to Calais, then hire a waggon or cart and several mules to make his way through the Low Countries, from Ghent to Brussels to Cologne to Frankfurt. Perhaps 450 miles.

If it took Shakespeare three days to get the 100 miles from Stratford to London, that would suggest at least a fortnight's journey just to get here. And was it worth it? Or was the Buchmesse, then as now, not so much about the physical books themselves but the titles on offer and the deals that can be done?

Stuttgart

Stuttgart was such a different experience after all the generous warmth I have received elsewhere. I wasn't allowed to turn the pages myself. Dr Hermann did this, wearing white gloves, until his younger colleague spoke to him quietly in German and he removed them. It's generally agreed now that your hands (as long as they are clean) are less likely to tear the fragile pages than the fabric of the gloves. It says in pencil on one of the first blank pages that it is another near perfect copy. All the German copies seem to boast this. There are a few annotations here and there, and the Duke's speech in *As You Like It*, 'Sweet are the uses of adversity', is underlined.

I felt deflated after the meeting and decided I would cancel my hotel room and see if I could fly home that night. Maybe after forty folios, I was getting folio-fatigue.

A Digression: Hand-marbled Endpapers

One of the largely unremarked features which distinguish each First Folio is the hand-marbled endpapers. The manufacture and application of these beautiful pages involves an ancient art. In Japan, where it emerged in the twelfth century, it is known as *suminagashi*, or 'floating ink', a perfect description of the craft of pouring, sprinkling or spattering different coloured paints into an alginate solution (which might include carrageen seaweed and tragacanth gum), then gliding a comb or stylus through the pigments and finally capturing the mesmerising swirls and curls by rolling on the surface single sheets of paper.

In the Ottoman Empire, where it had arrived by the fifteenth century, it was called *ebru* (*ibri* in Persian), or 'the art of clouds', a name which expresses exactly how hand-marbling evokes natural forms: shells, lichen or feathers, or the ice ferns on my childhood bedroom window. In Italy, where the skill arrived a century later, the technique is known as *marmorizzazione*. If ever Tony and I were in Florence, we would go to an old shop near the Pitti Palace where they had been hand-marbling paper for six or seven generations, and buy a few sheets with their tactile, kinetic patterns.

Kinetic and hypnotic, like those lava lamps in the sixties, with their endless psychedelic trip of wax and water, the effect of hand-marbled paper is of fluidity. Of movement suspended, of molten colours mingling and writhing in a serene abstraction. Like microbiological organisms cultivated in a Petri dish, or the rainbow slick of colour on an oily puddle, or some oceanic tide of phytoplankton in a deep algal bloom.

Some endpapers have a dark carnelian tone, combed into peacock-tail patterns, with ripples of peach and pigeon blue. But there are so many different types. The tones of the hand-marbling can be muted and subtle: a misty vegetation of olive and juniper, set against midnight blue with pale glow-worm dots. Others may be a pale butterfly wing of eddying pastel, a languid undulation of coral and soot and buttermilk and cornflower blue.

Looking at some marbling feels like peering into a rock pool, where pink and raspberry anemones float on a bedrock of sage and slate, rising from jet-black obsidian depths, while a vibrant ochre sky is reflected on the shimmering surface.

★ ★ ★

In 1987, the year Tony and I met, I found a shop selling photograph albums covered with beautiful hand-marbled paper. They were the old-fashioned sort with thick black leaves requiring gummed photo corners and a white ink pen. I bought several, and enjoyed selecting and compiling these albums so much that I started to do one every year. One day when I popped into this paper emporium, the owner told me that she had decided to retire and was closing the shop. As I had been such a regular customer, she offered me a discount on any of the remaining stock. But as by now I had one for every year Tony and I had been together, how many should I get? I filled the last album in 2021, the last year of Tony's life. So now I have a shelf of thirty-five beautiful albums, full of memories and smiles, and holidays and family life events. They stand in sunny contrast to the black diaries Tony filled with some of his darkest thoughts. The last two, his *Dying Diaries*, are still waiting to be read.

Chapter Six
The Great Libraries of Dublin, Cambridge and Oxford

Trinity College Dublin

> Books give a soul to the universe
> Wings to the mind,
> Flight to the imagination,
> And life to Everything.
>
> Attributed to Plato

A sign above the library at Thebes was said to read, *the place of the cure of the soul.*

Some great libraries I have had the privilege of visiting, some I know of by reputation and some because they have inspired the locations for film sets. The library that the Beast shows Beauty in the Disney live-action version of *Beauty and the Beast* is based on the Baroque Joanine Library in Coimbra in Portugal. It harbours a colony of bats to protect the books. Yes, there are bats in the Biblioteca, silky bats to be precise. The shelves have leather blinds, which every morning are wiped clean of the guano produced overnight. But the silky bats eat any of the insects that intend to feed on the irresistible glue bindings.

The Old Library of Trinity College Dublin has also been said to have inspired a film location. The Jedi Archive in the *Star Wars* prequel, *Attack of the Clones*, is based on this amazing space. There is the barrel vault stretching far into the distance, and the multiple levels of book stacks, and even the busts of great authors; although the 'bronzium' busts are one of the film's in-jokes (according to

Wookipedia) because they include George Lucas, the creator of *Star Wars*, as well as the visual effects supervisor and the co-creator of Pixar. In fact, when Trinity College realised the striking similarity between their Library and the Jedi Archive, and that they had not licensed their likeness, the film company quickly denied that there was any connection between the two.

Who cares? The Old Library is a breathtaking space.

On our visit, my sister Jo and I have been marvelling at its treasures. The Old Library contains the Book of Kells, and the oak and willow harp, said to have belonged to the High King of Ireland Brian Boru in the tenth century, the national symbol of Éire (and of Guinness, Jo reminds me*). And they look after the only copy of the First Folio in Ireland. It has one or two intriguing features: a burn mark, the paw print of some animal and a series of notes in an as yet undeciphered shorthand. But I am intrigued by what the folio means here in Ireland.

Also on display in the Long Room is one of the founding documents of Ireland. Just as many American libraries treasure the 1776 Declaration of Independence, here is one of the few remaining copies of the 1916 Proclamation of the Irish Republic, which was read outside the General Post Office on 24 April 1916 by Patrick Pearse at the start of the Easter Rising.

Professor Andy Murphy from the English Department here at Trinity has written eloquently about the coincidence of the Easter Rising, and the Shakespeare tercentenary, which occurred that same Easter weekend in 1916. He describes Patrick Pearse's love of Shakespeare, noting that one of the senior figures in Nationalist circles at the time had said: 'If England has only Shakespeare and Milton and the rest, the Fenians would not be against her.'

He is persuasive in his argument that the schoolteacher and playwright Pearse learned a great deal from Shakespeare about the power of rhetoric. What Pearse and James Connolly, his fellow Nationalist, and the Commandant-in-Chief of the Irish Citizen Army had in common was their intense devotion to Shakespeare, and what they

---

*When the new Irish state chose the symbol in 1922, it had already been licensed to Guinness for over sixty years, so the state had to distinguish their emblem by having a harp that faced right, whereas the Guinness emblem faces left.

derived from it: 'a sense of the political value of theatre, and the theatricality of politics'. They had both been involved in theatre, and in Professor Murphy's phrase, 'for them theatre and political action became fused virtually to the point of indistinguishability'.

Militant Irish Nationalists, for all their rejection of other aspects of British culture and identity, were heavily drawn to the cultural force of Shakespeare, and elevated him to the position of supreme 'supra-national' playwright. They understood in their 'messianic patriotism' that symbolism was the dominant power, the certainty of immediate failure over long-term triumph. The Easter Rising, celebrated in Yeats's great poem, was a failure in the short term, but paved the way for Irish independence. 'A terrible beauty is born.'

During our trip to Dublin, Jo and I were honoured to be invited to tea with Michael D. Higgins, and his wife, Sabina, at the President's Residence, Áras an Uachtaráin. President Higgins had visited the RSC in Stratford during a state visit to England in 2014. He had spoken then about the English language and about the shared dialogue between our two islands:

> Today I want to acknowledge a great truth: the English language that we share, if it was once the enforced language of conquest, it is today the very language in which we have now come to delight in one another, to share our different and complementary understandings of what it means to be human together in this world, transacting in the currency of words.

★ ★ ★

There is another First Folio, intimately entangled both with the history of the British Empire and with the Irish struggle for independence. It belonged to Lady Louisa Lennox Tighe. Her father had been Lord Lieutenant of Ireland from 1807 until 1813, when he moved his family to Brussels as storm clouds heralded the bloody climax to the Napoleonic Wars. At the British Embassy, Louisa's mother hosted a ball for the soldiers and their wives. It was made famous by Lord Byron, for during the ball a call to arms was sounded:

> There was a sound of revelry by night,
> And Belgium's Capital had gathered then
> Her Beauty and her Chivalry, and bright
> The lamps shone o'er fair women and brave men;
> ... And all went merry as a marriage bell;
> But hush! hark! a deep sound strikes like a rising knell!
>
> Lord Byron, 'Childe Harold's Pilgrammage'

It was the eve of the Battle of Waterloo and, as the call sounded, thirteen-year-old Louisa buckled on the sword of her godfather, the Duke of Wellington.

Louisa would marry and move to Ireland. Her home was a grand eighteenth-century mansion called Woodstock House, in County Kilkenny. In order to create employment for local women she brought with her from Brussels the tools for setting up a lace-making workshop, one of the first in Ireland.

Her First Folio remained in the library of Woodstock House after her death in 1900 and was passed down in the family. But it must have been removed by 1922 when the house fell victim to that tumultuous period of Irish history. Following the failed Easter Rising of 1916, the Irish War of Independence led to the establishment of Northern Ireland in May 1921 and of the Irish Free State later that year. But in the very first week of the Irish Civil War that followed, the house was set ablaze by the IRA in order to prevent Free State forces regarrisoning it. Louisa's First Folio was eventually donated to the Love Library of the University in Lincoln, Nebraska, in 1991. It was their two-millionth volume.

Trinity College Cambridge

There are moments on my Folio Roadshow when the library itself threatens to upstage the object of my search. Today might be one of them.

Dr Nicolas Bell greets me at the gate of Trinity College. As we walk across Nevile's Court, I get my first view of the Wren Library, a great glazed Palladian bridge spanning the sunlit lawn that sweeps through the cloistered court, under the open arches of the colonnade, and down to the River Cam beyond. You immediately want to be in that high, floating ballroom with its walls of glass, which seem from below to stretch from floor to ceiling. But where, you wonder, are all the books?

Climbing the wide black marble staircase to the landing you realise the optical illusion as you enter. The windows form a clerestory above a long nave of books, filling the room with light. Ten feet below them and between each pier, the oak bookcases are arranged in rows perpendicular to the walls. At the end of each stack is a carving by Grinling Gibbons, in pale lime wood. The busts of great writers stare down from above, Classical authors to the left, British to the right, and at intervals down the black and white checkerboard floor stand plinths supporting busts of notable members of the college. Nicolas tells me that the busts at eye level are in marble by the French sculptor Louis-François Roubiliac, whereas the busts that look down from the top of the stacks are cheaper plaster copies.

At the end stands the statue of Lord Byron. It was intended for Poets' Corner in Westminster Abbey, but his scandalous reputation prevented its installation. Byron didn't actually get recognition in Poets' Corner until 1969.

★ ★ ★

Once we have scanned the folios, Nicolas brings out one of the Wren Library's more recent acquisitions. It is an album full of the work of the most notorious Shakespeare forger of the eighteenth century, William-Henry Ireland.

As a boy, Ireland had been inspired by the story of Thomas Chatterton, the Bristol-born poet, who committed suicide at the age of seventeen and became an icon of the Romantic movement. Chatterton had discovered an oaken chest of mediaeval manuscripts in a secret muniments room above one of the porches of St Mary Redcliffe Church. He whiled away his hours as a boy imagining himself back in the reign of Edward IV, and started to write poems in the manner of that period under the name of Thomas Rowley, a fifteenth-century monk. His work began to be noticed, but when he moved to London to build his career as a poet, he declined into a deep melancholia. Walking through St Pancras Churchyard one day, with a friend, he fell into an open grave. Three days later he committed suicide. The famous painting by Henry Wallis shows Chatterton with long Pre-Raphaelite locks, his skin pale as a tea rose, stretched out under the window of his garret in Brooke Street, Holborn, the bottle of arsenic whose contents he has just swallowed lying where it has fallen from his hand.

William-Henry Ireland's story, though not tragic, is nevertheless poignant. He longed for the approval of his Shakespeare-loving father Samuel, so he invented his own oaken chest, but this one was full of articles and items relating to Shakespeare. He pretended they had been supplied to him by a wealthy country gentleman who wished to remain anonymous. He was eighteen years old, and a clerk in New Inn. Among the first documents he showed his father was a deed signed by Shakespeare, and a letter addressed to the Earl of Southampton expressing gratitude for his patronage. More followed, including a personal declaration by Shakespeare of his Protestant faith, and a poem to Anne Hathaway:

> Is there inne heaven aught more rare
> Thann thou sweete Nymphe of Avon Fayre?
> Is there onne Earthe a Manne more trewe
> Thanne Willy Shakespeare is toe you?

It seems strange to us now that this risible ditty with its cod Elizabethan spelling can have taken in any but the most gullible. But as the documents continued to appear, their fame grew and the Ireland house in Norfolk Street off the Strand was frequented by some of the most eminent people in town. Even Dr Johnson's biographer, James Boswell, came to view the sacred relics. Here is an account of that visit in William-Henry Ireland's own words:

> At length, arising from his chair, he made use of the following expression: 'Well, I shall now die contented, since I have lived to witness the present day.' Mr. Boswell then, kneeling down before the volume containing a portion of the papers, continued, 'I now kiss the invaluable relics of our bard: and thanks to God that I have lived to see them!'

Boswell died three months later.

Emboldened by the glow of fame, William-Henry Ireland then produced his most audacious 'find': an entire Shakespeare play, *Vortigern and Rowena*. Samuel Ireland, the ambitious father, who believed completely in his son's secret source, provoked a bidding war between the two London theatres at Drury Lane and Covent Garden, for the 'new' Shakespeare play. Richard Sheridan, the proprietor of Drury Lane, won, agreeing to stage the play sight unseen.

But by now things had already started to unravel.

The most eminent scholar of the day was Edmond Malone. Malone waited until Samuel Ireland published a book of facsimiles of all the newly revealed documents and then set about writing a 400-page exposé of the fraud. Meanwhile, Sheridan's leading man, the actor John Philip Kemble, began having serious doubts about the script. He was cast, of course, as Vortigern. His sister, the remarkable Sarah Siddons, had already withdrawn from the role of Vortigern's queen, Rowena, citing ill health. Kemble went so far as to propose the play should open on 1 April, April Fool's Day, but Sheridan refused and the opening night was set for the following day, Saturday 2 April 1795.

On 31 March, Malone publishes his damning book, and London is split between believers and non-believers, and that is the crowd that forces their way into a packed Drury Lane that fateful Saturday night. Proud father Samuel Ireland is sitting with forty of his most loyal acquaintances, in the front of the gallery. His son remains backstage in the green room close to the stage. The first three acts seem to go relatively well, and the audience remain attentive.

The story tells of how Vortigern (with Macbeth-like ambition) kills the king and seizes the throne. And (also as in *Macbeth*) his wife goes mad, and kills herself. We are back in pre-Christian Britain (where *Cymbeline* is set), a tributary state of the Roman Empire. Vortigern is supported against the Romans by the Anglo-Saxon warriors Hengist and Horsa.

In the interval, the popular actress Dora Jordan gives William an encouraging smile and tells him it all seems to be going very well. William has secretly written the part of Flavia specifically for Mrs Jordan, on whom he clearly has a crush. Flavia plays to all of Dora's strengths; it is a breeches role, in which she can show off her legs, and she has a sweet song to sing. Act 4 opens with Dora, whom the Drury Lane audience adore.

But then the tide turns. The role of Horsa has been entrusted to the incompetent Mr Phillimore. In the fatal duel Phillimore manages to die right across the curtain line, with his head upstage and his feet facing the audience. So when the curtain descends, it not only splits him in half, but the weight of the curtain bar makes the dead body emit a terrible groan. When he then struggles to get up and extricate himself from the curtain, the audience are helpless with laughter. There is no way to rescue it. And Kemble, with marmoreal grandeur, deals its death blow. In Act 5, he has the line 'And when this solemn mockery is over'…

William-Henry is watching from the wings. This is how he tells the story:

> No sooner was the above line uttered in the most sepulchral tone of voice possible … than the most discordant howl echoed from the pit that ever assailed the organs of hearing. After the lapse of ten minutes, the clamour subsided; when Mr. Kemble, having again obtained a hearing, instead of proceeding with the speech at the ensuing line, very politely, and in order to amuse the audience still more, redelivered the very line above quoted with even more solemn grimace than he had in the first instance displayed.

Sheridan had promised Ireland Sr half the profits for the first sixty nights of the run. At the curtain *The School for Scandal* was announced for the next performance.

What I find most bemusing about the disaster is its effect on young William-Henry. Instead of meekly confessing to his forgeries, he produces a list of further Shakespeare treasures, including another play (about Henry II), two drawings of the Globe Theatre and a full-length portrait of Shakespeare in oil.

In the Wren Library, Nicolas Bell and I are gasping at the ineptitude of one of Ireland's forgeries in the album. It is clearly meant to be Shakespeare. It shows him in a striped doublet and falling-band collar with a quill in his hand. It could have been painted by a primary school child. The face and hands are in poster-paint pink, which is flaking badly. This album, *An account of the Shakespearian manuscripts etc*, is one of a number of attempts to publish his confessions that Ireland made after his downfall. His father went to his grave in 1800 refusing to accept that any of the documents were his son's forgeries.

An account William-Henry published in 1805 reveals in detail how he did it. There was no wealthy country gentleman who he said had supplied the documents but wished to remain anonymous; a bookbinder's journeyman had taught him how to mix three marbling fluids to make a plausible faded sepia ink; and he had baked the paper in an oven. And finally William-Henry writes: 'Here then I conclude, most sincerely regretting the offence I may have given the world, or any particular individual, trusting at the same time, they will deem the whole the act of a boy, without any evil or bad intention, but hurried on thoughtless of any danger that awaited to ensnare him.'

Bodleian, Oxford

The Roman emperors outside the Sheldonian Theatre look as overheated as when Zuleika Dobson trotted down 'The Broad' in her open landau at the start of Max Beerbohm's breezy 1911 satire on Oxford student life. To me the sweaty emperors look as though they have been simultaneously goosed from behind. I am contemplating just how gloriously awful they are when I spot Richard Ovenden, Director of the Bodleian, emerging from the Clarendon Building to greet me.

The busts, which were already a second generation to the seventeenth-century originals, had to be remade in the early 1970s, Richard tells me, because they had deteriorated so badly in the city's air pollution, and he isn't quite sure where the originals now are. Probably, he surmises, in various wardens' private gardens all around Oxford.

It is a treat to be shown around the Bodleian's estate by such an amiable and erudite guide. In his celebrated *The Burning of the Books*, a crucial history of the destruction of knowledge from the Library of Alexandria to the Windrush papers, Richard traces how the Bodleian itself fell victim to the purges of Edward VI's reforming commissioners.

Bodleian Library

He shows me into the oldest reading room, Duke Humfrey's* Library. Of the 281 books donated by the Good Duke on his death in 1471, only three remain in the library today. Richard shows me where the shadow of the original shelves stood before the plunder.

It was Thomas Bodley, during Shakespeare's own lifetime, who began the library afresh, although he would never have tolerated the presence of plays in his collection. He regarded them as 'baggage books', the equivalent of 'airport reading', worth a few hours of distraction on the flight, but not worth taking home. However, he did create a contract with the Stationers' Company, in which they agreed 'to send to the Library a copy of every book entered in their Register', making the Bodleian the first legal deposit library. When the Shakespeare folio was published, a decade after Sir Thomas's death, the Jaggards duly shipped an unbound copy to Oxford.

Back in Duke Humfrey's Library, Richard shows me where the books used to be chained to the shelves, and were placed with their spines towards the walls. It would be to such a shelf in this very library that any Oxford student interested in reading the new edition of Shakespeare's plays would have come.

---

* Henry VI's uncle who appears in *Henry VI Parts One* and *Two* as Good Duke Humph<u>rey</u> (sic).

So what about that First Folio? Where is it now? Believe it or not it seems the Bodleian got rid of it. And I am lucky enough to have an expert to tell me the story. Emma Smith has written extensively on the First Folio, and is Professor of Shakespeare Studies at Hertford College, Oxford. She makes a number of appearances in this narrative.

On a visit to the Weston Library, which houses the Bodleian's special collections, Emma told me how the Bod (as it is known) came to lose their First Folio. In a way, it is quite a straightforward proposition that when any new edition is published you might think of updating your copy. If it were a medical textbook you would do so without fail. When the Third Folio was published in 1663/4 the new edition boasted the inclusion of seven extra plays by the same author. The Bodleian fell for the sales pitch, bought the third edition and somehow got rid of the first.

It disappears for two centuries until 1905, when a Magdalen graduate walks into the sub-librarian's office with a book under his arm. It is a copy of the First Folio. But not just any copy. There is a bite out of the cover, which the canny sub-librarian, one Falconer Madan, recognises to be the mark left behind when the volume was ripped from its chain in Duke Humfrey's Library. The ex-student rejoices in the unforgettably Anglo-Saxon name of Gladwyn Turbutt.

An assistant librarian at the Bodleian called Strickland Gibson, who was an expert in bindings, examined the Turbutt Folio, and from the colour of the calfskin and the type of waste paper used to line the inside of the boards and spine, he identified it as the work of the master seventeenth-century Oxford bookbinder William Wildgoose. There were other identical bindings by Wildgoose still on the library's shelves. Thus, having identified beyond reasonable doubt that this was indeed the set of unbound sheets of the First Folio that the Jaggards had sent to the Bodleian, and which had then been bound by the Oxford binder, the Bod wanted it back.

But by now Gladwyn realised that the Turbutt family had something rather valuable on their hands and told the Bodleian they had been offered £3,000 by an anonymous American donor. As Emma points out, 'this is an absolutely unprecedented, crazy sum of money': the Bodleian have never spent more than £200 on a book in its entire existence. The First Folio has never sold for more than

£1,300, so 'It's a huge upping of the stakes because of the specificity of this volume to the Bodleian.'

Then, in what Emma calls 'a very unprofessional, amateurish way', the Bodleian tries to raise the money. It goes up to the wire. It looks as if they can't raise the money to bring it back to the Bodleian. There is a patriotic appeal in *The Times*, warning that unless the Bodleian copy can be recovered 'there will be an indelible blot on our scutcheon'. Finally, the sum is raised and the anonymous donor is seen off. 'The best thing about the story,' says Emma, 'is the list made by the librarian of all the notables and worthies in Oxford who did *not* contribute', a marvellously vindictive piece of Scrooge-shaming.

Alongside the Turbutt Folio, Emma showed me the Bodleian's second copy, owned by William-Henry Ireland's nemesis Edmond Malone. Malone was an eminent scholar but his own reputation isn't entirely untarnished. He was responsible for whitewashing Shakespeare's bust in Holy Trinity Church, unable to accept that the original was boldly painted. Professor Lena Orlin of Georgetown University, who did revelatory research on the funerary demi-figure, decries Malone's 'neoclassicising'. The vicar at the time later lamented the vandalism that had been caused during his watch and called Malone 'that miserable pretender to good taste'. Professor Orlin suggests that the disfigurement of the bust was 'probably Malone's worst crime' but accuses him, too, of creating the myth that Shakespeare's marriage to Anne Hathaway was miserable.

★ ★ ★

During my visit to Oxford I enjoyed checking out the copy of the folio at Queen's College, once owned by David Garrick, and the copy at Wadham which has a handwritten final page, the last page of *Cymbeline*. The scribe has made a pretty good job, and if I had not been preparing to direct that very play I might not have noticed the error.

In the final speech King Cymbeline prays to the gods for peace between Britain and Rome. Unfortunately, just four lines from the end, there is a mistake: an entire line is missing. Despite their painstaking effort to copy out the text with the neatest of hands, they have missed out the line 'And in the temple of great Jupiter'. I wonder if they spotted the error, could not face the task of rewriting the whole text, and concluded ... 'It's *Cymbeline*... who will ever know!'

A Note on Annotations

As I was preparing to direct *Cymbeline* at Stratford, I came across an annotation in a folio at the V&A. It was a copy owned by John Forster, the literary critic and friend of Charles Dickens. Rather discouragingly, above the title of *Cymbeline* is written *Not Shakespear's, any part of it*, and *Not Shakeapear's, scarce a word* above *Titus Andronicus*. Legible annotations are quite rare in the folios I have seen. My favourite has to be in a highly annotated copy in private ownership in Virginia. The annotation appears written vertically in the outer margin on the last page of *Hamlet*.

It reads: *But I desier the readeres mough to kis the wrighteres arse.*

Sir John Soane's Museum

The view from my office in Stratford looked out on the Great Garden of New Place, and at a curious monument to Shakespeare. It is an eighteenth-century alto-relievo by Thomas Banks RA. Shakespeare is perched precariously on a rock. To his left the dramatic muse with her lyre wafts a laurel wreath in his face. Shakespeare with a hazy look ignores the proffered chaplet and gazes far away. His right hand,

Annotation in V&A Folio

however, rests on the shoulder of the genius of painting, with her palette and brushes. And she with a pert smile gestures proprietorially at Shakespeare.

Why is Shakespeare abandoning his old flame Theatre and shacking up with Painting? The pediment below tells us it once stood in front of the Shakespeare Gallery in Pall Mall. The gallery was the brainchild of a City alderman called John Boydell, who had the ambitious idea of commissioning a series of oil paintings of scenes from Shakespeare from all the principal artists of the day. He would build a specially dedicated gallery to exhibit them and publish an illustrated folio of the plays 'of the utmost typographical magnificence'.

Eventually thirty-five artists contributed works, including Royal Academicians such as Henry Fuseli, George Romney and Angelica Kauffman and finally even the sceptical founding President Joshua Reynolds was secured 'with the judicious application of £500 note'. The gallery was a temple to Shakespeare. Henry Fuseli even suggested to Boydell that he paint the ceiling of the gallery in the manner of the Sistine Chapel, with characters from the plays. Fuseli had lived in Rome for nearly a decade, and spent days lying on his back, gazing on Michelangelo's peerless ceiling. By the end of the eighteenth century, bardolatry had achieved the status of a religious cult.

The gallery was open to the public and allowed an eager middle-class audience on payment of a shilling to have an access to art previously rarely available to them. However, according to one of the artists on display, James Northcote (apart from his own work and that of one or two others), the paintings in the exhibition were 'such a collection of slip-shod imbecility as was dreadful to look at'. Boydell himself admitted the challenge of translating Shakespeare into art. 'He possessed powers that no pencil could reach,' he wrote. 'It must not be expected that the art of the painter can ever equal the sublimity of our poet'; and again, 'what brush can give to his airy being a local habitation and a name'. Nevertheless, he would try.

Charles Lamb complained of the injury that Boydell's gallery did him. Why should he want to have 'light-headed Fuseli's Shakespeare', or 'deaf-headed Reynolds' Shakespeare', instead of 'my and everybody's Shakespeare. To be tied down to an authentic face of Juliet!', he cried, 'To have Imogen's portrait! To confine the illimitable!' Lamb had the same problem with actors, wailing that Shakespeare's plays were too great to be acted. He said he could no longer tell whether Hamlet's celebrated soliloquy 'To be or not to be' was any good or not, he had heard it 'so pawed about'.

Of the 167 works commissioned for the Shakespeare Gallery, ninety-nine have been lost. We have thirteen of the extant paintings in our collection in Stratford. They vary from the portentous to the mawkishly sentimental. The most exciting work is Fuseli's evocative close-up of the three weird sisters, 'each at once her choppy finger laying upon her skinny lips'. Fuseli said Shakespeare 'rushed on our heart with an irresistibility which now subdues it'.

★ ★ ★

Two of the paintings from the Boydell gallery were purchased by the neoclassical architect Sir John Soane for his prodigious collection in his eccentric house. The museum, with its claustrophobically jam-packed rooms, today occupies three houses on the north side of Lincoln's Inn Fields, and has to be one of the most bizarre museums I know. It also houses a First Folio, and its own Shakespeare shrine.

I am at the top of the house, with the archivist Sue Palmer in the private apartments with their folio open before me. It once belonged to John Philip Kemble. It's a large folio. Following the eighteenth-century mania to create 'pristine' copies, Kemble had the pages washed and pressed and every single one of them remounted on new paper, so the volume increases its own sense of importance.

Thomas Lawrence's portrait of Kemble in his most famous role as Coriolanus is at the Guildhall Art Gallery. The scale of the painting is monumental, over twelve feet in height, and makes Kemble seem even more imposing and heroic, as he stands there glowering before the gates of Antium, his dark, tousled, curly hair and jet-black eyes staring out of frame under angry eyebrows. A huge black-green cloak is swept around his folded arms. He has a true Roman nose, aquiline with nostrils flaring. His chin is strong, his neck muscular, but his mouth is oddly pinched. Kemble was forty-one when this portrait was painted in 1798.

We know that Sir John Soane saw Kemble on stage and was present on 5 June 1817 at his last performance as Macbeth with his sister

Sarah Siddons as Lady Macbeth. So Kemble's ownership of the folio added to its appeal.

Sue takes me back downstairs, through the middle building which was Soane's actual house. The museum is closed today, and the lights aren't on. It lends the house a crepuscular gloom which is in itself rather special. She points out the paintings he bought from the Boydell gallery. Dominating the staircase, exactly where Soane originally hung it in 1805, is a painting of Sir John Falstaff in *The Merry Wives of Windsor*, disguised as the wise woman of Brentford trying to escape Ford's house. It's by James Durno. He painted it in Rome, which may account for why the setting seems to be taking place in a Gothic church, with views over the Italian countryside, rather than rural Windsor.

Next to it is a narrow space on the landing with a functional cupboard at the back, where the tableware was stored. This small nook has been converted into the 'Shakespeare Recess'. The cupboard is surmounted by a bust of Shakespeare, a copy of the funerary monument in Holy Trinity Church. Carved cherubs adorn the ceiling. Around it hang numerous paintings and sculptures paying homage to the playwright.

★ ★ ★

Other than Thomas Banks (who carved the alto-relievo of Shakespeare), the only other sculptor commissioned by Boydell for his Shakespeare Gallery was a woman. Her name was Anne Damer, and she is one of the few women to have owned a First Folio.

Anne had a fascinating life. She was part of the social set surrounding Georgiana, the Duchess of Devonshire, and was painted alongside the Duchess and Lady Melbourne, the most famous political hostesses and society beauties of the day, as the three witches from *Macbeth*, but instead of tossing poisoned entrails into the cauldron, they are throwing flowers. Anne's husband died after a short, loveless marriage, and she was free to travel. In Paris, Napoleon gave her a miniature of his portrait encrusted with diamonds. She sculpted a bust of Admiral Lord Nelson in Naples, and he gave her the coat he had worn at the Battle of the Nile.

Bust of Antony Sher by Richard Sharples

Prospero and the Spirits by Antony Sher

John Kani and Antony Sher in *Kunene and the King*, Tony's last stage appearance

Visiting the town of Shakespeare, Ontario

Sidney Lee, who compiled the first census of extant First Folios in 1902, by Alfred Wolmark

Pregnant Juliet?: a portrait of Maria Touchet, Lady Thynne, whose story may have inspired *Romeo and Juliet*

The Rev. C. H. Hawkins (known to the boys of Winchester College as 'Chawkers') playing Hamlet; he donated a copy of the First Folio to the school

Portrait of Shakespeare by the notorious forger William-Henry Ireland

Sir John Suckling reading *Hamlet* in a First Folio, by Anthony Van Dyck

Richard Burbage, the first actor to play *Hamlet*

Visiting John Lowin, actor in the King's Men, at the Ashmolean Museum

Two seventeenth-century owners of First Folios: Lucy Hutchinson and Jane Lane

Keith Richards looking at a First Folio at the New York Public Library

First Reading of the Emancipation Proclamation of President Lincoln by Francis Bicknell Carpenter

'Ignudo' of Harrison Post, lover of the first verifiably gay owner of a First Folio

One of Japan's greatest actors, Masachika Ichimura, as the Shogun Tokugawa Ieyasu

Monument to Restoration playwright and First Folio owner
William Congreve, in Westminster Abbey

Procession of nine kings at the funeral of Edward VII in 1910

Statue of Shakespeare in Sydney, Australia

The work of the late Australian artist John Olsen projected on the Sydney Opera House during Vivid Sydney 2023

Statue of Sir George Grey, the colonial governor who donated First Folios to New Zealand and South Africa

The Buffalo syndicate who bungled the theft of a First Folio from Williams College, Massachusetts

The 'Altar' to Harry Elkins Widener, a First Folio owner who perished in the *Titanic* disaster

The George Peabody Library in Baltimore, Maryland

A 'typo' in a mediaeval manuscript at the Walters Gallery in Baltimore, Maryland

'Scissorhands' James Orchard Halliwell-Phillipps, the man who cut out the 'first state' Droeshout engraving from the RSC copy of the First Folio

The 'first state' engraving rediscovered at the Folger Library

The Haida Reconciliation Pole on the campus of the University of British Columbia in Vancouver

Our last photo taken together

She carved two bas-reliefs for Boydell's gallery. Both are scenes prominently featuring women. One portrays Coriolanus's triumphant return to Rome as he meets his mother and his wife.

Volumnia: Nay, my good soldier, up;
My gentle Marcius, worthy Caius, and
By deed-achieving honour newly named, –
What is it? – Coriolanus must I call thee?
But O, thy wife!
Coriolanus: My gracious silence, hail!
Wouldst thou have laugh'd had I come coffin'd home,
That weep'st to see me triumph? Ay, my dear,
Such eyes the widows in Corioli wear,
And mothers that lack sons.
Coriolanus (Act 2 scene 1)

Anne's friend Sarah Siddons posed for Volumnia and her brother John Philip Kemble for Coriolanus.

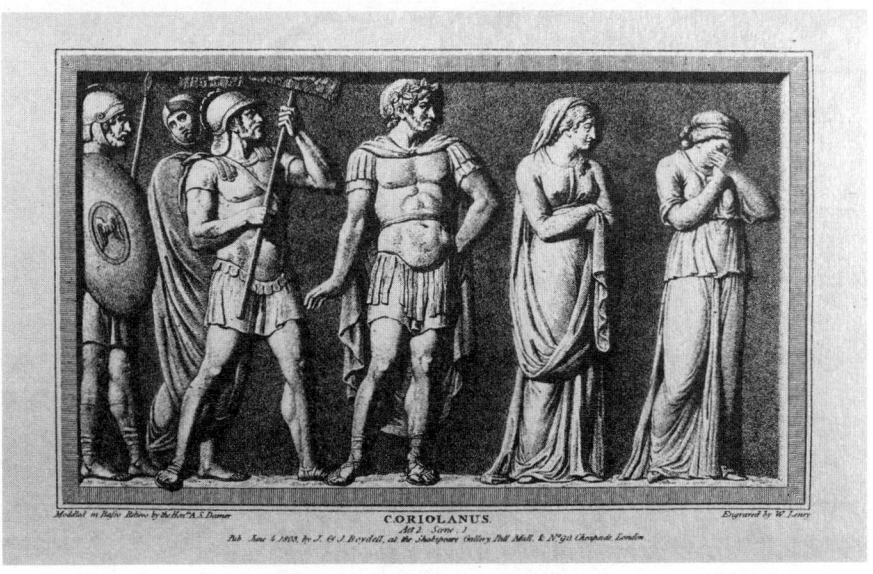

Coriolanus bas-relief by Anne Damer

The other bas-relief she sculpted depicts Cleopatra in the monument at the end of the play. She has just applied the asp to her breast, Iras lies dead at her feet, and Charmian laments at her side:

Now boast thee, death, in thy possession lies
A lass unparallel'd.

Antony and Cleopatra (Act 5 scene 2)

Both of her bas-reliefs have been lost, although engravings of them appeared in a huge atlas folio of prints from the gallery published by Boydell in 1803.

Sculpture was a rare craft for a woman to pursue in the late eighteenth century, and Anne's success in the field drew criticism. A cartoon called the Damerian Apollo appeared in 1798. It shows Anne seated behind the sculpture of a large figure of Apollo, who holds a phallic spear erect before him. Anne's chisel is placed between his buttocks, and she is about to wield a mighty blow with her hammer. She did in fact carve a statue of the god to stand in front of the Drury Lane Theatre. It disappeared when the theatre was demolished in 1794.

Cartoon of Damerian Apollo

Anne had a number of very close female friends. They included the Irish comic actress Elizabeth Farran, who starred at Drury Lane in roles like Lydia Languish in *The Rivals* and Lady Teazle in *The School for Scandal*. Their friendship attracted the vicious gossip of Georgian London. Mrs Thrale wrote in her diary that Mrs Damer is 'a lady much suspected for liking her own sex in a criminal way' and, later, 'It is a joke now in London to say such a one *visits Mrs Damer.*'

I feel pleased to have made the acquaintance of this pioneering woman, making a place for herself in the malicious milieu of late eighteenth-century society. Reading her notebooks I came across a passage she has translated from Cicero's comments on friendship, which I find moving:

> Who can have a true life, as Ennius says, who does not find pleasure in a friend's reciprocal friendship? What is sweeter than to have someone to whom you can dare to say everything as to yourself? What would be the great advantage of prosperity, if you did not have someone to rejoice in it, as much as you yourself do? Adversity indeed would be difficult to bear without one to take it harder even than you ... But indeed watching a friend is like watching a likeness of oneself.

But it's the last line that really strikes a chord:

> For this reason they are both present when absent, and abundant when lacking, and strong when weak, and something that is difficult to express, alive when dead.

PART FOUR

California Dreaming and a Great Literary Slug

'The Great Literary Slug'

Chapter Seven
California

There is a famous *Punch* cartoon by Eric Partridge showing a scowling Uncle Sam, with familiar goatee, striped slacks and tailcoat. Under his right arm he carries a large volume identified by a dangling label which reads 'Shakespeare First Folio 1623', and under the other a large framed painting labelled 'The Blue Boy. T. Gainsborough'. He is staring quizzically down at Shakespeare's tomb with its famous malediction: 'And curst be he that moves my bones.' Watching tremulously is the quivering wraith of William Shakespeare, as if he has just stepped down from his monument. Uncle Sam is saying: 'Now that's real disappointing. I'd set my heart on that skeleton.'

Partridge is satirising the flood of Shakespeare folios (and of great artworks) from British shores across to the States, which had accelerated since the turn of the twentieth century. The cartoon is dated 24 May 1922. *The Blue Boy* was purchased the previous year by the American railroad magnate Henry E. Huntington for $728,000, and its departure from England caused an outcry.

The painting's journey from London was tracked in the media as if he was a young rock star, with headlines shouting: '*The Blue Boy* is on a train', '*The Blue Boy* is crossing the ocean', '*The Blue Boy* is traversing across America', '*The Blue Boy* has arrived in California'. It still hangs in the Huntington Library in San Marino.

California has more copies of the First Folio than there are in the rest of Europe. In November 2022, I was invited to a Shakespeare conference at the Huntington and decided to take advantage of the trip to see as many of them as I could. My sister Ruth came from her home in Denver to join me on this next leg of my Folio Roadshow. We started in San Francisco.

San Francisco

The Palace was one of the great hotels of the Gilded Age. It was here in 1906 that the Neapolitan tenor Enrico Caruso had been staying during his appearance at the Grand Opera House a few blocks away, another of the splendid architectural treasures of the city built in the 1870s. Caruso was on tour with the Metropolitan Opera of New York and on the night of Tuesday 17 April he was appearing as Don José in *Carmen*. After his lauded performance, Caruso returned to the hotel and retired to his room at three o'clock.

The earthquake struck at 5.18. A minute later the city was in ruins.

The hotel 'seemed to dance a jig', someone recalled. The palm trees in the courtyard swayed. The horses took off from the front porch, wild-eyed and nostrils frothing, and the cobblestones in the streets were reported to be alive. When the Met conductor rushed to the great tenor's room Caruso was sitting bolt upright in bed, terrified. The hotel was destroyed in the earthquake and the fires that followed it.

This morning Ruth and I have breakfast in the hotel's gloriously restored fin-de-siècle double-storey ballroom. You can almost hear the echo of an orchestra playing that night, as the newly wealthy elite waltz on the edge of an abyss which was about to engulf their city.

Sutro Library

We head out to the Sutro Library at the North Campus of San Francisco State University. The Chief Librarian Mattie Taormina is waiting for us by Peet's Coffee. As we enter the library, there is a full-length portrait of its founder, Adolph Sutro, with his high, bald pate and fine silver mutton chops. He was a Prussian-born collector who was one-time mayor of San Francisco.

Sutro had made his money draining silver mines in the Comstock Lode in Nevada in the 1860s. On his return to San Francisco, he built himself a seven-storey 'gingerbread palace', up on the bluffs of Sutro Heights. He determined to build a world-class library to house his huge collection, which included not only rare books, but the only Egyptian mummy on the West Coast. Sadly, the library remained unbuilt on his death in 1898. Many of the precious items from his collection, including his copy of the First Folio, were stored in two warehouses, one that was fire-proof and one that was not.

When the great earthquake jolted the city to the ground in 1906, Sutro's daughter Emma drove her horse-drawn buggy through the burning city and rescued the folio from the second warehouse before it all turned to ash. It's a great heroic story, evoking spectacular shades of Rhett Butler and Scarlett O'Hara galloping through a burning Atlanta at the end of *Gone with the Wind*. In fact the Sutro have two copies of the First Folio. Mattie also shows us the unusual second copy. It is in twelve different volumes, identically bound in half-brown goatskin and has eleven complete plays, seven defective plays and fragments of three plays.

Berkeley

From the Sutro, we head north. As we cross the Bay Bridge on the way to Berkeley, I see a brown pelican flying lugubriously along up San Francisco Bay. The Berkeley campus is busy with students. We walk up through a wide pair of copper green gates, make our way to the library opposite the Bell Tower, the icon of the campus, and check in at the desk. In the reading room, the librarian, David Faulds, an expat Englishman, turns to the back of the Berkeley Folio, to the final two pages of *Cymbeline*, and asks me if I notice anything unusual.

'It goes from page 398 to page 993?' I venture.

'Yes,' he says, 'but the pagination is terrible throughout the book, and clearly here the compositor has placed the 3 at the wrong end. It should read 399, not 993. But that's not what I am referring to.' I take a closer look.

'No, not sure what you mean,' I admit.

'The whole page is a handwritten facsimile,' he smiles.

What! I can't believe it and peer more closely. 'You mean this is not printed type?'

'Nope, all written by hand, but intended to resemble the original as closely as possible.'

I am amazed. It is immaculate.

'Do we know who did this?' I ask.

Harris's signature on folio

'If you look very carefully,' says David, 'you will see he has signed it.' And he hands me a magnifying glass. While I scan the pages, David tells me about this celebrated facsimilist.

John Harris worked at the British Museum in the middle of the nineteenth century. He acquired a reputation as a master copier, working on early volumes of Chaucer, for example. The librarians at the museum were debating one day which of the pages were facsimiles created by Harris, and could not decide, so they called him in to identify his work. It was so unbelievably precise, down to reproducing tiny typographical irregularities in the original type, and using identical rag paper of the period, that Harris himself could not work out which pages were his own. From that moment on, it was decided that he should always sign his handiwork.

And suddenly I find the signature. There in the bottom left corner of the penultimate page, in a break in the inked ruling (and not much broader than that ruling) it reads 'FS by Harris'. Facsimile by Harris. Later I am absurdly proud to spot another Harris signature, this time within Ben Jonson's poem at the start of the volume.

As we Uber back across the Bay, the radio has an interview with Nancy Pelosi, the speaker of the House of Representatives, about a hammer attack on her husband, in their San Francisco home. With the mid-term elections happening here at the moment, you are made so aware of the rift between parties leading to intense tribalism. It feels like a tectonic crack, which could ultimately rip the country apart as effectively as the 1906 earthquake brought this city to its knees.

★ ★ ★

Los Angeles: the conference at the Huntington Library, at which I have been invited to speak, is called *Imagining Shakespeare in 2050*. It is convened by a Shakespeare pioneer, the charismatic Ayanna Thompson. She has assembled a remarkable group of American colleagues: among them Oskar Eustis from the Public in New York; Carl Cofield from the Classical Theatre of Harlem; Barry Edelstein from the San Diego Globe; Ian Smith from Lafayette College; and Nataki Garrett who revealed that in her time as Artistic Director of the Oregon Shakespeare Festival she has received multiple death threats for her programming choices. Mike Witmore, Director of the Folger, is also there. He tells me the Folger's brand new exhibition space is due to open for the Folio quatercentenary, and I must make sure to visit. I tell him it will be the climax of my whole journey. I start wondering if I can extend my Folio Roadshow even further.

UC Irvine

Before arriving at the Huntington, Ruth and I have three other folios to see. First we travel down to Orange County to UC Irvine, and arrive in the pouring rain. A flash-flood warning appears on my phone forecasting 'serious threat to life'. What happened to sunny California? But the following morning the sun appears, and an even sunnier smile on the face of our host, Professor Julia Lupton. Julia is the interim director of the University of California Humanities Research Institute, and she welcomes us to the library and introduces their debonair librarian, Derek Quezeda de Meneses, who takes us up to the special collections floor. Derek seems a little taken aback when I suggest that the copy in his care has a reputation as the 'stinky' copy, and he leads us back through the stacks to the metal cupboard where the volume is kept, so we can investigate.

It was owned by Dr Patrick J. Hanratty, a computer scientist who, because of his pioneering work in the field in the late 1950s, was referred to as the father of computer-aided design and manufacturing (CAD/CAM). He had been interested in Shakespeare ever since his parents involved him in the productions at San Diego's Old Globe theatre. When an opportunity came along in 1983 to buy a copy of the First Folio at the Heritage Bookshop in Beverley Hills, Hanratty leapt at it. In 1986, he donated his copy of the folio to UC Irvine (where he had done his doctoral thesis) after noticing 'the folio had begun to smell, and to smell very badly' from being stored in a vault. Derek and I take a sniff of the Irvine Folio, and I am relieved to report we can trace no offensive or mildewy odour today.

Loyola Marymount University

I already knew something of the provenance of our next folio. It was once in the library of Cross Hall near Ormskirk in Lancashire, the home of a branch of the Stanley family. The 5th Earl of Derby, Ferdinando Stanley, was the patron of the acting company that produced Shakespeare's early plays: *Titus Andronicus* and the *Henry VI* trilogy. The Earl died under suspicious circumstances, poisoned with mushrooms by the Jesuits, some said, or perhaps by the powdered unicorn's horn which was administered to cure him.

The Jesuit University of Loyola Marymount is located near Playa Vista, close to the airport, on the west side of Los Angeles. We are greeted by the librarian, Cynthia Becht, a bright-eyed woman with an ash-blonde ponytail. Cynthia tells us that their folio is one of the last-known specimens of the work of the legendary eighteenth-century bookbinder Roger Payne. It's a beautiful copy. Shakespeare's armorial shield has been placed on the cover, surrounded by a shimmer of dots. This spray effect represents the shaking of the spear ... a visual pun on the writer's name.

There is a striking engraving of Payne dated 1800 (Payne died in 1797). It shows a lean figure stooped over his book press in a wretched empty room with cracked plaster walls. He has a shock of unkempt white hair and looks gaunt and exhausted. His thin tailcoat

Roger Payne

is ripped under the arms, his skinny trousers have tattered hems and his feet in worn-down mules look cold. On the mantelshelf sit glue pots, or perhaps they are jars of the barley broth, for which 'he had an inordinate liking'. This is the only known engraving made of a bookbinder that century. Why, then, doesn't it celebrate his trade, rather than depict the squalor of his working conditions?

His story is one of genius, 'but of an entirely thriftless disposition and most irregular habits of life', wrote an admirer of his work. 'He lived without a rival, and died without a successor.' 'The scene closes with a lonely death in a comfortless garret.' And here Payne is in those dreary lodgings in Duke's Court opposite St Martin-in-the-Fields. He had a shop nearby in Leicester Square. But here we are in a library in California over 200 years later still admiring his marvellous craftsmanship.

Cynthia's words caress the volume. She points out the exquisite tooling sporting Druid acorns and lyre motifs. It is a superb example of eighteenth-century gilt brown russia, with its 'diced' or cross-hatched patterning, embossed by hand. Russia, she says, is very different from the usual goatskin morocco bindings you so often see. Both names reveal their origin. Most russia leather was made around

St Petersburg. Russia is reddish-brown calfskin. The calf, in Payne's day at least, was not necessarily bovine: it could be horse or reindeer. It was tanned with willow bark, then 'curried' with birch bark extract which gave it a distinctive smell.

In 1973 a quantity of eighteenth-century russia turned up off the Devon coast. In December 1786, the brigantine *Metta Catharina* set sail from St Petersburg with a cargo of leather hides and hemp on board. It was bound for the port of Genoa, when a storm forced it to seek shelter in Plymouth Sound. The crew were saved, but a fierce wind ripped the ship from its anchorage, and it sank. Nearly 200 years later, divers recovered the ship's bell and dozens of rolls of hide scattered on the seabed. They had been so well preserved in the black mud that, once cleaned, the hides not only showed the richness of their colour and their characteristic lattice patterning, but they still gave off the sweet, distinctive barky aroma for which they were so highly prized.

I try to catch the scent of the Loyola Folio, hoping to get a sense of its origin, expecting perhaps the ambery fragrance of Cuir de Russie, the dark, smoky perfume that Coco Chanel created in the 1920s evoking her brief affair with a green-eyed Russian Grand Duke exiled in Paris. But it just smells of old books. Musty not musky.

Then Cynthia tells us a remarkable story about how this copy of the 1623 Folio arrived at the university. Mrs T. Marie Chilton was a wealthy widow. 'I always tell my students, "Think of *Downton Abbey*. Mrs Chilton was like Cora, the wealthy American heiress who marries the Earl of Grantham, and brings her large dowry with her".'

'But we only met Mrs Chilton late in her life,' Cynthia continues. In 1959, the campus of Loyola University (not yet amalgamated with Marymount College) opened its first stand-alone library. The Von der Ahe Library attracted considerable attention in the press, and reminded citizens of the presence of the largest Catholic college in the Los Angeles area. 'Mrs Chilton reached out to us at that time,' Cynthia says. 'We believe she was a lapsed Catholic and having lost her husband was looking to re-establish a connection with the Church. So she invited Father Ted Marshall, the director of the library, to visit her home.'

She and her husband had bought a house on Camarillo Street, in North Hollywood, a palatial mansion with polished hardwood floors and a timeless elegance. Bing Crosby had been a close neighbour. She showed Father Marshall her impressive book collection, which not only included first editions of Austen, Dickens and Hardy, but an original edition of Mary Wollstonecraft's seminal feminist work, *A Vindication of the Rights of Women*. Mrs Chilton discussed a possible sharing arrangement with the new library.

A relationship was quietly established between the elderly widow and the Jesuit fathers. She was brought back into the Church and Father Marshall began visiting her to hear her confession. 'She would give him a sherry,' Cynthia continues, 'and then tuck a few books under his arm and say "take these back to the campus and share them with your students". These books included treasures such as the 1481 edition of Dante's *Divina Commedia* with illustrations by Botticelli, and Shakespeare's First, Second and Fourth Folio.'

At some point during the process, the conversation turned towards permanent donation, and she started buying books specifically with Loyola University in mind, including a Third Folio in order to complete the set. 'But then the story took a dramatic turn,' says Cynthia. Ruth and I glance at each other, gripped. 'One day Father Marshall went to visit only to find he was denied access ... we had been barred.' Cynthia is a fine storyteller. Neither of us could have guessed what happened next.

Mrs Chilton rented out a room in her mansion to a man called Bruce Dickerson Stevens, who worked his way into her life and, it seems, into her bed. For in 1968, Stevens takes his 85-year-old landlady, and whisks her off to Las Vegas, where he marries her. The next time Father Marshall visits, Stevens insists he return all the books his 'wife' had lent the university. Just as Mrs Chilton allowed God back into her life through the front door, the devil entered by the back door at roughly the same time.

The judgment of the Court of Appeal, Second District, Division 2, California (decided 25 May 1972), records 'the nefarious plans and schemes of Mr Stevens', and how he 'insinuated himself into Mrs Chilton's good graces, and turned her against others through fraud and undue influences'. He had inserted himself into the poor widow's will, and was set, on her death, to receive $50,000 in cash, and her house, and to be one of the two trustees of her estate. A psychiatrist who examined Mrs Chilton deemed her incapable of entering into any contract. 'Sadly,' Cynthia tells us, 'Mrs Chilton was so senile by that time, when the judge asked her to identify her "husband" in the court, she could not, and the marriage was dissolved.'

It all worked out well for Loyola Marymount. The university received an unrestricted gift of $3 million from the estate of Mrs T. Marie Chilton, the donation of her impressive collection of over 400 books, and even the finance to build a vault in which to house them.

The William Andrews Clark Library

The iconic Hollywood sign looks out over the urban sprawl of Los Angeles. The sign went up originally in 1923. That same year, a fire broke out in the home of William Andrews Clark Jr, in the West Adams neighbourhood of LA. The owner was a great bibliophile and he decided he needed to house his collection in a purpose-built library. His Beaux Arts library building was completed in 1926.

I am impressed as we arrive, that, in order to enter, visitors have to descend into a sort of tank within which the entire building is suspended, the result of recent rebuilding to accommodate seismic activity. Outside is a sundial by Eric Gill, showing one of his trademark nubile ephebes grinning while reclining, the semicircular dial resting on his naked body, with his hand provocatively caressing the gnomon. The inscription reads *WHEN THE SUN IS NOT SHINING I DO THIS FOR FUN.*

The librarian, Nina Schneider, takes us through the features of their folio. The striking bookplate with a writhing octopus reveals that it was owned by W. K. Bixby. 'The richest man in St Louis', William Keeney Bixby once made every railroad car in America. In the corner, a more sedate black leather bookplate, tooled in gold, bears the figure of an owl perched on a book of law with a globe, and the name of the owner, William Andrews Clark Jr.

Andrews Clark Sr was a mining tycoon known as 'the Copper King of Montana'. Mark Twain wrote of him: 'He is as rotten a human being as can be found anywhere under the flag; his proper place was the penitentiary, with a ball and chain on his legs.' His son was once described as 'prickly and aloof', and one historian wrote of him 'there are icicles in his handshake'. Andrews Clark Jr became one of the richest men in Hollywood in the twenties. He launched the LA Philharmonic, and established the Hollywood Bowl.

But, as Nina shows us around the Beaux Arts building, William Andrews Clark Jr's interests begin to become more apparent. His collection of Oscar Wilde is the largest and most significant in the world and includes nearly every edition of every printed book by and about Wilde. In the reception room, there is a rather dramatic and tender portrait of tousled-haired John Ogilby, a dancer in Jacobean Court Masques. The barrel vaulting of the vestibule entrance hall is painted to resemble the Sistine Chapel. And then we notice that the ignudi, the hunky male nudes languidly draped around the garlands of fruit, all have the same features. They are portraits of Clark's 'assistant librarian', Harrison Post.

Post was Clark's lover. He installed him in a Mediterranean-style villa across the road from his house and bought him a Rolls-Royce convertible. I am delighted to have identified my first verifiably gay owner of a First Folio. Not perhaps surprising that it should be here in California, since the 1970s seen as the most liberal of all the American states with regard to gay rights.

The Huntington Library

The Blue Boy has had a facelift, a hundred years after it first crossed the Atlantic. It is now on display in the Thornton Portrait Gallery at the Huntington. Since Ruth and I got here, I have been keen to show her the restored painting. It now hangs brightly alongside other portraits in the grand manner, eighteenth-century duchesses and fine ladies in their silk dresses and high-coiffured hair. Here is Joshua Reynolds' magnificent Sarah Siddons as the Tragic Muse, the original of a tarnished copy I had seen at the Dulwich Picture Gallery.

Today on the opposite wall *The Blue Boy* faces Kehinde Wiley's response *Portrait of a Young Gentleman*, which reconceives Gainsborough's icon. Wiley is famous for his colourful paintings which insert Black subjects into canonical European settings and ornate decorative patterns, like his recent painting of Barack Obama.

The acquisition of the Wiley portrait celebrates the 100th anniversary of the purchase of the Gainsborough painting by Henry and Arabella Huntington, the founders of the institution.

★ ★ ★

Stephen Tabor, the Curator of Rare Books here at the Huntington, is wearing a Covid mask and it is not until we take a selfie together at the end that I realise he has a short, neatly clipped white moustache which with his round, gold-rimmed glasses and short back and sides make him the epitome of an American gentleman academic.

Stephen looks after the four copies of the First Folio the Huntington possess. The Bridgewater copy is undoubtedly their finest. Remarkably, it is still in its original calf binding. It is one of the very few folios that have remained in the possession of the same family for nearly three centuries of its existence, until Henry Huntington bought it in 1917. Stephen very carefully opens it up for me to see. The copy has quite a lurid back story and potentially a strong connection to John Milton.

It was purchased by the 1st Earl of Bridgewater, John Egerton. In 1633, John Egerton was installed as the new Lord Lieutenant of Wales, and Milton was commissioned to write a masque to celebrate his arrival. He produced *Comus*, with music by Henry Lawes, in the Great Hall of Ludlow Castle. It was quite unlike any of the masques seen at court, and rejoiced in the triumph of the 'Sun-clad power of Chastity' over carnality and licentiousness. It was written for the Earl's children to perform, his two sons and his daughter Alice (fifteen) as the Lady. The children are led through a dark wood, where the Lady is accosted by the figure of Comus and his bestial rout. She censures his court in remarkable language:

> If every man that pines with want
> Has but a moderation and beseeming share
> Of that which lewdly-pampered luxury
> Now heaps upon some few with vast excess
> Nature's full blessings would be well dispersed
> In unsuperfluous even proportion
> And so no whit encumbered with her store.

I am struck by how Milton's lines echo King Lear's epiphany when he sees the poor naked wretches who haunt the heath:

> Take physic pomp
> Expose thyself to feel what wretches feel
> That thou mayest shake the superflux to them
> And show the heavens more just.
>
> *King Lear* (Act 3 scene 4)

It is possible that *Comus* was written to clear the family name. The Earl of Bridgewater's wife, Frances, was the daughter of Milton's patron, the Dowager Countess of Derby. The year before the production of *Comus*, Frances's sister Anne had been dragged through a very public scandal when her husband, Mervin Touchet,* the Earl of Castlehaven, became the only Member of Parliament (before or since) to be executed for a non-political crime. The charge was rape and sodomy. Castlehaven had repeatedly raped his wife, and kept a household in which he conducted open relationships with two of his male servants. One of the footmen, Lawrence, was referred to throughout by his nickname 'Florence'. Castlehaven had even tried to make one of them inseminate Anne to produce a male heir, in order that he could then disinherit his own son. Milton's elegant promotion of chastity in *Comus* was an attempt both to eradicate the memory of humiliation done to the Earl's sister-in-law, and to counter the licentiousness of the Caroline court.

★ ★ ★

The Huntington has three other 1623 Folios: the Roxburghe-Chatsworth copy references both the Duke whose vast collection was the spur for the foundation of the famous bibliophilic Roxburghe Club, and Chatsworth, the family estate of the Dukes of Devonshire, where the book resided until it was privately sold to Huntington. Another folio, known as the Halsey copy, used to live close to Stratford-upon-Avon in a house now long gone called Grove Park,

---

* Brother to the Maria 'Mall' Touchet who had married Thomas Thynne in the Longleat version of *R & J*.

and belonged to Sir John Baptist Joseph Dormer, who painted exquisite watercolours of the Levant. It was then owned by the mistress of Charles Yerkes, a millionaire streetcar tycoon. The Church copy (named after its owner, Elihu Dwight Church) is the only copy I have seen so far where *Troilus and Cressida* appears after *Timon of Athens* and before *Julius Caesar*.

I ask Stephen about two other precious items in the Huntington's admirable collection. I know they have a copy of the so-called 'Bad Quarto' of *Hamlet*. The First Quarto of *Hamlet* (1603) is known as the Bad Quarto, as it contains, for example, the line 'To be or not to be, I, there's the point'. There are only two copies. One of them connects to the notorious James Orchard Halliwell-Phillipps and is in the British Library. The other is here. 'Ah,' says Stephen, 'the Bad Quarto, that's in deep freeze. It's a bit like Timothy Leary's brain, we are waiting for the technology to catch up.' He explains: 'The original quarto was at some stage cut up and inlaid in frames, made of heavier material, so the paper started to pop, making it very fragile.'

'And what about the Perkins Folio?' I ask tentatively.

'Yeah,' Stephen shakes his head reluctantly, 'that's another thing we tend not to show.'

The story of the Perkins Folio introduces us to another of the nefarious characters that haunt the history of the First Folio: John Payne Collier. The very name Collier sends a shiver down the collective spine of Shakespearean scholarship.

Chapter Eight
'The Great Literary Slug'

In the spring of 1849, the eminent Shakespeare scholar John Payne Collier was browsing in Thomas Rodd's bookshop in Great Newport Street, London, when a parcel of books arrived 'from the country'. Rodd opened the parcel in front of his friend, but there was nothing much that interested Collier. There were, however, two large books that caught his eye.

The first was a splendid copy of John Florio's magnum opus, *New World of Words*, the 1611 edition of the lexicographer's Italian–English dictionary. The second volume, in rough calf, was a battered copy of the 1632 Folio of Shakespeare's plays. 'The book,' he wrote, was 'in a very shabby condition ... many stains of wine, beer, and other liquids are observable: here and there, holes have been burned in the paper, either by the falling of the lighted stuff of a candle or by the ashes of tobacco. In short to a choice book-collector no book could well present a more forbidding appearance.'

But despite its greasy cover, and the fact that it had been heavily cropped, Collier decided to buy it along with the Florio edition, for thirty shillings, thinking it could help 'complete' another copy of the Second Folio in his possession. It had, he wrote 'nothing more to commend it'. When he got it home, he found that the two leaves he needed to perfect his own Second Folio were unfit for the purpose. They were damaged and defaced, and too short anyway. 'Thus disappointed I threw it by.'

It wasn't until he was packing to leave for the country with his family, and decided to take the Second Folio with him, that he removed it from an upper shelf and happened to look inside. He wrote later of his surprise to find that it contained notes and emendations 'in a handwriting not much later than the time when it came from the press'. No page had less than ten to thirty of these emendations. There were over 20,000 of them.

There was a name inscribed at the front, one Thomas Perkins. Collier thought briefly that this might be the actor Perkins who scored a hit playing Barabas in the 1633 revival of *The Jew of Malta*, but that turned out to be Richard, not Thomas, Perkins. Collier surmised from the number of passages that had been ruled through that perhaps the Perkins Folio had been used in preparing texts for performance. Hundreds of stage directions had been added, and indications as to which lines should be delivered as asides. The unknown hand, which Collier began to refer to as the old corrector, had also excised 'some expressions and lines of an irreligious or indelicate character'. The coarse joke in *The Taming of the Shrew*, about the wasp's sting (the tongue-in-your-tail 'rimming' joke), was crossed out.

In 1853, Collier revealed to the world his amazing discovery and published a book: *Notes and Emendations to the text of Shakespeare's Plays, from Early Manuscript Corrections in a copy of the Folio 1632, in the possession of J. Payne Collier Esq*. He acknowledged that some of the emendations in this 'singular and interesting volume' had subsequently been picked up by other editors, 'but in not a few instances the sense of the poet has been elucidated in a way that has not been anticipated'.

Lady Macbeth's line to her husband when he starts getting cold feet about the murder of King Duncan: 'What *beast* was't then that made you break this enterprise to me?' is rendered by the old corrector as 'What *boast* was't then …'. Collier agrees: 'Surely it reads like a gross vulgarism for Lady Macbeth to ask "What beast?" but no one has hit upon this improvement, so trifling as regards typography, but so valuable as respects the meaning of Shakespeare.' He is enraptured. 'It cannot be denied by the most scrupulous stickler for the purity of the text of the Folio 1623, that the mere substitution of the letter "o" for "e", as it were magically conjures into palpable existence the long-buried meaning of the past.'

Collier's unmitigated praise for the old corrector knows no bounds. He writes of another correction: 'The blunder has lasted two or three centuries, and might have lasted two or three centuries more but for the discovery of this corrected folio.'

And the old corrector not only amends, but inserts new lines, too, lines which according to Collier he may have had directly from the actors in the original productions, or from manuscripts which are no longer available. In *Henry VI Part Two*, the lords determine to remove the Good Duke Humphrey from his position as regent to the young king, and insist that he return his staff of office. Following the first line of his response, the old corrector has added a line (here in italics) to make a rhyming couplet. Humphrey says:

> My staff? Here noble Henry is my staff
> *To think I fain would keep it makes me laugh.*
> *Henry VI Part Two* (Act 2 scene 3)

Collier writes, 'It seems impossible to doubt the genius of the insertion', and promptly announces that he will be incorporating all the emendations in a new edition of Shakespeare. But the more Collier insists how impossible it can be to deny the genius of the old corrector, the more he defies anyone to challenge their obvious merit, the more doubts grow.

Someone threw the first stone. In 1855 a pamphlet titled *Literary Cookery* appeared casting aspersions on Collier's good faith. Stung, Collier took out an affidavit, swearing that he had not added a single emendation to the Perkins Folio, and accused the publisher of libel. The case went to court, but the judge (an old acquaintance of Collier) refused to rule, considering Collier 'a most honourable man'. But this was now a major cause célèbre and the public was agog.

Collier managed to elude the problem of producing the Perkins Folio for inspection by presenting it to his quondam benefactor, the 6th Duke of Devonshire. He had been the 'Bachelor' Duke's librarian thirty years before. However, when the Duke died, the folio became the property of his cousin, the 7th Duke, who presently turned it in for inspection at the British Museum.

Sir Frederic Madden was not only Keeper of Manuscripts at the museum but one of the greatest British palaeographers of the century. Initially, Madden was kindly disposed towards Collier, counting him as a friend. But he was a man of Victorian rectitude, and he proceeded to subject the Perkins Folio to the very latest scientific analysis, including microscopic and chemical tests.

Pencil marks are discovered under the ink. The ink turns out to be sepia-coloured paint over erased pencil annotations. They conclude that the emendations are 'incontestable forgeries', and not only that, the handwriting though superficially similar to a seventeenth-century secretary hand is 'most certainly in a modern hand' and, worse, it bears an 'extraordinary resemblance to Mr Collier's own hand'. Madden declared in his journal, 'I now give up Mr Collier altogether, and think he deserves to be chased from all literary Society.'

At seventy-two, John Payne Collier had been exposed as a fraud, who had fabricated evidence. The Perkins Folio was a sham. His seemingly unassailable reputation as the foremost scholar of his generation, as the first historian of English drama, as the pre-eminent Shakespeare editor of the day, all lay in ruins.

Every document he had ever touched now came under scrutiny. Shakespeare's name had been introduced into a list of the shareholders of the Blackfriars Theatre in 1589. A note had been added to a letter dated 1608 and signed by the Earl of Southampton suggesting that Shakespeare and Burbage were both 'of one countie, and indeed almost of one towne'. Collier had produced 'indisputable' evidence of a performance of *Othello* at Harefield House in August 1602, pre-dating the play's composition by two years. All forgeries.

Attention turned to the documents Collier had been examining in the library of Dulwich College. He had published an edition of the Memoirs of Edward Alleyn in 1841, and, four years later, the first published version of Philip Henslowe's Diaries, that most invaluable document on the day-to-day workings of the theatre in Shakespeare's day. It turned out that the librarian had allowed Collier to take Henslowe's account book home with him indefinitely.

Collier's nemesis was a solicitor called Clement Ingleby, whose detestation of Collier is evident in the following damning statement about the Alleyn and Henslowe archives: 'We know that the great literary slug has crawled over both. What wonder if we shall still be able to trace his slime.'

Professor Schoenbaum (in his definitive *Shakespeare's Lives*, which gives a full account of the scandal) is unequivocal about Collier's guilt. 'No extenuation can be offered for Collier, he forged in deadly earnest for glory, and staked his reputation on his discoveries ... The pity is that Collier was an excellent scholar.'

★ ★ ★

When John Payne Collier was just seventeen he bought what he thought was a First Folio at a bookshop in Baldwin's Gardens. That very copy is now part of the SBT Collection in Stratford-upon-Avon. Browsing through it, I found a note in Collier's hand scribbled on the leaf facing the title page dated 1876. Seventy years after that youthful purchase, Collier, now eighty-seven, recalls the excitement of that teenage transaction: 'I fancied it the first edition and a great prize; and what pleasure I had in making up its deficiencies.'

The folio was missing its title page, which is possibly why the young man rashly and excitedly presumed it was the 1623 Folio. In fact it was not a First Folio, but the second impression of the Third Folio, published in 1664, on the first and otherwise uncelebrated centenary of Shakespeare's birth. It was the first Shakespearian publication since the Restoration. I take a look at the title page. By this time young Collier had realised it was a Third Folio, and he lovingly and painstakingly supplied his own copy of the title page in ink. But the old John Payne Collier's note continues, 'I was then properly ignorant, and was only beginning what I wish I had never begun! J.P.C.'*

Why did he do it? Stephen Tabor has a theory. 'You love your subject so much you want there to be more.' I think that might have been true for Lewis Theobald, and arguably for William-Henry Ireland, but with Payne Collier it seems like plain self-serving skulduggery. The dishonesty was shocking and the impact longterm. How many documents had he forged? And how many scholars who came after Collier had believed those systematic falsifications and drawn conclusions based on flawed evidence?

---

* John Payne Collier is the source for another piece of Shakespeare apocrypha, which I hope one day will prove *not* to be a baseless story. Sidney Lee mentions it in the introduction to his 1902 census, in his account of eighteenth-century sales. He writes '... but nothing is known of the copy, which John Payne Collier reported that he saw in 1869 in Joseph Lilly's shop, bearing in old handwriting, the names of Garrick and Mrs Siddons; it was apparently a gift from the veteran actor to the young actress at the opening of her great career.'

In 1850 he was regarded as one of the foremost scholars of his day, a pre-eminent editor of Shakespeare and the author of over forty books on his subject. A decade later he was the object of universal contempt and execration. His name is ranked among the most infamous in literary history.

I thank Dr Tabor for allowing me to take up so much of his time. But before leaving I ask him what he would save from the Huntington's Collection in the event of a fire. His answer makes me laugh. 'Well, not the First Folio, that's for sure. There are folios enough to pelt dogs with.' He chooses the Ellesmere Chaucer, the unique illuminated manuscript with all those famous illustrations of the Canterbury pilgrims, including Chaucer on horseback.

Chapter Nine
January 2023

I am lying in a bed in intensive care. A nurse has just come to ask me if I know where I am.

'In hospital,' I say. 'Queen Square?'

'You are in the ICU of the Neurology and Neurosurgery Hospital in Queen Square,' she nods. There are various leads attached to me. 'You might have had a stroke,' she adds. 'They're doing some tests.'

I am meant to be heading to Heathrow for a flight to New York for an RSC Development Event with AMEX at Carnegie Hall. But as I was packing this morning the side of my left hand went numb, and it seemed to stretch up the side of my face. I phoned my brother Mark, who told me to dial 999 immediately. My nephew Evan, who has been staying with me, dashed back from the gym the shock on his pale face the most distressing thing about the whole episode. Within half an hour, three ambulance crew were in my living room, and I was having a Zoom consultation on my iPad, before being 'blue-lighted' here, sirens blaring. Now I await results. It's January 2023, the start of the First Folio's quatercentenary year.

I reflect on the last hectic couple of months. Alongside preparing to direct *Cymbeline*, and auditioning actors, I had been packing up the Stratford house, ready for the move back to London before I start rehearsals. I have had a checklist in my head for months and run through it now.

Tony's archive: I shifted most of Tony's artwork to the RSC Collection in Arden Street – the cabin trunk of his acting scripts, the manuscripts of all his journals and novels, and the large plastic storage box of his old diaries, his make-up box, the much-repaired smock he used to paint in, and though the move felt right – the

RSC Collection would be able to care for the whole archive together – nevertheless not having those familiar objects around me is harder than I imagined it would be.

I still haven't moved his toothbrush from the pot on the sink in the bathroom; his towel from the rail; his hairbrush from the shelf; his Filofax from his desk or his crocs from underneath it. I know it's over a year, but I haven't yet moved his clothes from the bedside or his jacket from its hanger in the hall. I can't decide what to do about the sundial. I had had it made for our Stratford home, in 2016, the centenary of the house, with its gnomon representing Shakespeare marching northwards, and the motto: 'Life's but a walking shadow'.

They come to move me upstairs for a CAT scan of my brain. I ask if they think I will still be able to make my flight this evening. They don't know. Intimations of my own mortality are crowded out by checklists. The Islington house now has its new roof. But for months the place has been pestered with Sainsbury's jumbo bags waiting to be emptied, and cluttered with endless cardboard boxes. Jo has shifted piles of clothes to the Shakespeare Hospice and whole shelves worth of books to Oxfam.

The CAT scan done I am returned to the ICU. But the nurse says the blood thinner they have given me means that they have to keep me in overnight for observation, and someone will be moving me upstairs to the ward when a bed becomes free. So not heading to New York tonight. But if I have had a stroke, will they let me travel at all? The doctor arrives to confirm that though the signs are good they do need to keep me in tonight. In the ward, the young Black guy opposite is a great favourite with the staff. He seems very cheerful, but his stroke has robbed him of the power of speech. He keeps smiling across at me and raising a thumb. The old lady in the next bed to me howls throughout the night.

In the darkness of the ward, I find myself reviewing the last year. I lit a Yahrzeit memorial candle on the first anniversary of Tony's death in December. I found the black hardback diaries he had written during his final months. And while clearing his desk I had found his *Dying Diaries* and realised he had begun to shape his thoughts about his cancer into something he intended to publish. I still can't bring myself to read them. Not yet.

And do I move the sundial?

I lie there knowing how lucky I have been but wondering if I care. I will be getting back on a plane, and doing a workshop intended to excite and inspire people about Shakespeare and the work of the RSC and see another eight First Folios at the start of this centenary year. But why?

New York Public Library

The trip to New York was successful. I had to delay my flight by two days, but the workshop was exhilarating. Stephen Greenblatt and I riffed together on Shakespeare and the actors did beautiful work. Alexandra Gilbreath revisited her Olivier-nominated performance as Olivia and heart-rending Hermione, and Lucy Phelps, Tony Byrne and James Cooney reprised their roles in the *Measure for Measure* we had been doing when Covid hit.

They perform the scene in the prison where the Duke, despairing of life, can't see the point of fearing death. He tells the young Claudio to 'Be absolute for Death', complaining even if you reach old age and are prosperous, you have lost your desire, your looks, and your appetite, and no longer care. So what's the point?

> When thou art old and rich,
> Thou hast neither heat, affection, limb, nor beauty
> To make thy riches pleasant. What's yet in this
> That bears the name of life?
>
> *Measure for Measure* (Act 3 scene 1)

I feel shaken by how closely the Duke's words seem to resonate with me.

Then, Claudio, facing a death sentence, tells his sister Isabella of his horrible apprehensions about death: 'Aye, but to die, and go we know not where / To lie in cold obstruction and to rot', ending 'Sweet sister, let me live'. I am moved by how Shakespeare counterbalances the older Duke's despair with the young man's appetite for life.

My visit to the New York Public Library is invigorating. Michael Inman (Curator of Rare Books) and Declan Kieley (Director of Exhibitions) go out of their way to show me around, and the pleasure

Facsimile of Droeshout engraving by Harris in NYPL

they take in their work is palpable and stimulating. First, before the doors open to the public, they show me one of their six folios which is on display in the Polonsky Treasures exhibition. Then there are three folios laid side by side in the Astor Room. My fascination with Harris facsimiles reaches a new high when Michael reveals that one of the folios has two Droeshout engravings, one by the punctilious Harris, that I can genuinely only recognise as a facsimile because of his signature.

I tell my hosts of the torn corner I had found in the 'perfect' copy in Cologne, and Declan tells me what happened when the Irish writer Colum McCann visited the library to view their first edition of *Ulysses*, signed by James Joyce.* As they were putting it away in its box, a minuscule flake fell out. McCann stared at it. And then he writes, 'I did what any heartsick lovesick booksick wordsick world-sick joycestick fool would do. I ate it.' Perhaps I should have been nifty enough back in Cologne to lick my finger, tap up

---

★ The story appears in *Know the Past, Find the Future*, published to celebrate the NYPL's centenary.

the consecrated fragment and pop it on my tongue, though I am not sure what my German hosts would have made of my secular communion.

So many famous folk have come here to see the First Folio. Michael showed Keith Richards a folio. The Rolling Stones guitarist, once dubbed 'the world's most elegantly wasted human being', was promoting his autobiography *Life* when he visited the library in 2010. They were photographed in the majestic Rose Main Reading Room.

Michael points out the rusty imprint of a pair of embroidery scissors in *Romeo and Juliet*; perhaps the owner was sewing while she read, was interrupted and could never remember again where she put them. Declan points out a fascinating quirk in a volume known as 'Lenox Collection Copy A'. At the bottom of the title page it says 'Printed by Isaac Jaggard, and Ed. Blount 1622'.

'1622?' I'm bewildered. 'So is this a genuine early copy?'

Backlighting reveals that the date has been tampered with and the final 2 appears to have been made by overlaying paper to obscure the lower portion of the printed 3 and then overwritten in ink. 'Basically it's a fraud,' says Declan. 'A deceitful owner's attempt to present this volume as the very earliest, in order to increase its value.'

One of the copies of the First Folio the library has was owned by the New York socialite Mrs Mae Caldwell, who once exchanged her million-dollar Fifth Avenue home for a string of pearls. Another by a lawyer who took on the corrupt 'Boss' Tweed and his Tammany Hall Gang. Then they take me out to Long Island City to their conservation lab to show me another two copies that are being prepared for an exhibition of all six folios, later in the year.

We spot a reddish-brown blotch in a sort of stain pool in the gutter of *Love's Labour's Lost*, and wonder whether it's a squashed flea. Everyone is pondering the problem, and sharing thoughts. I sit back and bask in their intense knowledge and excitement about books. Then Michael and Declan outdo themselves by actually walking me to my next folios, down Madison Avenue at the Morgan Library. I am overwhelmed by their kindness and generosity, and promise to keep in touch. The Morgan Library's two copies are going to have a struggle to match up.

But, of course, the Morgan does not disappoint.

This fine library and museum houses the collections which the railroad financier John Pierpont Morgan built at the height of the city's age of elegance. Stepping inside, several worlds converge and collide: from its classical façade and marble interiors inspired by Renaissance Italy, with book-lined rooms adorned with majestic tapestries and high decorated ceilings, all seamlessly integrated around the modern glass piazza (with café), to the elegant freestanding brownstone on the corner of Madison and 36th, which now houses the shop. This was once the home of J. P. Morgan's son Jack, who opened his father's collection to the public in 1924. It is all created from the desire to collect, to preserve, to interpret and to share the treasures of the past.

I am hosted by curator Jesse Erickson in the North Parlour, where his team are laying out the Morgan's two First Folios ready for me to see. The first contains a note boasting it is 'the largest and finest copy known'. It certainly bears two handsome crests on both front and back, belonging to Robert Sidney, 2nd Earl of Leicester (1595–1677), nephew to the great Elizabethan poet Philip Sidney. But it's another fraud. The book's previous owner, James Toovey, exchanged the volume's binding for this one in order to present a more prestigious provenance. Mr Toovey bought the volume for £255 in 1887. J. P. Morgan purchased it twelve years later, unaware of the binding's substitution, for in excess of £1,000.

Intriguingly, this copy has a 'cancel leaf', the final page of *Romeo and Juliet* with the first page of *Troilus and Cressida* on the reverse of it, as well as the Prologue to *Troilus* and reprint of the first page. This is further evidence of the confusion caused when the publishing syndicate failed to secure the rights to *Troilus and Cressida* before they started printing. The original plan had been to place *Troilus and Cressida* after *Romeo and Juliet*, but when they realised that they could not establish the rights, having already started typesetting the play, they had to rethink. While they did so, this 'cancel' page was left in.* Paper was too expensive to waste, and this copy went on sale with the corrected page still there. A copy at Meisei University in Japan is one of the early copies that was purchased without *Troilus and Cressida* before the rights issue was resolved.

---

* There is another cancel page of the last page of *Romeo and Juliet* in Folger 11.

Eventually the printers were instructed to replace *Troilus and Cressida* with *Timon of Athens*, which, in most folios, follows *Romeo and Juliet*. This explains one of the many pagination oddities in the folio, as *Romeo and Juliet* jumps from page 77 to 79, and is then followed by page 80, the first page of *Timon*. And, finally, when the rights were secured, instead of removing *Timon*, and placing *Troilus and Cressida* where it was originally intended, they crammed it in between the Histories and the Tragedies.

This caused its own problems, as the last of the history plays, *Henry VIII*, finished on the left-hand side (the verso) of the page, the same side that the already printed first pages of *Troilus and Cressida* had been printed. Therefore an entire recto page had to be filled. Thus, the long prologue to *Troilus and Cressida* ('In Troy there lies the scene ...') was given an entire page to itself. As it appears in neither version of the quarto editions published in 1609, it is intriguing to know whether it comes from Shakespeare's own manuscript (known as 'foul papers'), or perhaps from the theatre's prompt book copy.

On the frontispiece of the Morgan's second copy of the folio in light brown ink are the words *Ex biblioteca H. A. Hadermanni.*

It is the first known acquisition of a folio in Germany. Johann Heinrich Hadermann (1710–85) was the rector of a school just north-east of Frankfurt. I recall the discussions I had in Frankfurt about the German love of Shakespeare. Perhaps it is not a coincidence that the first completed German translation of Shakespeare's plays appeared in the eighteenth century, during Hadermann's lifetime, while three King Georges served simultaneously as dual monarchs of England and of Hanover. How it got from Germany to Madison Avenue, however, is a mystery.

Chapter Ten
Stratford, Westminster Abbey, Windsor Castle

Cymbeline

The rehearsals for *Cymbeline* began at the end of February 2023, and the first preview coincides with the annual celebrations in Stratford for Shakespeare's birthday in April. At dawn that day I walked along the Avon to Clopton Bridge, to the place I had scattered half of Tony's ashes just a year ago, and threw a small, dried protea into the river. The nurses from the Shakespeare Hospice who had laid out his body the morning after his death had found the flower in a vase in the kitchen and, unaware that it was the national flower of South Africa, had laid it on his pillow.

I miss Tony all the time, but I wish especially that he was with me today. I have been offered the Pragnell Shakespeare prize. He would have felt such 'nachas' from that. I can hear him relish the guttural joy of the word. 'Nachas' – it's a Yiddish expression describing the pride folk get from the accomplishments of their kids. Without him by my side the day will feel thinner.

The Pragnell is to be presented that afternoon at the birthday lunch, in a huge marquee erected on the lawn in the Theatre Gardens. I am honoured and flattered; it's a prestigious award. The only trouble is we are scheduled to be doing our dress rehearsal that afternoon, which means I won't be able to attend. The producing team, in consultation with the crew and backstage staff, make the unprecedented call that, barring any hiccups, they can bring the dress rehearsal forward and complete it in the morning, at least in time for me to get to the post-lunch presentation.

The dress went smoothly, and I felt that evening's preview would be fine, but nevertheless my head was full of notes of the things I wanted to change, of lines we could cut, of sequences that still needed clarification, of cues I could tighten, of themes I wanted to strengthen, and I arrived at the marquee feeling ruffled and distracted and calculating how long it would be before I could get away. And then one of those moments occurred which stops you in your tracks, and slaps your preposterous ego across the face.

On the stage delivering the toast 'to the immortal memory of the Bard' is a Ukrainian professor called Nataliya Torkut. She is Head of the Ukrainian Shakespeare Centre in Zaporizhzhia, and this is the first time she has left Ukraine since Russia invaded in February 2022. She has been continuing her work hosting online seminars, and taking part in academic events, often from bomb shelters. As I stand and listen, she is talking about how important it is for people during the war to survive not only physically, but spiritually and mentally as well. 'We keep reading Shakespeare,' she says, 'because we need something that helps us to feel that life is worth living.'

'Shakespeare has always been a manifestation of our resistance to Russian colonial oppression,' said the professor. In 1863, when Ukraine was part of the Russian Empire, Russian leaders banned the translation and staging of Shakespeare in the Ukrainian language. 'Nevertheless, the first translations of Shakespeare appeared at this very time, and amateur companies performed *Hamlet*,' she said. 'Since that time Shakespeare is considered to be the person who helps us demonstrate our disobedience to the imperial power of Moscow.'

President Volodymyr Zelenskyy himself quoted *Hamlet* in a speech to the British Parliament weeks after Russia's full-scale invasion. 'The question for us now is: To be or not to be?' he said. 'We decided "to be",' said Professor Torkut, 'and we decided to fight.'

Overnight, Ukraine reported a wave of Russian aerial attacks across the front lines, from Kharkiv in the north-east to Odessa in the south-west. Professor Torkut has been glued to her phone for updates on these latest airstrikes. She is anxious to hear from her son who is fighting on the frontline. She has found numerous parallels with Ukraine's situation in Shakespeare's works, comparing

Zelenskyy with Henry V. 'His evolution from Prince to King, we have seen it with our own eyes.' Henry's rousing St Crispin's Day speech bolsters his small army, which is unexpectedly victorious against the more numerous French. 'At the very beginning of the war, we felt like those soldiers – with no weapons, no support,' said Professor Torkut. 'Zelenskyy is appealing to the nation, to those on the frontline.'

'I do believe that William Shakespeare, and culture in general, can help us survive this cruel war. It is the essence of our human nature that we can't live without beauty, without something that is much more important than our everyday situation.'

That night at our first preview, with Professor Torkut in the audience, we heard so many lines with different ears, like Cymbeline's lines about Rome's invasion of Britain:

> Caesar's ambition
> Which swelled so much that it did almost stretch
> The sides of the world, against all colour here,
> Did put the yoke upon's, which to shake off
> Becomes a warlike people ...
>
> *Cymbeline* (Act 3 scene 1)

As the preview drew to a close, and against all odds Britain had overcome the might of Rome, Cymbeline's prayer for peace sounded more fresh and urgent:

> Laud we the gods;
> And let our crooked smokes climb to their nostrils
> From our blest altars.
>
> (Act 5 scene 5)

As the company turn to the sun, and Stephen Brimson Lewis's dazzling solar disc burns brighter and Paul Englishby's uplifting score rises to its sublime climax, I feel the company have allowed the hope in Shakespeare's late play to be fully realised in our world now; and that with a few more tweaks and a bit more tightening, I can be proud of this production to stand as my RSC swan song.

The Coronation

In the summer of 2022, Prince Charles had agreed to show me the First Folio held at Windsor Castle. 'Now the man is king,' I thought, 'he'll be far too busy.' Then, suddenly I received an invitation to the Coronation. Now here I am sitting in Westminster Abbey. There have been calls that it is an extravagance during a cost-of-living crisis, while others insist that it boosts trade. It has been scaled back. The late Queen Elizabeth had 8,000 guests in the Abbey. Today I am one of only 2,000, and feel all the more honoured to be among the company.

The gentleman sitting next to me in the Abbey is resplendent in full tartan regalia with kilt. He is Ian from Dundee. His partner is in the procession and recently accompanied the Stone of Scone from Scotland when it was returned to be replaced in the Coronation chair last month. He tells me how moving it was to be so close to such a resonant relic. The Stone of Destiny. John Major returned it to Scotland in the 1990s, Ian says, to stave off calls for independence. It took a good deal of complex manoeuvring to get it back in place in the throne.

As I settle waiting for the ceremony to begin, I start to ponder how many coronations I have staged in my time. In our open rehearsal project on *Henry VI Part One* two summers ago, I had the props department dust down the Coronation Chair we had used in the King and Country cycle. Chris from Props had travelled up to Westminster Abbey and we had been allowed to measure the actual chair, and they had reproduced it faithfully, right down to the latticework under the seat, and the graffiti on the back. That prop throne travelled the world with us and toured to China and the United States.

Henry VI opens with the funeral of the hero warrior-king Henry V, but his son, the saintly Henry VI, is not crowned until the start of Act 4 in Paris, amid turbulent attempts to secure the French territories won by his father. The crown will be tossed backwards and forwards through the Wars of the Roses plays, featuring a mock coronation of York with a paper crown by the ferocious Queen Margaret. Then, last year in *Richard III*, any coronation splendour was immediately undercut as Richard realised there was no joy in being enthroned if the Princes in the Tower were still able to challenge his right to reign.

My first coronation was Anne Boleyn's in *Henry VIII*, a grand display of Magnificence, accompanied by gilded heraldic beasts held aloft. The Macbeths had a rather dour ceremony in our production with an acclamation blasted out through tinny loudspeakers. In *King John* the neurotic king insists on a second crowning to secure his shaky position, an act derided by his courtiers who cry:

> To guard a title that was rich before,
> To gild refined gold, to paint the lily,
> To throw a perfume on the violet …
> Is wasteful and ridiculous excess.
>
> *King John* (Act 4 scene 2)

I had spotted the State Trumpeters of the Household Cavalry assembling up in a gallery across the nave by the great west door, their trumpets hung with the sovereign's standard. The clock ticking towards eleven. And with a loud flourish the Coronation began.

The procession moved past me through the body of the Abbey, from the stone flagging in the nave to the royal blue carpet in the quire, to the golden-yellow carpet where the Chairs of Estate are placed in what the order of service describes as the 'Theatre of Coronation' reminding me of how theatrical all this is, how carefully stage-managed, how deliberately designed for maximum impact. The Coronation Chair is placed on the great Cosmati pavement facing the high altar.

And thrillingly theatrical is the first beat. A child greets the King saying with great confidence: 'Your Majesty, as children of the kingdom of God, we welcome you in the name of the King of kings.' He is a young chorister from the Chapel Royal. His welcome prompts a reply from the King which seems designed to set the tone for the ceremony and by extension for the reign: 'In his name and after his example I come not to be served but to serve.'

The poignancy and power of the ceremony is deeply enhanced by the singing of that most iconic anthem composed by Handel for the Coronation of George II in 1727, describing the anointing of King

Solomon. As it builds slowly through its incredible sustained crescendo, rising in anticipation and excitement before bursting into the acclamation 'Zadok the Priest', I can't help but find myself incredibly moved. And I know it's all designed to have precisely that effect. Nevertheless, it is an overwhelming feeling to be here in this place where kings have been crowned for nearly a thousand years, and to witness the solemn anointing of a man I have come to know as President of the RSC for the last thirty years. He is the thirty-ninth British monarch to be crowned in this very place.

Windsor Castle

> Not all the water in the rough rude sea
> Can wash the balm off from an anointed king;
> The breath of worldly men cannot depose
> The deputy elected by the Lord …
>
> *Richard II* (Act 3 scene 2)

Despite my misgivings, the King kept his promise and in July invited me to see the folios held in the Royal Library at Windsor Castle. He is after all a genuine Shakespeare enthusiast.

The Windsor First Folio was purchased by the Prince of Wales, later George IV, for his library at Carlton House. I had already seen the inferior copy he inherited from his father, which he donated to the British Library. But it is the Second Folio held here that I want to see. There were relatively few changes made between the First and Second Folio, published nine years later in 1632. A number of typographical errors were corrected, *Troilus and Cressida* is finally included in the contents page and a new and uncredited dedicatory poem has been added: the first published poem by a 24-year-old John Milton. It contains the lines:

> Thou in our wonder and astonishment
> Hast built thyself a lasting monument.

The striking fact about Windsor's Second Folio is that it was read by King Charles I while he was imprisoned at Carisbrooke Castle, on the Isle of Wight, before his execution. His initials are written in the frontispiece along with his motto *Dum spiro, spero* – 'while I breathe, I hope'. We are being filmed for a documentary to coincide with the quatercentenary year. An old friend, the eminent Shakespeare scholar and writer Jonathan Bate, is on hand to provide expertise.

'Do we know what he was reading?' says the King. He'd want cheering up, wouldn't he? And the evidence points towards that. We look at the annotations Charles I made in the copy, in particular to the titles of the plays on the catalogue page. For example, *Twelfth Night* is Malvolio; *As You Like It* becomes Rosalind; and *A Midsummer Night's Dream* is Pyramus and Thisbe. The King is clearly naming the plays by their most significant characters so he can remember which is which, as their titles are otherwise enigmatic.

Jonathan has discovered that according to John Milton, Charles I not only read the plays at Carisbrooke, but had also read them when he was briefly held here at Windsor. Milton published a report to Parliament* in which he writes: 'The King is pretty merry, and spends much time in reading of Sermon Books, and sometimes Shakspeare and Ben Johnsons Playes.' And later Milton provided further evidence for Charles I's attachment to Shakespeare's works towards the end of his life, describing the folio as 'the Closest Companion of these his solitudes'.

'I never knew that King Charles I had annotated this copy,' says the King. 'Whenever I go up to see one of the plays at Stratford,' he continues, 'I will write down some line I have heard that I particularly want to remember, and then I will put it into my own copy when I get home.'

'Forget the folio,' I say, 'that's the edition of Shakespeare that I want to see.'

And to my surprise the King says: 'Well, come along and I'll show it to you if you like.'

After the filming session, as we walk through the State Apartments our conversation turns to the Coronation.

'Did you know … I certainly didn't,' he says, 'that the area in the Abbey where the actual Coronation took place is called the Theatre?'

---

* Milton's report from Windsor was published in the semi-official mouthpiece of Parliament, *Perfect Occurrences of Every Daies Journall in Parliament, 22 to 30 December 1648.*

And we ponder the similarities in terms of presentation and ritual of performance. I say the music was magnificent, in particular the music chosen for before the ceremony. 'Yes,' he laughs, 'I rather missed all that.'

We walk through into the private apartments and into his study. The King moves to his desk and picks up his complete works. Not a grand copy, but one he was given on his twenty-first birthday. And he hands it to me for my inspection. It is stuffed with small notepad pages on which he has scribbled lines he wants to remember.

Many of them are about kingship. I turn to a page in *Henry V*. It's the night before the Battle of Agincourt, when the young king goes about among his army to test the mood of his men, what that unreliable narrator the Chorus describes as 'A little touch of Harry in the night'. He is shocked to discover their animosity and defends the role he is set to play:

> I think the king is but a man, as I am: the violet smells to him as it doth to me: the element shows to him as it doth to me; all his senses have but human conditions: his ceremonies laid by, in his nakedness he appears but a man; and though his affections are higher mounted than ours, yet, when they stoop, they stoop with the like wing. Therefore when he sees reason of fears, as we do, his fears, out of doubt, be of the same relish as ours are: yet, in reason, no man should possess him with any appearance of fear, lest he, by showing it, should dishearten his army.
>
> *Henry V* (Act 4 scene 1)

King Charles has marked the speech which follows it, in which Hal is disconcerted by his encounter with the common soldiers, Williams, Bates and Court. He turns from prose to introspective verse:

> Upon the king! let us our lives, our souls,
> Our debts, our careful wives,
> Our children and our sins lay on the king!
>
> We must bear all.
>   O hard condition,
> Twin-born with greatness, subject to the breath

> Of every fool, whose sense no more can feel
> But his own wringing!
>   What infinite heart's-ease
> Must kings neglect, that private men enjoy!
> And what have kings, that privates have not too,
> Save ceremony, save general ceremony?
>   … No, thou proud dream,
> That play'st so subtly with a king's repose;
> I am a king that find thee, and I know
> 'Tis not the balm, the sceptre and the ball,
> The sword, the mace, the crown imperial,
> The intertissued robe of gold and pearl,
> The farced title running 'fore the king,
> The throne he sits on, nor the tide of pomp
> That beats upon the high shore of this world,
> No, not all these, thrice-gorgeous ceremony,
> Not all these, laid in bed majestical,
> Can sleep so soundly as the wretched slave …
>
>   (Act 4 scene 1)

Here is a note in *Richard II*. The death of kings. And the King begins to read it – 'and there the antic sits, grinning at his state and scoffing at his pomp, allowing him to monarchise, be feared and kill with looks, infusing him with self and vain conceit' – and I am able to complete the quotation for him from memory:

> … As if this flesh which walls about our life,
> Were brass impregnable, and humour'd thus
> Comes at the last and with a little pin
> Bores through his castle wall, and farewell king.

The mention of death has recent poignancy for us both.

'How are you coping?' he asks, putting his hand on my arm.

'It hurts,' I say. 'It just hurts.'

Chapter Eleven
'Slippery Times'

> What subject can give sentence on his king?
> *Richard II* (Act 4 scene 1)

There are two folios and two portraits I encounter on the Roadshow that tell the story of the troubled decades of the mid-seventeenth century. One folio was owned by a man who signed Charles I's death warrant; one by a man who helped the king's son escape after the Battle of Worcester. One a Puritan Parliamentarian, the other a Royalist sympathiser. Of the two portraits, the first is of a man we have already met: the King's Man whom the owner of the Glasgow Folio knew *by eye-witnesse*, John Lowin.

By the time the Second Folio is published in 1632, Hemmings and Condell have both died, the old guard left over from the Lord Chamberlain's Men have finally passed, and Lowin and Joseph Taylor are left running the King's Men. They are challenging times. For the last two years, Charles I has embarked on a period of personal autocratic rule, having refused to call Parliament.

That same year, as well as the Second Folio, a book called *Histriomastix, or The Players' Scourge* is published by the extreme Puritan William Prynne. It runs to over a thousand pages and is the most notorious attack on theatre in English history. Prynne fizzes with fury at the state of the kingdom, and fulminates against all stage plays, masques and every kind of entertainment from bear-baiting to maypoles. The book dares to criticise the queen herself, and the triviality of her court. Prynne is tried by the Star Chamber, imprisoned, whipped, has his ears lopped and his nose split. Change is in the air.

At the centre of Queen Henrietta Maria's court circle is Sir John Suckling.

His full-length portrait by Anthony van Dyck is part of the Frick Collection in New York. Here the young spark stands 'a slight-timbered man, and of middling stature' in his Prussian-blue knee-length tunic, with a scalloped cape draped over one shoulder, and a pair of tan mid-calf Roman booties. Suckling stares into the middle distance trying to insist we take him seriously. But we can't. The book he is so ostentatiously holding is a Shakespeare Folio, and it is open at *Hamlet*. It is the first depiction in art of the First Folio.

Suckling's exotic costume may well be from a production of his own play *Aglaura*, a tragedy set in Persia. *Aglaura* marks the tipping point not only for the King's Men but for the decline of early modern drama. It was produced at Blackfriars not because of its merit, but because Suckling paid for the costumes – embroidered with gold and silver thread. When it was performed at court the following year, Suckling gave the play a happy ending to suit its audience's frivolous taste, then published it in a grandiose folio edition.

On the rock against which Suckling leans in the Van Dyck portrait, an inscription reads *Ne te quaesiveris extra*, or 'Don't seek outside yourself'. It is from the Roman poet Persius. Is it advocating self-reliance, or neurotic self-confident egotism? Suckling, the spendthrift lothario with an addiction to gambling, is here adopting a pose as a serious thinker. He surely bears a closer resemblance to the waterfly Osric than to the moody Dane.

When the king recalled Parliament in 1640, Suckling was returned as an MP. But in the chaos that followed he was embroiled in a plot to rescue the Earl of Strafford, an ardent supporter of the king, from prison. He was charged by Parliament with high treason and fled to Paris, where John Aubrey says, 'reflecting on the miserable and despicable condition he should be reduced to, having nothing left to maintain him, he took poison, which killed him miserably with vomiting'. He was thirty-two.

★ ★ ★

1640 is the date John Lowin has his portrait painted. It is held at the Ashmolean in Oxford but is not on display. The museum's Director, Xa Sturgis, kindly agreed to take me down to the store to see it. You can see what good casting Lowin must have been for Henry VIII, which he was playing on the afternoon the Globe burned down in 1613. I try persuading Dr Sturgis just how important I feel this portrait is. It is one of only a handful of pictures we have of the actors of the King's Men, along with the Chandos portrait of Shakespeare himself in the National Portrait Gallery, and the Dulwich portraits of Richard Burbage, 'Nid' Field and William Sly.

Here is Lowin aged sixty-four, about to face the most catastrophic period in theatre history. Two years after it was painted, on 22 August 1642, the king raised his standard at Nottingham and effectively declared war on his own people and Parliament. Within a fortnight the theatres were ordered to close. Lowin and Taylor were among many of the actors in London to sign a desperate petition called The Actors' Remonstrance appealing against 'the silencing of their profession and banishment from their severall play-houses', to no avail.

With the theatres closed, the audience's appetite for plays could only be satisfied by reading them. In 1647 a new folio edition of collected plays joined the folios of Jonson and Shakespeare. Beaumont and Fletcher's plays had been a core part of the repertoire of the King's Men. Fletcher had succeeded Shakespeare as the chief dramatist of the company. The publisher, Humphrey Moseley, wrote:

> For since we saw no plays this cloudy weather
> Here have we brought ye our whole stock together.

The dedication to this new folio was signed by a number of the now unemployed actors in the King's Men, including Joseph Taylor and John Lowin.

On 5 February 1648, Lowin and Taylor were appearing in a clandestine production of *The Bloody Brother* at the Cockpit when the theatre was raided by Parliamentarian soldiers. The actors were hauled off to prison in their costumes. Within a week a much more severe act of Parliament was published. *An Ordinance for the utter suppression and abolishing of all Stage-Plays and Interludes* provided for the demolition of theatre seating, fines for any spectators and the treatment of actors as 'rogues'. The Globe was eventually pulled down 'to make tenements in the room of it', the Fortune met with a similar fate, and at the Hope Theatre one Saturday morning in February 'Seven of Mr Godfrey's bears ... were shot to death by a company of soldiers'.

John Lowin went to run a pub, the Three Pigeons in Brentford, and died at the age of eighty-two in 1659.

★ ★ ★

> We charge you, that you have contrived to take
> From Rome all season'd office and to wind
> Yourself into a power tyrannical;
> For which you are a traitor to the people.
>
> *Coriolanus* (Act 3 scene 3)

There are two folios owned by military men on either side of the political divide in the English Civil War.

Colonel John Hutchinson sat on the panel of judges charged with deciding the fate of King Charles I, and was one of the fifty-nine signatories to his death warrant in 1649. Two years later, in 1651, Colonel John Lane helped King Charles II escape from the Battle of Worcester.

But it is the women in their lives whose stories fascinate me: Colonel Hutchinson's fiercely loyal wife Lucy, and Colonel Lane's courageous sister Jane. The different paths they both took, and the choices they both made, demonstrate the divisions of those 'slippery times'.

Lucy Hutchinson's *Memoirs of the Life of Colonel Hutchinson* was only found in the nineteenth century, in an old trunk. It became an influential perspective on the causes and progress of the civil war. Here Lucy describes the king's trial in January 1649 at which her husband reluctantly served as a commissioner:

> The king was brought to his trial, and the charge drawn up against him for levying war against the parliament and people of England, for betraying the public trust reposed in him, and for being an implacable

enemy to the commonwealth. But the king refused to plead, disowning the authority of the court, and after three several days persisting in contempt thereof, he was sentenced to death.

Ten days after the trial, on a cold January morning, the execution scaffold had been erected outside the Banqueting House in Whitehall. Inside, Charles must have stared up at the magnificent coffered ceiling he himself had commissioned twenty years before from the great Flemish artist Peter Paul Rubens. It depicts the apotheosis of King James I, assumed into a heavenly pantheon, and was intended to celebrate the achievements of his father and of the Stuart dynasty. King Charles stepped out through the open window and onto the black-draped scaffold. One witness commented: 'There was such a groan by the thousands then present as I never heard before and desire I may never hear again.'

★ ★ ★

In 1651 the Coronation of Charles I's son took place at Scone, in the heart of Perthshire, the last king to be crowned there. Young King Charles had returned from exile in Paris to claim his father's throne. Once crowned, he rallied an army in Scotland and marched south. But Oliver Cromwell, leading his New Model Army, in a force which vastly outnumbered the king's troops, pursued him to the city of Worcester.

The king watched the battle rage around the city walls from the tower of the ancient cathedral. When Cromwell's Parliamentarian soldiers overwhelmed the Royalist sympathisers, the king and his closest allies made a dash for it and galloped through the St Martin's Gate to the north-west. The most iconic episode in the king's escape took place near Boscobel House. The king himself recounted the story many years later to Samuel Pepys:

> We went and got up into a great oak, that had been lopped some three or four years before, and being grown out again, very bushy and thick, could not be seen through, and we stayed all the day ... while we were in this tree we see soldiers going up and down, in the thicket of the wood, searching for persons escaped.

It was soon decided to move the king to Bentley Hall, to the protection of Colonel John Lane. His sister Jane had been granted a permit to travel to Bristol where a close relative was due to give birth. The king would accompany her as her manservant, in a suit of grey cloth. He would be referred to as William Jackson for the duration of the journey.

Jane rode pillion behind her servant Jackson. She was accompanied by her sister and her husband, and Henry Lassells, a Royalist officer relation. Henry Wilmot travelled with them but refused to go in disguise so rode on about half a mile ahead. They made their way south.

As the party approached Wootton Wawen, about four miles outside Stratford-upon-Avon, they encountered a troop of Parliamentarian soldiers blocking the road outside an inn. Jane's sister's husband refused to go on as he had been beaten by soldiers in the past, and they had to make a detour. The party waded across the Avon at Stratford (one of the arches of Clopton Bridge having been destroyed by Parliamentarian forces) and finally travelled via Chipping Camden and Cirencester through Chipping Sodbury to Bristol, to Abbots Leigh on the other side of the Avon Gorge. Here George Norton's wife was very close to giving birth. In the three days the party spent under their roof, the Nortons never suspected they had a royal guest.

One morning, the king came down and found some of the servants at breakfast. One was giving an account of the Battle of Worcester and turned out to have been in the king's own regiment. Fearing discovery, they decided it was too dangerous to stay in Abbots Leigh.

> But the night before we were to go away ... Mrs Norton who was big with child, fell into labour, and miscarried of a dead child, and was very ill; so that we could not tell how in the world to find an excuse for Mrs Lane to leave her cousin in that condition, and indeed, it was not safe to stay longer where there was so great resort of disaffected idle people.

They faked a letter from Jane's father saying he was close to death and she must return. Jane continued with the king until they reached Trent, and then returned with Henry Lassells to Bentley Hall. The king and Wilmot made their way down to the south coast and eventually found shipping to France. When Jane got back home she discovered that her part in the king's escape had been reported, and the Council of State had put out a warrant for her arrest. If she were to be caught her sentence would certainly have been death. Audaciously, she disguised herself as an ordinary country woman, and walked south, a journey of nearly 150 miles, crossing to Yarmouth on the Isle of Wight. When she arrived in Paris in December 1651, the king greeted her with 'Welcome my life'.

★ ★ ★

He would be crown'd:
How that might change his nature, there's the question.
It is the bright day that brings forth the adder;
And that craves wary walking.

Julius Caesar (Act 2 scene 1)

During the interregnum, Cromwell took control of the country. Under his protectorate, the Hutchinsons decided to retire to their family estate in Owethorpe. John Hutchinson suspected Cromwell not only of aiming for the presidency for life, but for the crown, and eventually broke entirely from him. Cromwell died in 1658, a disillusioned man. He had failed to create a working Parliament and his incompetent son and heir, Richard, was forced to resign as Lord Protector. Rather than endure another civil war, Parliament invited the late king's son to return to rule.

★ ★ ★

At the Restoration in 1660, in the Act of Oblivion, King Charles II promised pardon for all crimes committed during the Commonwealth period except for those regicides responsible for the execution of his father, primarily the fifty-nine men who had signed the death warrant. Cromwell had been buried in the aisle of Westminster Abbey. The new king had him dug up, dragged to Tyburn, and his corpse hanged, drawn and quartered. The decapitated head was then placed on a spike above Westminster Hall, the very place where Charles I had been tried. Colonel John Hutchinson's life hung in the balance, until eventually he was spared execution. Lucy describes her husband's final imprisonment at Sandown Castle, in Deal in Kent, 'a lamentable old ruined place', until at last: 'The Lord of hosts sent his holy angels to fetch him out of their cruel hands up to his everlasting and blessed rest above.'

★ ★ ★

A portrait of Jane Lane showing her holding a crown partially covered by a veil, demonstrates her role in concealing the identity of the monarch, and delivering him from the hands of his enemies. A scroll of script hanging from a nail in the corner reads *sic, sic, iuvat ire sub umbra*. It is a line from Book IV of Virgil's *Aeneid*: 'Thus, thus, I am pleased to go into the shadows'. They are the final words of Queen Dido after Aeneas abandoned her and sailed from Carthage to his destiny, the founding of the Roman nation. *Sic, sic* ('Thus, thus') she cries as she stabs herself with her lover's sword, claiming she is content to go to the land of shades. Some think that Jane Lane fell in love with the young king, and that the scroll casts her as the abandoned Dido, lamenting the sacrifice she made.

I find it fascinating that these two families, the Lanes and the Hutchinsons, on either side of the political divide, should have owned First Folios. We can't know how deeply they read Shakespeare, or whether or not they found their own perspectives accommodated in his words. Part of the supple genius of his work is his ability to articulate both sides of the story.

★ ★ ★

After the Restoration the ban on theatre was lifted and two new companies were granted royal licences: the King's Company under Thomas Killigrew, and the Duke's under Sir William Davenant. And in 1663 a new edition of the folio was prepared for publication, with a second issue appearing the following year. The publishers clearly thought they needed to include some added incentive to persuade people to buy the Third Folio, so seven new Shakespeare plays were added. Only one of them, *Pericles*, do we now regard as by Shakespeare. The others included a play about Sir John Oldcastle

(Shakespeare's original name for Falstaff for which he had to publish a retraction: 'for Oldcastle died a martyr and this is not the man'), another about Thomas Cromwell, as well as *The London Prodigal, The Puritan Widow, Locrine* and *A Yorkshire Tragedy*.

Two years later, when the Great Fire of London broke out in 1666, the stationers ran with as much stock as they could carry into their chapel, St Faith's under St Paul's, in the crypt of the cathedral. They were not to know that the flames would rage so fiercely that the six acres of lead on the roof of St Paul's would melt and cascade through the vaulted roof, break into St Faith and incinerate all the stock. According to diarist John Evelyn, it burned 'for a week following'. Among that stock were all the unsold copies of the new folio edition. That is why the Third Folio is the rarest of all the four seventeenth-century editions today.

PART FIVE

'I' th' east my pleasure lies':
Japan, Australia, New Zealand and South Africa

Bronze of Shakespeare in Auckland Public Library

Chapter Twelve
Japan and 'The Unknown World'

Friday 2 June 2023

The captain has just welcomed us on board, tells us the flight time to Tokyo is expected to be around eleven hours and announces that, as we can no longer fly over Russian airspace, our route today, instead of taking us north, will be taking us south. Normally the flight path heads through Scandinavia, above the Arctic Circle and over the Siberian Plain.

A few hours on, and I open the in-flight map to find out where we are. The plane is flying across a large body of water. I don't recognise the names of the cities or the coast below me: Ardesen, Batumi, Poti and Zugdidi. Then I track up above the horizon line and see names which over the last year we have learned how to pronounce: Kharkiv and Donetsk. Names that have become bywords for struggle, defiance and endurance.

So this large body of water below me is the Black Sea, the edge of the known world to the Greeks, the world of the Argonauts, of Colchis and the Golden Fleece. These are the distant lands known to Shakespeare as Tartary, home to Scythians and Cimmerians and Mithridates, King of Pont. Othello calls this ocean the Pontic Sea:

> Whose icy current and compulsive course
> Ne'er feels retiring ebb, but keeps due on
> To the Propontic and the Hellespont …
>
> *Othello* (Act 3 scene 3)

We will be flying over Tbilisi, and following the route of the Silk Road into Armenia and Uzbekistan. Then we will skirt

North Korea, fly across South Korea and land at Haneda Airport in Japan.

My room at the Metropolitan Hotel in Ikebukuro won't be available until 3 p.m. I ring my host, Matthew Knowles, the head of the British Council in Japan. Within half an hour he greets me at the wheel of a driverless car and whisks me off to buy croissants. The car's owner, his neighbour Benoit, is sitting in the back seat and encouraging Matthew not to be nervous. But as we make our way over the high-sided freeways that loop over the city, every time Matthew lets go of the wheel the car threatens to veer into the barrier. I suspect the technology has some way to go.

We go over the week's schedule. I am visiting First Folios in Kobe tomorrow, then at Meisei University and in Kyoto, and delivering a lecture for the Daiwa Anglo-Japanese Foundation at the British ambassador's residence. Then Matthew gives me a little reminder of the bewildering contrasts of ancient and modern in this remarkable country. First in Shibuya, he takes me to a junction where several roads meet amid neon-clad skyscrapers. At one end of a zebra crossing I notice that there are four other pedestrian crossings spanning the space and every one of them is crowded with people waiting to cross. Suddenly all the traffic lights change together and a tide of humanity surges across. As many as 3,000 people use the Shibuya Scramble Crossing every two minutes. It is the busiest pedestrian intersection in the world.

Lines from Wordsworth's *The Prelude* pop into my head. Having left the Lake District, he sees London stretched out before him from the top of Highgate Hill:

Thou monstrous Anthill on the plain of a too busy world.
Thou endless stream of men and moving things.

As we hit the centre of the junction, amid the ordered chaos Matthew takes my photo, and tweets it with the Wordsworth quotation. Welcome to Tokyo.

Kobe

I am on the Shinkansen to Kobe to see my first Japanese 1623 Folio. From the moment the Shinkansen first drew out of Tokyo Station in

1964 it was nicknamed the bullet train for the speed of its service: 1964, the year of the Tokyo Olympics and of Shakespeare's 400th birthday. 'The Shinkansen is symbolic of Japan's economic recovery, and future drive and remains a source of national pride', my twenty-year-old guidebook tells me. We speed past the unmistakable flanks of Mount Fuji as the sacred mountain rises suddenly and steeply from the Kantō Plain.

Andrew Eglinton, a lecturer in performance studies here at Konan Women's University, is my guide for the day. He tells me that the university is very familiar with the performance of Shakespeare's plays. Since a production of *As You Like It* in 1966, they produced one a year, spoken in English with an all-female cast. Sadly, Covid interrupted the tradition, and this year Andrew tells me they are producing Ibsen's *A Doll's House*.

Leafing through Konan's Folio, one of the cleanest and brightest I have seen, I come across some tiny crosses in *The Comedy of Errors*. One is inked alongside a line of Egeon's. He is the father of the twins around whom the mistaken identity plot revolves, and he has spent years trying to find his sons:

Five summers have I spent in farthest Greece,
Roaming clean through the bounds of Asia ...
The Comedy of Errors (Act 1 scene 1)

I find the serendipity of that piece of common-placing rather pleasing as, in Western terms at any rate, here I am on my quest 'roaming the bounds of Asia'. I wonder what significance those lines had for the original owner.

Konan University's fine collection affords me a very special opportunity to compare three of their different manuscripts. I turn to *Henry V* in the 1623 Folio, to Mistress Quickly's touching speech about the death of Falstaff in Act 2. Here it is, exactly as it is set out in the folio, with the folio punctuation, capitalisation, italics and spelling:

Hostesse: Nay sure, hee's not in Hell: hee's in *Arthurs* Bosome, if ever a man went to *Arthurs* Bosome: a made a finer end, and went away and it had beene any Christome Child: a parted eu'n just betweene Twelve and One, eu'n at the turning o' th' Tyde: for after I saw him fumble with

> the Sheets and play with Flowers, and smile vpon his fingers end, I knew there was but one way: for his Nose was as sharpe as a Pen, and a Table of greene fields ...
>
> *Henry V* (Act 2 scene 3)

You can follow its easy, chatty flow, an erratic accumulation of detail until that last phrase: 'for his nose was as sharp as a pen ... *and a table of green fields*'.

Then we get out the Konan University's copy of Alexander Pope's 1725 edition and read his notes on the same passage:

> These words, *and a table of green fields* are not to be found in the old editions of 1600 and 1608. This nonsense got into all the following editions by a pleasant mistake of all the Stage-editors, who printed from all the common piecemeal-written Parts in the Playhouse. A Table was here directed to be brought in, (it being a scene in a tavern where they drink at parting) and this direction crept into the text from the margin. Greenfield was the name of the Property man at that time who furnish'd implements &c for the actors.

I find this an incredible proposal, lacking in any sense of the realities of performance, quite apart from there being not a shred of evidence for the existence of any property man called Mr Greenfield. Can you imagine the boy actor playing Mistress Quickly tasked with delivering this speech, certainly one of the most moving prose speeches in the entire canon, allowing the stage crew to interrupt it by coming crashing on with a pointless table. But then we compare the next eighteenth-century editor on the subject, a man who will become Pope's arch-rival, Lewis Theobald.

> Mr Pope has observ'd, that these Words *and a table of greenfields*, are not in the old 4tos. As of the History of Greenfield he was then Property-man, whether it was really so is a point which I shall not contend about. But were we to allow this marginal direction and suppose that a Table of Greenfield's was wanting, yet it never was customary in the promptor's book (much less in the peacemeal parts) where any such directions are marginally inserted for properties or

implements, to add the Property-man's Name, whose business it was to provide them. Besides the furnishing Chairs and Tables is not the province of the Property Man but of the Scene-keepers.

Theobald makes his own assessment of the problem, realising that it probably results from a confusion by the compositor of the letters 't' and 'b'. He amends the text to 'a' babled o' green fields'.

Theobald's solution, that the delirious Falstaff nearing his end, his mind straying perhaps to the Elysian Fields, should babble incoherently is both brilliant and ineffably beautiful, and became so widely accepted that it appears in every edition available today. I've seen for myself, in the edition held at Winchester, how obsessively 'piddling' Lewis Theobald could be, but for this emendation alone I salute him.

Meisei

Meisei is a private university which opened in the boom year of 1964. Originally it had one department, the Faculty of Science and Engineering, now its most famous asset, and the one it features most prominently on its website is its large Shakespeare Collection.

The library sits on one of its two campuses at Hino, in western Tokyo. Matthew drives me out there in his non-self-driving car. We chat about the event last night for the Daiwa Anglo-Japanese Foundation, at the ambassador's residence. It was gratifying to see so many familiar faces. Masachika 'Ichi' Ichimura is one of Japan's great actors. I have directed him twice, once as Shylock and once as the shogun Tokugawa Ieyasu in a play about the first Englishman to arrive in Japan in 1600. When the production came to Sadler's Wells, Ichi was proclaimed by *The Times* as 'one of the finest actors on the planet'. Another honoured guest is Hideki Noda, one of Japanese theatre's innovators. He is a director, writer, actor and currently artistic director of the Tokyo Metropolitan Theatre.

Over dinner Ichi tells me he wants to play King Lear and wonders if I would consider directing. Although I think he could be a great Lear, I couldn't face directing that particular play again, after Tony's death. But there is a very merry banter as I suggest that Ichi and

Noda alternate the roles of King Lear and the Fool. Noda is a great comedian.

* * *

On our arrival at the Kodoma Memorial Library, we are greeted by the Meisei Librarian, Ms Miki Ishii. She has been expecting us. The folios are kept in a vault, and are brought out one by one, for us to inspect. The most notorious folio in the large collection is Meisei 11. It has a bullet hole going through it. Above the catalogue page you can clearly read the signature of its owner, the Restoration playwright William Congreve. The author of *The Way of the World* and *Love for Love,* Congreve penned the famous line often misquoted as 'Hell hath no fury like a woman scorned'. Perhaps he was speaking from the heart when he wrote those words.

You can imagine Congreve sitting happily reading his folio by candlelight one evening when the door creaks open, there is a rustle of silk and a small flintlock is drawn from a hand-warming muff, it is primed and loaded, and levelled at its target, the trigger is pulled, there is a flash. What is the horrified playwright to do but protect himself with the only thing he has at hand, his copy of Shakespeare. As he raises it, the lead shot pierces the cover and lodges in the rag paper pages, saving his life. As we peer at the copy, we can trace the bullet's path (albeit now expertly repaired), all the way through to *Much Ado About Nothing.*

Congreve never married but had relationships with several women, including his leading lady, Anne Bracegirdle. He also had a long affair with Henrietta, the married daughter of the Duke of Marlborough, with whom he is said to have fathered a child. When Congreve died in 1729, Henrietta had a marble monument erected to him in the south aisle of Westminster Abbey, with an inscription which read: 'this monument is sett up by HENRIETTA, Dutchess of MARLBOROUGH as a mark of how dearly she remembers the happiness and honour she enjoyed in the sincere friendshipp of so worthy and honest a man'. When Horace Walpole chastised her for exposing herself 'by placing a monument and silly epitaph of her own composing and bad spelling to Congreve', her mother, quoting those words, said, 'I know not what pleasure she might have had in his company but I am sure it was no honour'.

When Meisei bought this copy in 1991, their application for an export licence was challenged on the grounds that it was part of the country's national heritage. The challenge was unsuccessful.

★ ★ ★

If nothing else the Meisei Collection demonstrates 'the great variety of readers' the 1623 Folio has enjoyed in its time. One copy was owned by the manager of the Rothschild bank in Turin during the 1860s railway boom; another by a doctor who pioneered the study of acute infectious respiratory diseases; yet another by a book collector who drowned with his wife in a canoeing accident in Maine in the summer of 1881. Meisei 6 was owned by two famous lyricists, who lived two centuries apart.

One of my favourite pieces of music is a sublime countertenor aria by Handel, 'O Lord, whose mercies numberless'. It is sung by David (the young shepherd who stood up to Goliath) in the oratorio *Saul*. George Frideric Handel wrote it in 1738, when he was recovering from a stroke which he thought would end his life, and it never fails to make me weep within the first few bars, it is so ravishingly beautiful. The words were written by Charles Jennens who also contributed to some of Handel's other great works, including *Belshazzar* and *Messiah*. Jennens not only owned a First Folio but himself edited several of the plays and published them in individual volumes, the first time that edited versions of Shakespeare's plays were available in single editions.

By a strange coincidence, 200 years later the very same copy owned by Jennens was purchased by another lyricist. In contrast to Jennens's spiritual oratorios, Paul Francis Webster wrote the lyrics to *Spiderman*. I can still remember the theme song to the TV show from my childhood in the sixties, warning you to listen bud, 'cos he has radioactive blood.

I never quite expected to use the words 'Shakespeare' and 'Spiderman' in the same sentence. Webster described his Shakespeare Folios (he had copies of all four) as standing 'like giant redwoods' above the other books in his library. A very Californian way of putting it.

Webster's copy is not the only folio to have connections to Hollywood. John Lloyd Balderston was a playwright whose adaptation of a stage version of *Dracula* formed the basis of the 1931 Universal Pictures hit starring Bela Lugosi, the first talkie made of Bram Stoker's novel. Balderston bought his folio in Los Angeles in 1939. It is now held at the University of Illinois, at Urbana-Champaign. However, there is another folio here I really want to see. Meisei 2 belonged to Apsley Cherry-Garrard, the youngest member of Scott's ill-fated Terra Nova Expedition to the South Pole. His book, *The Worst Journey in the World*, recalls his time in the Antarctic. It is quite simply the best piece of travel literature I have ever read. I have been longing to see his copy.

But it seems there is a problem. It's not here. In my experience, the polite Japanese never want to let you down, and hate saying no. Initially my enquiry was met with evasion. Ms Ishi tells me the library had decided that with so many copies they had a responsibility to 'share them with the world'. But over a sandwich lunch I discover what has really happened. Presumably the university in the wake of Covid needed to bolster its funding base. So Meisei 2 was sold, but Ms Miki Ishi does not know who bought it.

As we leave she very graciously presents me with a facsimile of Meisei 1, which they produced in 2014, in commemoration of the fiftieth anniversary of the founding of the university – an excellent way of sharing their treasures with the world. It's highly annotated in a seventeenth-century hand by one William Johnstone. And from the dialect in which the annotations are written, Mr Johnstone seems to have been a Scot. On closer inspection the densely written script reveals that he is scribbling notes on the plot and the characters as he goes, and I realise they are very similar to the way I mark up any of the Jacobethan repertoire I read. I jot down in the margin who is who, and what is happening so I can keep track, particularly if I have to break off and pick up the reading sometime later.

Back home in the UK, I get an email from Ms Ishi. She sends me a photograph from a newspaper report. From a wrinkle in the Droeshout engraving she recognises it as Meisei 2. It has been purchased by a university in Canada.

The Imperial Residence

I have been granted a private audience with the Emperor of Japan.

Emperor Naruhito ascended the Chrysanthemum Throne in 2019, on the abdication of his father Akihito, and is now in his early sixties. The British Council has arranged the visit in cahoots with the British Embassy. And we meet there. It is a distinguished address, located at No. 1 Ichiban-cho which, as Matthew points out, means No. 1, Number One Street. The Embassy lies just west of the Imperial Palace.

The ambassador Julia Longbottom is joining us. She has not met the emperor since she presented her credentials to him in 2021. We take a selfie before clambering into one of the Embassy's glossy limousines. With the Union Jack fluttering on the bonnet, the guards open the gates, stop the traffic and sweep us across the dual carriageway.

It is a short journey over the moat and into the densely wooded Imperial Park that sits right at the centre of Tokyo city. Within minutes we are crunching up the perfectly raked gravel drive of the Fukiage Palace. The Imperial Residence is a low building with tiered dove-grey roofs, surrounded by clipped hedges. As we draw up under the carriage porch, a fleet of footmen surge forward to open the doors and usher us inside.

The hallway leads into wide corridors clad in mellow wood, and lined intermittently with planters of immaculate bonsai trees, with plush, plump cushions of vivid green, ancient, contorted dwarf juniper and pine that look so artificial they must be real. The soft carpets are the colour of oysters and pearl.

First we have a rehearsal, as the chamberlain instructs us how we will be introduced to the emperor. We are to line up before one of the fusuma sliding screens of wood and Japanese paper. When they draw back, the emperor will be standing before us. I am to go forward first, and introduce myself, but am gently reminded not to hold out my hand as the emperor will not be shaking hands. Then I pass on to the ambassador and to the director of the British Council. After the allotted twenty minutes or so, the chamberlain will rap softly on the screen behind us, a signal that the audience is at an end.

We are conducted back to a side room to put on our Covid masks and wait to be called. Although the wearing of masks has been relaxed in Japan, the emperor and empress are due to go on their first state visit in a week's time, to Indonesia, and an aide has just returned from Jakarta with Covid, so restrictions have been reapplied in the Imperial Residence. I find myself struggling with the same problem I had throughout the pandemic: when wearing a mask, how on earth do you prevent your glasses from steaming up. Just as I am wiping my specs, and rehearsing the ceremonial choreography in my head, we are called in. As the screen slides back, there is Emperor Naruhito, who unexpectedly comes forward, hand extended, and welcomes me into the room.

As a young man he had studied at Merton College, Oxford, and has good English, which allows our conversation to flow. I have brought with me the folio facsimile given to me at Meisei. As I bring it out onto the table to show him, he tells me how he visited Stratford in his Oxford days to see productions of various Shakespeare plays.

The gentle Naruhito's chosen field of research at Oxford had been river transportation in eighteenth-century England, and in his book he explains why. He had had a keen interest in roads since childhood. 'On roads, you can go to the unknown world,' he wrote. 'Since I have been leading a life where I have few chances to go out freely, roads are a precious bridge to the unknown world.'

Under the Japanese constitution, Naruhito's role is defined as entirely ceremonial. Not only is he not allowed to make political statements, but his movements, too, are strictly confined. He loves jogging but has only the palace grounds in which to do so. Reading his book I had been struck by a paragraph where he acknowledged the frustrations of his confinement as a child within the huge Akasaka Palace where he then lived. Built during the Meiji period, the neo-Baroque palace was said to be a copy of Buckingham Palace outside and a copy of Versailles inside. One day, at around the time he started school, he was wandering in the gardens when he discovered a sign which read *Ōshū Kaidō*.

The Ōshū Kaidō was an ancient highway which connected Edo (modern-day Tokyo) with the northern provinces of the country. It was part of a network of roads established by the shogun Tokugawa

Ieyasu to speed the passage of personnel and dispatch boxes which were crucial to the shogunate's attempts to rule the country. The sign indicated that this ancient highway once ran through the Akasaka Palace grounds.

Then later as a teenager Naruhito had read his mother's copy of *The Narrow Road to the Deep North*, by the great Japanese poet Bashō. *Oku no Hosomichi* describes an epic thousand-mile journey made by the seventeenth-century poet on foot. I couldn't help but equate the young Naruhito's love of roads with a desire to break free from his confinement. Bashō had made his life a journey. At the start of his most famous work, he writes, 'Every day is a journey, and the journey itself is home'.

I want to discuss how immersion in Shakespeare is a form of escape, of travelling beyond, of exploring the 'unknown world'. But then there is a soft rap on the screen behind me and the audience comes to an end. 'Every day is a journey, and the journey itself is home.' As we drive back to the Embassy, I wonder if, following Bashō's words, my own travel is in fact just a desire to find home. But what is 'home'? For the last thirty-five years home was wherever Tony was. So where is it now?

Kyoto

The eye of the cloud dragon follows me around the chamber. Wherever I walk in the dharma hall, the swirling dragon painted in a lightning blue ring in the ceiling above me keeps watch with his all-seeing eye. Tenryū-ji is a fourteenth-century temple in Kyoto, and a registered World Heritage Site. It is a favourite spot of Jason James, who runs the Daiwa Foundation, and he has brought me to this beautiful site on our way to my final Japanese folio, for a moment of peace and serenity.

When we arrive at Kyoto Foreign Studies University, a man in a black suit dashes out to the gate to open the doors of the taxi to greet us. Mr Hiyasugi seems to dash everywhere. He dashes ahead to call the lift, dashes again to check the president is ready to welcome us, and at the end of our visit will dash off to fetch a taxi.

There is quite a welcoming party in the president's office where we are offered green tea. Besides President Takahiro, there are several associate professors, two of whom are English, and the librarian who kicks off proceedings with a little speech, before inviting the president to speak. He quotes *Julius Caesar*, 'There is a tide in the affairs of men', and talks about how his university strives to cultivate individuals with an unwavering spirit who can advance towards the goal of 'pax mundi per linguas' (world peace through language). Shakespeare's ability to speak to the whole world, he says, makes him a perfect exponent of their motto.

I am not quite sure if I am expected to reply to the president's paean to the universality of Shakespeare, so I pick my cue and rise to tell the assembled staff that when we were touring *Macbeth* here, Harriet Walter (Lady M) asked a largely female audience at a Q&A session why they thought that particular play was so popular in Japan. Easy, came the reply, because in Japan women are the real power behind the throne. Polite laughter. I should have asked the emperor yesterday what his wife thought about that. As we head to the library, Felicity, who teaches Shakespeare, says she fears the subject is losing popularity in Japan.

The Kyoto University's First Folio has only one known previous owner, a veteran war correspondent. Rowland Denys Guy Winn wrote for the *Daily Telegraph* in the Spanish Civil War and was condemned to death. He fought in the Second World War, was mentioned in dispatches and awarded the Croix de Guerre, and he was a volunteer in the Korean conflict, before becoming a Conservative MP. Having seen and commented on so much in various theatres of war, I wonder what passages in Shakespeare might have appealed to him. *Troilus and Cressida* perhaps? Maybe Thersites's coruscating line 'Lechery, lechery, wars and lechery, nothing else holds fashion'. I turn to look.

In the Kyoto copy there is a surprise. At the bottom of page 80 in *Troilus* (the third page of text) are written the words 'turn 7 leaves back'. And later, 'And turne over leaf'. They are contemporary scribbled notes to the binder giving specific instructions about where *Troilus and Cressida* should be placed. It gives a real sense of how individual these folios are with variations in how and when they were originally bound together.

One theory is that when the negotiations for the rights to *Troilus and Cressida* stalled, Hemmings and Condell decided to replace it with another play. This tantalisingly suggests that they had a pile of plays by (or co-authored by) Shakespeare that they considered for inclusion but rejected on whatever grounds. Why did they not choose to include *Pericles*, or *The Two Noble Kinsmen*? Whatever the reason, the printers removed what had already been set up of *Troilus and Cressida* and replaced it with *Timon of Athens*.

Once the folio had started to appear on bookstalls in London, it seems Henry Walley, the bookseller who originally bought the rights to *Troilus and Cressida*, came to his senses, didn't want to lose potential profits and agreed to lease his rights to the syndicate. But as the printers had already set the type for *Timon*, they decided to leave it in. Otherwise we would have no knowledge that Shakespeare had ever written (or collaborated on) such a play as there is no other contemporary reference to it.

As we close the covers of the Kyoto Folio, I notice two of the university's other wondrous treasures. On the cabinet next to me are two globes: one terrestrial, one celestial. They are the size of a pair of crown green bowls. They were made in the workshops of the Dutch cartographer Willem Jansz Blaeu (1571–1638) who was an apprentice to the great Danish astronomer Tycho Brahe. He got the contract to supply these globe pairs for all the ships of the Dutch East India Company. I peer at them, these rare, beautifully crafted objects, four centuries old, with their ocean-braving galleons and spouting sea monsters.

In the play *Anjin: The English Samurai*,* William Adams presents the shogun at the end of his life with a globe: 'Great Lord,' he says, 'may I offer you the world?' The shogun points with his fan at their two little islands, much the same size, on either side of the globe and wonders at the world he never got to see. As the shogun takes his last breaths he speaks lines from the famous Noh play *Atsumori*:

Why should it be
That a man glories in the strength of his body – so weak a thing
For the soul that knits its sinews – giving it life and movement –
Soon takes wing to the pale, silent moon,

---

* By Mike Poulton with Shoichiro Kawai, which I commissioned and directed in Tokyo in 2009.

Leaving only a desolate ghost – naked, shivering with cold –
To howl in the winds of autumn: Alone! Alone! Alone!

Ichimura delivered this speech with the haunting inflections and tonalities of great Noh performers to a gentle melancholy underscore of a shakuhachi flute. And I thought of Hamlet asking, 'And yet to me, what is this quintessence of dust?'

★ ★ ★

Japan had been an unexpected addition to my Folio Roadshow, but inevitably it prompted an ambition to see more folios around the world. I knew there were copies in Australia and New Zealand, but doubted I would be able to finance the trip to see either of them. And then by a strange coincidence an email dropped into my inbox.

Occasionally, Tony's agents inform me of royalties which he earned and which have now been paid into my account. They are usually a few pounds, from the odd TV jobs he did. Tony did very few films. But one day the phone rang at our home in Stratford. It was Peter Jackson asking Tony to be in the second part of his *Hobbit* trilogy, *The Desolation of Smaug*. Jackson had a challenge on his hands. Tony hated any kind of fantasy film, so he had seen neither *The Lord of the Rings* trilogy nor the first *Hobbit* film.

Jackson explained that the role was Thráin, the King of the Dwarves, father to Thorin Oakenshield. After the Battle of Azanulbizar against the Orcs, Thráin has been captured, held prisoner in the ruined fortress at Dol Guldur and been driven mad. Gandalf finds him and brings him to his senses, but, as they escape, Thráin is grabbed by one of the black tentacles of the Necromancer and dies. Tony didn't have a clue what he was talking about. Apparently Ian McKellen (Gandalf) had agreed to film this extra plot line as long as Jackson could persuade Tony to play the insane dwarf king. So, because McKellen had asked and they loved working together, Tony said yes. Months later Jackson rang again in abject apology to say the entire plot had ended on the cutting room floor.

However, because the scenes had been included in the Director's Cut, Tony was entitled to a royalty. I was astonished at the size of the cheque: it would certainly get me as far as New Zealand, which holds the furthest flung of all the folios. Ironically, it felt comforting to know that Tony's reluctant week's work on *The Hobbit* would underwrite the Antipodean leg of my quest.

Chapter Thirteen
Australia

> Will your grace command me any service to the world's end? I will go on the slightest errand now to the Antipodes that you can devise to send me on ...
> *Much Ado About Nothing* (Act 2 scene 1)

Sydney: Monday 12 June 2023

I arrive in Sydney on the King's birthday. It is the first time that the annual holiday weekend has been renamed in honour of the new King, even though it's not his birthday. I am meeting up with my cousin Frankie. She moved to Australia many years ago and married an Aussie called Steve. They live in Melbourne and have flown up for the weekend. We sit sipping cold Foster's lager in the sunshine on Circular Quay in the harbour, overlooking the sails of the famous opera house.

Recently the state premier, Chris Minns, declined to light the iconic building to celebrate the King's Coronation, although the famous concrete shells of Jørn Utzon's design had controversially been used as a giant billboard to promote a horse race a few years ago. The republican premier suggested the sails were being lit too often, and cited the financial burden to the taxpayer.

'So what do Australians think about Charles III being King of Australia?' I ask my companions.

'Having a monarch feels irrelevant to most of us,' says Steve. 'It's kinda anachronistic. It's just a reminder of a tricky colonial past.' Though one in three Australians wants the country to become a republic as soon as possible, a recent Australian poll suggested that as the King is more popular than any Australian politician, they are happy to wait. Some people are proud of having a king, many are embarrassed about it but most don't care. Most suspect he will be the last King of Australia.

'And there is a generational divide,' Frankie interjects. 'Young Australians are much less enthusiastic than their older counterparts.'

★ ★ ★

And Sydney feels like a very young city. My visit coincides with the Vivid Festival, which transforms the city every year with amazing outdoor immersive light installations. I can't wait to see the light show here in the harbour later tonight. But first I've been invited to meet one of Australia's best known theatre companies.

The Bell Shakespeare Company have moved into their new premises in one of the piers in the renovated finger wharves in Sydney Harbour. Their director, Peter Evans, shows me around. He is justifiably proud of the Nutshell Theatre, where I would be speaking later. 'We named it after Hamlet's line,' says Peter: 'I could be bounded in a nutshell, and count myself a king of infinite space.' Peter boasts that with its open, light position surrounded by water, the Nutshell must be the most beautiful rehearsal room in the world. I disagree: that accolade belongs to the Ashcroft Room in Stratford, but I graciously concede that the Nutshell comes a close second. Peter is about to open their first show here, a 'stripped back' production of *Romeo and Juliet*.

The Bell Shakespeare Company was set up in 1990, and I am really honoured that their legendary founder, John Bell, arrives to hear my talk. He has been instrumental in shaping Australian theatre and was named by the National Trust of Australia as one of the country's Living Treasures. John, like me, attended the Bristol Old Vic Theatre School, and spent some of his early career at the RSC. He was in the 1965 season in which John Schlesinger directed Paul Scofield in *Timon of Athens*. His daughters were both born in Stratford while he was in the company. He introduces me to one of them. Lucy is presently playing the nurse in their new touring production. Having directed so many of the plays, and played so many of the great roles, it must be good to see your own legacy flourish.

★ ★ ★

I am heading to the State Library of New South Wales to see their First Folio, the only one in Australia, and one of only three in the entire Southern Hemisphere.*

The library stands in Shakespeare Place, and as I approach I spot the Shakespeare monument on a traffic island in the middle of the busy freeway in front of it. I dodge the traffic and dash over to grab a selfie. The inscription informs me that the monument was presented to the city in August 1914, by Henry Gullet.

In the pre-war fervour for Empire, Shakespeare's reputation for greatness had been consolidated. He could be held up as an improving spiritual inspiration for all mankind. Gullet had chosen to approach an Australian sculptor for the monument. Bertram Mackennal had left his native Melbourne to become one of the leading sculptors of the Empire. His statues of Queen Victoria can be seen across the globe from Blackburn to Bangkok. Another of his imperial commissions, a statue of Lord Curzon, stands in the Viceroy's House in Delhi. But Mackennal is probably best known for carving the marble effigy of King Edward VII (and his queen, Alexandra) on his tomb in St George's Chapel, Windsor.

Nine kings on horseback followed Edward's cortège at his funeral in May 1910. Nine sovereigns of European states riding together in an unprecedented tribute. 'The sun of the old world was setting in a dying blaze of splendour never to be seen again,' wrote the historian Barbara Tuchman of that pivotal moment in the history of Empire.

By 1914, the British Empire had grown to become the biggest in the history of the world, ruling a quarter of the earth's surface. Australia had officially become a dominion in 1901. By the time of Henry Gullet's death in August 1914, Britain had declared war on Germany, and the Empire was drawn into the conflict. Few countries made such a heavy sacrifice as Australia during the First World War. Haunted by the huge ANZAC losses incurred at Gallipoli in

---

* Tasmania subsequently acquired a copy in 2024.

1915, Antipodean enthusiasm for Empire began to diminish. By the end of the war, those nine kings who had ridden flank to flank in the splendour of that imperial May morning in 1910 had lost their kingdoms and three great empires of Russia, Germany and Austro-Hungary had been swept away, with the Ottoman Empire soon to follow.

Mackennal's statue was finally unveiled on Shakespeare's birthday, 23 April 1926, the same year the British Commonwealth of Nations was founded, in which it was agreed that, though all her dominions owed allegiance to the king and queen, the United Kingdom did not rule over them. Nearly a hundred years later, attitudes to that imperial conception of Shakespeare are being challenged. The library's Director, Dr Vallance, later tells me that there are moves afoot to change the name of the street where the library stands, Shakespeare Place, to something with a stronger connection to the land.

Here on the traffic island, Romeo embraces Juliet, Hamlet broods, Portia points to the bond and Falstaff strokes his beard and chuckles. Mackennal chose these particular characters because 'they seemed to embrace the cardinal features of humanity, with all its greatness and weakness woven into imperishable thought'. At the apex of Mackennal's design, Shakespeare contemplates his quill feather, perhaps pondering his posthumous reputation.

Colourful banners hanging between the pillars of the portico of the library announce 'Pride (R)evolution', a free gay pride exhibition, which 'takes a queer lens to the State Library's vast collection' and as I enter, another exhibition calls for us 'to pause and consider the devastation of colonisation for Aboriginal people, and to remember the complex and painful legacies of this history'.

★ ★ ★

I discover some unexpected connections between the library in Sydney and its counterpart in Birmingham. Both have Shakespeare rooms, both with elaborately carved bookshelves, created to hold precious volumes of Shakespeare plays and books about him. When Maggie Patton (Head of Collection, Acquisition and Curation) shows me the Sydney Library version I recognise their original shared ambitions. She tells me that the wood used in the room is

Tasmanian blackwood, dyed in order to have the appearance of English oak and carved into linen-fold panelling. There are stained-glass windows depicting the Seven Ages of Man, and the coats of arms of Queen Elizabeth I and of Shakespeare. There is even a Tudor-style three-legged chair which includes a sliver of the mulberry tree which Shakespeare is said to have planted at New Place. As in the Birmingham Library, the actual volumes are nowadays safely stored in secure and air-conditioned stacks. The books in the room are all modern duplicates from the collections.

In the folio, Maggie shows me a pair of signatures on two different plays. She is sure they are romantically related. At the end of *Hamlet*, a woman has written in a beautiful looping script *Elizabeth Windebank: Her Book*. And in what seems like a response, at the end of *Antony and Cleopatra*, three plays further on, you read *the unworthiest of your servants Tho. Hurst*. Has Thomas Hurst chosen to sign this play of gaudy obsessional love to convey a coded message to Elizabeth Windebank? Maggie is sure he has.

Then, as a special treat, I am taken backstage to see the box the folio came in. And here is the second connection with Birmingham.

The folio was the gift of a Cornish engineer and manufacturer who built his works in Birmingham. His name was Richard Tangye. He and his brother George came to fame in 1858, when their hydraulic jacks were used to launch Isambard Kingdom Brunel's steamship, the SS *Great Eastern*. 'We launched the *Great Eastern*,' he wrote, 'and she launched us.'

Then, in September 1878, one of the firm's great engineering achievements was the use of their hydraulic jacks in placing Cleopatra's Needle on the Thames Embankment. Tangye proudly asserted that it took just four men and four of Tangye's Patent Hydraulic Lifting Jacks to raise the 186-ton granite needle from Heliopolis. One of the jacks was placed in a recess under the monument as a memorial, where it remains to this day. As their business expanded the Tangye brothers opened offices in Johannesburg and Sydney.

In *One and All: An Autobiography of Richard Tangye*, Tangye describes his impressions of the city:

> Everybody knows that Sydney is noted for its beautiful harbour; the citizens are justly proud of it, for it is one of the most beautiful sights

on the face of the earth. But Sydney has other things to be proud of : the Botanical Gardens are lovely beyond description ... There is a fine library of books, free for the use of the citizens, including a copy of the 'First Folio' of Shakespeare; but Sydney neither does itself justice, nor its collection of books, nor the loving care bestowed upon them by the worthy librarian, in the building which it has provided for their accommodation.

What underpins the wealthy industrialist's indignation is not only that he donated the folio to the library, but that he had a special casket made 'from wood from the Forest of Arden' to house it in. And in front of me now is that very casket. It has been undergoing some restoration prior to inclusion in an exhibition. The box looks like a large wooden tea caddy lined with velvet in imperial purple.

After my library visit, I strolled through the Botanical Gardens so admired by Tangye, lush with strelitzia and agave flowering in orange spikes, past massive gum and eucalyptus trees, and sunny lawns stalked by white ibis and pied crows.

★ ★ ★

On my last night in Sydney, I make my way back down to the waterfront. Large crowds are moving towards the harbour to watch a light show called *Written in the Stars*. A bank of drones in grid formation rise in front of the Harbour Bridge and glide across the water. There must be 200 points of light. They scatter and regroup into wonderful shapes, like stars dancing: a huge southern right whale surfacing in a pool of ripples; a spiralling cosmic pinwheel; and then an entire revolving globe, with the terrier-headed continent of Australia sparkling brightly.

But what moves me most is the light show projected on the opera house. Ochres echoing the outback, Australia's red centre, dust the iconic sails, then blot and stain into wetland blues and greens, then become a lily pond haunted by jacanas and frogs with impossibly long legs and toes. The teeming imagery is boisterous, ebullient, optimistic. Colours drain and dribble, seep and sprawl to a soundtrack of trumpets and Aboriginal voices, as giddily lit tourist boats trip over the bright reflecting pool of the harbour.

Lighting of the Sails: 2023 is a tribute to a quintessentially Australian artist, John Olsen, who passed away at the age of ninety-five just a month before the Vivid Festival began. He said that his work in capturing landscape was intended to be more of a sensory experience rather than a purely visual one. Paul Klee, one of Olsen's inspirations, wrote: 'Art does not reproduce the visible, rather it makes visible.' Klee famously talked of his art 'taking the line for a walk'; Olsen dances with it.

Lighting of the Sails is subtitled *Life Enlivened*. As I leave Sydney that's exactly how I feel, enlivened by its vibrancy, its innovation, its art.

Chapter Fourteen
New Zealand and a Māori Love Story

The pōhutukawa tree is sacred to the Māori. The English settlers named it the New Zealand Christmas tree. And as they arrived on 26 December 1849, Boxing Day, the tree would have been an explosion of midsummer blossom, each a tiny crimson firework.

The men had paddled their canoes across to Mokoia Island from the mainland. Lake Roturoa lies in an ancient caldera, which accounts for the number of hot springs that fringe the island. And it was into one of these *waiariki* that the men lowered themselves. The governor unbuttoned his shooting jacket, took off his battered hat but remained out of the spring, and sat up on the rocks in the shade of the fine pōhutukawa tree. That was when the old chieftain approached. He told the governor that this particular hot spring was the setting of a famous love story. As the wind had started to freshen, and they would be unable to paddle back for a while, the governor, who loved collecting 'native' stories, asked the old chief to sit and recount the legend, and called some of his men to take down the story verbatim, while he himself copied down the detail in his notebook.

The tale of Hinemoa and her beloved Tūtānekai is one of New Zealand's most famous legends, a story of forbidden love, Aotearoa's own *Romeo and Juliet*. This was the first time the story would ever have been committed to paper.

Hinemoa was the daughter of a proud chieftain on the mainland, far above the hopes of Tūtānekai, who lived with his family on Mokoia Island. But at one of the tribal gatherings they had caught each other's gaze and fallen in love. Hinemoa listened every evening as Tūtānekai played his flute and the mournful melody drifted across the calm water of the lake. Eventually one night she decided she would take one of the canoes and cross over to her beloved, but her family, suspecting her attraction to the beautiful young man, had hauled all the canoes high up onto the beach and Hinemoa could not shift them.

But as the beguiling song of Tūtānekai's flute continued to play, she felt, the old chieftain said, 'as if an earthquake shook her', and she grew even more determined. So she slipped off her clothes, strapped six gourds to either side of her body and swam out into the water. Halfway across, the old narrator said, 'she reached the stump of a sunken tree, which used to stand in the lake and she clung to it with her hands and rested to take breath'. Then she swam on, and every time she felt exhausted she would float in the water supported by the gourds. Eventually, guided by the sound of the flute, she reached the island at the very pool where the governor was now sitting, and slid into the warm water to relax.

At this point the story of Hinemoa and Tūtānekai more closely resembles the legend of Hero and Leander, but whereas it was Leander who swam to his beloved Hero across the Hellespont, here it is the woman who enacts that heroic challenge.

The old chieftain's story, as told to the governor that morning, is embellished with all sorts of hilarious details as Tūtānekai sends his boy down to the water to fill a calabash for him to drink, and Hinemoa, hiding her nakedness, puts on a gruff voice, takes the calabash, drinks its contents and then smashes it. When this has happened three times, the furious Tūtānekai himself comes down to the shore to find out who this uncouth 'rascal' who has smashed all his calabashes is. When she hears Tūtānekai's voice, Hinemoa, the narrator says, 'rose up in the water as beautiful as the wild, white hawk, and stepped upon the edge of the bath as graceful as the shy white crane'.

The story of Hinemoa and Tūtānekai does not end tragically. In fact, as told by our genial old chieftain, there is further comedy when Tūtānekai does not turn up for breakfast in the village that following morning, and his father sends a messenger to check on him.

> Then the man who was to fetch him went and drew back the sliding wooden window of the house, and peeping in, saw four feet. 'Oh!' he was greatly amazed, and said to himself, 'Who can this companion

of his be?' However, he had seen quite enough, and turning about, hurried back as fast as he could to Tūtānekai's father and said to him, 'Why, there are four feet, I saw them myself, in the house.' The father answered, 'Who's his companion, then? hasten back and see.' So back he went to the house and peeped in at them again, and then, for the first time he saw it was Hinemoa. Then he shouted out in his amazement, 'Oh! here's Hinemoa, here's Hinemoa, in the house of Tūtānekai!' And all the village heard him, and there arose cries on every side. 'Oh! here's Hinemoa, here's Hinemoa with Tūtānekai!' And his elder brothers heard the shouting, and they said 'It is not true'; for they were very jealous indeed. Tūtānekai then appeared coming from his house, and Hinemoa following him, and his elder brothers saw that it was indeed Hinemoa; and they said, 'It is true, it is a fact.'

I hear in the telling of this story a vivid account of how oral tradition is handed down, as the old Māori raconteur shapes the detail of the story to suit his audience on that summer Boxing Day afternoon, by the hot sulphur spring under the shade of the beautiful pōhutukawa tree. As he tells it, the story is one of female determination and courage, or the yearning of young love, but its conclusion (the two families are eventually reconciled) is joyful and, though romantic, is without sentimentality. But I can also hear the actual moment when a tradition, subject to infinite variety, becomes fixed on paper, no longer flexible but official.

The governor, listening so attentively to that story, published it in a book he called *Polynesian Mythology and Māori Legends*. I have a copy of the second edition, published in 1885 in both English and Māori. Its pages are the colour of nicotine and as brittle as baking parchment, and it smells quite unlike any other second-hand book I own, of woodsmoke and hot ash. The governor's own preface seems stained, too, with the patina of another age, although some of the attitudes he expresses and their legacy are very much felt in New Zealand today.

The governor's name was George Grey.

At thirty-three, Grey had been appointed Governor of New Zealand. He had already served as Governor of South Australia, which he had been offered on presenting to the Colonial Office a plan of forced assimilation of the Aboriginal peoples with the settlers. His governorship there had drawn severe criticism from some quarters, with one Melbourne newspaper leading the charge against him with a headline borrowed from *Richard III*: 'Think upon Grey and let thy soul despair.' The situation between settlers and the Māori in Aotearoa would be even harder to deal with.

In his first term of office (1845–53), Grey earned the respect of many Māori chieftains, reflected in his efforts to understand their culture. One of them, Rangikāheke, who helped Grey learn the Māori language, wrote to Queen Victoria describing the great *mana* (honour) in which Grey was held, commending the way he looked after both the Pākehā* and the Māori.

I am in Aotearoa to see their First Folio. It was donated by Sir George Grey. In the rare books room of the Auckland Library which houses the Grey Collection, Jane Wild, the library curator, has the folio ready for me to view, alongside a quarto of *Pericles* (the only quarto in New Zealand). Grey's motive in making the generous donation of his huge library is clarified when you read the address he delivered. Shakespeare, he claimed, clearly demonstrated the supremacy of the English language, and that superiority justified the drive to adopt English universally across the Empire, and the necessary suppression of indigenous languages.†

Perhaps I can now also understand a little more fully a recent spat in Wellington which reached the British press. A headline in the *Guardian* read, 'New Zealand pulls funding for festival of Shakespeare citing canon's imperialism'. The row ignited over a secondary schools' Shakespeare festival that had been running for three decades. The advisory panel of the funding body, Creative New Zealand, questioned whether 'a singular focus on an Elizabethan playwright is most relevant for a decolonising Aotearoa in the 2020s and beyond', and that the festival 'missed the opportunity to create a living curriculum'.

A lecturer at Victoria University made an interesting claim: 'Wouldn't it be great if young people could come home and say:

---

* New Zealanders of European descent.
† The Māori language was suppressed in schools under colonial rule, and was only made an official language of New Zealand under the Māori Language Act 1987.

Hey, Mum, Dad, I just found this story and it is really similar to Hinemoa and Tūtānekai. It's called Romeo and Juliet. That would be an awesome act of decolonisation.'

Jane Wild has brought out something else for me to see: Shakespeare with a facial tattoo. The right-hand side of his face is covered with the swirling markings of the Māori Moko. A long pendant hangs from his left ear, and around his neck he wears a pekapeka, a necklace worn as a symbol of status and cultural identity. It's an arresting image. Shakespeare as Māori.

The image was created* in 2000, for an edition of the sonnets translated into Te Reo Māori by Merimeri Penfold, a champion of the Māori language. Jane has invited a contemporary New Zealand poet to join us. He is the Fijian-born Daren Kamali; he is the Heritage Pacific adviser for the Auckland Libraries, and he uses the sonnets in his outreach work with homeless groups in the city. Of the nine sonnets Merimeri Penfold translated it is Sonnet 60 I want to hear: 'Like as the waves hasten to the pebbled shore, So do our minutes hasten to their end.' The author promises that despite Time's 'cruel hand' to which every living thing is subject, the memory of his beloved will eternally be preserved in words.

Penfold wrote that translating Shakespeare's 'fascination with highly wrought intricacies of language' and 'his feeling for the rhythmic energies of the spoken word' was a real challenge, but the cross-cultural exercise of discovering that the Māori language, despite differing constructions, vocabularies and histories, could accommodate such intensity of thought was powerful and enriching. Listening to this familiar sonnet, a meditation about time and the inevitable process of decay, but in a language as ancient as Māori with its multisyllabic liquid eloquence and staccato rhythms, is beautiful and moving. And despite the way that Shakespeare played a critical role in establishing British cultural dominance in colonies like Aotearoa, it is marvellous to hear his words reappropriated.

★ ★ ★

* By Māori artist Cushla Parekowhai.

Old Government House, where Lord Grey once held sway, sits in Albert Park on the university campus. Now it is a rather drab and run-down municipal place, but in its glory days there were grand reception rooms, parlours furnished with gleaming wooden furniture and a chandeliered ballroom, festooned with ferns and aspidistras. As I reach the top of the sweeping staircase, my host suddenly says, 'Ah, here is George Grey.' I turn to find a rather elderly Burmese cat, with a sleek lilac coat, who deigns to let me scratch his head.

The British Council have organised a group of historians to help me understand Grey's substantial role in the history of New Zealand. Judith Bassett is a retired teacher and unashamed Anglophile; Linda Bryder, a historian with a focus on the social history of medicine; and Rowan Light, a young professor in his thirties, is a historian of memory and commemoration, interested in public uses of the past.

'If Grey had finished his time in New Zealand at the end of his first period as governor he would be remembered as a good man passionate about Māori culture, and an excellent negotiator and conciliator,' says Judith. 'It was the second term when things fell apart.' Not all of her colleagues agree about Sir George's reputation, but the conversation establishes him as a deeply controversial figure. My knowledgeable experts tell me about the crucial Treaty of Waitangi signed in 1840 between the British and the Māori, over the sale of land to the settlers. 'Grey made a rushed land grab,' one of them sums up. 'It betrayed all the care he had taken to appease the indigenous population and went against the treaty, which was regarded by the Māori as a sacred covenant guaranteeing their rights.' War quickly followed. Grey's crackdown was severe, as if he revealed through impatience what had in fact been the colonial imperative all along.

My head buzzing with the significance of all this information, I take a stroll in the garden of Government House. Here is a tree Grey himself planted. The plaque at its base tells me it is a flame tree, *Erythrina indica*, but someone later tells me the plaque got it wrong. It seems, like many of the historical facts I am learning, to be in dispute. I spot George Grey, his feline namesake, peering down at me from a second-floor window, with an inscrutable look.

Later in Albert Park, on a drizzly afternoon, I ponder the marble statue of this contentious figure. A clipping from one of the New

Zealand newspapers from 2020 shows Grey's statue with hands, face and chest drenched in blood-red paint, and the word RACIST scrawled across the pedestal. The assault occurred in the wake of the murder of George Floyd and the protests that followed, which, in England, swept Edward Colston's statue into Bristol harbour. A statue of Captain Cook here in New Zealand was daubed 'Black Lives Matter … and so do Māoris'.

In Sonnet 55, Shakespeare uses the idea of marble and brass to stand for longevity, which only his poetry will outlast:

> Not marble nor the gilded monuments
> Of princes shall outlive this powerful rhyme,
> But you shall shine more bright in these contents
> Than unswept stone besmeared with sluttish time.
> When wasteful war shall statues overturn,
> And broils root out the work of masonry,
> Nor Mars his sword nor war's quick fire shall burn
> The living record of your memory.

But the very durability of these monuments can encourage us to think of them and what they stand for as eternal, whereas our collective memory depends on shifting cultural and political debate.

★ ★ ★

If the row over the Schools' Festival had provided a platform for heated debate about Shakespeare's position on the curriculum, I discovered his place in the theatrical repertoire is more secure. I had been invited to the press night of *King Lear* by the Auckland Theatre Company. I had given a couple of workshops for the younger members of the company, and I was looking forward to seeing their work. Just not that play. It was the last play in which I had worked with Tony.

The avalanche of cards and emails I received when Tony died expressed sorrow and regret. Most, unsurprisingly, found it hard to know what to say. Some retreated to winsome banalities: 'He'll be there in the wind, or in the lapping of the waves on the shore.' I could only remember King Lear's last words as he cradles his dead daughter in his arms:

> Thou'lt come no more,
> Never, never, never, never, never.
>
> *King Lear* (Act 5 scene 3)

I had always wondered in rehearsal why Shakespeare had Lear repeat the word 'never' five times. Now I know. They express the seeming impossibility of comprehending a raw reality. I will never, never, never, never, never see Tony walking through the front door again. Though harsh, I prefer Shakespeare's assessment of that reality than the limp sentimentality of imagining him looking down from a fluffy cloud. That just isn't helpful. To me anyway.

The Auckland production of *King Lear* was presented on a proscenium arch stage, but in a traverse formation with a bank of seats on the stage facing the audience. I was given a seat in the middle of the front row on stage. Very visible. Very lit. No hiding. The production was terrific, with a diverse cast, and excellent performances from the leads including veteran Michael Hurst as Lear. I spent most of the last act surreptitiously wiping away tears, and preparing myself for 'that' line, girding myself for the impact of its brutal punch. But suddenly we were at the end of the show, and the cast were rising to bow. Had I zoned out? Had my brain protected me from the pain of hearing that line?

At the party in the foyer I told Michael Hurst how much I had enjoyed his performance as Lear and he invited me to brunch the following morning, a Sunday, with his wife, Jennifer Ward-Lealand, who played Kent in the production. She is tall and striking, he short and stocky, with bright eager eyes. We talked about their ambitions for theatre in the country, and the challenges of an industry that no longer has the repertory system where they had learned their craft. After a couple of mimosas, I congratulated Michael again on his performance, for which he thanked me but suddenly said, 'You must have noticed though?'

'What?' I asked.

'I managed to miss out one of the most famous lines in the play, right at the end,' he confessed.

I suddenly felt rather guilty, as if my own anxiety had somehow communicated itself to the actor, and slipped that famous line out of his brain. I thanked him for accidentally relieving me of a painful memory.

Chapter Fifteen
Cape Town

Sitting in Terminal 3 of Singapore's massive Changi Airport after a flight of over eleven and a half hours from Auckland, I am feeling giddy. I have a wait of about four hours until the flight to Cape Town via Johannesburg, which leaves at 1.30 in the morning. I won't get to Cape Town for another fourteen hours after that. Over a day spent on a plane. Suddenly the reality of this crazy quest hits me. WHAT AM I DOING?

Many hours later, the captain has put on the seat belt sign: we have begun our descent into Cape Town. Tony always sat in the aisle seat on long-haul flights, but whenever we came into Cape Town we would swap seats. He wanted to watch as the plane approached his home city and Table Mountain came into view.

Table Mountain, its top flattened by aeons of wind erosion, forms a dramatic backdrop to Cape Town. It even has its own cloud cover, the tablecloth. The plateau, two miles wide, is flanked by Devil's Peak to the east, and by Lion's Head to the west which sits above the suburb of Sea Point, the place where Tony was born, and where until the age of eighteen he grew up. As we came in to land, and that great mass of sandstone at the tip of Africa finally swung into view, Tony would well up, his eyes filling with tears. He was coming home.

As I look out of the window today, we are flying through a cloud bank. It seems to go on for ever. My head starts to jerk forward. I should have swapped seats with Tony by now. Where is he anyway? Perhaps it's the lack of sleep, but I feel as if I am in some grey limbo. Where is Table Mountain? Perhaps I have died. Where am I going? What am I doing?

Then there is a bump.
'Welcome to Cape Town.'

★ ★ ★

In April 1856, three years into his governorship of the Cape Colony, Sir George Grey had an almost incredible event to deal with. On the eastern coast of South Africa, 800 miles away from Cape Town, is the Wild Coast. It was here that this strange eventful history unfolded. The region had been declared a Crown colony since 1847, when it was annexed by the British. It was the traditional homeland of the Xhosa people, but now it was to be known by the clumsy title of British Kaffraria.

One morning a young Xhosa girl and her friend went out to scare birds from her uncle's crops in the fields at the mouth of the Gxarha River which ran down to the ocean. Her name was Nongqawuse. Rising from the sea mist she saw the spirits of two of her ancestors who told her that her people should slaughter all their cattle and destroy all their crops. When they did so their dead would arise and sweep the white men into the sea. Behind them from their caves under the water would follow fresh, strong, beautiful cattle to fill their kraals, and grain enough to fill all their store houses.

Nongqawuse ran home and told her uncle. At first he did not believe her, but when she described one of the spirit ancestors, her uncle recognised his own dead brother from her description. He then went straight to the king, who declared that what the young girl had said was true and that they must all obey the prophecy, and that in eight days' time the sun would rise blood-red, and then set and be followed by the crack of a mighty thunderstorm. Then if they had performed their instructions diligently, the dead would arise. In the days that followed, as incredible as it may seem, the Xhosa obeyed the words of the prophecy as Nongqawuse had revealed it to them. Word spread at speed. A cattle-killing frenzy ensued. It spiralled into a movement in which over 400,000 cattle were slaughtered.

The sun rose on the eighth day, as normal. But an apocalypse was to follow. With their cattle dead and their grain destroyed, famine set in. Sir George Grey wrote: 'I at once hurried North to grapple with it. I could not have believed it so serious, until I was actually on the spot. Here were nearly a quarter of a million kaffirs on the advice of a prophetess, destroying the cattle and produce and looking forward eagerly to a triumph over the whites.'

His action took some courage on his part. 'I went among the chiefs, although I was warned that I endangered myself unduly, hoping to check the movement.' But it was a useless task, as an entire nation seemed gripped by mass hysteria. Grey's imperative was to secure the Cape Colony, to ensure that the frontier settlers (most of them English, Scottish and Irish families) should not be massacred. But as Grey's Edwardian biographer recounts: 'The blood-red sun did not flame in the East, neither did the moon in any of her humours light the ancient chiefs along, the now precious cattle with them.' How to account for it? Was it mass suicide, or mass resistance, in the face of what seemed like insuperable odds? By the end of 1858, it is estimated that approximately 40,000 of the Xhosa people had starved to death.

Grey's part in this millenarian event* is contested. Some argue that he cynically took advantage of this opportunity to destroy a possible obstacle to British expansion. By only allowing food to those who would agree to sign a contract to move west into the Cape Colony and work for the settler farmers, at whatever pay was offered, he not only broke the back of Xhosa resistance, he sent many thousands of them into what was effectively slave labour. His biographer, driven by the same certainty in his faith and in his empire as Grey, concludes: 'Civilisation drove forward in a mortuary cart; but it was civilisation.'

It was in that same crusading spirit of the civilising influence of the British Empire that George Grey donated a second copy of the First Folio, along with another very considerable book collection, to Cape Town and established a fine library where it still stands today in what are known as the Company Gardens.

In front of the library is another statue of Grey, though here he appears as a younger man than the elderly gent on the marble monument in Auckland. Here, in the butterscotch light, his image conveys a man of vigour, in his frock coat, dress sword, high-waisted trousers and tunic buttoned up to his ribboned medallion (probably the KCB he was awarded in 1848). His left hand rests on a pile of books.

---

* It was echoed in the Ghost Dance of the Native American nations in 1890.

I peer to see if the one on top is meant to represent the First Folio, but can't tell.

I have brought quite a party with me to visit the Cape Town National Library. It includes some Cape Town friends: Janice Honeyman and her partner Liza Key (Janice directed Tony with John Kani, in his last ever performance, in *Kunene and the King*), and actress and activist Buhle Ngaba. Chris Thurman runs a research unit of the University of the Witwatersrand, which concentrates on the significant but often neglected history of translating Shakespeare's plays into African languages. It is called the Tsikinya-Chaka Centre. Tsikinya-Chaka is 'Shake-spear' translated into Setswana. And we are joined from England by Professor Emma Smith. Emma is a world expert on the Folio but, despite having seen many of them around the globe, she has never had the opportunity to see the Cape Town Folio so jumped at the invitation.

None of the party, Cape Townians or otherwise, has ever seen this folio. It is the only one in the entire continent of Africa. The Chief Librarian, Najwa Hendrickse, is very welcoming, but tells us that there have been no other plans to display the folio in its 400th anniversary year, and that she has had no other requests to view it. I begin to think of this copy as unloved. We spend a very agreeable couple of hours examining the book, as Emma and I share a sort of double act, of her substantial academic expertise and my amateur enthusiasm. I note an inscription – F. Herbert – and ponder if this might be the 'lost' copy which must once surely have been presented to the 'incomparable brethren' William Herbert and his brother Philip, the book's original dedicatees.

As we leave, Emma shares her thoughts with me. Wherever we have been in this folio year, the volumes have been celebrated, but here it feels as if we were standing around the hospital bed of a sick patient. 'I've always experienced the folio as a wonderfully charismatic book,' she says, 'raising questions about creativity and craftsmanship and value. But here its presence seemed entirely muted, as if it had nothing at all to say.'

As we walk back through the gardens, past Sir George Grey, just up the path is another statue. Diamond magnate, politician and arch-imperialist, Cecil Rhodes seems to be waving his brazen hand towards his fellow colonialist as if in greeting or perhaps just warning what might lie ahead. In fact Rhodes is pointing north, as the inscription on the plinth informs you, his hand indicating the direction for further colonial expansion: 'Your hinterland is there.'

The Rhodes Must Fall movement began at Cape Town University before moving on to Oxford and elsewhere. Just around Table Mountain the university's Rhodes monument, seen as a memorialising of white supremacy, was smashed a few months ago. When we take a closer look at his bronze statue here, we notice a slice in his ankle. An angle-grinder has been applied, although without success, to his Achilles heel. So perhaps it is not surprising that the Cape Town First Folio, for ever associated with the controversial figure of Sir George Grey, should be neglected, and that Shakespeare is regarded either as irrelevant or as a hated colonial imposition.

★ ★ ★

I am joining the people who run the South African Shakespeare Schools' Festival. We meet in a café on Bree Street. The festival's managing director, Blythe Stuart Linger, introduces me to his young team. They have just concluded a month-long festival, with schools from across the Western Cape, Gauteng, Kwa-Zulu Natal and the Eastern Cape. Since its inception, Blythe tells me, the festival has become Africa's largest Shakespeare youth drama programme. 'We are working with over four hundred and ninety schools, nine thousand youth and six hundred and seventy teachers.' No wonder Blythe looks tired, but his ready statistics are impressive.

Buhle Ngaba joins us. I have known Buhle since 2016, when she was a recipient of the Brett Goldin Bursary. Brett was a young actor playing Guildenstern in Janet Suzman's Baxter Theatre production of *Hamlet*, which had been invited to the Complete Works Festival in Stratford in 2006. The night before they left Cape Town he and a friend were brutally murdered. Tony, Janet and I (with other colleagues) set up a bursary in his name to give young South African actors the opportunity that Brett missed, to come and spend some time with the RSC as part of the company, and work alongside us for a month. Buhle was one of the last two bursary winners in 2016. She talks fondly of her time in Stratford and how it changed her relationship with Shakespeare.

'Point being,' she says. 'I never thought I would ever "understand" Shakespeare let alone perform or teach it. Yet it kept finding and (re)finding me. Growing up, my associations and ideas around what Shakespeare was, was that it was a fancy way of speaking that only rich white people could access. I felt it was something reserved for the elite. So, when I won the bursary to the Royal Shakespeare Company, I made a pledge that I would teach whatever I had learnt in my time there to actors/storytellers at home that might be loaded with the same anxieties I had. I think the most valuable thing I took away from the RSC was that I had no reason to fear Shakespeare. If anything, I had all of the reason in the world to feel exhilarated by the challenges his work presents to me as an actor.'

Buhle is now in her stride. She has brought something to show us. Wrapped in a small cardboard box is a book titled *Dintshontsho Tsa Bo-Julius Kesara*. It is her grandmother's copy of *The Tragedy of Julius Caesar*, translated into Setswana by Sol Plaatje* and published by Wits Press in 1937, before Bantu education was implemented in South Africa.

Buhle is unstoppable. She has become involved in any number of Shakespeare projects, as well as the Shakespeare Schools' Festival, as actor, teacher, writer. 'Sol Plaatje created an entry point for me into Shakespeare's stories,' Buhle continues, 'by nullifying the language barrier. I learnt that ultimately, Shakespeare's works are stories about the human condition. They are stories about love, passion, murder, betrayal, they are stories that I have heard in different variants within all sorts of contexts. Romeo and Juliet in Verona could very well be Jabu and Khanyisile in Huhudi township, Vryburg South Africa, whose parents are involved in taxi wars. I discovered that these stories are mine as much as they belong to any other person, because I too have lived these stories. I too have seen reflections of them throughout my own life.'

As Buhle sits down, she concludes: 'When you start looking at Shakespeare, you find so much. The more you know, the more it unfolds for you and the more you get the magic.'

---

* Plaatje was a founding member of the South African Native National Congress, which became the African National Congress (ANC).

Our lunch has been exhilarating, so unlike the dry experience of the unloved First Folio in the South African Library in the morning. With Buhle and her bright young associates at the Shakespeare Schools' Festival you feel a genuine sense of regeneration, untrammelled by the necessity to connect directly with the 400-year-old book. They are on a mission to prove resoundingly that William Shakespeare has something to say in today's South Africa.

★ ★ ★

Now I had seen the furthest travelled of the extant First Folios, I realised that if I was going to be really serious about my folio odyssey in the quatercentenary year, then I needed a plan. Most of the 1623 Folios migrated to the States during the first decades of the twentieth century, and are widely scattered across the country. The largest collection is held at the Folger Library in Washington, DC. Every Ivy League university boasts at least one copy, and others are distributed in colleges and public libraries from Chicago to Dallas and from Buffalo to Boston. I needed a map, and some serious scheduling skills.

This is now officially an obsession.

PART SIX

North American Folio Roadshow: Chicago to Texas

Worn binding on sammelband of sermons by Henry Smith

Chapter Sixteen
North American Folio Roadshow I: Chicago to Boston

Chicago

I am beginning the next leg of my Folio Roadshow here in Chicago, the 'Windy City' or sometimes the 'City of Big Shoulders'

Today is Labor Day, Monday 4 September, the unofficial end of summer. The city is sweltering, heaving with visitors sizzling barbecues under the trees in Lincoln Park, jet-skiing round Navy Pier or clambering on board one of the river cruises to admire the city's amazing range of architecture: the Tribune Tower, like Rouen Cathedral on steroids, or the Wrigley Building, clad in white terracotta and as dazzling as a chewing-gum smile.

I head for a more modest building at the other end of the Magnificent Mile. It's a water tower. It looks like a miniature mediaeval castle, with a Rapunzel turret fifty-five metres high, clad in limestone. Oscar Wilde called it 'a crenellated monstrosity with pepper pots stuck all over it'. But to Chicago, the Water Tower is a symbol of resilience and regeneration. It was the only building in the burned zone to survive the Great Fire of Chicago in 1871.

They say it was Mrs O'Leary's cow which started it, kicking over an oil lamp in her barn during milking. That was probably just prejudice towards the Irish immigrant community in the city. The real reason for the devastating spread of the flames was the long drought and the high winds, and the fact that the old city was largely made of wood, right down to the sidewalks. The conflagration destroyed over three square miles of buildings, killed 300 people and left 100,000 homeless. Among the livelihoods lost, the household belongings gone for ever, the whole districts and neighbourhoods destroyed, one Mr J. W. McCagg lost his most precious possession, his 1623 edition of William Shakespeare's plays. So the first copy of the folio on this leg of my pilgrimage no longer exists. Or did it ever exist? If so, it would have been one of the first copies ever to reach the Mid-West. Or was it just part of the folklore surrounding the First Folio?

Sidney Lee lists McCagg's folio as one of two 'destroyed' copies. In 1854, a New York lawyer called Almon W. Griswold purchased a folio and had it shipped from Liverpool aboard the paddle steamer SS *Arctic*. In a thick wall of fog, fifty miles off Newfoundland, the wooden steamer collided with the steel hull of the *Vesta*, a fishing vessel, and 300 souls perished. The protocol of 'women and children first' made famous later in the *Titanic* disaster but heroically established two years before in 1852 when the Royal Navy troopship HMS *Birkenhead* struck a sunken reef near the Cape of Good Hope was roundly ignored. Of the eighty-five survivors from the SS *Arctic*, sixty-one were crew and twenty-four were male passengers. No women or children survived the wreck. And Almon W. Griswold lost his copy of the First Folio.

★ ★ ★

I take part in an event at the Newberry Library with Barbara Gaines. Barbara founded the Chicago Shakespeare Theater thirty-five years ago, saw its relocation to the Navy Pier (in a new theatre inspired by the Swan in Stratford) and now, at the age of seventy-seven, has just stepped down. Her passion for Shakespeare burns through her. She has done so many of the plays, some like *Troilus and Cressida* and *Cymbeline* (her favourites) two or three times. She has the spritely energy of a Puck (and I suspect the ruthless tenacity of a Lady Macbeth), and her welcome is joyful.

Jill Gage (Custodian of the John M. Wing Foundation at the Newberry) shows me their First Folio. The singular annotation in the volume is curious. It is a name, and it appears in *The Two Gentlemen of Verona*, next to the title and above one of Proteus's speeches, to which it seems to relate. It is the moment when Proteus confesses to the audience that he has fallen for his best friend's girlfriend, Sylvia. He is already in a relationship with the devoted Julia, but is prepared to sacrifice both her love and his friendship with Valentine. Oh, the tangled complexities of young love! Some unknown writer has penned in an elegant hand 'Ann Park is'. If the invitation is for us to continue on to the Shakespeare text which follows below then it would read:

Ann Park is ... That I did love.

So a rejected lover perhaps? It continues:

> ... for now my love is thaw'd;
> Which, like a waxen image, 'gainst a fire,
> Bears no impression of the thing it was.

What can the writer be doing? Has he read the passage of Proteus's self-justification for his switch of allegiance from one girl to another, and felt compelled to declare his own parallel situation? Does he expect anyone else to read and decipher his coded betrayal? Does he feel trapped in a relationship he can't get out of and need to offload his secret despair, covertly revealing his secret somehow, like the servant in Ovid whispering to the rushes that King Midas had ass's ears? There are other folios I have seen with female names tantalisingly inserted. In the copy in Auckland, New Zealand, the name Anne Hearle appears twice above the final scene in *Othello*, the murder of Desdemona. Why? The most curious insertion of a female name alongside a particular piece of text I have so far encountered is contained in a folio held at a gentlemen's club in Pall Mall. In *Richard III*, as the two murderers wake the sleeping Duke of Clarence, he cries out:

Clarence:	Your eyes do menace me: why look you pale?
	Who sent you hither? Wherefore do you come?
Both:	To, to, to—
Clarence:	To murder me?
Both:	Ay, Ay.

Richard III (Act 1 scene 4)

Chicago Police escorting the First Folio in 1964

Against this darkly comic, menacing little exchange someone has written 'Janice Weston 1775'. Of course the writer may have chosen a random space to scribble their signature, unrelated to the text. Otherwise it is a rather ominous choice. When I checked the name out on Google, a slew of references showed up immediately. The first read: 'The mysterious unsolved murder of Janice Weston'. But this Janice Weston was a solicitor, brutally murdered in a lonely lay-by on the side of the A1 in Cambridgeshire in 1983. I can make nothing of the weird coincidence that connects the eighteenth-century Janice Weston with her tragic twentieth-century namesake. It seems like the plot of a novel.

Jill tells me that the Newberry Folio arrived with other books as part of the 'Silver Collection' in 1964 and she shows me a photo of the folio entering the library under armed guard. Somehow the folio surrounded by guns seems a distinctly Chicago image.

Toronto

Sitting at Gate E4 at Chicago's O'Hare Airport at 4.30 a.m., I watched 'heaven's artillery thunder in the skies'. My flight to Toronto was severely delayed. When we eventually landed, Toronto was sweltering and humid. I didn't have time to check in at the hotel, and headed straight for my appointment at the library. The taxi driver informed me that some of the surrounding roads were closed due to Freshers' Week, so I grabbed my case and waded through the crowds of very fresh-faced students. I made my sweaty way between two protest groups, one pro- and one anti-abortion, waving banners and shouting the other side down. I lugged my case up what seemed like an unnecessarily long flight of stairs and arrived in the lobby of the Thomas Fisher Rare Books Library, exhausted and sodden.

'You made it then,' a cheery voice behind me laughed, and I turned to find the very welcome face of Steve Rebbeck. I have known Steve since doing the York Mystery Plays in millennium year. He then took over as the RSC Technical Director. He now lives in Canada, and is going to accompany me on my Folio Roadshow for the next couple of days.

The Thomas Fisher Rare Books Library is a beautiful space. The reading room sits at the bottom of a five-storey hexagonal light well of ancient books. David Fernandez has risen through the ranks at Toronto University, where he was an undergrad, to become the Head of Department. This is his domain. 'They call this the Rosebud Folio,' he says, immediately conjuring up the murmured enigma of the dying words of Citizen Kane, as he drops the snow globe and whispers 'Rosebud'. So what riddles does the Toronto Folio contain? Surprisingly a real rosebud has at some time in its past been clamped between its pages, and left a ghostly imprint. 'I just can't remember where it is,' says David.

I ask him how he uses their copy of the folio. David is originally from Venezuela and his South American background contributes to his determination to set the book in a contemporary global context for the students. He suggests that acknowledging the challenges of Shakespeare's function as a colonial imposition is not to deny its intrinsic greatness, in fact it only deepens its significance. Just as mining the text for frequently suppressed expressions of same-sex love, and embracing those references with LGBTQ+ students, can create unexpected gateways into the plays.

I tell David about one of the lines that took my breath away when I was directing *Cymbeline* last year. Imogen, dressed as a boy, has

Scorpion/Rosebud in Toronto Folio

just encountered Belarius and the two boys in the Welsh mountains. She is overwhelmed by their generosity, and their kindness towards her. She turns to the audience and says: 'I'd change my sex to be companion with them.'

David finds the rosebud. It is the outline of a small bud, a dark yellow stain on the page in the last great scene of *Cymbeline*. But looking closely at the shadow of the rosebud, something else occurs to me. With its long stem in segments it also looks remarkably like a scorpion's tail. And then I spot the word it seems to be pointing to: 'Scorpion'.

So who knows, perhaps the image is more complex than the romantic associations of a pressed flower? Perhaps, like the Sphinx-like riddle of Citizen Kane's rosebud, there's a sting in the tail.

Stratford Festival Theatre, Ontario

Steve Rebbeck drives me out from Toronto to visit the Festival Theatre in the 'other Stratford' (Stratford, Ontario). There is no First Folio here: I just want to reach out a fraternal hand to our Canadian namesake. En route, we arrive in a little town called Shakespeare. It has a population of 160, a Shakespeare Truck Center, Shakespeare Pies and a Shakespeare Optimist Hall. Just seven miles further down the road from Shakespeare is Stratford. Steve and I wonder, as we stroll around the luxuriously expansive campus of the Festival Theatre, which came first: the town or the theatre? Is it just coincidence that they built a Shakespeare Theatre in a town called Stratford and that the willow-lined Avon River flows past it? We head up to the stage door to meet Antoni Cimolino, the Festival Theatre's dynamic director for the last decade.

Antoni and I have a similar career trajectory. He started as an actor at this theatre in 1988, and for the last decade he has been its Artistic Director. We are doing an event together at six, so he has a little time to show us around. As we approach the Festival Theatre, it appears like some grand jousting pavilion on the crest of a grassy hill, heralded by flags. Antoni reminds us of its history. The original theatre was indeed constructed in a tent, which was eventually replaced with a building that would recognise its original design. As we wander into the foyer, there are reminders of some of the great talents that Tyrone Guthrie attracted to the theatre in the early days. Here is a portrait of Alec Guinness as Richard III.

Antoni sneaks us into the back of the theatre for a few moments where a performance of *King Lear* is taking place. You can immediately see the brilliance of Guthrie and Tanya Moiseiwitsch's innovative design: a thrust pulling right down into the audience, who are wrapped around the space, with exits provided through sunken vomitoria allowing the staging to be dynamic and fluid. This theatre's influence on the theatres in Chichester and Sheffield, and on the Olivier at the National Theatre, is evident. The scene on stage is the fight between the feuding brothers, the disguised Edgar and the devious Edmund, while the fractious sisters bicker on the sidelines. Goneril has poisoned Regan, jealous of her claims on Edmund. As Regan clutches her stomach and groans, 'Sick, O sick', Goneril responds 'If not I'll ne'er trust poison'. Wonderful horrid laugh.

Buffalo

The Amtrak train crosses the Canadian border at Niagara Falls. I clamber off for the passport check and clamber right back on again for the twenty-odd more miles to Buffalo. I have come to see two copies of the First Folio here. One is kept at the Buffalo and Erie

County Public Library, on Lafayette Square, the other at Capen Hall on the campus of the University of Buffalo.

I make my way to Lafayette Square to meet librarians Susan Buttaccio and Amy Pickard, who take me down to the vault. Buffalo-born Colonel Charles Clifton, a major figure in the early days of the automative industry, secured a fascinating copy of the First Folio apparently owned by one of the King's Men. 'Samuel Gilburne' is written next to that name on the page listing the 'Principall Actors'.

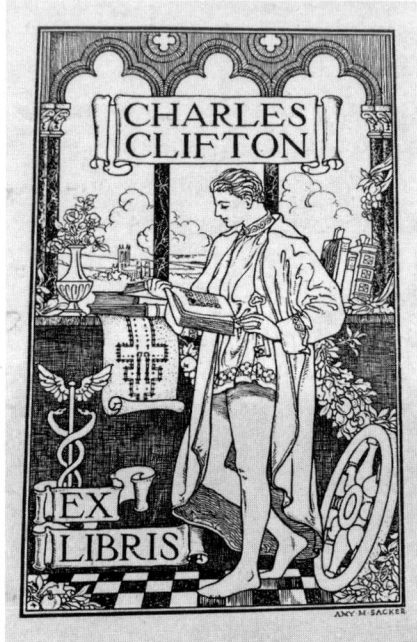

The Clifton bookplate

We know very little about the actor Samuel Gilburne, except that he was apprenticed to one of the original sharers in the Globe Theatre, Augustine Phillips. When Phillips died he bequeathed forty shillings to Samuel, along with his 'mouse-coloured' velvet hose, his black taffeta suit and white taffeta doublet, as well as his purple cloak, his sword, his dagger and his bass viol.

Henry Clay Folger, who had failed to see the reference to the Gilburne copy in the sales catalogue, was furious that he had missed a folio which evidently belonged to one of Shakespeare's own company and offered to swap Clifton's Folio for a much 'better' copy.

Folger could be dogged in pursuit of a folio he wanted, though the evidence that this copy ever belonged to Gilburne was flimsy at best. In the end, Folger had to trade not only a First Folio, but a set of all four folios and a copy of the 1640 Poems. And here they all are before me. Colonel Clifton's bookplate of a young squire in mediaeval dress reading an illuminated manuscript also references Clifton's job as an automobile manufacturer: a wheel is propped up behind him.

When I ask the 'what would you save in the event of a fire' question, Amy and Susan are already prepared. One of the County Library's most treasured possessions lies in its green cloth box on the table. It is the handwritten manuscript of Mark Twain's *Huckleberry Finn*. The first page contains a message to the reader which states *Persons attempting to find a motive in this narrative will be prosecuted. Persons trying to find a plot in it will be shot. By order of the Author.*

I love the chapter where one of the pair of charlatans posing as English actors deliver a faux-Shakespeare soliloquy:

> To be, or not to be; that is the bare bodkin
> That makes calamity of so long life:
> For who would fardels bear, till Birnam Wood do come to Dunsinane.
> But that the fear of something after death
> Murders the innocent sleep,
> Great nature's second course,
> And makes us rather sling the arrows of outrageous fortune
> Than fly to others that we know not of.

At Capen Hall on the university campus I am greeted by Jim Maynard in the Silverman Library. One fascinating textual anomaly unites the two Buffalo folios. It is a stage direction in *King Lear*. In the university folio it reads: '*H edis*', and in the Public Library folio it reads: '*H e dis*'. These two variants are uncommon: only twenty of the extant copies have one or the other of them. In well over half the copies the stage direction reads '*He dis*'. The compositor for this section of the folio is a seventeen-year-old apprentice and he makes a lot of mistakes, necessitating the careful scrutiny by his master, the printer, possibly Isaac Jaggard himself. Rather sadly he is the only compositor for whom we have a name: John Leason. Poor Leason has several goes at getting the stage direction right before he finally produces the correct version. The stage direction occurs as the old king expires, and should of course read '*He Dies*'.

★ ★ ★

I found out just how difficult setting type could be when I had a go myself at a workshop arranged by Judith Buchanan, Master of St Peter's College, Oxford, to celebrate the Folio quatercentenary. It took place in a letterpress workshop in the corner of the Quad of the Old Bodleian Library. The room is crammed with ancient printing machines and presses, trays of metal type and shelves of paper, and draped with washing lines on which various block prints have been pegged out to dry. The presiding genius is a tall, white-bearded gent called Richard Lawrence, wearing an inky pinafore. He splits the party up into five small groups and we are each tasked with setting a single line from the opening chorus of *Henry V*. I have the first line, 'O, For a Muse of Fire'.

I am given a composing stick, a small wooden tray about four inches long, to hold in my left hand and must place individual bits of metal type into it from 150 separate compartments in two sloping trays in front of me. The upper case holds the capital letters and the lower case, as you might have guessed, holds the lower-case letters. It's very tricky. You have to put them into the composing stick backwards and upside down, from right to left. There are blocks to place for spaces in the text. Each metal letter has a small nick at the top side, so you can tell it if you have placed them correctly.

You also have to trust that the type has been returned to the right box on the tray after its previous use. A laborious ten minutes later, carefully holding all the assembled letters, punctuation marks and blank spaces in place with my thumb, I take my completed composing stick round to Richard to be placed in the 'forme' for the whole page. But we discover I have placed a 'W' instead of an 'M', which when printed out would've read: 'O, For a *Wuse* of Fire'. Richard discreetly picks it out with a pair of tweezers and replaces it with the correct letter.

The task of typesetting the text could be challenging even for the original compositors. In one extant copy of the folio, the very first letter of the first word spoken was set incorrectly. The large decorated 'B' of the word 'Boatswain' has been placed upside down and was printed before anyone noticed the mistake and could correct it. Richard has chosen to set up the type for that very page, the first text page in the 1623 Folio, page 1 of *The Tempest*, so we can see how the printing press works. The page of metal type lies on the table of the press, with the ink applied. The slightly dampened paper ready for printing is placed on to the press's tympan, a fabric-covered frame set at an angle to the print bed. The paper is fixed behind the frisket (another great word), a sheet of oiled paper with a rectangle cut out of it which matches the size of the area to be printed.

We each bring a clean sheet of paper, place it under the frisket, lower the tympan onto the type and crank round a lever to produce the correct pressure between type and paper. The type has to 'kiss' the paper, we are told, not 'bite' it. I lift my paper off the type, and rejoice in my printed page. We are then all allowed to take them home with us like proud schoolchildren. The Bodleian printing workshop made me realise how fiendishly fiddly the work of the compositor could be. I began to reassess my opinion of poor John Leason, the much-maligned apprentice.

Woodcut of 'The Printer' from *The Book of Trades*

Cornell

It's Monday 11 September. The breakfast TV screens this morning are full of shattering imagery of the collapse of the Twin Trade Towers, twenty-two years ago today. Despite the over-familiarity of the footage, time has hardly diminished the shock. It reminds me of Shakespeare's Sonnet 64:

> When I have seen by Time's fell hand defaced
> The rich proud cost of outworn buried age;
> When sometime lofty towers I see down-razed
> And brass eternal slave to mortal rage …

'Lofty towers down-razed.' In the same sonnet Shakespeare seems to capture the anxiety attendant on political change:

> When I have seen such interchange of state,
> Or state itself confounded to decay …

Shakespeare moves from the global to the personal in the last quatrain. He captures a dreadful sense of apprehension which feels familiar to me:

> Ruin hath taught me thus to ruminate,
> That Time will come and take my love away.
> This thought is as a death, which cannot choose
> But weep to have that which it fears to lose.

I meet up with Ruth for the next cross-country stretch of my Folio Roadshow. She doesn't think it is safe for me to drive across the States by myself, and I manage to prove her not entirely wrong when we stop for gas and I deluge us both in gasoline as I try to fill the tank.

Today, we are in Ithaca, at Cornell, the first of the Ivy League universities on the journey. Cornell prides itself on being, since its founding, a co-educational, non-sectarian institution where admission has not been restricted by religion or race. The campus is situated on the top of a high hill with magnificent views over the Finger Lakes.

In the lobby of the Carl L. Kroch Library we are admiring a sculpture crafted of 'Brazilian granite, lapis lazuli motherlode' in the shape of a mighty book when a man with the broadest of beaming smiles says, 'Greg, right?'. Theo Black, a lecturer in the Department of Performing Arts, has come to join us, and, wheeling a trolley bearing precious cargo, Katherine Reagan, the Curator of Rare Books, appears and takes us all down to the reading room fifty-two feet underground in the basement of the building.

Ezra Cornell, who founded the university in 1865, believed that his students should learn about their subjects directly from the original printed matter, whether that be a Shakespeare First Folio or printed pamphlets from the French Revolution. One of Theo's students joins us. Tess has been studying Shakespeare directing and asks me how I use the First Folio as a director.

I made very particular use of the folio directing *Cymbeline* earlier this year, adding into the rehearsal script every case of capitalisation in the play to see what options for emphasis they might afford. For example, the very opening line of the play immediately sets a curious tone of anxiety. The First Gentleman says: 'You do not meet a man but Frowns.' The word 'Frowns', having a capital 'F', contributes to that mood. A little later in the scene, Posthumus's father is referred to. He died, before Posthumus was born, of grief for the loss of his two older sons in the war. But the simplicity of the phrase chosen to express the manner of his death is poignant: 'He quit Being.' Not he quit his life, or quit living, but (again fortified by the capital letter) 'He quit Being'. It's a very special experience to be sharing these thoughts using the First Folio itself for reference.

As we make our way back down the hill, one of the lawns is filled with little Stars and Stripes flags. There are 2,996 of them for both the victims and the hijackers who died in the Twin Towers of the World Trade Center that day.

Colgate University, Hamilton, New York

Ruth and I drive across state from Ithaca to Hamilton, 200 miles of rolling countryside, cornfields and grain silos and russet-red barns. Colgate University, like Cornell, sits atop a hill overlooking the wooded valleys of upstate New York. In the Case Library Xena

Becker, Special Collections librarian, has laid out all four folios as part of a 'Folio Fest'. We spend an hour or so enjoying the detail of their First Folio. There are three unidentified autographs: Mary Shipp, James Foreman and Ravenscroft. I wonder if this could be Edward Ravenscroft, the Restoration dramatist who wrote *The London Cuckolds*, and adapted *Titus Andronicus*, which he revived at Drury Lane in 1686, although he called it 'the most indigested piece in all his Works ... rather a heap of rubbish than a Structure'.

I am not expecting the surprise of opening their Third Folio and seeing a drawing of Anne Hathaway. It's a picture I have seen many times in reproduction, but here is the original, dated 1708. It looks like it has been drawn from an oil painting. Its delicate brown/red pencil lines reveal an enigmatic face with a clear stare and a faint smile. It is accompanied by a parody of the Ben Jonson lines on the Droeshout engraving:

> This figure, that thou there see'st put
> It was for Shakespear's consort cut

A note pasted into the volume claims the drawing was made by the owner's great-grandfather, Sir Nathaniel Curzon of Kedleston. The printed verses, it suggests, 'were made for the very rare edition of 1663, printed without the seven additional plays'. Anne Shakespeare (née Hathaway) died just months before the First Folio was published in 1623.

Williams College, Williamstown, Massachusetts

On 8 February 1940, an English professor called Sinclair E. Gillingham, carrying a briefcase and a raincoat over his arm, appeared at the Chapin Library in Williamstown asking to see their copy of the First Folio. He presented as his credentials a letter of recommendation from the President of Middlebury College in Vermont. The librarian seated him in a reading room and brought out the precious volume in its special protective cover and hand-marbled slipcase for examination. Some time later the professor said he was going to fetch his wife, but never returned. When the assistant librarian went to retrieve the book, she discovered that the folio was gone and a copy of *Reynard the Fox* (illustrated edition) chopped down to the exact size of the folio had been put in its place. A $1,000 reward was announced and the FBI were involved.

In fact, Professor Sinclair E. Gillingham turned out to be a shoe salesman called Donald Lynch from Hudson Falls. Mr Lynch had been promised payment of $1,000 by a Buffalo syndicate to steal the book, but they were slow in coming up with the money, and then only paid him in paltry instalments. Eventually, six months later, a disgruntled Lynch got drunk in a bar in Albany one night and, unaware, spilled the beans to the police. The syndicate were arrested.

Anne Peale, the present-day curator in the Chapin Library, shows me a scrapbook the library kept at the time. There are press cuttings about the whole drama, including mugshots of the thief and a photograph of the syndicate. They look like spivvy hoodlums from a Damon Runyon short story.

The whole scandal became headline news all over America. Even the famous newspaper journalist Walter Winchell in his syndicated *On Broadway* column referred to it. The men were arrested and charged and the folio came back to the Chapin Library unharmed. Anne Peale even shows me a copy of a letter from the Director of the FBI, J. Edgar Hoover, presenting an account of the whole saga.

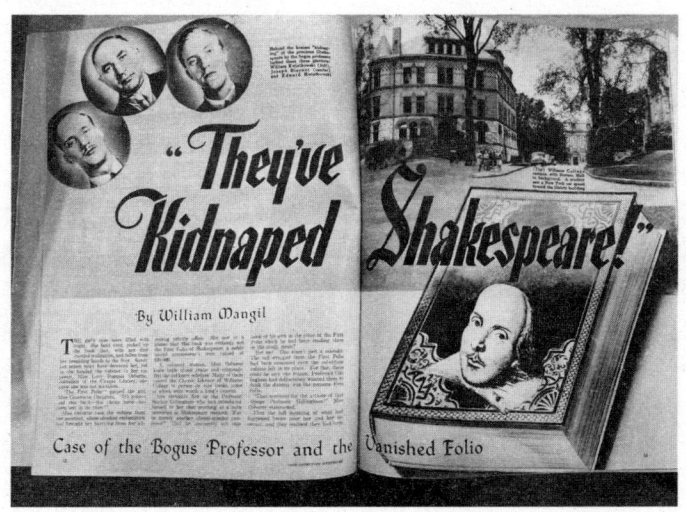

Magazine feature about the folio theft

★ ★ ★

There is an entire history of stolen folios. The Christie Library at the University of Manchester was inordinately proud of its First Folio. They acquired it in 1898, and went to the trouble of commissioning a specially designed glass-topped display case in light polished oak with appropriately Tudorbethan features: bulbous balusters, side panels carved with grapes and vine leaves, and decorative moulding called, splendidly, 'gadrooning'. It is a sumptuous marriage of Edwardian revivalism, and civic-minded bardolatry.

Normally a facsimile was placed on show, and the genuine folio was only displayed when the library was entertaining distinguished visitors. Unfortunately, on the night of Thursday 13 July 1972, the original folio was on exhibition, when thieves entered the library, smashed the plate-glass top and stole the folio.

The theft occurred just a week before a merger between the University Library and the Rylands was to be announced. Was the theft a protest against the merger, designed to spoil the celebrations? Could it have been an inside job? There was no sign of a break-in – the thieves apparently had a key. The Christie Library Folio has never been recovered. The case now stands forlornly empty in the university's Christie Building.

Dartmouth College, Hanover, New Hampshire

The entrepreneurial Matthew Ritger, Assistant Professor in the English Department, has invited me to join his Shakespeare class with freshers. He has persuaded the Head of Special Collections to share Dartmouth's First Folio with his students. They have carried it across the Green from the Rauner Library. I can't help thinking that Matthew's class is a pretty special start to their freshman year. Perhaps the most distinctive feature of the Dartmouth College First Folio is the presentation box it is stored in. It's a grandiose affair.

The first confirmed owner of the Dartmouth copy was Judge Willis Vickery from Cleveland, Ohio. He was a member of the exclusive invitation-only Rowfant Club, one of the oldest book clubs in America. It is still in existence and still exclusively male. On his retirement from the Bar, in February 1913, the members decided to present him with a gift. They had the Rowfant Club's own bindery make a case in which to keep his most prized possession, his Shakespeare First Folio. The elaborate box is a mock book in green morocco. You open the cover to reveal two hinged doors, decorated like a pair of swirly wrought-iron gates in gold. They suggest the promise of wonders beyond them, like the pearly gates opening onto paradise. And perhaps, like the gates of heaven (and the Rowfant Club), also guarding the entrance from those considered unworthy. Once opened, the folio lies in the cavity lined with green silk.

Perhaps the Rowfant members thought that Judge Vickery's folio needed the extra protection of a substantial box. Matthew shows the class photos from a family album in the college archive of the judge relaxing at his home, surrounded by pets, including a large marmalade cat, a blue budgerigar, and, looking in at the window, three hungry-looking raccoons he invited in on occasion. Behind his armchair, on a low shelf, sits the First Folio in its case alongside copies of the Second, Third and Fourth Folio. As Matthew said: 'Good thing his folio had that raccoon-proof box.'

Boston Public Library, Boston, Massachusetts

'This is probably the most boring copy of the First Folio that ever existed,' laughed the librarian at the Boston Public Library. There are no annotations and the copy has been scrupulously washed and trimmed and mended. So I don't feel so bad that I can't actually thumb my way through it as I have with every other copy I have seen so far on the Roadshow. It is behind glass on public display in the Special Collections Room. But instead, in contrast, they have pulled out their substantial collection of Shakespeare quartos for me to see. 'So quartos are the little cheap paperback editions of single plays that were published first, right?' Ruth asks. She has seen several folios by now, so showing her the difference between quartos and folios makes a nice change.

The first two we look at are both quartos of *Richard II*. The first copy, printed in 1598, has no abdication scene. The Duke of York arrives in Westminster Hall to tell Bolingbroke and the assembled lords that he has come from 'plume-pluckt Richard' who has agreed to yield his 'high sceptre' into Bolingbroke's hands. York tells him to ascend the throne and cries 'Long live Henry, fourth of that name'. The Bishop of Carlisle then makes his long, direful warning against the deed, is arrested by Northumberland for treason, and Henry declares he will be crowned 'on Wednesday next'. And there the scene ends. It adequately serves its purpose, and follows the historical record, as Richard II never actually made a public abdication in Westminster Hall, but stayed in the Tower throughout.

The next quarto we see is the 1615 quarto of *Richard II*. The title page advertises that it contains *new additions of the Parliament scene and the deposing of King Richard*. Turning to the same scene in this quarto, you have the dramatic arrival of the 'skipping king', and his virtuoso display of volatility, ricocheting from wallowing self-pity to petulant preening, capricious, provocative and hurt. It's at once a spectacular performance and a howl of despair. Did the play as performed originally include the abdication scene but the 1598 quarto excluded publication of it out of fear of retribution, only too aware of Elizabeth's sensitivity around any discussion of the succession? Or was the abdication scene written especially for performance on Saturday 7 February 1601, the eve of the Essex Rebellion* (as has recently been suggested) when Shakespeare's company was paid forty shillings by Essex's supporters to revive that particular play for a single performance, to stir the city to support their cause? The company certainly got themselves into hot water for presenting the play that night, as the queen knew precisely what the choice of play implied. 'I am Richard II,' she cried, 'know ye not that?'

The new scene runs over four and a half quarto pages, and contains perhaps 165 lines, which would be a running time of ten to twelve minutes. That is quite a long additional scene to write on demand, let alone learn, rehearse and insert at two days' notice, into a play that had been out of the repertoire for some years, and already would have required substantial re-rehearsal.

I find the question enthralling. If Shakespeare actually wrote that scene to order, during the lifetime of Queen Elizabeth, it would surely convey his political affiliations more directly than he ever does elsewhere, a daring, subversive but atypical act defining his own

---

*The unsuccessful uprising by the Earl of Essex against Elizabeth, for which he was beheaded.

attitude with dangerous potential consequences. Who knows? But looking at the two versions printed in these two quartos seventeen years apart, the issue feels very alive.

★ ★ ★

The next quarto we are shown is *Pericles*, advertised as *The late and much admired play*. *Pericles* is the one significant play not to appear in the First Folio, although, as this quarto copy makes clear, it had been printed by then, in 1609. Then we examine a quarto of *Much Ado About Nothing* (dated 1600) which belonged to George Steevens, one of the great eighteenth-century editors of Shakespeare. He has had the quarto remounted with wide paper margins so he can write his notes on the text. It's compelling to read his editorial thoughts as they occur to him, and he scribbles them in pencil down the side.

In Act 2, Benedick has been tricked into believing Beatrice is in love with him. A surly Beatrice then arrives and says: 'Against my will I am sent to bid you come in to dinner.' After a little rude banter she exits, leaving Benedick to replay the conversation. In one of the sure-fire laughs in the play, Benedick then says: 'Ha! "Against my will I am sent to bid you come in to dinner;" there's a double meaning in that!' In his margin note, Steevens rather misses the point of the joke and unpicks a double meaning suggesting a coded reference to the author and writes in the margin: 'My Will-I-am!'

George Steevens left his initials with its trademark asterisk G★S against every Shakespearian entry he could find in the Stationers' Register, including against the entry for the 1623 Folio. An eighteenth-century version of 'Kilroy was 'ere!'

Ruth flies back to Colorado tomorrow. I have the Rosh Hashanah weekend to myself.

Boston: Europa in America

A free Sunday in Boston. I arrive at the Isabella Stewart Gardner Museum on the Fenway as the doors open and head straight up to the third floor in order to beat the crowds and look at one of the most influential and iconic Renaissance paintings in America. Isabella Stewart Gardner was one of the great art collectors of the Gilded Age, and in 1896 she acquired a painting that she later called 'a whacker'. And here it is: Titian's *Rape of Europa*. It was one of a series of paintings which Titian executed for his patron King Philip II of Spain, all based on stories from Ovid, including 'Venus and Adonis' and 'Diana and Actaeon'. *The Rape of Europa* was hanging at Cobham Hall in Kent when the owner of the house, the 6th Earl of Darnley, saddled with mounting debts and a son and heir who 'spent money like water', decided he had no option but to sell it.

Isabella's young friend and scout, the handsome art connoisseur Bernard Berenson, advised her that the painting could be hers if she acted swiftly. There was a public outcry in Britain. Too many of the aristocracy, faced with plummeting revenues from their estates, were selling off the family treasure, and too much of that was heading across the pond to the United States. Nevertheless, Isabella paid a staggering £20,000 for it.* More than had been paid for any other painting at the time.

As I walk around Isabella Stewart Gardner's faux-palazzo in the late summer sunshine, I become aware of just how seriously she took her passion to introduce the glories of Western art to her homeland. Around the mock Venetian courtyard, plush with blue and white delphiniums, and dotted with Roman sarcophagi and statues, wind three floors of treasures. All acquired (or elegantly plundered) with her enormous wealth. Giottos and Botticellis, a gorgeous close-up of Christ carrying the cross from the school of Bellini, Veroneses and Guardis, tapestries and altarpieces.

There is a magnificent portrait by Rubens of Thomas Howard, the 14th Earl of Arundel. Rubens painted the Earl in armour, but his reputation relied more on his work as a diplomat and as a collector. He was known as the Collector Earl, as he made his name as the original 'Grand Tourist', during the reigns of James I and Charles I. While in Rome he was allowed to conduct an archaeological dig, and 'discovered' a number of ancient Roman statues, which had probably been planted for him to dig up. They now form the basis of the long sculpture gallery at the entrance to the Ashmolean in Oxford.

---

* Perhaps £3,500,000 in today's money.

In his time in Italy he collected over 600 paintings, and drawings by Leonardo da Vinci, which are now in the Royal Collection at Windsor. Ironically the portrait is rather upstaged by the blank wall spaces on either side of it. Two great Rembrandt paintings, one of a Lady and Gentleman in black and the other of Christ in the storm on the Sea of Galilee, were stolen from the museum in a heist in 1990 along with Vermeer's *The Concert* and several drawings by Degas.

★ ★ ★

Just as the passion of people like Isabella Stewart Gardner and Henry Huntington to share the culture of the Old World with their home country has blessed Boston and Los Angeles with resplendent collections, so the bibliomaniacal bardolatry of people like Henry Clay Folger has given the States – and the world – its most exceptional Shakespeare Collection. About 60 per cent of the surviving First Folios are here in North America. And of those 144 folios, eighty-two are at the Folger Library in Washington.

In Boston I hear news that the long-awaited opening of the new exhibition space at the Folger Library slated for this fall has been delayed. Disappointingly, it would not open at all in 2023, and will not now be welcoming visitors until an unspecified date in the future. With the Folger out of the picture for now, I decided that at the end of this leg of the Folio Roadshow I would head down to Texas instead, adding another four folios I was not expecting to see to my total, and 1,500 miles to the distance travelled. Meanwhile, on to my next folio date in Massachusetts.

Harvard University, Cambridge, Massachusetts

> Some books are to be tasted, others to be swallowed, and some few to be chewed and digested.
> From Francis Bacon's essay 'Of Studies'

The left shoe on the otherwise weathered-bronze statue of John Harvard in Harvard Square has been rubbed to shiny copper. I suspect it's a tradition, akin to kissing the foot of St Peter's statue in his basilica in the Vatican, for prayers to be answered, presumably in this case those of generations of Harvard students hoping to pass their exams. The breasts of the statue of Juliet in Verona have received similar attention from those hoping to be lucky in love, while the brazen testicles of the Charging Bull on New York's Wall Street positively gleam.

John Harvard is described as the founder of Harvard University, though his statue is a Victorian sculpture and, as there were no existing portraits of Harvard himself, it was modelled on a student called Sherman Hoar (Class of 1882) dressed in the Puritan garb of the 1630s. John was a graduate of Cambridge University in England, and emigrated to America in 1637. The following year, he died of tuberculosis, leaving his library and estate to the college, who decided to rename the institution after him.

John's grandfather, a butcher named Thomas Roger, came from Stratford-upon-Avon. He served as an alderman for the Stratford Corporation alongside William Shakespeare's father John. Thomas lived in a fine house on the High Street (next to the Garrick Inn). The gabled Harvard House, with each of its three storeys jutting a little further out into the street, is the most splendid timber-framed building in the town. Thomas Roger rebuilt the house after a fire swept away a number of the houses in Stratford in 1594. He carved his own initials and those of his second wife, Alice, onto one of the beams. His daughter Katherine married one John Harvard in 1605, and it was their son, also John, who became the benefactor of this university.

But it is the story of another Harvard man that I have come here today to discover. So I leave the statue (foot unrubbed) and make my way among the students, dashing in the rain from one class to another, up the steps of a monumental building emblazoned with the name The Harry Elkins Widener Memorial Library.

Harry Elkins Widener (Harvard Class of 1907) was a prodigious book collector. He came from a Philadelphia family whose immense wealth was derived from railroads, steel and tobacco. His indulgent mother Eleanor encouraged his passion by giving him not only a copy of Shakespeare's First Folio, but a Second, Third and Fourth Folio as well. At only twenty-seven, he owned a library of 3,000 books, including a Gutenberg Bible, and was already a member of

New York's prestigious Grolier Club (another private establishment for prominent bibliophiles).

In the spring of 1912, Harry was on a 'quick trip' to Paris and London. He was travelling with his father George D. Widener and his valet Edwin, his mother Eleanor and her maid Amalie. His father was looking for a chef for his new hotel in Philadelphia, the Ritz Carlton. Harry, meanwhile, had managed to purchase a first edition of Francis Bacon's *Essays* (1597). The quarto edition could easily fit in his pocket. Harry wrote a letter to a friend setting out his travel plans: '[we] return on April 10th, on the maiden voyage of *The Titanic*'. As Harry helped his mother and her maid into the fourth lifeboat, the story goes that he ran back to his cabin to fetch his copy of Bacon's *Essays*. Another version of the legend suggests he said to his mother, tapping his pocket, 'Little Bacon goes with me'.*

I wonder what, if any, sustenance or consolation he might have received from Francis Bacon on that terrible night among the icebergs in the North Atlantic. In his essay *Of Death* Bacon writes: 'But above all believe it, the sweetest canticle is *Nunc Dimittis* ['now let thy servant depart in peace'] when a man hath obtained worthy ends and expectations.' And though at twenty-seven Harry Elkins Widener cannot have been said to have fulfilled his potential, he was able to pass on a considerable legacy. Harry's mother and her maid were picked up by the *Carpathia* when the *Titanic* foundered. Both her son and her husband perished. Their bodies were never recovered. On her return home Eleanor gave a grant to Harvard to build a library in memory of her son and to house his book collection, including his Shakespeare Folios.

From the security gate at the entrance to the library you can see up the stairs to a portrait framed by huge doors. As you enter and cross a white marble hall, it strikes you that this is an extravagant mausoleum built by a grieving mother for her son. His picture is

---

* Some believe that Harry went back to retrieve a book whose safe transportation across the Atlantic he had been entrusted with. *The Great Omar* was a copy of Edward Fitzgerald's *The Rubáiyát of Omar Khayyám*, sumptuously bound by Sangorski & Sutcliffe in 1912, with 100 square feet of 22-carat feathered gold leaf in the tooling and edges, decorated with over a thousand semi-precious stones: peacocks with ruby eyes and topaz in their tail feathers, surrounded by vines of amethyst grapes. The book sank with the ship and was never recovered.

an altarpiece to a young man whose life was cut tragically short and who will now always be defined by his death.

★ ★ ★

I am shown the folio that Harry owned along with the other Harvard Folio, by Matthew Wittmann, Curator of the Harvard Theatre Collection, and his associate Dale Stinchcomb. We are in the Houghton Library, in an oval room of genteel Georgian opulence named after Dr Samuel Johnson and under the quizzical gaze of the great panjandrum himself, in a portrait by John Opie. Professor Stephen Greenblatt arrives from his office in the English Department next door, to share the viewing with us. Stephen's peerless book *Tyrant* has been my constant companion directing Shakespeare's history plays.

We enjoy other treasures: two prop handkerchiefs, spotted with strawberries, from the production of *Othello* with Paul Robeson, and a letter dated 1944 from a theatre owner in Waco, Texas, saying that if the production toured there it would be impossible for 'the whites and the negroes' to be seated together. Robeson's production did not tour the Southern States.

Brandeis University, Waltham, Massachusetts

> This precious book of love, this unbound lover,
> To beautify him, only lacks a cover
>
> *Romeo and Juliet* (Act 1 scene 3)

The Brandeis copy of the First Folio was a surprise. It has been 'disbound'. The folio, which librarian Susan Shoemaker carefully lifts from its case, has had its binding and cover painstakingly removed. The previous nineteenth-century binding of blue morocco with a gold-tooled border sits abandoned beside it. The folio looks rather vulnerable, stripped naked. What has happened?

The volume was deliberately 'disbound' by the Northeast Document Conservation Center back in 1998, in order for it to be digitised by the Perseus Project, and made available online through Internet Shakespeare Editions. Despite its forlorn state, the Brandeis

Folio gives a clear insight into how these folios were bound. You can see every stab hole the binder's needle made, how the separate gatherings, or individual quires of pages have been stacked up and sewn together. On the spine, the five band ridges are visible, the cords affixed to the signatures and used to hold the book together. Scruffy remnants of the animal glue used to attach the spine are still evident. The 'disbound' Brandeis copy reminds me of another folio.

A 1623 Folio in Durham was also 'disbound', but in truth it was ripped apart. It was kept in the episcopal library of the Bishop of Durham, a beautiful seventeenth-century wood-panelled library built in 1669, known as the Cosin's Library, and situated in the close of the ancient cathedral on Palace Green. In December 1998, the folio was on display along with other rare books in the library when it was stolen. It disappeared for a decade, until one summer day in 2008 when a man walked into the Folger Library in Washington, DC, asking for help in identifying a book in his possession.

He produced a First Folio in a very sorry state. He said he had been given it in Cuba, where it had been kept in a box by the mother of a major in Fidel Castro's army. The librarians knew in a matter of minutes what this battered copy was. They asked the man if they could keep it in overnight to examine it. The man agreed. His name was Raymond Scott.

While on holiday in Havana, Scott had fallen for a nightclub dancer half his age. He somehow needed to fund the playboy lifestyle to which he felt he was entitled, and he thought the First Folio might buy that for him. What Scott didn't know was that as a physical object the First Folio is perhaps the most studied volume in the world. Every bookplate, every single manuscript annotation, every watermark and rust spot, every tiny piece of foxing or damage or repair has been checked and catalogued. The Folger librarians knew almost immediately that this was the stolen Durham Folio. Scott was arrested for handling stolen goods.

Raymond Scott projected himself as an international playboy. He was not only a fantasist, but also a flamboyant narcissist. He arrived to answer bail at Durham city police station in a gold-coloured stretch limo flanked by burly minders, wearing a full-length sable coat, Tiffany shades and silver crocodile-skin shoes by Versace. He was clutching a bottle of Dom Pérignon, a large Cuban cigar and a

Pot Noodle. But despite his claims of an extravagant lifestyle with a home in Monte Carlo, the prosecution revealed that in fact he had been amassing huge credit card debts of over £90,000, while living on the dole with his eighty-year-old mum in a modest terraced house in Tyne and Wear, not ten miles from the scene of the crime.

In 2010 Scott was given an eight-year prison sentence for handling stolen goods. The severity of the sentence shocked many. What danger was he to the general public? Many standard sentences for rape are not that long. But perhaps that is the point. Somehow Scott's crime was not regarded just as petty theft. The First Folio was not just a book, it was an object sacred to our shared heritage, and its mutilation at his hands was an act of sacrilege. Scott quoted Andy Warhol saying that in the future everyone would be famous for fifteen minutes. After two years of his harsh custodial sentence, Scott was found one morning in his cell with his throat cut. He had committed suicide.

The ultimately tragic story of the Durham Folio is a potent reminder of the dangers of fetishising the First Folio, and the costs incurred. The price Raymond Scott paid was far too high.

Chapter Seventeen
The Book World's Jekyll and Hyde

Before heading to Providence, Rhode Island, I want to revisit the story of a man who haunts the history of Shakespeare scholarship. James Orchard Halliwell-Phillipps is a controversial figure who had deep but complex associations with Stratford-upon-Avon. He is also the man responsible for removing the Droeshout engraving from the front of our RSC copy of the First Folio.

The Shakespeare Birthplace Trust (SBT) in Stratford was set up by Halliwell-Phillipps, so it feels a little disloyal (albeit entirely accurate) for their website to describe their founder as 'the Book World's Jekyll and Hyde'. But they can present as evidence of his "Hyde crimes" shelves and shelves of his uniformly bound scrapbooks (he made hundreds of them) into which he has pasted items cut out from rare editions of seventeenth-century plays and books, including, for example, leaves from Ben Jonson's 1616 Folio. In one such scrapbook at SBT he has clipped out a woodcut of eglantine, from a copy of *Gerard's Herbal* of 1597, and one of knotgrass (Lysander calls Hermia 'You minimus of hindering knot-grass made').

In the process of this wanton vandalism he destroyed some 800 books, and made 3,600 scraps. It has been argued in his defence that making scrapbooks was common practice in the Victorian period and we have no evidence of disapproval of his behaviour from any of his contemporaries. So it is perhaps not surprising that he took his scissors to our own copy of the First Folio. But the reason he removed the Droeshout engraving was, it turns out, because it was a very important print of that engraving, in what is referred to as 'the first state', before it was retouched. The 'second state' has the added shadow on the standing collar. There is even a 'third state', in which minimal and almost imperceptible changes have been made: a stray hair, and an adjustment to the highlight in the eyes.

So who was this young book collector with an eye for a rarity?

The young James Orchard Halliwell made a considerable name for himself. By the age of nineteen he had been made a Fellow of the Society of Antiquaries and a Fellow of the Royal Society, although he left Cambridge without taking his degree. He had built up a remarkable book collection, and published his first work on Shakespeare, and was busy editing the Coventry Mystery Plays, Dr Dee's private diary and the letters of the astrologer Simon Forman. It was at this point that he came to the attention of the greatest private book collector England had ever known, Sir Thomas Phillipps, who invited this young prodigy to Middle Hill, his country estate in Worcestershire. The house, built in 1724, still stands today.

About half an hour's drive from Stratford-upon-Avon is Broadway Tower. The famous turreted folly stands on top of the beautiful Cotswold escarpment overlooking the handsome honey-coloured village from which it takes its name. Since 1822 the Tower had become known as the *Lighthouse of Wisdom*, when Thomas Phillipps set up a press inside it to issue catalogues of his ever-expanding book collection. Middle Hill lies just below the Tower. Perhaps Phillipps invited James for a brisk climb up to the *Lighthouse of Wisdom*, on one of those bright crisp February mornings during his visit. Perhaps they were accompanied by the widowed Sir Thomas's three daughters. Certainly James, a tall, slender twenty-year-old, made an impression on the eldest, Henrietta, who later described him as 'fair but pale and with blue eyes – well-tempered and as kind as possible to me'.

Over the next few months, Halliwell was invited back to Middle Hill on a number of occasions. The house had twenty-one rooms, sixteen of which were devoted to Sir Thomas's huge and immensely valuable book collection. Phillipps was paranoid about their safety. He had specially designed cases made to store them, so they could be swiftly transported away if fire broke out. But then with a weird, chopped logic, he created a potential fire hazard by placing piles of logs in the rooms to distract beetles away from the books, and prevent their predations.

At some point that spring, James proposed to Henrietta. The swiftness of that proposal might suggest opportunism on the young book collector's part. If at first Sir Thomas considered the match favourable, he soon changed his mind and became implacably opposed to it. However, the determined Henrietta was quietly resolute, and on the morning of Tuesday 9 August, her sisters Mary and Kate helped her dress, and afterwards, as she writes in her diary, 'marching along the plantation to the top of the lane ... I met my intended and walked with him down to the church'.

The beautiful old church, on Snowshill Road, dates back to the twelfth century and is dedicated to St Eadburgha. That morning it was filled with well-wishers, many of whom threw flowers into the chaise as the newlyweds sped off to Cheltenham to begin the journey by rail and ferry to their honeymoon on the Isle of Wight. The only question her angry father had about the wedding ceremony was who had given his daughter away. Phillipps never forgave Henrietta, or her husband. In fact, he did everything he could to cut her off from her inheritance and to prevent his collection falling into his wretched son-in-law's hands. Even before James and Henrietta married, the fifty-year-old Sir Thomas had taken a wife nearly half his age. 'The bride is very fair with tight ringlets, short, rather stout and twenty-seven years old,' Henrietta confided tartly to her diary.

Later Sir Thomas bought an entirely new property to house his massive collection, on which his family would have no claim. Thirlestaine House (now part of Cheltenham College) had galleries so long you could ride a horse through them. He left Middle Hill to rot.

Two years after the wedding, in 1844, Halliwell was plunged into a crisis which would stigmatise him for the rest of his life. The British Museum discovered it had several books in its possession which had been stolen from the library of Trinity College Cambridge, where Halliwell had matriculated as a student in November 1837. The theft was traced back to Halliwell, who had sold the books to the BM. The official investigation was followed by a national outcry and Halliwell was banned from the British Museum. The case was never proved, but the ban was never rescinded, so the suspicion remained.

Later in his life Halliwell was to be accused of an even more heinous crime. In his business dealings in the book trade he was accused of selling two precious 'Shakespeare' items to the British Museum:

the mortgage deed to the Blackfriars Gatehouse (with one of the few genuine Shakespeare signatures) and a copy of the First Quarto of *Hamlet*. The First Quarto of *Hamlet* was a very rare item indeed. Known as the Bad Quarto, it is thought to be a memorial reconstruction of the text. Only two copies were known to exist. One had been discovered in a closet in a Suffolk manor house in 1823 and was now in the possession of the Duke of Devonshire,* and the other, according to one of the many catalogues of his books, belonged to Sir Thomas Phillipps. Had Halliwell stolen not only Sir Thomas's daughter but also his rarest treasure?

Halliwell provided unequivocal evidence of where he had purchased the rare quarto, but his reputation for light-fingered larceny persisted. Long after his death, the writer E. V. Lucas, who once met Halliwell, wrote: 'He had no scruples about taking something he thought he was more worthy to possess or able to protect.' The British Library still hold that copy of the Bad Quarto of *Hamlet*. It is missing its first page, which could well have once held a Middle Hill stamp or the bookplate of Sir Thomas Phillipps.

By his mid-forties Halliwell had become recognised as an eminent Shakespeare scholar. He had forged a close relationship with Stratford-upon-Avon, and was joint secretary of the tercentenary celebrations there in 1864. He had also set about purchasing the land on which Shakespeare's house, New Place, was built; rescuing from dilapidation the house in Henley Street where Shakespeare was born; and trying to retain as much of the town Shakespeare knew as still existed. It is at about this time that he buys the folio: our Theatre Copy.

By the age of fifty, he had abandoned textual analysis of Shakespeare and devoted himself to elucidating his life. This retreat from the battlefield of academia might have been prompted by the need to look after his wife, after a riding accident led to her slow mental decline, and ultimately to being placed in a care home. After the accident, and just five years after Thomas Phillipps had died, James Halliwell secured his own inheritance by legally adding his father-in-law's name to his and thus becoming James Orchard Halliwell-Phillipps. Halliwell-Phillipps became

---

* This is the copy now in "deep freeze" at the Huntington Library.

highly proprietorial of the archive and the Trust he had curated in Stratford and was suspicious of any attempts to siphon potential funds away from it.

When Stratford decided it wanted to build a theatre in Shakespeare's name in the town, Halliwell-Phillipps felt it would divert too much attention away from the Birthplace Trust, and was fiercely opposed. He wrote that the different parties competing to secure funding for their projects in the town became 'as frantic as lions and tigers in the Zoological Gardens when feeding time approaches'. He became the inveterate enemy of the man who largely funded the Shakespeare Memorial Theatre, Charles 'Self-Raising' Flower. Halliwell-Phillipps called Flower at one point 'His Imperial Majesty King Charles III of Stratford'. Just under a month before the theatre opened, Henrietta (his beloved 'Harry') died. Though how much they had grown apart during her decline might be measured by the fact that he married a woman called Mary Rice Hobbes on 21 June, within three months of Henrietta's death.

The year the Shakespeare Memorial Theatre opened, 1879, was also the year that Halliwell-Phillipps's relationship with the whole of Stratford began to break down. His biographer, Marvin Spevack, calls it a 'painfully disappointing split'. As well as Flower, he had also fallen out with the vicar of Shakespeare's church, Holy Trinity, the redoubtable Rev. George Arbuthnot, whose 'so-called' restoration of the church Halliwell-Phillipps regarded as 'a serious piece of vandalism'. Halliwell-Phillipps's antipathy for the church and the theatre was soon matched by his fury at the town, and after a fierce row with the corporation in 1884, he left Stratford for ever. Yet Stratford was where his soul lived. It was like Coriolanus turning his back on Rome. But was there a world elsewhere?

★ ★ ★

In his last decade the increasingly erratic Halliwell-Phillipps (he called himself 'a retired old lunatic') created a ramshackle home on the South Downs. Hollingbury Copse was an assortment of build-it-yourself bungalows, roughly attached together, which he called his 'rustic wigwam'. He stored his collection here, and in the dining room he proudly showed his guests his prize possession: the

Droeshout engraving in its original state. This was the engraving he had cut out of our Theatre Copy of the First Folio. But where did it go after his death?

Looking again at the Sidney Lee Census two things strike me. First the statement: *sold with other books from Halliwell-Phillipps's library in July 1889 for £95, when it was acquired by Charles Edward Flower, of Stratford-on-Avon, for presentation to the Memorial library there.* It's ironic that the copy was acquired for the library by Halliwell-Phillipps's arch-enemy, Flower. Then a sentence whose significance had escaped me the first time I read it: *To this copy originally belonged the early proof impression which was detached by Halliwell-Phillipps, and was sold with the Halliwell-Phillipps Shakespearean Collection in 1897, to Marsden J. Perry, Esq., Providence, Rhode Island, U.S.A.* When I visit Brown University in Providence on my Folio Roadshow tomorrow, I am going to see if I can track down that first state engraving that James Orchard 'Scissorhands' Halliwell removed from our folio. If I do, I shall ask for it back.

Brown University, Providence, Rhode Island

Brown University possesses two 1623 Folios. The first one is at the John Hay Library. But on opening it I quickly realised that this could not be the copy with our Droeshout engraving as all the preliminary pages turn out to be facsimiles. So I put my scalpel knife away.

Two of the bookplates in this volume belong to owners from Stratford-upon-Avon. The first is the Rev. John Day Collis. He was the vicar of Holy Trinity in Stratford until 1879, the year the Memorial Theatre opened, and was the immediate predecessor to Halliwell-Phillipps's adversary the Rev. Arbuthnot. We have him to thank for building the river terrace to the east of the church. Collis also moved the altar rails 'downstage' of the Shakespeare family gravestones, which meant the general public had to pay their respects to the funerary monument from the chancel floor. There are two small stained-glass lancet windows in the porch of Holy Trinity Church celebrating the life and good works of the Rev. Collis and his wife, Elizabeth.

The John Hay copy also has a bookplate for one Captain William Jaggard. Jaggard claimed descent from the original printer of the First Folio, William Jaggard. From 1910 until his death in 1947, Captain Jaggard ran the Shakespeare Bookshop in Sheep Street in a building dating back to 1490. It is now the popular restaurant Vintners.

Brown's second 1623 Folio is held at the John Carter Brown Library, just a few minutes' walk across a small park called Quiet Green from the John Hay Library. It proves not to be the beneficiary of our Droeshout engraving either, as it is in fact one of those very fourteen perfect copies (*Class 1 Division A*) identified by Sidney Lee's census. So I seemed to have drawn a blank in my search for our missing Droeshout and decided I wouldn't be going home in triumph with our errant frontispiece. But then I remembered another detail in the Lee Census: the man in Providence, Rhode Island, who purchased the Halliwell-Phillipps Collection. Who was Marsden J. Perry Esq.?

Marsden Jaseal Perry had the Midas touch, a fabulously wealthy man who bought up much of the town's utilities, from gas and electricity companies to the streetcars that ran on that electricity. He became known as 'the man who owned Rhode Island'. He was also a bibliophile and a great collector of Georgian furniture and Chinese porcelain, but as the son of a farmer and despite his financial clout he was looked down upon by the old money in town. I find a cartoon of Marsden J. Perry sitting on the Union Trust building, a steel-frame, brick and stone office building constructed in 1902, and at the time, the tallest in Providence. It's right down the street from my hotel.

Perry amassed a vast collection of Shakespeare material, but when he lost out on the sale of the Duke of Devonshire's library to a higher bidder, he decided to give up collecting if he could not be the best. And when his fortune was decimated by the Panic of 1907, the first worldwide banking crash (known as the Knickerbocker Crisis), he sold his entire collection ... including the James Orchard Halliwell-Phillipps Collection ... to Henry Clay Folger. So ... Folger Library watch out! When you finally do reopen, I am coming to find out which of your folios has the RSC Folio's engraving in it, or if in one of those many possibly uncatalogued boxes amassed

Cartoon of Marsden J. Perry

by Halliwell-Phillipps, and bought by Folger, there is an unattached original Droeshout in search of a home.*

★ ★ ★

While awaiting my appointment at the John Carter Brown Library, I dawdle in the dappled shade of Quiet Green. In the corner is a ninety-five-foot-high campanile clocktower. It is an icon of the Brown campus. The Carrie Tower was built by a grieving husband for the wife he lost.

Count Paul Bajnotti was an eccentric globetrotter from Turin. In 1875, while serving as a diplomat he fell in love in Rhode Island with Carrie Mathilde Brown, the granddaughter of Brown University namesake Nicholas Brown Jr. After sixteen years of happy marriage,

---

*The Folger finally reopened to the public in June 2024.

Carrie caught the flu, which progressed to pneumonia, and she died. In his grief, Bajnotti paid for the construction of this tower in her memory, and named it after her. Over the lintel there is an inscription from the Song of Solomon which reads: LOVE IS STRONG AS DEATH.

It catches me out. It seems like a reproof, or an accusation of betrayal. Perhaps in trying so hard to forget what happened, I have forgotten to remember.

Chapter Eighteen
North American Folio Roadshow II: Connecticut to Texas

Yale University, New Haven, Connecticut

The visit to Yale starts badly.

I am sitting in a reading room at the Beinecke Library, waiting to see their First Folio, when a person leans against the doorpost and announces that they have some bad news. Crossed wires: the folio isn't there, it's in conservation, and can't be seen. Eve Houghton, my host for the day, is embarrassed. But I persist, and ask if we can go and see it in the conservation lab, adding that the New York Public Library took me to theirs in Long Island City and it was one of my most interesting visits. Our adversary doesn't think that would be convenient. I say I have come rather a long way to see it and of all the folios I have seen I wouldn't want to miss out the Yale Folio.

In the meantime, Eve takes me to see Yale's other folio in an exhibition she has curated in the Sterling Memorial Library. As we leave the Beinecke I marvel at its innovative architecture. At its centre is a six-storey book tower enclosed in glass, surrounded by outer walls of tiles of thin, translucent, veined marble from Vermont, which diffuse the light and bathe the lobby in a soft amber gloaming.

The Sterling Library on the other hand was modelled on Salisbury Cathedral. And whereas the Beinecke is refreshingly and uncompromisingly modern, this library, and much of the Yale campus, is deliberately made to look ancient and studiously august. Eve's exhibition is called 'The First Folio: Shakespeare for all time?' The title echoes Ben Jonson's famous assertion that Shakespeare was 'not for an age but for all time', but the provocative question mark at the end invites us to question the values (aesthetic, monetary and ethical) that we have come to ascribe to Shakespeare. The First Folio is here under glass, and though I don't get to examine it intimately, other wonders are constellated around it.

Delia Bacon's copy of Shakespeare is here. Born in a log cabin in Ohio, Delia was one of the first to question the authorship of Shakespeare, and her copy is covered in her bizarre scribbled notes. In *Love's Labour's Lost*, next to Moth's line to Don Armado ('I will add the l'envoy: say the moral again'), Delia writes: 'I will add the sense "Say the word Raleigh again"' – evidently revealing that Sir Walter Raleigh is the true author of the play. And next to Costard's line 'O, marry me to one Frances', Delia writes 'Bacon', asserting that her namesake (though no relation) Sir Francis Bacon might also be a candidate. Further irrefutable evidence towards her mission to prove that the plays were not written by the man from Stratford.

She once spent a night in Holy Trinity Church intending to dig up Shakespeare's tomb to find hidden relics to prove Bacon's authorship, but she became spooked when she heard a noise in the dark church (it was the sexton who had come to check what she was doing) and she ran away. Shortly afterwards she was admitted to a lunatic asylum, and finally was returned to the States. Eve tells me Delia is buried here in New Haven.

In the next case, there is an unbound half-sheet of one of the many editions of *Richard III*. And a quarto of *Romeo and Juliet* in which Elisabeth Rotton has worked out a wry anagram of her own name: 'Her lot is to b neat'. And I learn another marvellous word on my Folio Roadshow, along with 'pilcrow' and 'deckle'. A 'sammelband' is a set of disparate texts, separately printed and later gathered in a single binding, in this case Ben Jonson's plays.

As I am examining it, Eve gets news that we can indeed see the folio in the Gates Lab. We Uber across town to Yale's new book conservation facility, and meet Paula Zyats, Head of Rare Books and Manuscript Conservation. I have the pleasure of slowly leafing through the folio while receiving Paula's expert knowledge. She makes a distinction between book restoration – trying to make a book look as good as new – and book conservation, her job, the object of which, as Paula puts it, is 'to maintain its place in time'. 'This one looks like it's been run through heated rollers,' she laments, 'so none of the letter press is preserved – you should be able to feel the individual letters on the page.'

She rails about how so many old books like the one in my hands have been 'restored', i.e. cleaned up, washed in chemicals to remove any annotations, bleached to restore their whiteness (a process which ironically renders them yellow with time), and then flattened so that, for Paula at any rate, they lose all their character. Paula echoes the feelings of the nineteenth-century bookseller Thomas Rodd: 'I have great dread and horror of all washed books, having seen many of them crumble to pieces in the hand from the powerful acids employed ... I would rather see a book black as the ground than after its undergoing the ordeal of the infernal wash-tubs and lies.'

My trip to Yale is completed with a visit to the Elizabethan Club, the 'Lizzie' as they call it, situated in a federal-style white clapboard house with mallard-green shutters on College Street. A portrait of its founder, Alexander Smith Cochran, hangs above the fireplace in the parlour. He was a carpet tycoon, who was known as the richest bachelor in New York until he married a Polish opera singer who couldn't sing.* Cochran cunningly stole a march on all the other wealthy Shakespeare bibliophiles at a much-anticipated sale of the vast book collection of Henry Huth, including four folios and 100 Elizabethan and Jacobean books. The day before the first sale began in London in November 1911, Cochran bought up the entire collection for £40,000, promptly donated it to his alma mater, Yale, and set up the Elizabethan Club to house and celebrate it.

After a brief tour of the house with its comfy lounges and sitting rooms, Eve shows me 'The Vault'. It is a safe straight out of central casting, requiring both of us to wheel open its massive door. But such security is well warranted by the treasures inside: quartos and folios, Jacobethan plays, essays and poems, an overwhelming feast of riches.

Eve and I settle in the garden with a nice cuppa (the Lizzie's own blend of oolong tea) and slices of cinnamon toast. The day may have started inauspiciously, but it has ended very well indeed.

---

* Ganna Walska inspired aspects of the screenplay for *Citizen Kane*, when her fourth husband promoted her career, and even bought her a theatre.

Columbia University, New York

The Amtrak from New Haven arrives in Penn Station, and suddenly the pace of everything changes. To start with I can't even find the way out, there are so many people in this vast underground space below Madison Square Garden. I finally spot daylight, find myself on Eighth Avenue, but can't work out which way is uptown and which way is down. And the sidewalks seem so cracked that I keep stumbling with my heavy wheelie case. Thankfully I spot a Yellow Cab, and fall into it. New York.

The pace slows back down later in the afternoon as I walk into the grand campus of Columbia University in Morningside Heights. This leisurely, wide-open space, like an Ancient Greek agora, fills several city blocks. The university, founded in 1754, was originally called Kings College, but, after the Revolutionary War, styled itself Columbia and chose the architecture of the Roman Empire rather than the British one. Hence the square is dominated by a pantheon, the Low Library, and on the steps leading up to it sits the statue of *Alma Mater*, the goddess Athena, her arms raised in welcome and a large book on her knee. I have come to see another big book in the Butler Library opposite, an ionic colonnaded neoclassical temple. And I am meeting an old friend.

Noma Dumezweni has made her life here in the city. I first met her nearly a quarter of a century ago, when she auditioned for the RSC in 1999, and was cast as one of the weird sisters in *Macbeth*. She caused a little controversy in London when she was cast as Hermione in the stage hit *Harry Potter and the Cursed Child*. That show then brought her to New York. She is in the recent Disney live-action remake of *The Little Mermaid*. And now her work life embraces stage, film and TV, though much of that has been curtailed recently because of the Screen Actors' Guild strike which has shut down the industry since early May. She's looking stylish, as always, with a new silver braid in her hair.

As we enter the rare books department on the sixth floor, our host, Emily Runde, points out a black-painted mantelpiece. 'It's called the Raven Mantel,' Emily says; 'it's the last remnant of the room in which Edgar Allan Poe penned his most famous poem.' I briefly imagine the ghastly raven perched on the fireplace answering the poet's restless imploring: will he ever recover from the grief of losing his beloved? Will his soul find happiness again? The raven croaks ominously *Nevermore*. Poe carved his name on the mantelpiece, but Emily says it's been painted over.

Noma is excited to see her first First Folio. I love the way actors respond to seeing this book. It is radioactive, releasing a particular energy, emitting exhilaration. We spend a happy couple of hours poring over the book and laughing at the compositors' errors. In Act 5 of the folio text of *Hamlet*, the gravedigger declares: 'I have been sixteen, man and boy thirty years.' How can he have been sixteen for thirty years – it's a typo of course: it should read 'I have been *sexton*, man and boy thirty years' – and in *Lear* the distracted king declares, 'I shall go *mads*.'

And then it's time to go. Emily's students are waiting outside to attend her class. We retire for something to eat and Noma takes me down to the chic Cafe Luxembourg, where we discuss everything: life, Tony, the future… When we part Noma gives me a big hug, and as I head back up Broadway, an old lady passes me and says, 'Wow, that was some hug!'

Return to the New York Public Library, New York

I decide to go and see the exhibition of the NYPL's six First Folios that Michael Inman and Declan Kiely were preparing when I visited back in January. Here they all are in splendid array. Of course, the very fact that there are six folios is another reminder that the First Folio is not a rare book. The exhibition contains a much rarer one: a Gutenberg Bible. It's not the world's oldest printed book. That comes from ninth-century China. But it's the first substantial book printed in Europe, and it heralded a radical shift in the way the world communicated.

As Michael points out, 'With the mass production of identical texts … people were able to debate the same ideas, in the same language.' It has been called 'arguably the greatest achievement of the second millennium'. The Gutenberg Bible in front of me now was part of the collection of James Lenox and was the very first copy in America. On its arrival in 1847, Lenox issued instructions that the officers at the Customs House were to remove their hats on seeing it, in due reverence for such a rare and important work.

Imagine my delight when I discover that *Gutenberg! The Musical!* is in preview on Broadway. The premise of the show is that a pair of down-on-their-luck actors have written a musical about Gutenberg and are doing a one-off presentation for the first time in front of a live audience. As there isn't a lot of factual information about Gutenberg ('on Google') they have made stuff up (there is a wicked monk and a sexy heroine called Helvetica). It is very funny indeed.

Penn Station, Lower Manhattan, New York

The rain in New York City seems more deliberately determined to drench. Summer is definitely over. The weather guy on CNN said so, and the news seems just as gloomy, as Americans prepare for the likely US Federal Government shut-down next Monday, due to stalled budget negotiations between Congress and the White House. If that happens, my visit to the Library of Congress won't go ahead. As I watch New Yorkers crink and crank between each other at the zebra crossing ahead, a cockapoo stops dead, refusing to obey the tugs on his lead. He looks as if he has decided to 'quit Being'. But suddenly he shakes himself out, soaking other pedestrians, and walks nonchalantly on.

The taxi passes Lincoln Plaza, the home of the Met Opera. It was here on the grandest of opening nights in 1964 that Samuel Barber's *Antony and Cleopatra* was premiered. The extravagant production by Zeffirelli included camels (he wanted elephants) and hundreds of extras. The new stage turntable had broken during technical rehearsals, entailing reblocking much of the action. Leontyne Price as the Queen of the Nile made her first entrance from a huge pyramid which opened to reveal her, but when the cue came the damn pyramid wouldn't open and she had to start singing from inside.

I haven't managed my customary walk in Central Park this trip because of the deluge. Normally I pay my respects to the Shakespeare Statue at the end of the walk of American elms, and wanted to visit the Bethesda Fountain to see the famous Angel of the Waters since hearing that the sculptress Emma Stebbins based it on her lover, the Shakespearean actress Charlotte Cushman.

As we continue down the island of Manhattan, I remember that Tony and I visited the Players, a club in Gramercy Park, when we were here in 2015, with *Richard II* and the *Henry IV*s. The club was opened in 1888 by the most famous American actor of the nineteenth century, Edwin Booth, in his own house. We were taken on a special tour, including his apartment at the top of the house.

Sitting on a cabinet was a skull. It's the one Booth used playing Hamlet. They let me examine it. Inked on the front like a tattoo was a crescent moon and star, the symbol of the Ottoman Empire. No one could tell me why it was there, and we speculated that perhaps it signified that this was not a Christian skull, and therefore in the eyes of club members and their guests not a problem to have on display. However, the story goes that this particular skull originally belonged to Edwin's father, Junius Brutus Booth, also a renowned Shakespearean actor. His Yorick was originally the cranium of a horse thief called Fontaine, who left it to Booth Sr after his execution.

There are so many Shakespeare associations here in New York. From up in Harlem, where Orson Welles directed (and certainly took most of the credit for*) the so-called voodoo *Macbeth* in 1936, down to the Center Theatre (which no longer exists) where Louis Armstrong starred in the forgotten *Swingin' the Dream*, a musical version of *A Midsummer Night's Dream*, which flopped spectacularly in 1939.

I didn't get time to see an old friend, Oskar Eustis, who runs the Public Theater (they produce Shakespeare in the Park, every summer in Central Park). Their home is in Astor Place, the scene of the famous riots of 1849, which broke out when the British actor William Macready appeared in the city at the same time as the American actor Edwin Forrest, in exactly the same play, *Macbeth*. Between twenty and thirty of the rival factions were killed in the rioting which ensued. It was the deadliest civic disturbance in Manhattan, to that date.

Eventually the taxi deposits me at Penn Station, for my onward journey to Princeton.

---

* See the account of this production in James Shapiro's *The Playbook*.

Firestone Library, Princeton University, New Jersey

> I felt rather lonely this morning at breakfast so I went and unboxed a Shakespeare. 'There's my comfort'*
>
> John Keats

So wrote John Keats in a letter to his siblings while on holiday on the Isle of Wight. It is one of the items on display in a thoughtful exhibition at the Firestone Library in Princeton University, called 'In the Company of Good Books'. Keats's letter reflects my own mood this morning, wondering why I am so far from home and what I am doing. But the purpose of travel is not to get to where you are going, but to enjoy the journey. And I constantly find that encountering yet another folio is a thrill (Princeton's trio are numbers 97, 98 and 99 on my Roadshow).

One of two copies owned by the Scheide Library, its librarian Eric White tells me, is the oldest copy of the 1623 Folio in America, signed by an American, Samuel Parker, in 1791. Amos Prescott Baker Esq. of Boston was given it by his aunt Rebecca in 1864, the year of Shakespeare's tercentenary. He used it as an autograph book to capture the signatures of some of the greatest American Shakespeare actors of the day. So here, of course, is *numero uno*, Edwin Booth, who played Macbeth in Boston in November 1868, and signs the copy with his Lady Macbeth, the Czech-born Fanny Janauschek.

Here is the name Tommaso Salvini, the great Italian actor, who came to the States, and played Othello opposite Booth as Iago. He performed in Italian, while Booth and the rest of the company spoke the lines in the original English. What a feat of listening, and of understanding the rhythm of the lines that must have been.

Here is the great French actor Constant Coquelin, who created the virtuoso role of Cyrano de Bergerac by Rostand in 1897. He then toured the States in 1900 with Sarah Bernhardt as Roxane (she was sixty-six at the time). Here, too, is the signature of my latest crush, Charlotte Cushman. Abraham Lincoln once told her that he hoped to see her as Lady Macbeth someday, a wish that came

---

* 'Here's my comfort', as Stephano, the drunken butler in *The Tempest*, says of his bottle.

Charlotte Cushman as Romeo

true when he saw her in his favourite play, in October 1863, eighteen months before his assassination. But the really startling thing about Cushman was that she played many male roles as well, including Hamlet, and in *Henry VIII* even alternated the roles of Cardinal Wolsey and Katherine of Aragon on different nights. Her most famous role, Romeo, which she played opposite her sister Susan, is celebrated in a Staffordshire porcelain figurine.

Charlotte had many often turbulent and flamboyant affairs with different women. They were tolerated by a public who thought of women's romantic friendships as chaste. Her exceptional celebrity at the time, and certainly her subsequent reputation, was eventually tarnished by the public response to her sexuality. We should know her better today.

On Shakespeare's 300th birthday, an actor we have now forgotten signed the Scheide copy. Edward Everett played Cassius to Booth's Brutus. His signature is accompanied by a heartfelt message:

> It is said that the manuscript of the Pandects of Florence used to be exhibited with lighted tapers as a sacred relic. I should be more inclined to pay that honour to a copy of the First Folio of Shakespeare.
> Edward Everett, Boston 23 April 1864

The Pandects of Florence were ancient texts, a digest of Roman law from the time of the Emperor Justinian, discovered in Amalfi in 1135 and brought to Florence where they were venerated, and could only be seen by candlelight in the presence of two magistrates and two monks with bared heads. For good or bad, the folio does draw, if not quite that level of veneration, then certainly a sense of proximity to a great spirit gone.

Free Library, Philadelphia, Pennsylvania

Today the sun came out in Philadelphia and I saw my 100th First Folio. It is held in the Free Library on Logan Square, and has many annotations in a seventeenth-century hand.

I am greeted by Kelly Richards, the Director of the Library, who ushers me into his new office. He has only been in position for nineteen months and joins the library at an exciting time in its development, having recently been granted a large loan by the city to expand its operation. When I ask him how he got into books his answer is surprising. He was a cop, in his hometown of Flint, Michigan, in his early twenties. One day he found himself called to a library where he got talking with the librarian about the work they did in the community. And he had a Damascene epiphany. Now, thirty years later, he has risen up the ladder in his field. He was the first Black man to serve as president of the American Library Association and is now the boss in Philadelphia Free Library. He tells me he is going to leave me in the capable hands of some of his staff to see the folio and I am to come back and tell him what I think.

In 2019, Claire Bourne, an associate professor in the English Department here at Penn University, wrote about the annotations in this copy, how the author of those notes had fixed textual mistakes, finessed the metre and added alternative readings from the quartos. She tweeted her findings, including pictures of the handwriting. Then Jason Scott-Warren, a scholar at Cambridge University, thought he recognised that handwriting, cross-checked with other sources and emailed the Penn scholar back to say he thought the author of these annotations was none other than the young John Milton. When they shared their astonishing findings on Twitter the world agreed. The greatest playwright of the seventeenth century being closely analysed by the century's greatest poet. John Payne Collier once announced that there was such a copy, owned and annotated by Milton, but after his fall from grace, no one believed him.

We could justly claim Milton as one of the first editors of Shakespeare. I am taken by a line from *Hamlet* where the Prince describes Claudius as the '*blunt* king'. Milton adds the quarto reading 'the *bloat* king'. Each suggests entirely different interpretations about how Hamlet regards his uncle, either as impotent and crude, or as insatiable and indulgent. Milton doesn't cross out one and substitute the other; he lets both stand, allowing for interpretation and choice admitting the plural nature of the text. (When I did the play with Patrick Stewart as Claudius we went for the 'blunt king'). When I return to Kelly's office, I tell him that, with the Milton connection, the folio he has in his charge is one of the most exciting folios and probably one of the most valuable I have seen.

In the afternoon I move on to the Van Pelt Library. Here in a small case, like Snow White's glass casket, are the charred remnants of a folio owned by the great Shakespeare actor Edwin Forrest (Macready's American rival). They burned in a fire in his home shortly after his death. Actually, it turns out the pages are from a Second Folio, but the librarian Mitch Fraas shows me remaining First Folio pages from *Timon of Athens* which also survived that fire. Somehow, the way these pages have been placed in this reliquary is further testimony to the manner in which this book has been venerated to absurdity in the four centuries of its existence. Though a hundred folios into my Folio Roadshow, I am aware how perverse that last comment might sound.

I am also very pleased to see yet another Yorick. This skull was a prop used at the Walnut Street Theatre here in Philadelphia, which originally belonged to a stagehand called John 'Pop' Reed, who worked at the theatre for fifty years in the first half of the 1800s. He left his skull in his will to the theatre. The various Hamlets who used it have inscribed their names upon it, and include the now familiar list of Booth, Cushman and Forrest.

Bryn Mawr and Haverford, Pennsylvania

In the library of Bryn Mawr College, deep in the wooded hinterland of Philadelphia, is a copy of Shakespeare's First Folio with an

Blake bookplate

enigmatic bookplate. It shows a figure trying to get to the moon on a ladder.

It comes from William Blake's *The Gates of Paradise* (1793). What is it meant to express? Is it man's aspiration to achieve the impossible? You can hardly get to the moon on a long ladder. Is it mocking that ambition? Is the cry in the caption 'I want, I want!' a childish tantrum, or an unconquerable human urge? Is Blake describing the lonely journey of the poet determined whatever the odds to escape the bonds of earth and reach for the moon? Or is he satirising the destructive worldly drive to have more and more, whatever the cost? When you realise that the owner of this bookplate trained under Freud in Vienna, then perhaps her choice of image is deliberately intended to analyse your own response, to discover what that may say about you.

Bryn Mawr's copy of the folio is one of the few copies acquired and donated by a woman.

Caroline Newton was born in Philadelphia and studied psychoanalysis under Freud. She was the first female member of the International

Psychoanalytical Society, and worked at Bellevue Hospital in New York. In the thirties, she also generously supported the novelist Thomas Mann, author of *Death in Venice*, when he fled Hitler's Germany where his books were being burned, providing her house in Rhode Island as a refuge. Caroline Newton had a rival patron for Mann's attention, the philanthropic wife of the owner of the *Washington Post*, and both women were possessive and needy for his affection.

Newton was also a patron of W. H. Auden, whose friend Charles Miller cruelly called her 'short, plump and round-faced with lots of loose brown hair, greying. Despite her furs and expensive clothing she managed to look disheveled ... blinking behind glasses.' Auden's biographer described her character as demanding and irritating: 'She had been psychoanalysed by Freud but despite setting up in psychiatric practice herself she remained a neurotic and even risible figure. She was self-absorbed, histrionic and self-important.' This portrait of a rich but vulnerable woman unfairly undermines her achievements, but to me those contradictions also deepen her interest as a study in human nature.

I wonder what she saw in Shakespeare, and, as I pore over her volume, secretly hope she will have annotated those passages which offer the most complex portraits of 'unaccommodated man': the disintegration of Lear, or Ophelia; the mental stress of Angelo's hypocrisy, or Macbeth's ambition. I turn to *The Winter's Tale* to read that most knotted and nettled tumble of a speech of Leontes, describing his descent into destructive morbid jealousy:

> Inch-thick, knee-deep, o'er head and ears a fork'd one.
> *The Winter's Tale* (Act 1 scene 2)

Alas, no psychological insights are recorded.

In the afternoon, to another folio just a few miles further on, at Bryn Mawr's sibling Quaker college at Haverford. This copy was owned by the great American impresario Augustin Daly, who owned theatres in both New York and London, and mounted spectacular Shakespeare productions which were roundly despised by George Bernard Shaw. Shaw objected among other things to him regendering characters in the plays, and savagely cutting ('slaughtering') the text. Shaw describes his frail hope that eventually innovative ideas will dry up and Shakespeare will be left to speak for himself: 'Every revival helps to exhaust the number of possible ways of altering Shakespeare's plays unsuccessfully, and so hastens the day when the mere desire for novelty will lead to the experiment of leaving them unaltered.' In *A Midsummer Night's Dream*, Daly introduced an entirely pointless 'illusion of the passage of Theseus' barge to Athens' so perhaps Shaw had a point.

West Chester to Washington, DC

The copy at West Chester University was once owned by Richard Oswald, who led the British side in the negotiations for peace with America in 1782. In Benjamin West's unfinished painting of the subsequent Treaty of Paris, the British delegation are not depicted. Oswald, who had by then been roundly criticised for giving the Americans too much, had no desire to commemorate Britain's defeat and declined to pose. Instead, he retired to his estate in Auchincruive in Ayrshire. Is it perhaps this folio, then, that his famous neighbour Robert Burns was thinking of when he wrote 'The Book Worms':

> Through and through the inspir'd leaves,
> Ye maggots, make your windings;
> But oh! respect his lordship's taste,
> And spare his golden bindings.

Dead maggots, wick trimmings, quill shavings, nail parings and even brass binders' pins have been discovered in the gutter sweepings of different folios, but in 1952, in a copy of the Fourth Folio held at West Chester, they found an eighteenth-century beauty spot made of silk court plaster.

My stately progress became a mad dash today. I nipped across from Philadelphia to West Chester, managed to spend an hour with the Oswald Folio and its genial librarian Ron McColl, and then grabbed an Uber and hurtled down to Washington, DC to the Library of Congress in order to see their First Folios, before the anticipated government shutdown closes the library for what could be months.

Michael North, the Head of Reader Services at the Library of Congress, is a gentleman, polite, punctilious, white-haired. He has very kindly kept me informed of the progress of negotiations with regard to the federal shutdown and has prepared both their First Folios for me to see. 'We don't get asked for them very often,' he explains, 'because of that building over there.' He points to the roof of the Folger Library which you can just see through the window. 'Yes,' I say, 'well, they do have eighty-two copies!' But the Library of Congress Folios are intriguing.

By now I am very used to seeing beautiful nineteenth-century bindings by Rivière or Bedford or Zaehnsdorf. But the first 1623 Folio that Michael shows me looks like our old family Bible. It is white leather with gold lettering. This folio was bound in 1982, and the description reads 'full, white pigskin, alum tawed, in immaculate condition'. Beyond its curious cover, the volume has few annotations and is fairly ordinary. But the next folio he shows me is an entirely different kettle of fish.

To begin with, it would not be out of place on the shelves of our prop store in Stratford-upon-Avon. It looks like a stage property that has suffered the wear and tear of a long run. The moss-green velvet tabs with little metal Tudor roses at each end which once held the book closed have torn off and sit in the case. The scarlet cloth cover is frayed and worn, and the silver-encased fore-corners and engraved oval centrepiece could do with a bit of Duraglit.

Whereas the Rasmussen/West catalogue has the usual four pages of notes on annotations, watermarks, damage repairs and press variants, for the white 'Bible' copy there are ten densely packed pages of content. It was given to the library by John Davis Batchelder in 1936. The book is a glorious mishmash of various copies with some very battered pages front and back. But the most intriguing element is the Droeshout engraving. It seems the frontispiece is a facsimile, but a copy of the original Droeshout has been stuck on top of it. And only one corner seems still to be attached. A receipt in the folio slip case is made out to John D. Batchelder Esq. (November 29 1922), for £200 *received with thanks* from Frank T. Sabin, Bookseller, New Bond Street, for *the original Droeshout portrait of Shakespeare for the 1st folio*. I wonder if this is somehow the page that James Orchard Halliwell-Phillipps cut out of our Stratford copy, and am pondering slipping it into my pocket when Michael comes back to tell me that it is already five o'clock and the library has to close.

United States Capitol, Washington, DC

Freedom is imprisoned.

The statue which stands on the pinnacle of the US Capitol dome in Washington, DC, is hidden in a cage. A scaffolding structure surrounds the bronze figure while she is being restored. She regularly gets struck by lightning, and the conductor rods constantly need replacing. She also needs to be inspected, cleaned and have a layer of protective coating reapplied.

I am being told all this in Emancipation Hall in the Capitol Visitor Center, next to the original plaster nineteen-foot-tall model of Freedom, by my special guide Jessica Wall, one of the comms team staff, who has graciously agreed to show me a particular painting, even though it's actually her day off. Emancipation Hall is an appropriate place to start our visit, because the painting I want to see is entitled *First Reading of the Emancipation Proclamation of President Lincoln*. It's not on the official Visitors' Tour, so I have been allowed 'backstage' to see it.

Jessica is married to one of the tour guides, and as we walk around the building she introduces me to her husband, and other members of the staff who ask her why she is in today. 'Do you live here now?' one of them laughs. Jessica tells me that so many of the team have met and married here that their wedding photos look like staff meetings.

The picture I want to see was painted by Francis Bicknell Carpenter during the American Civil War, and his account of that period, *Six Months in the White House,* provides an insider's view of the sixteenth President, and the conversations they had as he sat for his portrait. One afternoon the artist tells Lincoln that Edwin Booth is to perform *Hamlet* at the Grover's Theatre that evening. The President becomes animated with his enthusiasm for Shakespeare. 'It matters not to whether Shakespeare be well or ill-acted,' he tells Carpenter, 'with him the thought suffices.' He then reveals his admiration for Claudius's speech where he admits his guilt for the murder of his brother, Hamlet's father: 'O my offence is rank, it smells to heaven.'

'It always struck me as one of the finest touches of nature in the world,' says Lincoln. Then to Carpenter's surprise: 'He repeated the entire passage from memory with a feeling, an appreciation unsurpassed by any actor I ever witnessed on the stage.' Lincoln went on to discuss the lines which open *Richard III*, 'Now is the winter of our discontent'. He then repeats the speech 'unconsciously assuming the character', and Carpenter lays down his palette and brushes and applauds him.

'His favourite diversion was reading Shakespeare,' Carpenter reveals (apparently Lincoln never read a novel in his life). One day, in the spring of 1862, on campaign in Fort Monroe, before the capture of Norfolk, he called to his aide, and read him sections of *Hamlet* and *Macbeth*. He then read the passage in *King John* where Constance bewails the capture of her son Arthur. Then he closed the book and repeated the words:

And father Cardinal, I have heard you say
That we shall see and know our friends in Heaven:
If that be true, I shall see my boy again –

King John (Act 3 scene 4)

Carpenter continues with Lincoln's words: '"Colonel, did you ever dream of a lost friend, and feel you were holding sweet communion with that friend, and yet have a sad consciousness that it was not a reality? – just so I dream of my boy Willie." Overcome with emotion, he dropped his head on the table, and sobbed aloud.' In contrast, the young artist adds a feature of the President's character of which I knew nothing – his laughter. 'Mr Lincoln's laugh stood by itself,' Carpenter writes. 'The neigh of a wild horse on his native prairie is not more undisguised and hearty. That laugh has been the President's life-preserver.'

When Jessica and I arrive at the staircase where the painting is now exhibited, the police officer tells us we shouldn't be in that part of the building. Jessica is embarrassed, and says it is because it's the weekend. During the week all the police know her. But I tell her it's fine. In truth, the painting is rather poor, and it's very badly lit in its current position, and what it represents is more important than its execution. When it was finished Lincoln himself could only manage to say it could not be better than it was.

The painting shows Lincoln presenting his draft of the Emancipation Proclamation to his cabinet. Someone said it looks like a group of men sitting around a table waiting for their pictures to be taken, but it was a moment that led the way for the abolition of slavery in America.

As we walk back through the Capitol, we pass a staircase heading down to an outside door. 'That corridor leads to the West Terrace tunnel,' Jessica says quietly. It was the scene of some of the worst violence on that terrible day of 6 January 2021, as the guards fought the rioters for three hours trying to repel them, unaware that they had broken in elsewhere and were roaming the building. It was from that door that the police officer was dragged out by the crowd, beaten unconscious with pipes and poles and an American flag, tasered and tear-gassed as he pleaded 'I got kids', the appalling footage captured on his body cam. But none of the mob got into the Capitol through the West Terrace tunnel.

It was a year later, at the start of 2022, when rehearsals were due to start for *Henry VI Part Two* (which we called *Henry VI: Rebellion*) that the footage of those Proud Boys and Oath Keepers, and the QAnon shaman in his buffalo horns and face paint, came back onto our screens. Those images reminded us of the violent Jack Cade inciting the murderous London crowd to riot, while being manipulated by York behind the scenes. Just as Trump had stoked the crowd, telling them to 'fight like hell', and ignited the events which still traumatise America today. 'You can bet if those rioters had been Black they wouldn't have gotten anywhere near the Capitol,' comments Jessica wryly. She is a Black woman from the state of Virginia.

For many the Emancipation Proclamation represents a pivotal moment in American history, in *our* history: the beginning of their road to freedom. Just as 6 January 2021 marked a moment when our democracy was damaged and warns us to be vigilant of any further erosion of our freedom, the freedom represented by that statue in her scaffolding cage on the top of the Capitol Dome.

Georgetown University, Washington, DC

This afternoon I am at Georgetown University with Jay Sylvestre, the Curator of Rare Books in the Lauinger Library here. We are staring together through a magnifying glass at the final page of *The Merchant of Venice*. The full stop at the end of the title is curious.

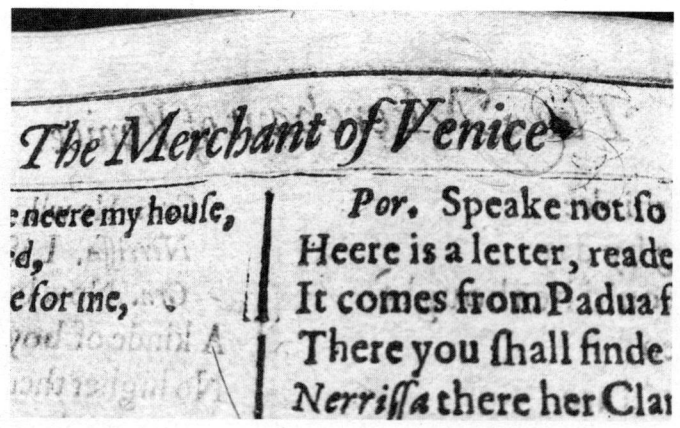

Trapped curlicue of hair

There are faint little curly ink stains around the full stop which must have been made as the ink was still wet. The inkblot seems to have trapped a wisp or two of hair. And when Jay blows on it, it moves.

'So, is that what I think it is?' I say rather tentatively.

'It's a little curlicue of hair embedded in the ink which has survived,' he confirms.

'From 1623? But that's amazing,' I splutter.

'It would seem so,' he smiles.

I am ridiculously excited by our find: the actual DNA of one of the original typesetters. Just as the 'vatman's tears' in the Bute Folio transported me back to the Normandy paper mill where the paper was manufactured, now I feel present in the Half Eagle and Key as the book was being printed.

Baltimore, Maryland

Shakespeare looks like the sexy scar-faced Bond villain in *Casino Royale*.

I am in an airy reading room in an Italianate palazzo, overlooking a croquet lawn … in Baltimore. It was the Gilded Age mansion of the Garrett family, who made their money in the railroad business. Daniel McClurkin picked me up at Penn Station and has whisked me through green suburbs of Baltimore to the Stern Center of the Evergreen Museum, where he is a 'Curatorial Postdoctoral Fellow'.

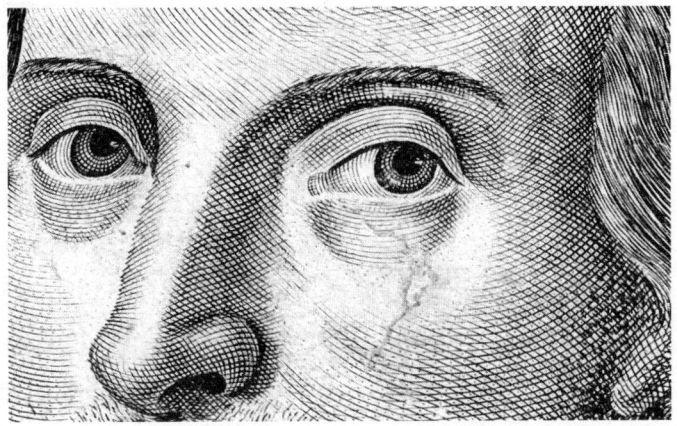
Evergreen Droeshout engraving with scar

The Evergreen houses Johns Hopkins University's rare book collection.

The Droeshout engraving has a mended tear under his left eye, making him look sinister. The first known owner of this folio is T. Harrison Garret (1849–88). He was something of a prodigy, running away twice at the age of twelve in an attempt to join the Confederate army, and attending Princeton from the age of fourteen. He acquired his First Folio as a sophomore at fifteen. His life ended in tragedy when his yacht *Gleam* collided with a steamer in Chesapeake Bay, and he drowned, aged thirty-nine.

Daniel brims with erudition and enthusiasm. He shows me a storybook of *Hamlet* beautifully illustrated with woodblock prints, made in the late 1940s. And here is a 1676 edition of *Hamlet*, which has been marked up for production, with whole sections crossed through. An address to the reader begins: 'This play being too long to be conveniently acted, such places as might be least prejudicial to the plot or sense, are left out upon the stage.' Daniel is hoping to try it out by putting it on next spring.

My host graciously drives me back into town for my next appointment. I am surprised by the elegance of the Mount Vernon–Belvedere Historic District, Baltimore's old quarter. He drops me in a square by a towering column, a monument to George Washington, and the oldest statue of the first President in the country. Daniel urges me, before I arrive at the Walters Art Gallery for my next encounter, to enter the building just across the road, even if just for a second to see their library. I check my watch. 'Really,' he says, 'you won't be disappointed.'

The Peabody Library takes your breath away. I feel like Jonah in the gigantic ribbed belly of the whale or as though I have entered the ark, or some vast Grecian temple. Five tiers of ornamental cast-iron balconies, each filled with books, rise from a black and white marble floor, to a frosted glass ceiling more than sixty feet above. Thanks, Daniel. That was quite a gift.

The Walters Gallery is closed today, so Dr Lynley Anne Herbert, the Curator of Rare Books, greets me at the staff entrance. They are hosting a press reception to welcome a new acquisition, a stained-glass window by Kehinde Wiley. It complements the Walters' collection of mediaeval stained glass, and sets up a conversation with it. We go behind the scenes to Lynley's office. The folio is washed, trimmed and 'clean', but I do find some legible annotations in *Hamlet*, and a number of Harris facsimile pages.

We discuss the ways in which rare books are perfected. I tell Lynley about the copy at Wadham College, with its missed-out line at the end of *Cymbeline*. She has an even better example and she fetches me a precious thirteenth-century missal with lustrous illuminations. Under the account of the crucifixion of Christ, the funeral of Reynard the Fox with its animal mourners processes mischievously over several pages. By mistake the scribe left out a line of text. So he has written it out at the bottom of the page, and then drawn a little figure clambering back up the text, with a rope attached to the stray line, and his hand pointing to its proper position.

I ask Lynley if this is the book she would save in the event of that hypothetical fire. She has another precious contender for that choice, and shows me an eleventh-century missal. She reminds me of the story of St Francis of Assisi and his three young companions. They have been discussing what to do with their lives and decide they should go into the church of San Nicolò, and open the Bible three times, once for each of them, and attend whatever wisdom it imparts. On each page, they read an exhortation to give up all their worldly goods and follow God. 'And that is how the Franciscan order began,' says Lynley. Unbelievably, the book before me is that very Bible, preserved from that very church, and now Franciscan monks from all over the world come in devout pilgrimage to the Walters Gallery in Baltimore to see it.

I make my way down to the harbour to sit in the sunshine and contemplate Baltimore's unexpected marvels, and ponder the next leg of my Roadshow, down to Texas.

Dallas, Texas

Misty wasn't answering my emails. It didn't bode well.

I only stopped in Dallas, en route to Austin, in order to see their First Folio and if for some reason the library manager, Misty Maberry, hadn't been getting my emails, and there was no one there to show me the book, then that felt like a disappointing start to my Texas trip. I made up my mind just to turn up and travel with hope. The J. Erik Jonsson Central Library is 1980s modernist and monumental. The temperature outside was heading for twenty-seven degrees Celsius. Inside the lobby, people had clearly come in just to keep cool. On Floor Seven, I ask at the reception desk if by any chance Ms Maberry was around, I had come to see the Shakespeare First Folio. 'Oh, that's over there,' the young lady said, pointing to a darkened room behind me. 'I'll see if Misty is available.'

The room was like a small side chapel. It even had wrought-iron gates, painted black. Linen-fold oak panelling lined the walls, there was a low carved coffer chest between two seventeenth-century chairs, and at one end was the display case holding the folio on a cushion. The low level of light from two flickering candle bulbs was clearly designed to create an appropriate sense of devotion. The folio was open at *The Comedy of Errors*. I studied it a little wanly, worried that this was all I was likely to see of this copy. Then Misty arrived.

She was gracious. I apologised for bombarding her with emails. She said how nice it was for me to visit. The folio had come to them from the Dallas Shakespeare Club, and they had presented it to the library, in a new binding, on their centenary in 1986. The case was clearly staying shut. I said I noticed that the library had another treasure on display, a broadside copy of the Declaration of Independence, and I asked her if she would show me that, too. 'The great line at the start of Jefferson's Declaration, "We hold these truths

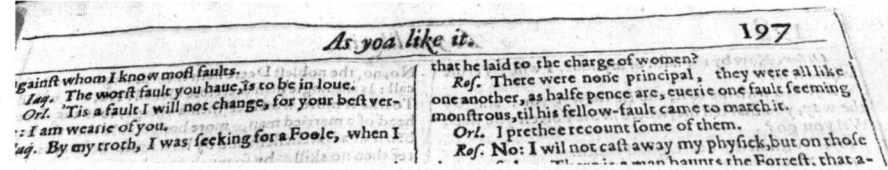

'As yoa like it'

to be self-evident", must count as the most famous iambic pentameter in American history,' I burble.

'And it's the first time the name *United States of America* appears in print,' she tells me. 'This is one of only about twenty-five known to exist. It's the only original copy west of the Mississippi.' As we walked along I filled her in a little on what I had been doing, of some of the folios I had met along the way, and of what I understood was so special about the copy in her charge.

Eventually Misty melted. To my relief she went to find a key, promising at least to show me the new binding. Once the altar gates had been closed and the case opened, and Misty's young assistant helped her lay the folio on a cushion on a trolley, I was able to share in detail what knowledge I had of this folio. Her assistant chuckled at some of the mistakes in the text, particularly how one of the pages is titled *As yoa like it*.

I turned to the end of the Histories, and the start of the Tragedies, to where most copies have inserted the folio's late entry, *Troilus and Cressida*, and as I expected there was no *Troilus*. But further on the play appears, bound in after *Timon of Athens*. I have only seen this once before, at the Huntington Library. I was glad that, with a little gentle persistence, Misty had allowed me to see the Dallas copy up close, and I think I was able to tell her a bit more about the volume in her charge. As she carefully placed the folio back in its case, she asked me what page they should leave open. 'What about *Hamlet*,' I said, 'where it jumps a hundred pages.'

'Oh, yeah,' said her assistant, enthusiastically.

Just before I left, Misty asked me what I had planned for the rest of my trip. 'The State Fair is on, you know,' she said, 'it's VERY Texas. There's a fun fair and rides, and livestock shows, and all the food stalls and beer tents.'

It didn't seem to be something to do on your own. So I waited for the heat to go out of the afternoon, and instead walked down to Dealey Plaza, and the grassy knoll, and the book depository building, and the painted cross on the road (which the city authorities keep erasing but which the people keep putting back) marking the spot where the motorcade was attacked and the thirty-fifth President of the United States was assassinated in November 1963.

Austin, Texas

It's not his baseball cap and denim jacket that make Dr Aaron Pratt the coolest curator of First Folios I have met, it's his forensic eye for detail and his ability to turn an engaging enthusiasm into accessible stories, despite the sometimes deeply arcane nature of his subject. The Carl and Lily Pforzheimer Curator of Early Books and Manuscripts (to give Aaron his full and proper title) fizzes with passion for his subject, and generously shows me around the exhibition he has curated, 'The Long Lives of Very Old Books', at the Harry Ransom Center, University of Texas.

The three folios the university possesses form the centrepiece of the exhibition. The first copy has a delicious description of the binding. It boasts an eighteenth-century 'diced russia binding' by Roger Payne, with 'tortoiseshell boards and a gingerbread spine'. The first known owner is Sir Richard Newdigate, a judge whom Oliver Cromwell threw off the bench. The last of the family to own it, Sir Francis Alexander Newdigate Newdegate, was a governor of Tasmania. He sold it in 1920, at Sotheby's for £2,000. Henry Clay Folger failed to get it, when he was outbid at auction.

The 'Foiling of Folger' is common to all three copies. When the Parsons copy (named after the last known owner, a New Orleans lawyer) was sold at Christie's for £4,000, Folger was again outbid. When Folger tried to buy the copy belonging to Rev. Fulford Adams, the rector of Weston Sub Edge, a Gloucestershire village just outside Chipping Campden, he told him decisively, 'I have no intention of selling my First Folio Shakespeare. It is something to have one.'

There are other fascinating items in the exhibition, including a 1606 account of the gunpowder trial, which ends with the speech Father Garnet made before his execution. Someone has added a gruesome little sketch of a man hanging from the gallows. I love Aaron's unalloyed pleasure in the objects in his care. 'I have got to show you this,' he says, 'it is so deeply whacky', or as I show him some of the photos of my folio encounters on my phone he says: 'That is really fucking weird, man', or 'That's awesome, I love that'.

Aaron shows me what was once regarded as one of the library's greatest treasures: a Bible that travelled to the New World on the *Mayflower* in 1620. It even has a sketch of Peregrine White, the first known English child born to the Pilgrims in America. Not until someone noticed that the Bible's dedicatory prayer to the monarch was addressed to King Charles I, who didn't ascend the throne until 1625, five years after the *Mayflower* sailed, was it finally admitted to be a fake. The Mayflower Bible was no doubt produced by sincere need. There must have been such a Bible on board, so there should be one. There is also a Jacobean playbook with Shakespeare's own notes in the margin ... found in 1794, by the young forger William-Henry Ireland.

Like Lewis Theobald uncovering Shakespeare's lost play, *Cardenio*, or John Payne Collier's Perkins Folio, the primary motive of these fraudsters was not financial gain, but a desire to make a connection with their beloved Shakespeare that would endow them with special status, an intimate, personal interaction with the soul of the great writer himself.

PART SEVEN

The Last Leg of My Quest

Apsley Cherry-Garrard

Chapter Nineteen
Vancouver

I am staring up at a totem pole carved from a single 800-year-old red cedar. It towers more than fifty feet into the air. The sun is starting to set behind it. We are asked what we see.

There are human and animal forms, masks with red mouths and big black eyes, two boats and a flying eagle on top. But the most apparent feature is the most unexpected: a grim doll's house high up in the centre of the pole dividing it in two. Our guide tells us something of this Haida reconciliation pole. You read the carving from the bottom, which symbolises the time before. There are salmon representing life and its cycles on a copper base. Above, a shaman stands between the legs of the bear mother. She holds her twin cubs in her paws and a raven peers out from between her ears. The middle section starts with the house. It is surrounded by children in uniform holding hands. They have no feet. Above them are carved four spirit figures: killer whale representing water; bear the land; eagle the air; and thunderbird the supernatural. This is the time during. Above is the time after. A longboat and a canoe travelling side by side — the symbolism respects difference, but most importantly shows us travelling together. Topping the pole, the eagle represents power, and the determination needed to look towards the future.

The house represents a national trauma. Canada's Indian residential schools were institutions run by the Church and funded by the federal government. They operated for more than a hundred years across the country, with the last one closing only in 1996. Over this time, more than 150,000 Indigenous children were taken from their families in order to 'kill the Indian in the child'. The schools were used to impose Western values and language on the children at the expense of their own unique cultures. Our guide knows whereof he speaks. He was one of those children. He points out the copper nails which have been hammered into the pole. There are more than 68,000 of them. Each nail commemorates a child who died in the schools. 'The everywhere of grief.'*

We are on the ancestral land of the Musqueam people at the end of a peninsula which looks out across deep straits onto high forested mountains dusted with snow on the north-west coast of the Pacific Ocean. Land. Water. Sky. Memory. Pain.

★ ★ ★

This is the campus of the University of British Columbia (UBC), a half-hour bus ride outside Vancouver. Our guide is Linc Kesler. Not only a professor here, he is the Senior Advisor to the President on Aboriginal Affairs. We are an eclectic international group. It is Shakespeare who has brought us all together. The university has acquired a First Folio. As the Folio's quatercentenary year draws to a close, I have been invited to join their conference, 'What's Past is Prologue', to celebrate the folio's arrival in Vancouver. Canada's second copy. It is the very copy I had hoped to see at Meisei University in Tokyo, the copy which once belonged to the young Antarctic explorer Apsley Cherry-Garrard.

The real benefit of these academic conferences occurs in between the various papers being delivered. I spent the bus ride out to the campus quizzing Aaron Pratt (from the Harry Ransom Center) about his paper exploding the idea that the First Folio was ever advertised at the Frankfurt Book Fair in 1622, which has become part of book's mythology.

Brandi Adams from Arizona State University talked about Shakespeare and a Black American readership. She shows a clipping from the *Chicago Defender* of 1910 describing two young Black men hauled up before the judge in Louisville, Kentucky, for crap-shooting. They both denied they had been 'rolling the bones' but had been attending a meeting of the Bacon Literary Society, and then regaled the court with long speeches from *Hamlet* and *Julius*

---

* From the poem 'Summer Song' by George Barker.

Caesar. They 'at once set the court room in such an uproar that the two prisoners were immediately discharged'.

Emma Smith, who had travelled out to Vancouver with me, provided fascinating insights about the folio's relationship with the slave trade. I know of one of the challenging figures she is discussing. 'Mad Jack' Fuller (1757–1834) instructed that his mortal remains should be buried under a pyramid in Brightling churchyard in East Sussex. It is said that twenty-two-stone Mad Jack, otherwise known as 'the hippopotamus', sits inside the mausoleum, with a glass of claret and a roast chicken by his side. But his reputation as an eccentric masked his vehemence as an anti-abolitionist and defender of the slave trade. One of the other follies he built stands close by, a large stone sugar loaf, indicating the source of that vast fortune, his sugar plantations in the West Indies. It was his copy of the folio that found its way to Mills College in Oakland, California, and which they sold in 2020 at auction to help clear their debts. It went to Stephan Loewentheil, a Brooklyn book dealer, who bought it for the record sum of just under $10 million.

I am on a conference panel with Rodrigo Beilfuss. Rodrigo describes himself as a Brazilian-born Canadian actor-director with a German last name. His personality is as bright as the sunny yellow jersey he wears. He is currently the director of Shakespeare in the Ruins, Manitoba's leading classical theatre company. His infectious enthusiasm for the event was amply demonstrated when he turned up at breakfast on the second day of the conference sporting a tattoo of the First Folio which he had just had inked on his right forearm.

★ ★ ★

On the final day of the Vancouver conference, Emma and I got a chance to see the Cherry-Garrard copy close up. UBC have assembled a group of librarians and staff from the English Department. Emma brilliantly puts their new acquisition in context for them. There are not too many unusual features in this folio: an odd bit of musical notation in *As You Like It*, and a date on the last page of *Two Gents* – 'Au: 15.th. 58' – to which no one has yet been able to attach any particular significance.

We look at *Measure for Measure*. There are some inky marks, which might be the fingerprints of the careless 'ink-devil' apprentices in the Jaggard workshop. Isabella's resolute couplet (Act 3 scene 1) expressing her decision to refuse Angelo's offer to release her brother in exchange for sex – 'Then Isobel, live chaste and brother die / More than our brother is our chastity' – has been marked with a cross at either end.

We turn to Claudio's terrible apprehension about death. I try to explain to the group why I find this passage so moving. How it seems to echo 'the thrilling region of thick-ribbed ice' that Cherry-Garrard describes in such appalling detail in *The Worst Journey in the World*. I read it out loud.

> *Claudio*: Ay, but to die, and go we know not where,
> To lie in cold obstruction and to rot,
> This sensible warm motion to become
> A kneaded clod; and the delighted spirit
> To bathe in fiery floods, or to reside
> In thrilling region of thick-ribbed ice,
> To be imprisoned in the viewless winds
> And blown with restless violence round about
> The pendent world; or to be worse than worst
> Of those that lawless and incertain thought
> Imagine howling – 'tis too horrible.
> The weariest and most loathèd worldly life
> That age, ache, penury, and imprisonment
> Can lay on nature is a paradise
> To what we fear of death.
> *Isabella*: Alas, alas!
> *Claudio*: Sweet sister, let me live.
>
> *Measure for Measure* (Act 3 scene 1)

I think of Tony. Of the dread he experienced. And my helplessness to relieve it.

Chapter Twenty
Foliomania

A third of all the known copies of the First Folio in the world are floating in the dark in a tank across the room ahead of me. I am in Folio-Mecca.

The building delays which had prevented the Folger Library opening in the Folio quatercentenary year were finally resolved. Mike Witmore had announced he was stepping down as Director, and the building would open briefly to host a farewell gala for him to coincide with Shakespeare's birthday in April 2024. I was being allowed a special preview peek at the new premises, and its marvellous new folio exhibition, before it closed again to prepare for the official reopening date set for June. It seemed only appropriate to conclude my foliomania at the unrivalled Folger. Everything smelled paint-fresh.

All eighty-two of the Folger Folios are here. The lighting is kept at a low level. Each folio is identified with a number, and uplit in its own spectral glow. They seem cryogenically suspended in 'hypersleep' like the crew of a starship awaiting resuscitation at some point in the future. And though I can hear the chatter of cleaners out in the corridor, here stillness reigns. A control panel in front of the case allows you to access information about each copy. It feels like a futuristic vending machine, though I doubt it would whirr into life, push the folio off its shelf and deposit it in a tray below to await collection.

This is not my first visit to the Folger: I have been several times when the RSC were performing at the Kennedy Center. Once, after Tony and I had done a production of *Titus Andronicus* in Johannesburg, I naively asked the librarian if they had a copy of the First Quarto of

Titus. She told me, no, they didn't have *a* copy of the First Quarto of *Titus*, they had *the* only known existing copy of the First Quarto of *Titus*. And she placed it in my hands. Its original bluish-grey soft paper covers now bound in smart black tooled leather.

This unique quarto turned up in the home of a postal clerk in Lund in Sweden in 1905. When news of its discovery reached Henry Clay Folger, he acted fast to beat the threat of an auction, and paid in cash, cabling $9,762.25 (£2,000), to the dealer. It was one of the greatest coups (and bargains) of his collecting career, and is now worth millions.

Today, two folios are out and open. Very pleased that the first is Folger 1, the Vincent copy that Henry Clay Folger fought so obsessively to wrest from Coningsby Sibthorpe. And there is William Jaggard's note presenting this early copy to Augustine Vincent, the Rouge Croix Herald. The other copy has the rusty outline of a pair of spectacles* on a page of *The Winter's Tale*.

By now I know the stories behind most of the volumes before me, presenting their gilded spines and red or green morocco bindings. Many, of course, have particular associations with the British Isles. Folger 28 was owned by the admiral of the HMS *Temeraire*. At a crucial moment in the Battle of Trafalgar, *Redoubtable* rammed into the side of Nelson's beleaguered flagship HMS *Victory*. A French musket fired from the mizzentop fatally wounded Nelson. Just as all seemed lost, *Temeraire* burst through the smoke and came to her aid. Its admiral, Eliab Harvey, ordered a broadside to be fired, reducing the *Redoubtable* to a wreck and forcing its surrender.

Harvey was determined that his part in the battle would always be remembered and bragged about it incessantly, to the fury of his fellow officers. Eventually he overstepped the mark, insulted a superior officer and was court-martialled.

Perhaps if he read his First Folio, Ulysses' words would remind him of Time's ingratitude:

> O, let not virtue seek
> Remuneration for the thing it was.
>
> *Troilus and Cressida* (Act 3 scene 3)

---

* No fewer than three Folger Folios have the imprint of scissors, perhaps left behind by careless binders.

The full title of Turner's famous painting at the National Gallery in Trafalgar Square is *The Fighting Temeraire, tugged to her last berth to be broken up, 1838*. Just as Time has largely forgotten Harvey, so the glorious achievements of the old battleship would not save her from being scrapped. In 2005, it was voted Britain's favourite painting.

The range of original owners of the Folger Folios is expansive: Edward Scarisbrick was a Jesuit priest accused by Titus Oates in his fabricated list of those plotting to assassinate Charles II; Sir Thomas Hanmer was the Speaker of the House of Commons who in his retirement produced an edition of Shakespeare (1744); Sir John Evans, whose study of the fossils of the archaeopteryx established the link between dinosaurs and birds, is perhaps more famous as being the father of Sir Arthur Evans, the archaeologist who excavated Minoan Crete.

There are folio owners who were British industrialists, scientists and artists: Richard Johnson was co-owner of a company that provided wire for the first successful trans-Channel telegraph cable in 1851; John Scott was a shipbuilder from Ayrshire; Benjamin Elden, a dyer from Norfolk; Norman Macleod Ferrers, a Cambridge mathematician who was ordained as a priest; the Rev. Samuel Crawford Crockett was a Victorian vicar who wrote novels like *The Play-Actress* in his spare time. Myles Birket Foster was an artist whose sentimental paintings of country scenes adorned Cadbury's chocolate boxes; while Alexander Bannatyne Stewart was a fanatical gardener who built a magnificent fernery (which has recently been rediscovered) at Ascog Hall, his estate on the Isle of Bute. One folio was owned by Elias Sutton, an apothecary who lived in the parish of St Giles Cripplegate, just a few hundred yards from the Half Eagle and Key, the Jaggard print shop at the Barbican.

Some Folger Folios remind me of the realities of how busy the Jaggard workshop was. In two different copies, traces of another book (a massive work by André Favyn called *The Theater of Honour and Knight-hood, Or Compendious Chronicle and Historie of the whole Christian World*) appear on leaves of *Richard II*, as wet ink on the tympan cloth of the press has been transferred by mistake onto the pages. There are copies with the Droeshout engraving in its first, second and third states; an early issue without *Troilus and Cressida* (like the one I saw in Kyoto); one with a cancel sheet of *Romeo and*

Juliet (like the Morgan Library copy) and folios which still have proof sheets where the printer has indicated corrections yet to be made in *King Lear* and *Othello*. In Folger 24 the capital B, the very first letter in the text of *The Tempest*, has been printed backwards. One Folger Folio is still in the loose sheets in which it was originally sold at Edmund Blount's shop, the Black Bear in St Paul's Churchyard.

The 'Feminist Folio' has the names of two women inscribed within it, and their extensive annotations. Elizabeth Brockett asserts her possession of the folio, and another writes in a mid-seventeenth-century hand: 'Mary Child is the true possessor of this book.' Many Folger Folios bear witness to a long history of female readership. The women who have signed and dated their Folios include Rachel Paule (1650); Mrs Mary Lewis (1685); a 'much tattered' copy belonging to Alice Stevenson (1723); Elizabeth Okell (1729); Miss Stoddart (1761) and Tamar Radford (1769). Folger 14 was owned by Abby E. Pope (1858–95), described as 'America's premier *femme bibliophile*'.

There is a copy which in the early nineteenth century was presented by Mrs Fortescue and Mrs Fillis to the Plymouth Public Library, with a note suggesting that the book became part of a circulating library. Imagine checking out a Shakespeare First Folio for a fortnight.

I have explored the provenances of many of the folios before me during my Roadshow. Here is the folio inscribed with the signature of the King's Men actor Samuel Gilburne that Folger swapped for the copy I saw in Buffalo & Erie County Public Library. Here are the folios owned by Colonel Hutchinson who signed the death warrant of Charles I, and the one owned by Colonel Lane, whose sister Jane helped Charles II escape on horseback. Here is the first copy to leave England, purchased by the Dutch poet and diplomat Constantijn Huygens. Here is the copy owned by the sculptress Anne Damer with a bookplate* designed by the sister of her lover Mary Berry. And a folio owned by George Nicol, the bookseller to George III, who claimed credit for the idea of John Boydell's Shakespeare Gallery. Here is the folio owned by Clement Ingleby, nemesis of the notorious Victorian Shakespeare forger John Payne Collier.

---

* Now missing.

Folger 5 is the very volume that provoked the *Punch* cartoon of Uncle Sam and Shakespeare. The Philadelphia book dealer A. S. W. Rosenbach, known as 'the Terror of the Auction Room', was involved in the sale of more than thirty First Folios,* dealing on behalf of many of the great book collectors in this story: Folger, Henry Huntington, J. P. Morgan and Harry Elkins Widener.

In 1922, Rosenbach purchased this volume at the London sale of the library of Angela Burdett-Coutts. Baroness Burdett-Coutts, who became one of the wealthiest women in the world when she inherited her grandfather's banking fortune, kept her precious folio in a casket (also in the Folger collection) which was presented to her by Queen Victoria and made from the wood of Herne's Oak which blew down in a gale in Windsor Great Park in 1863.

Rosenbach triumphantly bid for the volume, paying a record £8,600 and then, within a month, sold it to Henry Clay Folger for $52,070.

The same volume had previously been owned by the writer George Daniel, who bought it from his publisher, William Pickering in Chancery Lane, and carried it back to his home in Canonbury Square, Islington, 'in one of Pickering's best silk handkerchiefs'.

There is another folio story which involves an unusual method of transportation, though this one is more clandestine and involved being smuggled across state borders. It came from Ireland and is another folio to be embroiled in the fraught history of that country. A letter relating to this copy (Folger 76) is kept here at the Folger Library. It is dated 10 March 1934 and relates the folio's history.

The folio had been owned by the Bishop of Dromore. When he died in 1811, the 1st Lord Caledon 'returning from India' bought his library including a set of four Shakespeare folios. The books were housed at Caledon House in County Tyrone, Northern Ireland.

The author of this letter is Shane Leslie, an Anglo-Irish diplomat, first cousin to Winston Churchill, and a close neighbour to Caledon House. 'The present Lord Caledon is my best friend,' he writes. He describes how he was admitted to the Caledon Library 'shortly after

---

*Although Bernard Quaritch handled even more folios than Rosenbach. On his death in 1899 *The Times* called the Prussian-born book dealer 'the greatest bookseller who ever lived'. The Rasmussen/West catalogue mentions at least forty-five folio sales that he negotiated, including nineteen here at the Folger.

the recent civil war',* during which books had been sent for safety to Belfast but 'returned haphazard'. 'I found the First Folio lying on the floor,' he writes.

The following spring (1928) Shane Leslie invites a book expert to stay with him. It is none other than that 'very Napoleon of Books', A. S. W. Rosenbach. 'One afternoon we went over to Caledon and I let him loose.' At the end of their foray 'we crossed the Free State boundary carrying some of the rarest printed books known in a horse rug'.†

Rosenbach‡ sold Lord Caledon's folio to Henry Clay Folger. It was one of the last folios that Folger ever bought.

Henry and his wife Emily did not have children, but he used to refer to his folios as 'the boys'. Greg Prickman, the Director of Collections, takes me up to see their portraits. Folger never got to see his library open. He died of cancer aged seventy-two, the same age as Tony. Emily had his remains cremated and placed in a specially designed niche behind a panel in the Great Hall. Their two portraits hang on either side of the alcove.

Henry is pictured clutching the most expensive book he ever bought. Ironically, it isn't a First Folio. It's an infamous book known as 'the False Folio' printed by William Jaggard. In 1619, the bookseller Thomas Pavier assembled ten pirated quartos of Shakespeare's plays and attempted to publish them in a single volume, four years before the publication of the First Folio. But the King's Men enlisted the help of the Lord Chamberlain to prevent the sale of their works. Only two copies of the Pavier–Jaggard volume survived.§ When Folger was offered one of them he couldn't resist, especially as he knew his rival, Henry Huntington, had far more money at his disposal and would outbid him if he got the chance. But it was an astronomical asking price.

---

* The Irish War of Independence ended with the Anglo-Irish Treaty of 1921, and led in turn to the civil war from June 1922 to May 1923. Those supporting the Treaty opposed the establishment of an Irish Free State within the British Empire.

† The First Folio now held at the Bodmer Library in Geneva was once smuggled out of Dorchester House by Rosenbach in a butcher's cart.

‡ Rosenbach's obsession with books vied with his passion for angling. He spent his summers on board his fishing boats, *First Folio I* and *First Folio II*. He said on one occasion: 'I had more fun catching this channel bass than securing a Gutenberg Bible or a First Folio of Shakespeare.'

§ The other copy is held in the Special Collections, Texas Christian University in Fort Worth, Texas.

> What's aught but as 'tis valued
>
> *Troilus and Cressida* (Act 2 scene 2)

Folger was ridiculed in the press for the $100,000 he paid, but he knew he had secured a book rarer than any First Folio, and far more valuable. It would sit alongside his unique First Quarto of *Titus Andronicus* and his Vincent Folio as his most treasured possession, and the apex of all his foliomania.

Greg tells me how much he feels the whole library is indebted to Emily for its existence. She not only supported Henry, but influenced all his choices, and after his death oversaw the completion of their joint dream project. 'And you will notice,' says Greg, 'that the library is not called the Henry Clay Folger Library, but simply the Folger, acknowledging the debt to both.' Emily left instructions that when she died her body was to be cremated and her ashes placed next to those of her husband.

The Shakespeare Theatre in Stratford-upon-Avon and the Folger Library opened on the very same day, 23 April 1932. Both these art deco temples to Shakespeare have metopes adorning the front of the building. The Folger's depict scenes from the plays, ours represent 'emotions' in Shakespeare: Love, Jollity, Treachery, Martial Ardour and Life triumphing over Death.

★ ★ ★

I saw my 200th Folio in Padua with Emma Smith. It is the only First Folio in Italy.

It's at the University of Padua, 'nursery of the arts' as Lucentio calls the city in *The Taming of the Shrew*. There are annotations in it which suggest that it was marked up for performance sometime in the seventeenth century. That has led to speculation that it belonged to Sir Edward Dering, the first known purchaser of not one but two folios, who produced amateur performances of the plays at his home, Surrenden Manor, Pluckley, in Kent. Could this be his?

There is some uncertainty about how this folio got to Padua, but I have a theory which I try out on Emma. 'The Collector Earl', the 14th Earl of Arundel, whose portrait I had seen in Boston, was one of the richest peers in England, and one of the greatest art connoisseurs and bibliophiles in Britain. Arundel died in Padua in 1646. His body was returned to be buried at Arundel Castle on the South Downs, but his heart was buried under a marble slab in the Basilica of St Anthony here in his beloved Padua. After seeing the folio I ask Emma to come and help me find that memorial.

Arundel was a member of an elite circle known as the Whitehall Group, along with the Pembroke brothers, William and Philip Herbert, to whom the First Folio was dedicated. Arundel travelled frequently on the Continent as envoy to the king, and went on an extended tour of Europe accompanied by his friend Inigo Jones. In 1629, having renounced his Catholicism, he was made Earl Marshall, and then Lord Steward. But as the civil war threatened, Arundel fled England and returned to Padua. It was here that he returned to the Catholic Church, and here, too, in his last days that he entertained the diarist John Evelyn, who wrote how the Earl bewailed his hardships: 'The crosses that had fallen his family, [and] the misery of his country.' With no revenue from his estates in Britain he had been forced to sell off some of his prized collection.

Is it possible that during this time he made connections with the famous university? Might he have either donated or sold them his own First Folio? I have to admit to Emma that I have no actual evidence that Arundel owned a First Folio but his close connection to the Herbert brothers, his interest in the arts (which included drama – he presented a play at court attended by the king and queen) all suggest to me that he could surely have acquired a copy.

As we walk to the basilica in the hot sunshine Emma listens very patiently to my rambling postulations and nods sagely. Unfortunately the church is closed for the long Italian siesta. I felt somehow if I could have found Arundel's marble slab it would have provided invaluable support to my amateur theory. I then recall that St Anthony of Padua is the patron saint of lost causes. Emma suggests we get an ice cream. I agree.

★ ★ ★

That's enough foliomania now, I thought to myself. I would love to visit the copies I did not get to see at the Universities of Illinois, Indiana and Nebraska, or at Lehigh in Pennsylvania. But I doubt I would be able to track down all those in private hands, so the target was perhaps unrealistic anyway. The only one of Sidney Lee's perfect copies I have left to see is held at the Bodmer Library in Geneva, which is as I write closed for redevelopment.

Then, by a bizarre twist, I found one – a folio that did not appear in any of the censuses. I had been invited to dinner at a gentlemen's club in St James's, London. Boodle's was founded in the late eighteenth century and counted among its exclusive membership the Regency dandy Beau Brummell. I was seated next to a very distinguished lady approaching her ninth decade, who quizzed me about what I did. When I told her about my quest, she surprised me by saying brightly, 'Oh well then you must come and see ours.' I thought I knew about all the First Folios in England. 'Ah well, we don't like to shout about it,' she said, 'but do come down and see it, if you'd like to.' And that is what I did. So my tally of folios to date is 201.

★ ★ ★

As I was writing this coda, a wonderful thing happened. In Art Box D783 no. 1 (size S), the Folger found the Droeshout engraving in the first state, which James Orchard 'Scissorhands' Halliwell cut out of our Theatre Copy all those years ago. 'It had been hiding in plain sight the whole time,' said Greg Prickman, and he invited me back to the Folger to see it for myself. I feel inordinately happy, as if, like Jason, I have recovered the Golden Fleece, or like Galahad discovered the Holy Grail, or perhaps like Dorothy can find my way back to Kansas.

Epilogue

'For thy sweet love remembered'

G&T on a bench in their Stratford garden

Magdalen Tower, Oxford, May 2024

While tracking down the last few volumes in my Folio Roadshow, I was invited to become the Cameron Mackintosh Visiting Professor at Oxford University for the academic year 2023–4. My predecessors in the role had generally delivered an inaugural lecture in the Michaelmas Term, and then some other talk or workshop per term during their year in office. I suggested instead that I direct a Shakespeare play with the students.

The Two Gentlemen of Verona is a play about young people leaving home, making their way in the world, discovering who they are, falling in love and making horrible mistakes. As that pretty much describes my first year at university, it seemed like the ideal play to direct with students. As *Cymbeline*, one of Shakespeare's late plays and the final play in the folio, had seemed the right choice for my swan song at RSC in April 2023, so *Two Gents*, his earliest play, seemed the perfect choice for Oxford. And it was also the only play in the First Folio I had left to work on.

During the long Easter vacation, in a break from rehearsals, I finally read Tony's *Dying Diaries*. It had been two years and five months since he left. I had dreaded reliving the experience of the last few days of his life, and had tried to avoid thinking about them. But in trying to forget, I had forgotten to remember, to remember and to cherish the thirty-five years we had been privileged to enjoy together. Unexpectedly, I start to laugh. I feel an overwhelming sense of...release.

Then, on 1 May, I took part in one of Oxford's oldest traditions: I climbed the tower of Magdalen Church at 5.30 a.m. and listened to the choristers greet the dawn. The tower was completed in the year Henry VIII was crowned King of England. Looking over the crenellated ramparts, I can see dreaming spires, and the High Street a sea of faces, all looking towards us expectantly. Glancing the other way, I can see crowds gathering on Magdalen Bridge. A few intrepid students have hired punts and are gazing back up from the river below. I look eastwards across the mediaeval Magdalen cloister, and the classical colonnade of the New Building. ('New' in Oxford I discover generally means at least two centuries old.) Beyond the deer park, the water meadows are hauntingly beautiful, swathed in early morning mist.

Now the choir clamber up and start pulling their white surplices over their school blazers. The trebles and altos are arranged on the slope of the roof facing east, with the tenors and basses at the back. In the bell chamber beneath our feet, the bell tolls six o'clock. The choir master raises his hand and everyone falls silent. The *Hymnus Eucharisticus* has been sung to welcome in May on this spot for centuries. The choir's total concentration on their conductor is impressive. 'Te deum Patrem colimus.'

The presiding celebrant then calls us to prayer, addressing the Creator 'who spread out the heavens like a curtain', asking 'for the blessing of new life and hope, visible in the face of our mother the earth as she awakens to Spring': a nice syncretisation of the Christian and the pagan traditions represented by the revellers below, some of whom are dressed as green men in ivy leaves and bells. 'We celebrate before thee today the birth of an earthly morning', and as he says this he takes a generous sprig of rosemary, dips it in the bowl of holy water held by the curate at his side, and blesses the city, the university, and then as he blesses 'all those gathered here today', he asperges the choir, too, who giggle delightedly.

As they sang, and somewhere behind the cloud cover the sun rose, I thought of Tony's diaries, of how finally facing what had happened had brought his voice back into the room, and hearing that voice, and his laughter, had jostled those agonised last cries to the edge of memory, to be replaced by light and love. Death is the absence of presence, but when I had stopped running away I turned to find him there again, in his words. I can remember him again not in the last images seared into my brain, or the hollowness, the lovelorn last two years, but now in the laughter we shared, the jokes and the joy.

For thy sweet love remembered such wealth brings...

The choir launch into a medley of fa-la-la-ing. 'Now is the month of May', Vaughan Williams' setting of 'Linden Lea', and as a rousing finale to this sublime fifteen-minute dawn chorus, they sing the early American hymn so beloved by the Quakers, 'How can I keep from singing':

> I catch the sweet tho' far-off hymn
> That hails a new creation;
> Thro' all the tumult and the strife
> I hear the music ringing;
> It finds an echo in my soul –
> How can I keep from singing?

The hymn rises to a climax so jubilant that, as the crowds below erupt into applause and cheers and the bells ring out a clarion call to May, I cannot help but feel an echo in my soul, a sense of joy, and of hope, in these students, in their upturned shining morning faces, in their future lives, in what they will bring to the table.

We opened *Two Gents* for six rapturous performances in mid-May. If my contribution as Visiting Professor has given something to the students, they have also given something to me. As Shakespeare says in our play, *The Two Gentlemen of Verona*:

> Hope is a lover's staff, walk hence with that
> And manage it against despairing thoughts.
>
> (Act 3 scene 1)

Acknowledgements

Throughout my trek, I have been very grateful for the love and support of my family: Mark, Jo and Ruth, and of my dear friends Richard Sharples, James Robertson, Tony Mulholland, Martin Pople, Jim Hooper, Sue Powell, Mike Poulton, Lucy Shepherd, Steve Rebbeck, John Wyver, Patrick Spottiswoode, Jo Jelly, Vicki Heywood and Clive Jones.

I have been very lucky in enjoying the advice and friendship of some extraordinary people: in the world of academia, at Oxford: Emma Smith (Hertford); Judith Buchanan (St Peter's) and Richard Lawrence; Bart van Es (St Catherine's College) and Xa Sturgis (Ashmolean Museum); from Stratford: Robyn Greenwood (RSC Collection) and Michelle Morton; Michael Dobson and Ewan Fernie (Shakespeare Institute); Stanley Wells, Paul Edmundson, Paul Taylor and Emily Green (Shakespeare Birthplace Trust). And international friends and scholars including: Eric Rasmussen (Nevada) whose descriptive catalogue of Shakespeare's First Folios was my travel guide; Jonathan Bate and Ayanna Thompson (Arizona); James Shapiro (Columbia); Stephen Greenblatt (Harvard) and Ramie Targoff (Brandeis); and Zachary Lesser (Penn) and the invaluable Shakespeare Census.

I am very thankful for the international support of the British Council particularly: Matthew Knowles (Japan), Rebecca Simor, George Barrett (South Africa), Natasha Beckman and Richard Knowles (New Zealand); as well as Jason James (Daiwa Anglo-Japanese Foundation); Andrew Lamprecht (Iziko South African National Gallery); Peter Evans (Bell Shakespeare Co. Sydney); Antoni Cimolino (Stratford, Ontario); Barbara Gaines (Shakespeare

ACKNOWLEDGEMENTS

Theatre, Chicago), and friends and colleagues such as Dominic Riley; Buhle Ngaba; Jessica Wall, (Capital, Washington); Michael Hurst and Jennifer Ward-Lealand.

And of course my heartfelt thanks to all the experts and library staff who have helped along the way including : Tom Epps (Birmingham Shakespeare Library); Adrian Edwards and Christian Algar (British Library); Peter Ross (Guildhall Library); Simon Blundell (Reform Club); Peter Jolly (Dulwich College); Sue Palmer (Sir John Soane Museum); Simon Sladend (Victoria and Albert Museum); Catríona Cannon and team (Senate House, University of London); Jane Gallagher (Rylands Library, Manchester); Jan Graffius (Stonyhurst); Jenny Hill and Charlotte Craig (Craven Museum, Skipton); James Ford (Longleat); Richard Foster (Winchester College); Martin Meredith (Eton College); John Robinson (Arundel); Rhiannon Lawrence-Francis (Brotherton Collection, Leeds); the Durham team, including Judy Burg, Tony King and Liz Waller. In Cambridge : Patricia McGuire (King's); Nicolas Bell (Trinity) and the staff at Cambridge University Library. In Oxford I am grateful to Richard Ovenden and Andrew Honey (Bodleian); Matthew Shaw (Queen's); Tim Kirtley (Wadham). In Scotland and Ireland, to Graham Hogg (National Library of Scotland), Julie Gardham and Keira McKee (Glasgow); Elizabeth Ingham (Mount Stuart, Bute) and Andy Murphy (Trinity, Dublin).

In Germany, I enjoyed support from Claudia Olk, Roland Weidle and Anne Enderberg (German Shakespeare Association); Christiane Hoffrath (Köln); Joachim Seng (Goethe House, Frankfurt); Andreas Wittenberg and Silke Trojahn (Berlin) and library staff in Stuttgart. In Japan, Australia, New Zealand and South Africa I am very grateful for the help of Andrew Eglinton (Konan Women's University, Kobe); Miki Ishii (Meisei Library, Tokyo); President Takahiro and his team at Kyoto University; John Vallance and Maggie Patton (Library of New South Wales, Sydney); Jane Wild (Auckland Library) and Najwa Hendrickse (National Library, Cape Town).

In the United States and Canada, I was welcomed by Mattie Taormina (Sutro Library, San Francisco); David Faulds (Berkeley); Julia Lupton Derek Quezada Meneses, (UC Irvine); Cynthia Becht (Loyola Marymount); Nina Schneider (William Andrews

ACKNOWLEDGEMENTS

Clark Library); Stephen Tabor (Huntington); Declan Kieley and Michael Inman (New York Public Library); Jesse Erickson (Morgan Library); Jill Gage (Newberry Library, Chicago); David Fernandez (Thomas Fisher Library, Toronto); and staff at the University of British Columbia in Vancouver; Susan Buttaccio and Amy Pickard (Buffalo and Erie Public Library); Jim Maynard (Silverman Library, University of Buffalo); Theo Black and Katherine Reagan (Cornell University); Xena Becker (Colgate University); Anne Peale (Williams College); Matthew Ritger (Dartmouth College); the staff at Boston Public Library; Matthew Wittmann and Dale Stinchcomb (Houghton Library, Harvard); Sarah Shoemaker

(Brandeis); at Brown University: Mark Armstrong (John Carter Brown Library) and staff at the John Hay Library; Eve Houghton (Beinecke Library, Yale); Emily Runde (Columbia); Eric White (Scheide Library, Princeton); Kelly Richards (Philadelphia Free Library); Cary Mazer, Mitch Fraas and the team at the Van Pelt Library (Penn University); the Staff at Bryn Mawr College library; Sarah Horowitz (Haverford West); Ron McColl (West Chester); Michael North (Library of Congress); Jay Sylvestre (Lauinger Library, Georgetown); Daniel McClurkin (Evergreen Library, Baltimore); Lynley Anne Herbert (Walters Art Gallery and Library); Misty Maberry (Dallas Public Library); Aaron Pratt (Harry Ransom Center); and of course the Folger Library: in particular, Mike Witmore, Greg Prickman and Erin Blake.

There are also a number of people to thank who helped me to see further folios, which were too late for inclusion in this book, notably Samuel Lemley, (Carnegie Mellon University, Pittsburgh); Rigby Philips, (University of West Virginia, Morgantown); Amanda Nelson, (Olin Library, Wesleyan University, Middletown, Connecticut); as well as Rémy Cordonnier, (Bibliothèque d'Agglomération du Pays de Saint-Omer).

There are also a few particular individuals to whom I am very grateful for their generosity towards the project, including: Rick Adams, John Wolfson, John Murray, Lord Northampton, Lady Juliet Tadgell and Dr Christopher Tadgell, and the veteran folio hunter, Anthony James West for welcoming me into his home.

ACKNOWLEDGEMENTS

And finally to Bloomsbury. To Nigel Newton and Margaret Bartley for their kind encouragement. To Amy Whitaker, Elisabeth Denison, Anna Massardi and team for their hard work, David Mann for the jacket design and Tom Skipp for the audio book. To copy editor, Richard Collins, for his meticulous attention to detail, and to my infinitely perceptive editor, Ian Marshall.

Image Credits

INTEGRATED IMAGES

p. 3: John Kani and Antony Sher in *Kunene and the King* Photo by Ellie Kurttz (c) RSC
p. 13: 'Life's but a walking shadow' (courtesy of the author)
p. 24: Tony applying makeup backstage (courtesy of the author)
p. 34: Tony writing at his desk (courtesy of the author)
p. 43: Tony painting *Prospero and the Spirits* (courtesy of the author)
p. 59: 'Done from Death' by Tony Sher (courtesy of the author)
p. 76: 'Life triumphing over Death' bas-relief by Eric Kennington at the Royal Shakespeare Theatre (Alamy / Credit: Martin Bache)
p. 90: Portrait of Antony Sher by Guillem Trius (courtesy of Guillem Trius)
p. 103 **clockwise from top left:**
- Faceless Shakespeare: (reproduced by permission of the Provost and Fellows of Eton College)
- Spiral Droeshout (Image by Cushla Parekowhai for the cover of 'Nga Waiata a Hekepia / love sonnets by Shakespeare' 2000 marked a first on the world Shakespearean timeline. Holloway Press at the University of Auckland published nine sonnets translated into Te Reo Māori by the scholar Merimeri Penfold. PR:HOLL 2000, Auckland Libraries Heritage Collections.)
- Harris Facsimile of Droeshout (housed in the Rare Book Division of The New York Public Library)
- Quasimodo Droeshout (courtesy of the National Library of Scotland and reproduced under the CC BY 4.0 licence)

p. 106: Pope Paul VI watching the RSC recital (originally appeared in an article entitled '*Shakespeare company plays to Pope*' published in the *Sunday Telegraph* (number 198) on 15th November 1964)

IMAGE CREDITS

p. 119: Author's photos of child's pencil sketches (reproduced courtesy of the British Library)
p. 130: Dedication in the copy of *Sonnets* (1609) (image provided by The John Rylands Research Institute and Library, The University of Manchester)
p. 143: Greg reading a First Folio (courtesy of James Robertson)
p. 147: The Peacham drawing (image reproduced with permission of the Marquess of Bath, Longleat)
p. 152: Faceless Shakespeare (reproduced by permission of the Provost and Fellows of Eton College)
p. 160: 'Quasimodo' Droeshout engraving (courtesy of the National Library of Scotland and reproduced under the CC BY 4.0 licence)
p. 163: '*The Names of the Principall Actors in all these Playes*' (British Library archive / Bridgeman Images)
p. 167: 'The Papermaker' (Hans Sachs, *The Book of Trades (Ständebuch)* (1568; Dover Publications, New York, 1973): The book of trades (Ständebuch) : Sachs, Hans, 1494-1576 : Free Download, Borrow, and Streaming : Internet Archive
p. 178: 'The Bookbinder' (Hans Sachs, *The Book of Trades (Ständebuch)* (1568; Dover Publications, New York, 1973): The book of trades (Ständebuch) : Sachs, Hans, 1494-1576 : Free Download, Borrow, and Streaming : Internet Archive
p. 194: The Bodleian Library (courtesy of the author)
p. 197: Annotation of V&A folio (© Victoria and Albert Museum, London)
p. 201: Bas-relief of *Coriolanus* (reproduction from *Anne Seymour Damer: A Woman of Art and Fashion, 1748–1828*, by Percy Noble, p82, digitized by Google; courtesy of Wikimedia)
p. 202: Cartoon of 'The Damerian Apollo' (Alamy / piebags/LCB)
p. 205: 'The Great Literary Slug' (montage courtesy of Richard Sharples)
p. 210: Photograph of Harris's signature (courtesy of the Bancroft Library, University of California, Berkeley)
p. 213: Engraving of Roger Payne (Alamy / The History Collection)
p. 230: Harris facsimile of Droeshout engraving (housed in the Rare Book Division of The New York Public Library)
p. 253: Paul Beadle's bronze bust of Shakespeare (courtesy of Auckland Central Library, photo by Annette Hay)
p. 293: Worn binding on sammelband of sermons by Henry Smith (courtesy of Harry Ransom Center, The University of Texas at Austin)

IMAGE CREDITS

p. 298: Police escort for the First Folio at the Newberry Library in Chicago (courtesy of the Newberry Library)

p. 300: Scorpion/Rosebud in Toronto folio (courtesy of the Thomas Fisher Rare Book Library, University of Toronto Libraries)

p. 302: Colonel Clifton's bookplate (reproduction by permission of the Buffalo & Erie County Public Library, Bufallo, New York)

p. 305: 'The Printer' (Hans Sachs, *The Book of Trades (Ständebuch)* (1568; Dover Publications, New York, 1973): The book of trades (Ständebuch) : Sachs, Hans, 1494-1576 : Free Download, Borrow, and Streaming : Internet Archive

p. 309: 'They Kidnapped Shakespeare' (originally published in *True Detective* in June 1941; used with the consent of Chapin Library, Williams College)

p. 328: Marsden J. Perry cartoon (Small State Big History)

p. 338: Charlotte Cushman as Romeo (Alamy / Smith Archive)

p. 341: Bookplate engraving by William Blake (courtesy of Bryn Mawr College Libraries, Special Collections)

p. 348: Trapped curlicue of hair (author's photograph, reprinted with permission of Booth Family Center for Special Collections, Georgetown University Library)

p. 349: Droeshout with a 'scar' (courtesy of The John Work Garrett Library, The Sheridan Libraries, Johns Hopkins University)

p. 352: 'As yoa like it' folio page in a facsimile owned by Greg (courtesy of the author)

p. 355: Apsley Cherry-Garrard (Getty / Royal Geographical Society)

PLATE SECTION

p. 1: Bust of Antony Sher by Richard Sharples (courtesy of Richard Sharples)

p. 2: *Prospero and the Spirits* by Antony Sher (courtesy of Stewart Hemley)

p. 2: John Kani and Antony Sher in *Kunene and the King* Photo by Ellie Kurttz (c) RSC

p. 3: 'Welcome to Shakespeare' (courtesy of the author)

p. 3: Sidney Lee by Alfred Wolmark (© Royal Shakespeare Company / Bridgeman Images)

p. 4: Portrait of Lady Thynne (image reproduced with permission of the Marquess of Bath, Longleat)

p. 4: 'Chawkers' as Hamlet (courtesy of The Warden and Scholars of Winchester College)

IMAGE CREDITS

p. 4: 'Portrait' of Shakespeare by William-Henry Ireland (courtesy of the Master and Fellows of Trinity College Cambridge)
p. 5: Sir John Suckling by Anthony Van Dyck (Alamy / incamerastock)
p. 6: Richard Burbage (© Dulwich Picture Gallery / Bridgeman Images)
p. 6: Greg with portrait of John Lowin (courtesy of the author)
p. 6: Lucy Hutchinson (National Army Museum, London, UK / Bridgeman Images)
p. 6: Jane Lane, Lady Fisher (Alamy / Historic Images)
p. 7: Keith Richards looking at a First Folio in New York Public Library (Getty / Kevin Mazur)
p. 7: 'First Reading of the Emancipation Proclamation of President Lincoln' (Getty / Universal History Archive)
p. 8: 'Ignudo' with the likeness of Harrison Post (Allyn Cox (1896-1982). Detail from vestibule ceiling mural, ca. 1926) William Andrews Clark Memorial Library, University of California, Los Angeles.
p. 9: 'Ichimura' as the Shogun Tokugawa Ieyasu (courtesy of HoriPro)
p. 9: William Congreve's monument erected by his mistress the Duchess of Marlborough (© Dean and Chapter of Westminster)
p. 10: 1900s colour postcard by Henry Payne (courtesy of the author)
p. 10: Statue of Shakespeare in Sydney, Australia (courtesy of the author)
p. 11: Vivid Sydney (sourced from 'Art titan': City's tribute to national treasure – Yahoo News Australia)
p. 11: Sir George Grey's statue covered in red paint (Getty / Phil Walter/Staff)
p. 12: The Buffalo 'Syndicate' (originally published in *Buffalo Evening News* on July 9, 1940; used with the consent of Chapin Library at Williams College)
p. 12: The 'Altarpiece' for Harry Elkins Widener at Harvard University (courtesy of the author)
p. 13: Interior of the George Peabody Library (courtesy of the author)
p. 13: 'Typo' in a mediaeval manuscript (The Walters Art Museum, Baltimore)
p. 14: James Orchard 'Scissorhands' Phillipps (montage courtesy of Richard Sharples)
p. 15: Haida Reconciliation Pole (Alamy / Michael Wheatley)
p. 15: The 'first state' of the Droeshout engraving (ART Box D783 no.1, image 34537, Folger Shakespeare Library)
p. 16: Greg and Tony (courtesy of the author)

Index

Actors' Church, 63
Actors' Remonstrance, 245
Adams, Brandi, 358
Adams, Rev. Fulford, 353
Ahad, Nick, 127
Akihito, Emperor, 263
Algar, Christian, 115–18, 120
Alia, Dr, 16, 62, 86, 93, 96
Allam, Roger, 60
Alleyn, Edward, 125, 129, 224
American Civil War, 135, 345
American Declaration of Independence, 116, 186, 351–2
American Library Association, 339
Amman, Jost, 177
Anjin: The English Samurai, 267
Anne of Denmark, Queen, 125
anti-Semitism, 107–8
Arbuthnot, Rev. George, 325–6
Armstrong, Louis, 336
Ashcroft, Peggy, 142
Ashmolean Museum, 245, 314
Atsumori, 267–8
Aubrey, John, 244
Auden, W. H., 342
Audience with Kenneth Williams, An, 66
Austen, Jane, 215

Bach, Johann Christian, 72
Bacon, Delia, 331
Bacon, Sir Francis, 152, 161–2, 315, 317, 331
Bacon Literary Society, 358
Bajnotti, Count Paul, 328–9

Baker, Amos Prescott, 337
Balderston, John Lloyd 262
Banks, Thomas, 197, 200
Barber, Samuel, 335
'bardolatry', 121
Barker, George, 358n
Barnes, Peter, 53
Barton, John, 70
Bashō, 265
Bassett, Judith, 282
Batchelder, John Davis, 344
Bate, Jonathan, 240
Beale, Simon Russell, 108
Beatles, 52
Beaumont and Fletcher, 245
Becht, Cynthia, 212–16
Bechtler, Hildegard, 65
Becker, Xena, 307–8
Beckett, Samuel, *Krapp's Last Tape*, 50
Bedford, Francis, 174
Beerbohm, Max, 193
Beilfuss, Rodrigo, 359
Bell, John, 271–2
Bell, Nicholas, 188–9, 192
Benfield, Robert, 164–5
Benson, Frank, 149–50
Berenson, Bernard, 314
Berkoff, Steven, 52
Bernhardt, Sarah, 337
Berry, Mary, 364
Bespoke Overcoat, The, 50
Billington, Michael, 7
Bixby, W. K., 216
Black, Theo, 307
Blackfriars Gatehouse, 324
Blackfriars Theatre, 164, 224, 244
Blaeu, Willem, Jansz, 267
Blake, William, 341
Bloch, Cecil, 85

Blount, Edward, 124, 173, 180–1, 231, 364
Bodley, Sir Thomas, 194
Boleyn, Anne, 154
Bond, Edward, 52
Book of Kells, 186
bookbinding, 177–9
Booth, Edwin, 336–8, 340, 345
Booth, Junius Brutus, 336
Boswell, James, 190
Botticelli, Sandro, 215, 314
Bourne, Claire, 339
Boydell, John, 198–202, 364
Bracegirdle, Anne, 260
Brahe, Tycho, 267
Brando, Marlon, 66
Brendel, Alfred, 72
Brian Boru, High King of Ireland, 186
British Museum, 323–4
British Shakespeare Association, 137
Broadway Tower, 322
Brockett, Elizabeth, 364
Brontë sisters, 136–7
Brooke, Ralph, 155
Brown, Carrie Mathilde, 328–9
Brown, Lancelot 'Capability', 145
Brown, Nicholas, Jr., 328
Brummell, Beau, 369
Brunel, Isambard Kingdom, 274
Bryder, Linda, 282
Buchanan, Judith, 304
Burbage, Richard, 120, 123–7, 162–5, 224, 245
Burdett-Coutts, Angela, 365
Burns, Robert, 343

382

INDEX

Bush Theatre, 52
Buttaccio, Susan, 302–3
Bwindi Impenetrable Forest, 83
Byrne, Tony, 229
Byron, Lord, 136, 187–9

Caldwell, Mae, 231
Caledon House, 365–6
Callil, Carmen, 51
Callow, Simon, 75, 77–8
Campbell, Thomas, 136
Canwick Hall, 156
Cape Colony, 69, 287–8
Cape Coloureds, 62
Caplan, Esther, 50
Capote, Truman, 81
Carlton House, 239
Carpenter, Francis Bicknell, 345–6
Cartwright, William, 125
Caruso, Enrico, 208
Cary, Elizabeth, 164
Cary, Lorenzo, 164
Carysfort, 5th Earl of, 174
Castro, Fidel, 319
Cavendish, Dominic, 48
Chamberlain, John, 179
Chandos portrait, 245
Charlemont, Earl of, 160
Charles I, King, 125, 239–41, 243–7, 249, 314, 354, 364
Charles II, King, 246–9, 363–4
Charles III, King, 41, 237–42, 270–1
chasubles, 133–4
Chatsworth House, 219
Chatterton, Thomas, 189–90
Chaucer, Geoffrey, 210, 226
Cherry-Garrard, Apsley, 262, 358–60
Chicago Shakespeare Theatre, 296
Child, Julia, 63
Child, Mary, 364
Children of the Chapel Royal, 164
Chilton, Marie, 214–16
Christie's, 111, 139, 353
Church, Elihu Dwight, 220
Church, Tony, 105–6, 108
Churchill, Caryl, 8
Churchill, Sir Winston, 123, 365
Cicero, 203
Cimolino, Antoni, 301
Citizen Kane, 299–300, 332

Clark, William Andrews, Jr, 216–17
Clifton, Colonel Charles, 302–3
Cloud Nine, 52
Cobham Hall, 314
Cochran, Alexander Smith, 332
Cofield, Carl, 211
Coke, Sir Edward, 132
Collier, John Payne, 220–6, 339, 354, 364
Collis, Rev. John Day, 326
Collision Course, 53
Colston, Edward, 283
Condell, Henry, 1, 120–4, 148, 243
Congreve, William, 260
Connolly, Billy, 63
Connolly, James, 186
Cook, Captain James, 283
Cooney, James, 229
Coquelin, Constant, 337
Cornell, Ezra, 307
Coventry Mystery Plays, 322
Covid, 16, 22, 32
Cox, Brian, 69
Craig, Charlotte, 135–6
Crawford, William Stuart Stirling, 116
Crockett, Rev. Samuel Crawford, 363
Cromwell, Oliver, 247, 249, 353
Cromwell, Richard, 249
Cromwell, Thomas, 251
Crosby, Bing, 215
Cross Hall, 212
Crouch, Nel, 7
Curzon, Lord, 272
Curzon, Sir Nathaniel, of Kedleston, 308
Cushman, Charlotte, 336–8, 340

Dalí, Salvador, 152
Dallas Shakespeare Society, 351
Daly, Augustin, 342–3
Damer, Anne, 200–3, 364
Daniel, George, 365
Dante, 215
Davenant, Sir William, 250
Davidman, Joy, 137
Dawson, George, 113–14, 129
Dayan, Moshe, 39
Dee, Dr John, 322
Degas, Edgar, 315

Dekker, Thomas, 180
Dench, Judi, 48
Dering, Sir Edward, 367
Dickens, Charles, 197, 215
Dignitas, 35, 67
Djokovic, Novak, 30
Dobson, Zuleika, 193
Donne, John, 168
Doran, Jo, 17, 54, 88, 109, 166, 186–7, 228
Doran, Mark, 17, 33, 54, 66, 98–9, 227
Doran, Ruth, 17, 27, 53–4, 207–8, 211, 215, 217, 306, 313
Dormer, Sir John Baptist Joseph, 220
Dossor, Alan, 52
Doyle, Sir Arthur Conan, 132
Dracula, 262
Duke's Company, 250
Dumezweni, Noma, 333–4
Durning-Lawrence, Sir Edwin, 161–2
Durno, James, 200
Dutch East India Company, 267
Dutton, Richard, 138

Earle, John, 179
Easter Rising, 186–8
ebru, 182
Ecclestone, William, 164
Edelstein, Barry, 211
Edgar, David, 53
Edward IV, King, 133, 189
Edward VI, King, 193
Edward VII, King, 272
Edwards, Adrian, 115, 117–19
Egerton, John, 1st Earl of Bridgewater, 218
Eglinton, Andrew, 257
Eichendorff, Joseph Freiherr von, 78
Eichmann, Adolf, 107
Elden, Benjamin, 363
Elizabeth I, Queen, 141, 145, 165, 179, 274, 312
Elizabeth II, Queen, 141, 148, 153–4, 237
Elizabethan Club, 332
Elton Hall, 174
Emancipation Proclamation, 345–7
Enderwitz, Anne, 174
endpapers, hand-marbled, 182–3

INDEX

English Civil War, 168, 246–50
Englishby, Paul, 236
equivocation, 131–2
Erickson, Jesse, 232
Essex Rebellion, 312
Essiedu, Paapa, 108
Euro 2021, 23, 30
Eustis, Oskar, 211, 336
Evans, Daniel, 141
Evans, Peter, 271
Evans, Sir Arthur, 363
Evans, Sir John, 363
Evelyn, John, 251, 368
Everett, Edward, 338
Eyre, Richard, 52

Farley, Henry, 180
Farran, Elizabeth, 203
Faulds, David, 209–10
Favyn, André, 363
Fawkes, Guy, 131
Fawley, Molly, 150
Fernandez, David, 299–300
Fernie, Ewan, 112–14
Ferrers, Norman Macleod, 363
Field, Nathan, 164, 245
Fillis, Mrs, 364
Firth, Colin, 57
Fitzgerald, Edward, 317n
Flannery, Peter, 53
Florio, John, 221
Flower, Charles Edward, 110–11, 325–6
Floyd, George, 283
Folger, Henry Clay, 156–8, 302–3, 315, 327–8, 353, 362, 365–7
Folger Shakespeare Library, 125, 168, 211, 292, 315, 319, 327–8, 344, 361–7, 369
Ford, James, 145–6
Foreman, James, 308
Forman, Simon, 322
Forrest, Edwin, 336, 340
Forster, John, 197
Fortescue, Mrs, 364
Foster, Myles Birket, 363
Foster, Richard, 150
Fraas, Mitch, 340
Frankfurt Book Fair, 173, 176–7, 181–2, 358
Frankfurt *Ständebuch*, 177–9
French Revolution, 132, 307
Freud, Sigmund, 341–2
Fugard, Athol, 6

Fugard Theatre, 6–8
Fuller, 'Mad Jack', 359
Fulton, Missouri, 123
Fuseli, Henry, 198–9
Fust, Johannes, 176

Gage, Jill, 296
Gaines, Barbara, 296
Gainsborough, Thomas, 207, 217–18
Galba, Emperor, 153
Gale, Minnie, 18–19
Gallagher, Jane, 128–9
Gallipoli, 272
Garden Theatre, 18
Gardham, Julie, 162–3, 165
Gardner, Isabella Stewart, 313–15
Garnet, Fr Henry, 131–2, 353–4
Garret, T. Harrison, 349
Garrett, Nataki, 211
Garrick, David, 196, 225n
Gaysweatshop, 52
General Medical Council, 36
George I, King, 233
George II, King, 233, 238, 364
George III, King, 119, 233
George IV, King (Prince Regent), 119, 155, 239
Georgiana, Duchess of Devonshire, 200
Gerard's Herbal, 321
German Shakespeare Association, 173–5
Gibbons, Grinling, 189
Gibson, Strickland, 195
Gielgud, John, 142
Gilbreath, Alexandra, 229
Gilburne, Samuel, 302–3, 364
Gill, Eric, 216
Gillingham, Sinclair E., 308–9
Gillray, James, 154
Giotto, 314
Globe Theatre, 120, 122, 125, 132, 163–4, 192, 246, 302
Gloria, 46
Godfather, The, 66
Godfrey, Derek, 105–6
Goethe, Johann Wolfgang von, 176
Gogol, Nikolai, *The Government Inspector*, 52
Goldin, Brett, 290
Goldsmith, Oliver, 136
Gone with the Wind, 209
Goose-Pimples, 52

Graffius, Jan, 133–4
Great Fire of London, 123, 251
Greenblatt, Stephen, 229, 318
Greenwood, Robyn, 109–11
Grenville, Thomas, 116
Grey, Sir George, 279–80, 282–3, 287–90
Griswold, Almon W., 296
Grolier Club, 317
Grove Park, 219
Grover's Theatre, 345
Guinness, Alec, 301
Gullet, Henry, 272
Gunpowder Plot, 131–2
Günther, Frank, 177
Gutenberg, Johannes, 176
Gutenberg Bible, 116, 316, 334–5, 366n
Guthrie, Tyrone, 301

Hadermann, Johann Heinrich, 233
Halliwell-Phillipps, James Orchard, 110–11, 115, 160, 174, 220, 321–7, 344, 369
Handel, George Frideric, 238, 261
Hands, Terry, 52
Hands, Tim, 148
Hanmer, Sir Thomas, 363
Hanratty, Patrick J., 212
Harefield House, 224
Harley Street, 36–8
Harris, John, 210, 230
Harvard, John, 315–16
Harvey, Eliab, 362
Harvey, Tamara, 141
Harwood, Ronald, *The Dresser*, 6
Hathaway, Anne, 190, 196, 308
Hawkins, Rev. C. H., 148–50
Hawthorne, Nigel, 52
Hearle, Anne, 297
Heenan, Archbishop John, 106, 108
Hemmings, John, 1, 120–4, 148, 162, 164, 243
Hendrickse, Najwa, 289
Henrietta, Duchess of Marlborough, 260–1
Henrietta Maria, Queen, 243–4
Henry II, King, 192
Henry V, King, 140
Henry VI, King, 133

INDEX

Henry VII, King, 133
Henry VIII, King, 154, 371
Henslowe, Philip, 125, 224
Herbert, Lynley Anne, 350
Herbert, Philip, Earl of Pembroke, 121, 148, 289, 368
Herbert, William, Earl of Pembroke, 121, 148, 289, 368
Hermann, Dr, 182
Herne's Oak, 365
Hero and Leander, 278
Heywood, Thomas, 126
Higgins, Michael D., 187
Hill, Jenny, 135–7
Hill, Susan, 151
Hinemoa and Tūtānekai, 277–9, 281
History Man, The, 53
HMS *Temeraire*, 362–3
Hoar, Sherman, 316
Hobbes, Mary Rice, 325
Hobbit, The, 268–9
Hochhuth, Rolf, 107
Hoffrath, Christiane, 173–4
Hogg, Graham, 159
Holbein, Hans, 75
Holocaust, 107
Holt, Thelma, 48, 74–5, 83
Holy Trinity Church (Stratford), 63, 79, 82, 122, 137, 196, 200, 325, 331
Homer, 155
Honeyman, Janice, 6, 28, 45, 61, 88–9, 289
Hooper, Jim, 53, 60
Hoover, J. Edgar, 309
Hope Theatre, 246
Hopkins, Gerard Manley, 132
Houghton, Eve, 330–2
Houston, Keith, 118n
Howard, Catherine, 154
Howard, Charles, 11th Duke of Norfolk, 154–5
Howard, Henry, Earl of Suffolk, 154
Howard, Thomas, 14th Earl of Arundel, 314–15, 367–8
Howard, Thomas, 3rd Duke of Norfolk, 154
Huddington Court, 130–1
Huddleston, Archbishop Trevor, 52
Hughes, Arthur, 85, 126, 140
Humphries, Anne, 139
Huntington, Henry E., 207, 218, 315, 365–6

Huntington Library conference, 211
Hurst, Michael, 284
Hurst, Thomas, 274
Hutchinson, Colonel John, 246, 249–50, 364
Hutchinson, Lucy, 247, 249–50
Huth, Henry, 332
Huygens, Constantijn, 168, 364
Hymnus Eucharisticus, 371–2

Ibsen, Henrik, 257
Ichimura, Masachika 'Ichi', 259–60, 268
Ingelby, Clement, 224, 364
Ingham, Elizabeth, 165, 168
Inman, Michael, 229–31, 34
Ireland, Samuel, 190–3
Ireland, William-Henry, 151n, 189–93, 196, 225, 354
Irish Nationalists, 186–7
Irish War of Independence, 188, 366
Ishi, Miki, 260, 262

Jackson, Peter, 268
Jaggard, Isaac, 124, 181, 194–5, 231, 303
Jaggard, William, 120, 155–6, 158, 194–5, 327, 362–3, 366
Jaggard, Captain William, 327
James I, King, 120, 125, 165, 179, 247, 314
James, Jason, 265
Janauschek, Fanny, 337
Jefferson, Thomas, 351
Jelly, Jo, 68
Jennens, Charles, 261
Jesuits, 131–4, 212, 215
Joanine Library, 185
John XXIII, Pope, 107–8
John, Paul, George, Ringo, and Bert, 52
Johnson, Richard, 363
Johnson, Samuel, 115, 190, 318
Johnstone, Ollie, 18
Johnstone, William, 262
Jonson, Ben, 123, 126, 138, 148, 150–1, 164, 240, 245, 308, 321, 330–1
Jordan, Dora, 191–2
Joyce, James, 230
Justinian, Emperor, 339

Kamali, Daren, 281
Kani, John, 6–7
Kunene and the King, 6, 28, 44–5, 51, 289
Kauffman, Angelica, 198
Kawai, Shoichiro, 267n
Kayapo, 39
Keats, John, 337
Kemble, John Philip, 191–2, 199–201
Kemp, William, 163
Kennedy, John F., 353
Kesler, Linc, 358
Key, Liza, 289
Kieley, Declan, 229–31, 334
Killigrew, Thomas, 125, 250
King's Company, 250
King's Head Theatre, 52
King's Men, 120, 123–5, 164–5, 243–5, 302, 364, 366
Kinnock, Neil and Glenys, 52
Klee, Paul, 276
Knell, William, 122
Knickerbocker Crisis, 327
Knowles, Matthew, 256, 259, 263
Kyd, Thomas, 126

La Boétie, Etienne de, 80
Lamb, Charles, 198–9
Lane, Jane, 248–9, 364
Lane, Colonel John, 248, 364
Lapotaire, Jane, 153
Lassells, Henry, 248
Laughton, Charles, 159
Law, Matthew, 124
Lawes, Henry, 218
Lawrence, D. H., 'Snake', 53
Lawrence, Richard, 304–5
Lawrence, Thomas, 199
Leason, John, 303, 305
Lee, Sir Sidney, 109–11, 156, 173, 225n, 296, 326–7, 369
Leigh, Mike, 52
Lennox, James, 334
Leonardo da Vinci, 315
Leone, Sergio, 49
Leslie, Shane, 365–6
Levi, Primo, 44, 65
Lewis, C. S., 137–8
Lewis, Mary, 364
Lewis, Stephen Brimson, 236
Library of Alexandria, 193
Library of Congress, 335, 344
Light, Rowan, 282
Lighting of the Sails, 276
Lilly, Joseph, 225n

INDEX

Lincoln, Abraham, 337, 345–6
Linger, Blythe Stuart, 290
Liverpool Everyman, 50–2
Lloyd's of London, 157
Loewentheil, Stephan, 359
Longbottom, Julia, 263
Lord Admiral's Men, 125
Lord Chamberlain's Men, 120, 147, 243
Love Library, 188
Lowin, John, 163, 165, 243, 245–6
Lucas, E. V., 324
Lucas, George, 186
Lucian, 150
Lugosi, Bela, 262
Lupton, Julia, 211

Maberry, Misty, 351–2
McCagg, J. W., 296
McCann, Colum, 230
McClurkin, Daniel, 348–50
McColl, Ron, 343
McIntyre, Blanche, 140
McKee, Keira, 162, 165
McKellen, Ian, 52, 82–3, 268
Mackennal, Bertram, 272–3
McLaren, Malcolm, 116
Macready, William, 336, 340
Madan, Falconer, 195
Madden, Sir Frederic, 223–4
Mainz Psalter, 116
Major, John, 237
Makeba, Miriam, 86
Mala Mala, 39
Mallyon, Catherine, 15, 22, 38, 141, 153
Malone, Edmond, 191, 196
Mann, Thomas, 342
Mannix, Kathryn, 7
Mōri, 277–83
Market Theatre, 146
Marlowe, Christopher, 125
  The Jew of Malta, 222
marmorizzazione, 183
Marshall, Fr Ted, 214–15
Marshalsea prison, 155
Marston, John, 126
Mary I, Queen, 154
Mason, Jackie, 36, 39, 55, 60, 66
Mayflower Bible, 354
Maynard, Jim, 303
Maynardville Theatre, 50
Mays, Andrea, 157
Melbourne, Lady, 200
Meres, Francis, 129
Metta Catharina, 214

Michelangelo, 152, 198
Middleton, Thomas, 126
Miles, Sarah, 73
Miller, Charles, 342
Mills College, 359
Milton, John, 136, 186, 218–19, 239–40, 339–40
Minns, Chris, 270
Mrs Brown, 66
Mitchell, Adrian, 52
Modern Society, 128
Moiseiwitsch, Tanya, 301
Molière, 53
Montaigne, Michel de, 70, 80
Moore, Julianne, 46
More, Thomas, 133
Morgan, John Pierpont, 232, 365
Morricone, Ennio, 49
Morton, John, 133
Moseley, Humphrey, 245
Motion, Andrew, 52
Mount Fuji, 257
Mozart, Wolfgang Amadeus, 72
Murphy, Andy, 186–7

Napoleon Bonaparte, 200
Napoleonic Wars, 187–8
Naruhito, Emperor, 263–5
'necrophilia outrage' (Tunbridge Wells), 82
Nelson, Admiral Lord, 200, 362
Newdegate, Sir Francis Alexander Newdigate, 353
Newdigate, Sir Richard, 353
Newton, Caroline, 341–2
Newton, Edward, 174
Ngaba, Buhle, 289–91
Nicol, George, 364
Nile, Battle of the, 200
Ninagawa, Yukio, 52
Noda, Hideki, 259–60
Noh plays, 267–8
Nongqawuse, 287
Norris, Rufus, 48
North, Michael, 343–4
Northcote, James, 198
Norton, George, 248
Nottingham Playhouse, 52
Nussey, Ellen, 136
Nutshell Theatre, 271

Oates, Titus, 363
Obama, Barack, 218
Ogilby, John, 217

Okell, Elizabeth, 364
Oldcorne, Edward, 132–3
Oliver, Jamie, 83
Olivier, Laurence, 141
Olsen, John, 276
Once Upon a Time in America, 49
Opie, John, 318
Orlin, Lena, 196
Ōshū Kaidō, 264–5
Ostler, William, 164
Oswald, Richard, 343
Ovenden, Richard, 193–4
Overbury, Thomas, 126

Palazzo Pio, 105
Palmer, Sue, 199–200
Pandects of Florence, 338–9
papermaking, 166–8
Parekowhai, Cushla, 281n
Park, Ann, 297
Parker, Samuel, 337
Partridge, Eric, 207
Patton, Maggie, 273–4
Paul VI, Pope, 105–7
Paule, Rachel, 364
Pavier, Thomas, 366
Payne, Roger, 146, 212–14, 353
Peacham drawing, 146–7
Peale, Anne, 309
Pearse, Patrick, 186
Pelosi, Nancy, 210
Pendle witches, 135
Penfold, Merimeri, 281
Pepys, Samuel, 247
Perkins, Richard, 222
Perkins, Thomas, 222
Perry, Marsden J., 111, 326–7
Persius, 244
Phelps, Lucy, 229
Philip II, King of Spain, 314
Phillimore, Mr, 192
Phillips, Augustine, 302
Phillips, Sir Thomas, 322–4
Pickard, Amy, 302–3
Pickering, William, 365
pilcrow, 118
Pilgrim Fathers, 354
Plaatje, Sol, 291
Plato, 185
Players Club, 336
Plungyan, 55, 69
Poe, Edgar Allen, 333–4
Ponden Hall, 135–6
Pope, Abby E., 364
Pope, Alexander, 136, 150, 258

INDEX

Post, Harrison, 217
Poulton, Mike, 267n
Powell, Enoch, 52
Pragnell Shakespeare prize, 234
Pratt, Aaron, 353–4, 358
Prickman, Greg, 366–7, 369
Primo, 44, 65
Proclamation of the Irish Republic, 186
Prynne, William, 243–4
Punch, 207, 365

Quaritch, Bernard, 113–14, 365n
Queen's Men, 122
Quezeda de Menezes, Derek, 211–12

Rachmaninoff, Sergei, 84
Radford, Tamar, 364
Radio 4 *Front Row*, 127–8
Ramaphosa, Cyril, 22
Rasmussen, Eric, 111, 344, 365n
Ravenscroft, Edward, 308
Reagan, Katherine, 307
Rebbeck, Steve, 299–300
Reed, Isaac, 166
Reed, John 'Pop', 340
Rembrandt, 315
Repair Shop, The, 57
Reynard the Fox, 309
Reynolds, Joshua, 198, 217
Rhodes, Cecil, 289–90
Richard III, King, 133, 140–1
Richards, Keith, 231
Richards, Kelly, 339–40
Ritger, Matthew, 310–11
RMS *Titanic*, 296, 317
Robertson, James, 130, 133–6
Robeson, Paul, 318
Robinson, John, 153–5
Rodd, Thomas, 221, 332
Roger, Thomas, 316
Romney, George, 198
Room With a View, A, 72
Rose Theatre, 125
Rosenbach, A. S. W., 365–6
Ross, Peter, 120–1
Rothe, Hans, 177
Rotton, Elisabeth, 331
Roubiliac, Louis-François, 189
Rowfant Club, 310–11
Rowley, Thomas, 189
Roxburghe Club, 219
Royal Court Theatre, 52

Royal Society, 322
Rubens, Peter Paul, 247, 314
Rugby World Cup, 23
Runde, Emily, 333–4
russia bindings, 213–14, 353
Ryan's Daughter, 73
Rylands, Enriquetta, 128–9
Rylands, John, 128

Sabin, Frank T., 344
Sachs, Hans, 177
St Anthony of Padua, 368
St Francis of Assisi, 350
St Laurence Pountney, 123
St Mary Aldermanbury, 120–1
Saint-Omer, 132, 134
St Paul's Cathedral, 131, 179–81, 251
St Paul's Churchyard, 124, 155, 179–81, 364
St Paul's Cross, 179
Salmesbury Hall, 134
San Francisco earthquake, 208
Scales, Prunella, 8
Scarisbrick, Edward, 363
Schlegel, August Wilhelm, 177
Schlesinger, John, 271
Schneider, Nina, 216–17
Schoenbaum, Samuel, 224
Schöffer, Peter, 176
Schwarzkopf, Elisabeth, 78
Scofield, Paul, 271
Scott, John, 363
Scott, Raymond, 319–20
Scott, Robert Falcon, 262
Scott, Walter, 136
Scott-Warren, Jason, 339
Second Vatican Council, 107–8
Seng, Joachim, 176–7
Serengeti, 62–3
Serkis, Andy, 108
Seven Ages of Man, 274
Sex Pistols, 116
Shadey, 53
Shakespeare, John, 155, 316
Shakespeare Birthplace Trust, 107, 225, 321, 325
Shakespeare Folios
  annotations and inscriptions, 115, 129, 150, 182, 197, 224, 240, 262, 289, 296–8, 311, 319, 332, 339, 344, 350, 364, 367
  Arundel Castle, 153–8

Auckland Library, 280, 297
Berlin, 174–5
bindings, 213–14, 318–19, 344, 353
Birmingham Library, 112–14, 117n
Bodleian Library, 193–6
Bodmer Library, 366n, 368
Boodle's Club, 297, 369
Boston Public Library, 311–13
Brandeis University, 318–19
British Library, 115–20, 161
Brown University, 326–8
Bryn Mawr College, 340–2
Buffalo, 301–3, 364
Bute, 165–8, 348
Cape Town National Library, 288–90, 292
censuses of copies, 109–11, 135, 225n, 296, 326–7, 344, 365n
Chapin Library, 308–9
Chicago, 295–8
Christie Library, 310
Colgate University, 307–8
Cologne, 173–4, 230–1
Columbia University, 333–4
Cornell University, 306–7
Cosin's Library, 319–20
Craven Museum, 135–7
Dartmouth College, 310–11
Droeshout engraving, 111, 115, 119–20, 151–2, 159–61, 180, 230, 262, 308, 321–2, 326–8, 344, 349, 363, 369
Dulwich College, 125–7
Eton College, 151–3, 161
Evergreen Museum, 348–50
'False Folio', 366
'Feminist Folio', 364
Firestone Library, Princeton, 337–9
Folger Shakespeare Library, 361–7, 369
Frankfurt, 175–82
Georgetown University, 347–8
Glasgow University, 162–5
Guildhall Library, 120–5
hand-marbled endpapers, 182–3
Harris facsimiles, 210, 230
Harry Ransom Center, 353–4
Harvard University, 315–18

387

INDEX

Shakespeare Folios (cont'd)
  Haverford College, 342–3
  Huntington Library, 217–26, 324n, 352
  J. Erik Jonsson Central Library, 351–2
  John Rylands Library, 127–30
  Konan University, 256–9
  Kyoto University, 265–8, 363
  Longleat House, 145–8, 219n
  Love Library, 188
  Loyola Marymount University, 212–16
  Meisei University, 232, 256, 259–62, 264, 358
  Morgan Library, 231–3, 364
  National Library of Scotland, 159–62
  New York Public Library, 229–31, 330, 334–5
  Newberry Library, 296–8
  Perkins Folio, 220, 222–4, 354
  Philadelphia Free Library, 339–40
  publication, 123–4
  Queen's College, Oxford, 196
  rarity of Third Folio, 251–3
  RSC copy, 1, 105–11, 115, 324, 326–7, 344
  sale in St Paul's Churchyard, 179–81
  Senate House Library, 161
  Sir John Soane's Museum, 197–200
  State Library of New South Wales, 272–5
  Stockport, 138–9
  Stuttgart, 182
  stolen folios, 310, 319–20
  Stonyhurst College, 130–4
  Tasmania, 272n
  Thomas Fisher Rare Books Library, 298–300
  Trinity College Cambridge, 188–93
  Trinity College Dublin, 185–8
  UC Berkeley, 209–11
  UC Irvine, 211–12
  University of British Columbia, 358–60
  University of Illinois, 262, 368
  University of Padua, 367–8
  Wadham College, Oxford, 196–7
  West Chester University, 343–4
  William Andrews Clark Library, 216–17
  Winchester College, 148–51, 259
  Windsor Castle, 119, 237, 239–42
  Yale University, 330–2
Shakespeare Gallery, 198–202, 364
Shakespeare Hospice, 44, 94, 96–7, 228, 234
Shakespeare in the Ruins, 359
Shakespeare Institute, 112
Shakespeare Memorial Theatre, 111, 149, 325–6
Shakespeare works
  All's Well that Ends Well, 139–40
  Antony and Cleopatra, 202, 274, 335
  apocryphal plays, 251
  As You Like It, 109, 117–18n, 182, 240, 257, 352, 359
  Cardenio, 354
  The Comedy of Errors, 257, 351
  Coriolanus, 118, 201, 246
  Cymbeline, 109, 118, 142, 155, 191, 196–7, 209, 227, 234–6, 296, 299–300, 307, 350, 371
  Hamlet, 108, 126, 134, 197, 199, 220, 235, 244, 268, 271, 274, 290, 324, 334, 338, 340, 345, 349–50, 352, 358
  Henry IV Part One, 18–19, 85, 129, 336
  Henry IV Part Two, 119, 180, 336
  Henry V, 149, 236, 241, 257–8, 304
  Henry VI, 124, 150, 174, 194n, 212, 223, 237, 347
  Henry VIII, 118, 140–1, 154, 233, 245
  Julius Caesar, 1, 109, 220, 249, 266, 291, 358–9
  King John, 105, 118, 238, 346
  King Lear, 7, 53, 70–1, 85, 87, 108, 124, 126, 219, 259–60, 283–4, 301, 303–4, 334, 364
  Love's Labour's Lost, 231, 331
  Macbeth, 1, 109, 126, 131–2, 191, 222, 238, 266, 333, 336, 346
  Measure for Measure, 229, 360
  The Merchant of Venice, 107, 124, 149, 347–8
  The Merry Wives of Windsor, 200
  A Midsummer Night's Dream, 108, 124, 154, 240, 336, 343
  Much Ado About Nothing, 260, 270, 313
  Othello, 32, 52, 124, 224, 255, 297, 318, 364
  Pericles, 250, 267, 280, 313
  Richard II, 47n, 50, 124, 153–4, 239, 242–3, 311–12, 336, 363
  Richard III, 60, 62, 85, 112, 126, 133, 140–2, 237–8, 280, 297, 331, 346
  Romeo and Juliet, 124–5, 146, 231–3, 271, 277, 281, 291, 318, 331, 363–4
  Sonnets, 38, 129–30, 281, 283, 306
  The Taming of the Shrew, 129, 222, 367
  The Tempest, 1, 6, 108–9, 118, 134, 305, 337n, 364
  Timon of Athens, 220, 233, 267, 271, 340, 352
  Titus Andronicus, 124, 146–7, 197, 212, 308, 361–2, 367
  Troilus and Cressida, 118–19, 220, 232–3, 266–7, 296, 352, 362–3, 367
  Twelfth Night, 1, 107, 240
  The Two Gentlemen of Verona, 164, 296–7, 359, 370–3
  The Two Noble Kinsmen, 267
  Venus and Adonis, 74
  The Winter's Tale, 1, 78, 118, 126, 342, 362
Shapiro, James, 336n
Sharples, Richard, 87–8
Shaw, George Bernard, 121, 342–3
Shearman, Dr, 14–17, 19–21, 26–7, 36, 40–1, 98

INDEX

Sher, Antony
  acting scripts, 52–3, 227
  archive removed to RSC, 227–8
  The Audience, 152
  and bagels, 55–6
  his bust, 87–8
  Cheap Lives, 51
  citizenship, 69
  'Done from Death', 64
  as Falstaff, 41, 85
  and fear, 70–1
  The Feast, 51
  and First Folio quartercentenary, 108–9
  funeral, 61, 63, 79, 82, 137, 153
  Indoor Boy, 51
  Middlepost, 51–2, 62
  Joan, 23
  paintings and drawings, 28, 42, 45, 51, 61, 64–5, 72, 81, 126, 152, 227
  photograph albums, 183–4
  Prospero and the Spirits, 45, 61
  The Sea Point House, 52, 55
  royalties, 268–9
  'Seventy', 72
  and Shakespearean roles, 126–7
  'Sterre', 169
  his studio, 142
  Tammi, 23
  Telegraph obituary, 48–9
  Year of the King, 50
  Young, Marietta, 40, 44, 46–8, 56, 61, 64–5, 67–8, 72, 79, 85, 95
Sher, Beth, 54, 86
Sher, Joel (brother), 18, 54, 60, 63
Sher, Joel (grandfather), 69
Sher, Ralph, 52, 62
Sher, Randall, 18, 21–3, 50n, 60, 63, 72
Sher, Verne, 22–3
Sheridan, Richard, 191–2, 203
Shibuya Scramble Crossing, 256
Shinkansen (bullet train), 256–7
Shipp, Mary, 308
Shoemaker, Susan, 318
Sibthorp, Coningsby, 156–8, 362
Siddons, Sarah, 191, 200–1, 217, 225n

Sidney, Philip, 232
Sidney, Robert, 2nd Earl of Leicester, 232
Sinden, Donald, 149
Singer, 53
Six-Day War, 39
slave trade, 359
Sly, William, 245
Smith, Emma, 195–6, 289, 359, 367–8
Smith, Ian, 211
Smith, Sandra, 51, 61
Soane, Sir John, 199–200
Society of Antiquaries, 322
Solomon, King, 238–9
Sondheim, Stephen, 93
Sophie's Choice, 66
Sorrento's, 21, 32
Sotheby's, 111n, 116, 159, 353
South African Shakespeare Schools' Festival, 290–2
Southampton, Earl of, 190, 224
Southey, Robert, 136
Spencer, Stanley, 50
Spencer library, 128–9
Spevack, Marvin, 325
Spiderman, 261
SS *Arctic*, 296
Stanley, Ferdinando, 5th Earl of Derby, 212
Star Wars, 185–6
Stationers' Register, 124, 129, 194, 313
Stebbins, Emma, 336
Steevens, George, 110n, 115, 174, 313
Stein, Rick, 80
Stephens, Robert, 41, 52
Sternheim, Carl, 52
Stevens, Bruce Dickerson, 215–16
Stevenson, Alice, 364
Stewart, Alexander Bannatyne, 363
Stewart, Patrick, 135, 340
Stinchcomb, Dale, 318
Stoddart, Miss, 364
Stoker, Bram, 262
Stone of Destiny, 237
Stoppard, Tom, 52
Storm Arwen, 91
Stow, John, 179
Strafford, Earl of, 244
Stratford Festival Theatre, 300–1
Strauss, Richard, 78
Stravinsky, Igor, 78

Streep, Meryl, 46, 66
Sturgis, Xa, 245
Succession, 69, 80, 94
Suckling, Sir John, 244
suminagashi, 182
Sunday Bloody Sunday, 66
Supernova, 56–7
Surrenden Manor, 367
Sutro Library, 208
Sutro, Adolph, 208–9
Sutro, Emma, 209
Sutton, Elias, 363
Suzman, Helen, 52
Suzman, Janet, 290
Swanston, Clement Tudway, 114
Sylvestre, Jay, 347–8

Table Mountain, 8, 27, 286, 290
Tabor, Stephen, 218, 220, 225–6
Takahiro, President, 265
Tammany Hall, 231
Tangye, Richard and George, 274–5
Taormina, Mattie, 208
Tartary, 255
Tarzan's Last Stand, 52
Taverner, John, 66
Taylor, Joseph, 164–5, 245
Te Rangikāheke, 280
Teeth and Smiles, 52
theatre ban, 245–6, 250
Thebes, 185
Theobald, Lewis, 115, 150, 225, 258–9, 354
Theodorakis, Mikis, 46
Thirlestaine House, 323
Thompson, Ayanna, 211
Thomson, James, 136
Thorpe, Thomas, 129
Thrale, Mrs, 203
Thurman, Chris, 289
Thynne, Thomas, 145–6, 219n
Tick, Tick Boom!, 93
Tiecke, Ludwig, 177
Tighe, Lady Louisa Lennox, 187–8
Titian, 314
Tonson, Jacob, 115
Tooley, Nicholas, 164
Toovey, James, 232
Torkut, Nataliya, 235–6
Touchet, Maria, 145–6, 219n
Touchet, Mervin, Earl of Castlehaven, 219

INDEX

Trafalgar, Battle of, 362
Treaty of Waitangi, 282
Trojahn, Silke, 174
Tsikinya-Chaka Centre, 289
Tucci, Stanley, 57
Tuchman, Barbara, 272
Turbutt, Gladwyn, 195
Turner, J. M. W., 363
Tutin, Dorothy, 105–7
Twain, Mark, 216, 303
typesetting, 304–5
Tyreman, Ben, 66

Ukrainian Shakespeare Centre, 235
Uncle Sam, 207, 365
Underwood, John, 164
US Capitol, 345–7
Ustinov, Peter, 74
Utzon, Jørn, 270

Vadera, Shriti, 141
van Baerle, Suzanna, 168
Van Dyck, Anthony, 148, 244
Vaughan Williams, Ralph, 372
Vermeer, Johannes, 315
Vickery, Judge Willis, 310–11
Victoria, Queen, 174, 272, 280, 365
Vincent, Augustine, 155–6, 158, 362
Virgil, 154
Vortigern and Rowena, 191–2

Wagner, Richard, 177
Wall, Jessica, 345–7
Walley, Henry, 267
Wallis, Henry, 190
Walpole, Horace, 260

Walska, Ganna, 332n
Walter, Harriet, 255
Walters Art Gallery, 349–51
Ward-Lealand, Jennifer, 284
Warhol, Andy, 320
Warrington Library, 138–9
Washington, George, 349
Washington, Joan, 50
Waterloo, Battle of, 188
Webber Douglas Academy of Dramatic Art, 51
Webster, John, 126
Webster, Paul Francis, 261–2
Weidle, Roland, 173–4
Weismann Theatre, 50
Welles, Orson, 336
Wellington, Duke of, 188
Wells, Stanley, 123
West, Antony James, 111, 135, 344, 365n
West, Benjamin, 343
West, Samuel, 8
West, Timothy, 8
Westminster Abbey, 63, 189, 237–8, 240, 249, 260
Weston, Janice, 298
White, Eric, 337
White, Peregrine, 354
Whitehall Group, 368
Widener, George D., 317
Widener, Harry Elkins, 316–18, 365
Wild, Jane, 280–1
Wild Coast, 287
Wilde, Oscar, 217, 295
Wildgoose, William, 195
Wiley, Kehinde, 217–18, 350
Wilkinson, John, 135
William I, King of Prussia, 174

Williams, Kenneth, 66
Williams, Tennessee, 81
Wilmot, Henry, 248
Wilson, Richard, 65
Wilton House, 148
Wimbledon, 30
Winchell, Walter, 309
Windebank, Elizabeth, 274
Winn, Rowland Denys Guy, 266
Wintour, Helen, 130–1, 133–4
Wintour, Robert, 130–1
Witmore, Mike, 211, 360
Wittenberg, Andreas, 174
Wittmann, Matthew, 318
Wollstonecraft, Mary, 215
Wolmark, Alfred, 109
Wolsey, Cardinal Thomas, 154
Woodstock House, 188
Worcester, Battle of, 243, 246–8
Wordsworth, William, 136, 256
World According to Me, The, 60
Worldwide Fund for Nature, 39
Wren, Christopher, 123
Written in the Stars, 275

Xhosa, 287–8

Yeats, W. B., 187
Yerkes, Charles, 220
York Mystery Plays, 299

Zelenskyy, Volodymyr, 235–6
Zorba the Greek, 46
Zuma, Jacob, 32
Zyats, Paula, 331–2

A Note on the Author

GREG DORAN has been described by the *Financial Times* as 'one of the supreme Shakesepare directors of our era'. He joined the Royal Shakespeare Company as an actor in 1987 and was its artistic director from 2012 to 2022. He has directed and/or produced every single work in the First Folio of Shakespeare's plays at Stratford-upon-Avon. He was awarded the Sam Wanamaker Prize for pioneering work in Shakespearean theatre in 2012, and was knighted for services to the arts in 2024.